A Larger Hope?

A Larger Hope? Universal Salvation from Christian Beginnings to Julian of Norwich, by Ilaria L. E. Ramelli

A Larger Hope? Universal Salvation from the Reformation to the Nineteenth Century, by Robin A. Parry, with Ilaria L. E. Ramelli

A Larger Hope?

Universal Salvation from the Reformation to the
Nineteenth Century

A Larger Hope?

Universal Salvation from the Reformation
to the Nineteenth Century

by

ROBIN A. PARRY

with

ILARIA L. E. RAMELLI

CASCADE *Books* · Eugene, Oregon

Cascade Books
An Imprint of Wipf and Stock Publishers
199 W. 8th Ave., Suite 3
Eugene, OR 97401

www.wipfandstock.com

PAPERBACK ISBN: 978-1-4982-0040-0
HARDCOVER ISBN: 978-1-4982-8800-2
EBOOK ISBN: 978-1-4982-0041-7

Cataloguing-in-Publication data:

Names: Parry, Robin A., author. | Ramelli, Ilaria, 1973–, contributor

Title: A larger hope? Universal salvation from the Reformation to the nineteenth century / Robin A. Parry, with Ilaria L. E. Ramelli.

Description: Eugene, OR: Cascade Books, 2019 | Series: A Larger Hope? | Includes
bibliographical references and index.

Identifiers: ISBN 978-1-4982-0040-0 (paperback) | ISBN 978-1-4982-8800-2 (hardcover)
| ISBN 978-1-4982-0041-7 (ebook)

Subjects: LCSH: Universalism | Restorationism—History of doctrines | Universal salva-
tion—Biblical teaching | Hell—Christianity | Salvation—Christianity

Classification: BT263 P31 2019 (print) | BT263 (ebook)

Manufactured in the U.S.A.   02/12/19

To Peter Hiett
and Brad Jersak

Table of Contents

Acknowledgements

I WOULD LIKE TO thank Professor Ilaria Ramelli for the valuable research and material that she contributed to this book and for the inspiration that she always is. Much gratitude is also due to Dr. Anthony Cross, who managed to supply many rare and hard-to-access books for me for the research in this volume. I literally could not have written this work without his assistance. Finally, I want to acknowledge my eagle-eyed editor at Cascade Books, Caleb Shupe. His work was exemplary.

Material on Elhanan Winchester in chapter 6 is abbreviated from my "Between Calvinism and Arminianism: The Evangelical Universalism of Elhanan Winchester (1751–1797)." In *"All Shall Be Well,"* edited by Gregory MacDonald, 141–70. Eugene, OR: Cascade, 2011. Material in chapter 12 is in part drawn from my "Introduction to Thomas Allin (1838–1909)" in Thomas Allin, *Christ Triumphant*, edited by Robin A. Parry, ix–xxxvii. Eugene, OR: Wipf & Stock, 2015. Thanks are due to the publisher for permission to reproduce sections of those essays.

Introduction

THIS IS NOT REALLY a history book. It does contain a reasonable amount of historical information, but its primary goal is not to relate the "story" of universalism nor of any of the characters that might play a role in such a story. Neither is it chiefly an attempt to understand the fortunes and forms of the idea of universal salvation through the kinds of interpretative lenses that historians may employ. There is a tale to tell, and this book certainly provides windows through which to view that tale, but the task of telling it must belong to someone else. That task faces the challenge confronting any such endeavor, namely that most of the information we would love to have available in constructing it is long since gone. "History is at best a beggarly gleaner in a field where Death has gathered a bountiful harvest."[1] It may be, however, that this work might inspire a professional historian to write such a history of universal salvation or historical studies of some of the characters examined here. That would be very gratifying.

Instead, what this volume seeks to offer is a series of explorations into the theological ideas of certain interesting, but mostly long-forgotten, people. I have tried to situate those people in their historical worlds and to sketch certain biographical background information on them in order that readers might be able to go some distance toward situating their ideas in the right historical, cultural, and personal contexts. Ideas do not float around in space—they are embedded and embodied in contexts. I have also sought to highlight the key connections—at least, as far as I have been able to from the available evidence—between the different people studied here so that we can trace lines of influence as the universalist idea passes from one generation to another, or as it apparently gets

1. Brumbaugh, *History of the German Baptist Brethren*, xi.

1

spontaneously reinvented in one generation, and then in another. Some of the historical dimensions do come into the foreground at times, especially in the eighteenth century, where tracking lines of influence does require us to paint on a larger canvas, creating an interconnected triptych linking Continental Europe, Great Britain, and America.

I also need to explain in advance that some of our characters are treated not as main subjects of investigation, which they could have been, but as background linking-figures who can help us to better situate the main people selected for study. For instance, Johann and Johanna Petersen could easily be the subjects of detailed attention, but instead are treated more briefly as background for understanding the universalist groups within Radical Pietism. The work of Paul Siegvolk (a pseudonym), however, is taken up for closer inspection as an influential and representative work of early Radical Pietist belief in universal salvation. Others, such as Benjamin Rush, really draw the short straw—merely playing the cameo role of "interesting character who converted to universalism." Rush is a fascinating man, and in his day was both respected and influential; he could easily have been given more attention. But he did not make any theological contributions to universalist thought, so I pass him over in almost total silence. Choices have to be made, and I picked up on those which I felt gave a good flavor of belief in universal salvation in all its diverse configurations.

It is not my intention to assess the merits and demerits of the different theologies, though on occasion evaluative comments will slip out. For the most part, I simply describe what my different subjects taught and leave it to readers to assess those teachings as they see fit. Nor am I interested in passing judgment on the saintliness or otherwise of those I study, but again, occasional comments may make an appearance, though such comments mostly describe how some others in their day saw them, not how I do. The people included in this book—be they saints or sinners, profound theologians or somewhat inept Bible readers—are there simply because they had something interesting—maybe great, maybe small—to say about universal salvation. Speaking personally, I find myself warming to some of these people and feeling rather uncomfortable with others, both as people and as theologians. However, while I would have no qualms about offering sustained theological engagement with any of them, that would be a task for a different book, and not one I have plans to write. So here, for the most part, I simply set out what they thought and the impact those ideas had.

We pick up the fortunes of belief in final restoration in the Reformation period. In volume 1, Ilaria Ramelli charted the fate of this theological proposal from New Testament times into the Renaissance. By way of review, it would be useful to first sketch out the basic contours of what we might call the patristic doctrine of *apokatastasis*, as a background to the book that follows.[2]

THE PATRISTIC DOCTRINE OF *APOKATASTASIS*

Those in the Origenian tradition told the story of the cosmos as a great arc: God's creation of rational intelligences (*logokoi*), their fall, and the long process of God's restoring them to their earlier condition (*apokatastasis*). The beginning (*archē*) thus prefigures the end (*telos*), and the end will be like the beginning; but not *exactly* like the beginning, for the end will be *better*. Adam was created immature, and in the end, humans will be mature, never to choose evil again.

Creation

In the beginning, God created the rational intelligences (*logikoi*), which existed in unity, harmony, and the contemplation of God. All things were good and had a destiny (*telos*) in union with the divine.

Origen envisages a twofold creation: first a creation of *logokoi* in the image of God (Gen 1:26), and then a creation of the *logikoi* as materially embodied souls (Gen 2:7). So, the *logikoi* existed prior to the creation of the material world. The exact nature of this preexistence in Origen's theology is debated. Is this the literal preexistence of disembodied souls (Henri Crouzel, Michael McClymond)? Did the intelligences have spiritual bodies (Ilaria Ramelli)? Did they preexist only in God's foreknowledge (Marguerite Harl)? Did they preexist in God the Son prior to the creation of space and time (Mark Scott)? Were these preexistent *logikoi* existent beings or potential beings?[3]

---

2. The summary that follows is my attempt at drawing together threads from across Ilaria Ramelli's *Christian Doctrine of Apokatastasis*.

3. The preexistence of disembodied souls was condemned at Constantinople II in 553. Whether Origen's view was condemned depends on how one construes it. We maintain that it was not, for we would argue that, in his view, the *logikoi* were not disembodied, but had spiritual bodies. See Ramelli, *Preexistence of Souls?*

Fall

First some of the angelic beings chose to rebel against God, and then they incited the *logikoi* to rebel (the fall of humanity). The fall of the *logokoi* was not something that occurred in a single moment of time, but was a long, drawn-out "event." Laziness and negligence of God led to the gradual loss of the knowledge of God, and as creatures drift from the knowledge of God they fall away from goodness.

The fall of the rational intelligences saw a transformation of their bodies into mortal, heavy, corrupt, sexually differentiated(!), material bodies, subject to death: this was the "second creation." Now, some care is necessary here, for it is easy to misunderstand this idea. The Origenian views was *not* that the material creation was bad. *Christ himself* was the creator of this second creation. Material bodies are good, not evil, *but* they are temporary and must perish in the end because they are mortal. Mortality and death were actually a divine mercy granted in order to stop sin being immortalized in our souls.

Evil as non-substantial

A critical element in this tradition was the idea that evil has no substance; evil is not a thing, but a lack of goodness in a thing. This, of course, does *not* mean that evil is insignificant. What it does mean is that God did not create evil and that no creature has an evil nature. Rather, evil is rooted in the *will* of creatures. The significance of this understanding of evil for universalist eschatology will become clear soon.

Free will

Origen was strongly opposed to the idea that either our nature or the stars determined human actions, for this would remove the responsibility for our actions from us. It would also make God responsible for evil. No, we choose to do evil of our own volition.

However, people do not freely choose evil *knowingly*; they choose it because they mistakenly think it to be good (or they are under the influence of some freedom-restricting, nonrational compulsion). The notion of a fully informed choice of evil is, on this ethical intellectualist view, incoherent. That is why Satan had to *deceive* the woman and the man to eat the fruit of the forbidden tree.

Salvation involves the deliverance of our wills from the lies that bind so we are liberated to choose the Good. This requires education and illumination, enabling us to understand aright and therefore choose right. Thus, God does not force our wills, but instructs them, leading us toward salvation. Really, true freedom is the freedom to choose the Good. And in the end, when we are perfect, we will remain free, but will never choose evil.

Jesus and our salvation

How will God heal our broken souls? Our nature is healed through the Word-made-flesh. According to the Origenians, there is only one human nature in which we all participate. This whole nature was embodied in the two heads of the human race: Adam, who corrupted it, and Christ, who healed it.

Incarnation

Christ's incarnation is fundamental: "Christ has become the body of the whole of humanity, that, through the body that he was kind enough to assume, the whole of humanity might be hidden in him" (Hilary of Poitiers, *On Psalms* 51.16). "Flesh was taken up by the Logos to liberate all humans and resurrect them from the dead and ransom all of them from sin" (Athanasius, *Ep. Adelph.*). If Christ had not assumed our flesh, he could not have healed it.

Crucifixion

Christ's death too: "That corruption may disappear from all forever, thanks to the resurrection, . . . He has paid for all, in death, all that was owed" (Athanasius, *Apoll.* 9.3). "He died for all . . . to abolish death with his blood . . . he has gained the whole humanity" (Athanasius, *Letter* 10.10.23). Origen similarly affirms that there is "no salvation for anyone except in the blood of Christ" (*Hom. Josh.* 3.5).

Resurrection

But the cross is only salvific because of the resurrection: "The whole creation was restored through the Lord's resurrection" (Origen, *Comm. Rom.* 4.7.3). "Because the totality of the whole human nature forms, so to say, one living being, the resurrection of one part of it [Christ] extends to the whole, and, in conformity with the continuity and unity of the [human] nature, passes on from the part to the whole" (Gregory of Nyssa, *Or. Cat.* 32). "Just as the principle of death, becoming operative in the case of one human being [Adam], from it passed on to the whole human nature, likewise the principle of the resurrection, from one human being [Christ], and through it, extends to the whole of humanity" (Gregory of Nyssa, *Or. Cat.* 16). Jesus' resurrection is the resurrection of the whole human race in his humanity.

Understanding divine punishment

Punishment as corrective

In line with the view that evil choices are choices based on misperceptions of reality and that liberation of the will requires education, a particular educative interpretation of divine "punishment" was advanced: "God does not punish [*timōreitai*]—since punishment is the retribution of evil with further evil—, but corrects [*kolazei*] for the sake of those who are corrected, both in general and singularly" (Clement of Alexandria, *Strom.* 7.16.102.3). Origen says, "The Word of God is a physician of the soul and uses the most diverse, suitable, and seasonable methods of healing the sick" (Origen, *Philoc.* 27.4). Sometimes God even prescribes "very unpleasant and bitter medicine as a cure for ills; . . . in the last resort the ill is burnt out by fire" (Origen, *Princ.* 2.10.6). This leads toward a particular understanding of hell.

Hell is not forever

Hell, in accord with the view of divine punishment maintained in this tradition, is purifying. The fire burns away sin, not sinners: "Indeed, this fire of the corrective punishment is not active against the substance, but against habits and qualities. For this fire consumes, not creatures, but certain conditions and certain habits" (Didymus the Blind, *Comm. Ps.* 20–21, col. 21.15).

The fires of hell are, in fact, the burning conscience. The fire symbolizes the internal condition of guilt: "every sinner kindles for himself the flame of his own fire, and is not plunged into a fire which has been previously kindled by someone else or which existed before him" (Origen, *Princ.* 2.10.4). In this sense, hell is self-inflicted. God permits us to wound ourselves in this way so that we can learn.

Hell, understood as purifying fire, is therefore not forever, for that would utterly defeat its purpose. "Our Lord has freely forgiven many persons in their sins . . . but of the most serious sin retribution in Gehenna will be demanded . . . But not even this sin will be able to prevent a person from being justified. God, after giving retribution in Gehenna, will reward this person in the kingdom" (Ephrem the Syrian, *Commentary on Tatian's Diatessaron* 10.4). "[T]he *apokatastasis* that we expect to come to pass in the end, in the kingdom of the heavens: the restoration of those who had been condemned to Gehenna" (Gregory of Nyssa, *De Vita Mosis* GNO VII/1 57.8—58.3).

The unity of the divine attributes

Another foundational building block underlying this theology was the affirmation that God's love, justice, and mercy must not be set in opposition to each other; rather, they inhere in each other. "[I]t is proper to the wise neither to subvert justice nor to separate the good purpose inspired by love for humanity from the Judgment according to justice, but to join both these elements together in a fitting way, rendering to justice what it deserves, without parting from the goodness of the purpose inspired by love for humanity" (Gregory of Nyssa, *Or. Cat.* 26.64). Nowadays, one often hears people claim that while God is loving, *he is also* just, as if the two stood in some conflict. For the church fathers, God's love is just and his justice is loving. So, talk of divine justice and "wrath" must never be set up in opposition to divine goodness and mercy. Consequently, while God certainly destroys sin, he does so *in a manner fitting for God's goodness.* The implications of this for hell are spelled out most clearly by Isaac of Nineveh:

> If we said or thought that what concerns Gehenna is not in
> fact full of love and mixed with compassion, this would be an

opinion full of blasphemy and abuse against God our Lord. If we even say that God will hand us to fire in order to make us suffer, to torment us, and for every kind of evil, we attribute to the divine nature hostility toward the rational creatures that God has created by grace, and the same is the case if we affirm that God acts or thinks out of spite, as though he sought vengeance. Among all of his deeds, there is none that is not entirely dictated by mercy, love, and compassion. This is the beginning and end of God's attitude toward us. (Isaac of Nineveh, *Second Part* 39.22)

Consummation (*apokatastasis*)

The *telos* will come after the many aeons have reached their end: "Every knee will be restored to be one [John 17:21], and God will be 'all in all' [1 Cor 15:28]. However, this will not happen in a moment, but slowly and gradually, though innumerable aeons of indefinite duration" (Origen, *Princ.* 3.6.6). At that point, Christ will have subjected all creatures beneath his feet (1 Cor 15:24–28). This subjection, however, is not a defeat: "He will subject all beings to himself, and this must be understood as a salvific submission" (Eusebius, *Eccl. theol.* 3.15–16). The submission of creatures to Christ—their union with him in his body—must occur before Christ can submit to the Father on behalf of all creation. Christ's submission to the Father is the submission of his body, which at that point amounts to all creation. *Then* God will be "all in all" (1 Cor 15:28).

For God to be "all in all" requires that *no* evil be found in *any* creature:

> God will be "all" for this intelligence . . . because evil will exist no more for this intelligence, everything is God, who is untouched by evil. Therefore, if at the end of the world, which will be similar to the beginning, there will be restored that condition which the rational nature had . . . then for the creature, who has returned pure and unsullied, the One who is the only good God will become all. . . . [And] "in all" God will be all. (Origen, *Princ.* 3.6.2–3).

"It will be the case that God is 'in all' only when in the beings it will be impossible to detect any trace of evil" (Gregory of Nyssa, *In Illud* 17). "Evil must necessarily be eliminated, absolutely, and in every respect, once and for all, from all that is. . . . For, as evil does not exist in nature outside will, once each will has come to be in God, evil will be reduced to complete nothingness, because no receptacle will be left for it" (Gregory of Nyssa, *De anima* 101). Here we see the importance of the notion that evil has no substance: when God's good creatures are restored there is *literally nothing left* of evil. The annihilation of evil is thus inseparable from the salvation of creation.

In the end then, sin, death, and evil—not sinners—are forever destroyed. "There was a time when evil did not exist, and there will be a time when it is no more" (Evagrius, *Kephalaria Gnostika* 1.40, Syriac non-expurgated version 52). "We must understand the destruction of the last enemy as the destruction, not of the substance that was created by God, but of the inclination and the hostile will that stemmed not from God but from the enemy [Satan] himself. Therefore, he will be destroyed, not in order for him to exist no more, but in such a way as to no longer be 'enemy' and 'death'" (Origen, *Dial.* 26).

The *apokatastasis* also marks a return to the unity of creation: "Making us all one thing, so that we are no longer many, but all of us are one, made one with his divinity, . . . made perfect, not in a confusion of substances, reduced to one, but in the perfection of virtue brought to its apex" (Eusebius, *Eccl. theol.* 3.18). Note that the final unity is explicitly stated in non-pantheistic manner ("*not* in a confusion of substances"). It will also be marked as a resurrection of both body and soul, which is theosis.[4]

All will be saved

The universalism of this vision is already clear, but it is worth driving it home. No sin is too big to thwart God's purposes: "in souls there is no illness caused by evilness that is impossible to cure for God the Logos, who is superior to us" (Origen, *Cels.* 8.72). And all will be healed: "Every being that has its origin from God will return such as it was from the beginning,

---

4. Resurrection of the body is the destruction of sin and death and the door to "deification" (*theosis*): "Resurrection is a restoration to our original condition" (Eusebius, *Comm. Ps.* PG 23.1285.56). "After human beings have become pure of heart . . . restoration (*apokatastasis*) awaits them, in eternal contemplation. And they shall be gods" (Clement, *Strom.* 7.10.56.6).

Origen distinguished the metaphysical principle of identity of the body (*eidos*) and the material substratum of the body (*hupokeimenon*). In the resurrection, we will have a body, the same body, but it will be a spiritual body (*sōma pneumatikon*; 1 Cor 15:44), an ethereal body suitable to the heavens.

when it had not yet received evil" (Gregory of Nyssa, *In Illud* 14). Consequently, "no being will remain outside the number of the saved" (Gregory of Nyssa, *In Illud* 21). "The end will be the so-called *apokatastasis*, in that no one, then, will be left an enemy" (Origen, *Comm. Jo.* 1.16.91).

Origen and others who embraced *apokatastasis* were, however, very cautious about preaching it openly lest unspiritual and immature people use it as a license to sin (Origen, *Cels* 5.16; 6.26; *Comm. Rom.* 5.1.7; *Hom. Ezech.* 1.3.5). They would preach coming judgment and the fires of gehenna to the masses, often failing to mention that such fire was temporary, because they believed that fear was a factor that could help in restraining sin in some people.

This then is the basic shape of historic Christian universalism. As Ilaria Ramelli demonstrated in the first volume in this series, Origen's theology of *apokatastasis* was once widespread in the church, both among the laity and clergy, but under the influence of the Emperor Justinian in the East and Bishop Augustine in the West it fell out of favor, becoming a mere trickle in the mainstream Christian tradition. By the time of the Reformation it had been almost forgotten in the West. But, as we shall see, it is a hard idea to keep down.

Part I

The Sixteenth and Seventeenth Centuries
Reformation and Beyond

I

At the Radical Fringe of Reformation and Counter-Reformation

THE PROTESTANT REFORMATION WAS a time of massive religious, social, and political upheaval in Europe. Until that point, the church had kept a tight control over acceptable doctrine and the correct interpretation of Scripture, lest individuals get it into their heads that they were able to rightly interpret the Bible on their own and thus unleash upon the world a plethora of potentially heretical teachings, wrapped in the clothing of biblical authority. The Protestant demotion of the authority of church tradition and elevation of the Bible and its many individual interpreters changed all that. The Protestant cry was that "Scripture alone" was the authoritative source for Christian belief and life. Furthermore, discerning the meaning of Scripture, said the Reformers, was not the preserve of the church authorities, but of all true believers, for the Bible is *clear* when it read canonically and according to sensible grammatical-historical standards. Any Christian, they said, has the right to interpret the text and appeal to its authority, and if the Bible turns out to run counter to traditional Catholic teaching, then so much the worse for traditional Catholic teaching.

The Protestant Reformation very quickly generated not a single version of true biblical faith, but a wide range of different, not-fully-compatible versions of Christian religion all claiming to be the genuine manifestation of biblical teaching. The diversity was reflected even among the Magisterial Reformers like Luther, Calvin, and Zwingli, but was most clear around the margins of Protestantism, where individuals who considered themselves Spirit-led interpreters of the Bible were empowered to declare their new "discoveries" with confidence.

In this context, it is no surprise that the idea of universal salvation, which had for a long time been suppressed as "heretical" by the authority of the church, now began to re-enter through the crack in the door opened up by the Reformation. Its reappearance is hard to chart with any certainty. The Magisterial Reformers themselves never really questioned the traditional Western teachings on hell and heaven, taking them as given,[1] for their theological focus was elsewhere. Nevertheless, the idea of universal restoration did reappear quickly in some quarters. Thus Luther, in a letter to Hans von Rechenberg in 1522, wrote:

> For the opinion that God could not have created man to be rejected and cast away into eternal torment is held among us also, as it was at all times by some of the most renowned people, such as Origen and his kind. They regard it as too harsh and cruel and inconsistent with God's goodness. They based their opinion on Psalm 77[:7–9], where the Psalmist says, "Will God cast off forever, and never again be gracious? Has his steadfast love forever ceased? And his promises at an end for all time? Had God's forgotten to be gracious? Has he in anger shut up his compassion?" [They also cite] Paul, 1 Timothy 2[:4], "God desires all men to be saved and to come to the knowledge of all truth." Proceeding from this premise they argue that in the end even the devils will be saved and will not be eternally damned, etc., etc., one step following from the other.[2]

We are not certain who Luther has in mind here, but what is clear is that within five years of Luther nailing his ninety-five theses to the door of All Saints' Church in Wittenberg (1517), a trigger-event for the start of the Reformation, universalism was already poking its head around the doors of some Protestants.

Accusations of teaching the universalist heresy are especially common against Anabaptists—the radical wing of the Protestant Reformation. For instance, the Lutheran Augsburg Confession says that their churches "condemn the Anabaptists, who think that there will be an end to the punishments of condemned men and devils" (Article 17). In 1552/53 the Reformed English Church also intended to ratify one of its

1. Though they did come to reject purgatory, the *relatively* new kid on the eschatological block.

2. Luther, "Letter to Hans von Rechenberg," 51.

Articles of Religion against universalism, and it is generally thought that the article was directed against what was considered an Anabaptist belief: "All men shall not be saved at the last. They also are worthy of condemnation, who endeavor at this time to restore the dangerous opinion, that all men be they never so ungodly, shall at length be saved, when they have suffered pains for their sins a certain time appointed by God's justice" (Article 42). The ascent of the Catholic Queen Mary to the throne stopped the Articles making it to the statute books, and after Mary's death the Forty-Two Articles were reduced to the Thirty-Nine Articles, with the anti-universalism being dropped (presumably because the threat from universalism seemed to have diminished by 1571).

Accusations of universalism were repeated against one Anabaptist in particular—Hans Denck, an Anabaptist leader and humanist from Southern Germany. It is worth our while considering him in some more detail.

HANS DENCK (CA. 1495–1527)—ANABAPTIST

Hans Denck was a pious, intelligent, and often irenic man. Born in Bavaria, he studied at the University of Ingolstadt, where he seems to have been well regarded by his teachers, and on leaving edited a three-volume Greek dictionary before settling down to a quiet and respectable family life working as a headmaster in Nuremberg. However, his soul was restless, and he struggled with his inner sense of spiritual poverty despite his outward respectability. This led him to make contact with the Anabaptist Thomas Müntzer, who provoked Denck to significantly rethink his theology and practice. For this he was expelled from Nuremberg in 1525, when the city accepted the Reformation.

Denck was (re)baptized by Balthasar Hubmeier, an Anabaptist leader, in 1526, though he always maintained that it was the inner spiritual reality, not outward rituals like Baptism and Eucharist, that really counted. He was certainly harsh concerning what he regarded as legalistic religion based on the outward "dead letter," rather than the Spirit within. Denck then began preaching and publishing his ideas and became prominent within Anabaptist groups (and strongly disliked in Magisterial Reformation circles).

After his expulsion from Nuremberg, he remained "homeless" for the rest of his short life, moving to Augsburg, Strasbourg, Southern

Germany, and then on to Basel in Switzerland, where he died of the Black Death in 1527, aged only thirty-two.

Was Hans Denck a universalist? Possibly, though scholars continue to debate the issue and certainty eludes us. In 1525 Denck was imprisoned in Schwyz with the charge of teaching the salvation of sinners, and even the devil, from hell. In the same year, he was accused of disturbing the Anabaptists of St. Gall with similar doctrines.[3] Caution is always required when treating the accusations of opponents, and universalism was one of those "off-the-peg heresies" that was often used to dress one's enemies in this period. Charges of universalism were thus often leveled without accuracy—for instance, by some Catholics against all the opponents of the doctrine of purgatory—so that accusations alone are not enough to establish whether someone actually upheld a theory of universal salvation. Nevertheless, there is no smoke without fire, and the accusation seems to have had *some* basis in Denck's actual teachings.

Morwenna Ludlow notes Denck's stress, against the teaching of the Magisterial Reformers, on God's universal saving will grounded in his nature as Love. Denck writes, "He . . . offers his mercy to everyone with wholehearted earnestness and desires truly to accomplish all he promised."[4] Furthermore, Christ died for everyone in accordance with this desire of the Father to save all. This is suggestive, though it is not enough in itself to show that he was a universalist.

Another relevant element in Denck's theology is his belief that a "divine spark" from God resides in *all* people, even if they are not aware of it. This "spark" is God-within and offers a divine inner witness to God's truth: "This attestation is in all people and proclaims to each one in particular, according to how one hears him."[5] So none are completely without God's inner work, even if many are largely deaf to it. This provides a basis for God to draw even the most hardened of sinners to salvation, and he can do it even if those sinners have no access to Scripture. Denck appears to be what we would refer to as an inclusivist. But while such a theological idea could certainly fund universalism, it does not require it.

Does he go further than this? Yes. He rejects a retributive understanding of divine punishment and sees the suffering that results from sin to be a natural, self-inflicted consequence of such actions; consequences

3. Williams, *Radical Reformation*, 254.

4. Denck, *Was geredt sei*, 115 (*Hans Denck Schriften*, 46).

5. Denck, *Was geredt sei*, 89 (*Hans Denck Schriften*, 33).

designed by God for the purposes of reforming sinners. For Denck, Romans 11:32—"For God has bound everyone over to disobedience so that he may have mercy on them all"—was interpreted as applicable to individuals and their inner spiritual experiences. Johannes Steenbuch comments, "Human beings need to go through an existential experience of being lost and damned in order to come to faith and thus salvation."[6] So "hell" can be seen as an experience of divine abandonment followed by mercy. As Denck says, quoting 1 Samuel 2, "The Lord leads down into hell and up again."[7] However, it seems that the "hell" of which he speaks here is a "hell" experienced prior to death; he never clearly refer to post-mortem punishments, so caution is needed in assessing the implications of these ideas.

Sin itself is in fact part of the very purpose of God, part of the plan of salvation. God may use evil, but it will be more than compensated for in the end: "He who ordains evil [i.e., God] and yet can compensate with greater gains than the loss he cannot prevent is not to be blamed for evil."[8] God can and will overcome evil in creation: "For sin against God is to be reckoned as nothing; and however great it might be, God can, will, and indeed already has, overcome it for himself to his own eternal praise without harm for any creatures."[9] This flies close to the wind on the question of universal salvation, but remains frustratingly ambiguous.

In the treatise on *Divine Order* (1526), Denck writes, "God desires everyone to be saved, but knows full well that many condemn themselves. If then his will were to force anyone through a mere order, he could say the word this instant and it would happen. But this would diminish his righteousness." Here Denck sounds like what would today be called a freewill theist. He goes on to say that when a sinner rejects God, he "has come to the place for which he was predestined, which is hell." Again, thus far he seems not unlike Erasmus in his defense of human freedom (directed against Luther). The surprise comes in what follows. According to Denck, the sinner in hell "does not necessarily want to nor need he remain there, of course, for 'even hell is exposed before the Lord and damnation has no cover' (Job xxvi)."[10] The possibility of salvation from

6. Steenbuch, "Reconciling Conflicting Convictions," para. 15.

7. Denck, *Bekenntnis*, 61 (*Hans Denck Schriften*, 45).

8. Denck, "Whether God Is the Cause of Evil," 103.

9. Denck, "Whether God Is the Cause of Evil," 90.

10. Denck, *Ordnung Gotts*, 219 (*Hans Denck Schriften*, 92).

"hell" is very clearly proclaimed. However, a few lines later Denck can speak of people continuing to resist and thus submerging themselves in death, so yet again we must stop short of confident declarations on Denck's universalism.

While it seems clear that Denck believed that God works to redeem sinners from hell, it is not clear whether or not Denck thought that sinners could, in theory, continue to resist God forever, and thus unclear whether or not he was a card-carrying universalist. He certainly never explicitly claims in his published works that all will be saved. According to William Klassen and Morwenna Ludlow, Denck probably was not a supporter of universal salvation, even though he was accused of being one on at least three occasions.[11] However, his teaching on God's saving love for all, Christ's death for all, the divine spark in all, and his insistence on the therapeutic and purifying nature of punishments probably favored the accusations of universalism against him, and it is possible that his accusers were correct, at least in detecting the natural trajectory of his theology.

However, Denck's ideas, also spread by his follower Hans Hut, gained no favor in Anabaptist circles, despite the claims of their opponents, both Catholic and Protestant. Some other Radical Reformation theologians affirmed at least the possibility of universal salvation—Clement Ziegler, August Bader, and Anthony Pocquet, for instance, argued for the possibility of the salvation of the demons[12]—and future research may reveal other Reformation-period Christians with universalist sympathies.

UNIVERSALISM IN COUNTER-REFORMATION CATHOLICISM

Beyond Protestantism, in the Catholic world, universalism was equally rare. Here the church kept a very tight grip on what could and what could not be taught, and universal salvation was considered a dangerous heresy that would undermine righteous living. So it is little surprise that we see but fleeting glimpses of a wider hope. However, there were a few interesting exceptions, such as Giorgio Rioli, nicknamed Siculo (ca. 1517–51), a Benedictine monk who was the founder of the Georgian movement. He wrote in Sicilian and was killed in prison as a result of a religious

11. Ludlow, "Hans Denck," 257–74; Klassen, "Hans Denck."

12. According to Williams, *Radical Reformation*, 832–45.

trial by the Inquisition. In his most important published work, his *Letter* (*Epistla alli cittadini della riva Trento*, Bologna 1550), he proclaimed the final restoration of all people, which in his view will be made possible by Christ. (This work elicited a rebuttal from John Calvin, the Protestant Reformer, in 1551.)[13]

One Catholic thinker who warrants some more comment is a French mystic named Guillaume Postel. Postel is interesting not only for being a Catholic, but also for being a very clear example of a universalist theology deeply shaped by esotericism.

Guillaume Postel (1510–81)

Guillaume Postel—born in Normandy and educated in Paris—was a scholar of repute and a Catholic priest associated at various points with Ignatius Loyola and the Jesuits, though he was never a Jesuit himself.[14] Postel was a true "Renaissance man"—an accomplished linguist (able to work in Arabic, Hebrew, Syriac, Greek, and Latin), an astronomer, a cartographer, and a diplomat, serving in the French embassy in Istanbul from 1535 to 1536/7, when Francis I sought an alliance with the Ottoman Turks. While there, and on a later trip around the Holy Land and Syria (1548–51), he collected Eastern manuscripts for the King of France's royal library. When he returned to France he was appointed Professor of Mathematics and Oriental Languages at the Collège Royal. After some years, Postel resigned his post and traveled around Europe collecting Greek, Hebrew, and Arabic manuscripts and translating them.

His first universalist publication was *De orbis terrae Concordia* (*Concerning the Harmony of the Earth*) in 1544. Here he argued that all the religions of the world shared a common core—the love of God, the

---

13. Calvin, *De aeterna Dei praedestinatione*.

14. On Postel, see Bouwsma, *Career and Thought*; Kuntz, *Guillaume Postel*; Petry, *Gender, Kabbalah, and the Reformation*; Blanchard, *Will All Be Saved?* 83–86; McClymond, *Devil's Redemption*, 176–80.

worship of God, the love of humanity, and the importance of helping humanity. Christianity (the *philosophia Christiana*) was the best representation of this core, and the day was coming soon when all pagans, Jews, and Muslims would be convinced by this truth and convert to Christianity.

His universalistic optimism was grounded in his belief that Christ dwells within all, whether or not they recognize him. Given that Christ indwells all people, there is within them an impulse toward the good and toward their eschatological unification with God, an impulse that they cannot resist forever. This idea allowed him to identify godly people who were not Christians, but whom he considered members of the *ecclesia generalis*. These people—who would come to be called "anonymous Christians" in the twentieth-century Catholic thought of Karl Rahner—fell into different categories (e.g., those who had not heard of Christ, those who had heard but did not understand Christ, etc.). When all people are united in mind and spirit they will participate in the unity of God himself. For all things proceed from and reach their destiny in the divine unity. (This notion of the unity of all things with each other in God pervaded his thinking.)

His universalist inclinations became central to his life and mission through a life-changing relationship he developed in 1547–49. While he was working on translating mystical Jewish Kabbalistic texts in Venice,[15] Postel worked as a chaplain in the Hospital of Saints John and Paul, and became the confessor of a woman aged around fifty, an illiterate virgin named Johanna (1497–1549), who had given her life in service of the poor and sick at the hospital. She confessed to him that she had experienced visions, and he came to believe that she was a prophetess with global significance in the plans of God—a new Eve, Sophia, a Cosmic Mary, the "mother of the world," indeed, a female messiah. She would usher in a new age of political and religious harmony. He came to see himself as her spiritual son, with a divine destiny as a prophet and priest to unite the religions of the world in the coming cosmic restoration.

In Postel's view, Jesus had redeemed the superior, "masculine" part of the soul (associated with intellect), but not the inferior, "female" part of the soul (associated with emotion). He believed that Johanna, filled with Christ's spirit, had been sent to save the lower part of the soul, bringing to holistic completion God's salvific work in humanity.

15. The mystical theology of Jewish Kabbalah played a major role in Postel's own theology. His knowledge of it was extensive, and he was one of the first Christians to absorb it into his theology.

When Johanna died in 1549, Postel went into a coma for several weeks and believed himself to be possessed by her spirit. He claimed that she had communicated to him a message of universal pardon, universal restoration, universal baptism.[16] His function was to proclaim pardon and absolution to all people, thereby playing a pivotal role in the coming global restitution. In Postel's universalist future, all humans would be united within a reformed Catholic Church under the rule of the French monarchy. This would be the true reformation of the world, unlike the pseudo-reformation of the Protestants.

In 1553, Postel published two books based on his own visions, and this brought the Inquisition down on him, deeply concerned about his heterodoxy. Because of his longstanding connections with the Jesuits, who were conducting the Inquisition, he was not condemned as a heretic (a sentence that brought a death penalty), but was de-priested and declared insane, a verdict that was devastating to Postel. All his works, past and future, were put on the index of forbidden books in 1555, and he was confined to the papal prison in Rome and then the monastery of St. Martin des Champes in Paris. However, he continued to declare his idiosyncratic apocalyptic views—a blend of Christian theology, Jewish Kabbalah (mysticism), Islamic texts, and Mother Johanna's visionary teachings—until his death in 1581.

The Reformation opened a door to universalist speculations, but in both Protestantism and especially Catholicism these speculations only manifest themselves sporadically and at the fringes. None of the characters mentioned in this chapter—Denck, Rioli, and Postel—made any lasting impression on the theology of Christian universalism. They serve only to illustrate that here and there such matters were beginning to be considered. The seventeenth century was to witness some more overt manifestations of the wider hope in Protestantism, but as we shall see in the subsequent chapters, it was not until the eighteenth century that such ideas would really take root.

16. Kuntz, *Guillaume Postel*, 80–81.

2

Seventeenth-Century Troublemaker

Gerrard Winstanley

THE MID-SEVENTEENTH CENTURY WAS a time of great turmoil and increasing religious radicalism in England. As Andrew Bradstock notes, "the combined effect of three very bloody Civil Wars, the trial and execution of the Archbishop of Canterbury and the king, and the abolition of institutions such as the monarchy, House of Lords, Star Chamber, bishops and church courts combined to create a breakdown of censorship which allowed ideas hitherto considered heretical and kept underground to surface in print and word."[1] Among the many radical sectarian religious groups that arose in those apocalyptic, world-changing days of horrors and hope were the likes of the Baptists, the Levellers, the Diggers, the Ranters, the Quakers, the Fifth Monarchists, and the (wonderfully named) Muggletonians. And among the "heretical" ideas that manifested themselves, albeit not prominent among them, was the hope that in the end all would be saved. The man who first declared this in print was Gerrard Winstanley, leader of the True Levellers, or—as others called them—the Diggers.

1. Bradstock, *Radical Religion*, xiii.

GERRARD WINSTANLEY (1609–76) AND THE DIGGERS

The public ministry of Gerrard Winstanley was brief, a mere four years (1648–52).[2] For a while it burned hopefully; indeed, he became a figure of much discussion and debate in the capital, but it ended in disappointment.

"England is not a free people, till the poor that have no land, have a free allowance to dig and labour the commons..."
Gerrard Winstanley, 1649

Winstanley was born in Lancashire and moved to London, aged twenty-one, to work in the cloth trade, which he did until his business failed in 1643, perhaps as a result of the disruption caused by the English Civil War. He then moved near to Cobham in Surrey, where his father-in-law lived, to look after cattle. Here he fell upon hard times, especially following the harsh winter of 1647/48 and the failed harvest, which, combined with the huge increases in the levy demanded by the Army, drove Winstanley and many others into poverty.

Winstanley had grown up in an English parish church, being a committed churchgoer, moving with the cultural flow, but that changed after a religious awakening, possibly provoked by his own experiences of hardship. This moved him to denounce the established clergy and to leave the parish church and associate with those the authorities considered "sectarians."

Early in 1648 he started writing and took his manuscript, the first of twenty publications over the next four years, to the printers in London. This book, *The Mysterie of God, concerning the Whole Creation, Mankinde* (1648) is very possibly the first English-language defense of universal salvation in print.[3] It is all the more surprising given that it came out at a

2. On Winstanley, see Bradstock, *Winstanley and the Diggers*; Bradstock, *Radical Religion*, ch. 3; Boulton, *Gerrard Winstanley*; Gurney, *Brave Community*; McClymond, *Devil's Redemption*, 494–97.

3. Setting aside the implicit universalism in Julian of Norwich's *Revelations of Divine Love*. Winstanley's book was followed only a year later by Richard Coppin's *Divine Teachings* (1649) and *The Exaltation of All Things in Christ* (1649). Coppin's universalism did get him into trouble with the law and he was put on trial in Worcester for alleging "that all men whatsoever shall be saved, and there shall be no general day

time when public declarations of universalism were being made illegal in the Blasphemy Law of May 1648.[4] (The perceived need for the new law suggests that some were starting to teach universalism, or at least that the authorities feared that they were.) But Winstanley was not a man to be concerned about man-made laws if they went against what he considered the teachings of God.

It was not long after this publication that Winstanley's reconfigured faith was to take on a strong theo-political flavor in a theologically inspired form of proto-communism.

The year 1649 began with the execution of King Charles I—a tyrant in Winstanley's view—and a second catastrophic harvest failure, compounding the already-grim plight of the poor, with many starving. And Gerrard Winstanley had what he called a "trance" in which God spoke to him: "Worke together. Eat bread together." He believed that the Lord made clear to him that in creation all humans are equal, with none to rule over others, and that the earth had been given to *all* as "a common treasury." The landowners disenfranchised the poor by claiming the land as their private property, and the ancient rights of the people to use the land were gradually being eroded. So Winstanley and a handful of others felt led by God to engage in a prophetic act of land reclamation and community building. At the start of April, they set up a camp on (St.) George's Hill, Surrey, which was on common land, and planted beans, carrots, and parsnips. Hence they became known as Diggers.

---

of judgment." The Jury found him guilty of blasphemy, but the judge demurred. This story was repeated again at his second trial in Oxford in 1652. He continued to preach and get in trouble over the issue of universalism in the years that followed. Other universalist publications soon followed, two anonymous works: *God's Light Declared in Mysteries* (1653) and *Of the Torments of Hell: The Foundation and Pillars Thereof Discovered, Searched, Shaken, and Removed* (1660); the latter is often attributed to Samuel Richardson (fl. 1643–58), seeming to deny any hell in the afterlife.

4. "Be it further Ordained by the Authority aforesaid, That all and every person or persons that shall publish or maintain as aforesaid any of the several errours hereafter ensuing, viz. *That all men shall be saved*. . . . The party so convicted shall be ordered by the said Justices to renounce his said Errors in the publique Congregation of the same Parish from whence the complaint doth come, or where the offence was committed, and in case he refuseth or neglecteth to perform the same, at or upon the day, time, and place appointed by the said Justices then he shall be committed to prison by the said Justices until he shall finde two sufficient Sureties before two Justices of Peace for the said place or County (whereof one shall be of the Quorum) that he shall not publish or maintain the said errour or errours any more" (italics added).

Their intention was not to force any landowners off their land—indeed, Winstanley was consistently committed to non-violence throughout all his activity[5]—but to cultivate *common, untilled* land. His hope was that this act would inspire many more to join them and others to set up similar communities throughout the land. The plan was that, in the end, the landowners would find their supply of cheap labor drying up, as the poor now had land to cultivate on the commons and hills, and so landowners would be forced to reduce their holdings to a size they could tend themselves, eventually coming to see the truth that the land does not belong to them anyway.

This whole vision was couched in biblical language in Winstanley's many publications on it—it was, in his eyes, an eschatological recovery of creation, a liberation from oppressive political and economic tyranny. The Diggers were acting in the Spirit as part of the vanguard of new creation where the poor would feast on the fruit of the earth and none would hunger.

The community at George's Hill—and later on Cobham Heath, where it relocated—did grow (albeit at nothing like the rate Winstanley had hoped),[6] but it experienced fierce and sustained opposition from those with vested interest in the status quo: the Diggers were threatened often, physically attacked on numerous occasions; their houses were dismantled or burned down several times; their seeds and crops were spoiled; their property was confiscated; they faced spells in prison, were taken to court, and even to parliament; and all sorts of misleading stories were spread about them. In the end, in April 1650, around fifty men led by the local parson forcibly routed them, and the experiment came to an end.

Winstanley continued to write for two more years, seeking other routes to achieve the goal, but then he fell out of the public eye. We know little about his life after 1652. He associated briefly with the Quakers and then inherited his father-in-law's estate around 1657, becoming a "gentleman" and falling back into his pre-sectarian ways as a member of the parish church, even serving as a churchwarden (a fact that has flummoxed

---

5. "Victory that is gotten by the Sword, is a Victory that slaves get one over another; . . . but Victory obtained by Love, is a Victory for a King" (quoted in Boulton, *Gerrard Winstanley*, 62).

6. He had expected that, within ten days, four or five thousand people would come. The actual numbers were a tiny fraction of that.

some historians). After his wife's death, his father-in-law took away the estate again. He remarried and eventually became a Quaker.[7]

We do not know exactly when or how Winstanley came to affirm the final restoration. The preface to the *Mysterie of God* says that when he first encountered the idea he found it very strange and objectionable, but that God revealed its truth to him and he now sees great beauty in it. Beyond this we can only guess. He was certainly scathing about theological learning that came through books by "experts," and he claims that his own teachings came from two sources only—Scripture and his own inner experiences with God.[8] In his *Watch-word to the City of London and the Armie*, he writes that, after years of suffering, "my heart was filled with sweet thoughts, and many things were revealed to me which I have never read in books, nor heard from the mouth of the flesh." One of those revelations was that "the earth shall be made a common Treasury of livelihood to whole mankind, without respect of persons." Was universalism one of the others? That may well be the case. His universalism certainly has its own idiosyncratic feel, and there are no obvious direct sources from which he would have learned it.

WINSTANLEY'S UNIVERSALISM

The big picture:
The telos of humanity as the dwelling place of God

The Mysterie of God, concerning the Whole Creation, Mankinde, while not erudite, is full of theological interest. The book offers a short overview of what Winstanley perceives to be the story of God and creation from Genesis to Revelation. God's ultimate aim in creation was to fully indwell the humanity of Adam, but in the beginning God deliberately refrained from this. Adam was created pure and good, but God did not bodily indwell his humanity. In Winstanley's view, *Adam himself* was the Garden of Eden that God had made for his own delight, to inhabit and walk in. The lovely plants that grew in Eden were the holy virtues of love, joy, peace, humility, and the like. (He also thought that humanity was created as the biblical heaven, the dwelling place of God.) However, the

7. For an excellent discussion of Winstanley's perplexing final years see Boulton, *Gerrard Winstanley*, ch. 13.

8. See the appendix for a critique of McClymond's suggestion that Jakob Böhme was an influence.

very ontological "distance," as we might phrase it, between Creator and creation meant that without God's in-filling, when left to itself, creation would inevitably degenerate and fall away from goodness into self-love:

> But all these created qualities, and a Being distinct from the Be-ing of God; God knew and saw, that there would spring up as a weed, and the first fruits of it likewise, an inclinable principle, or spirit of self-love aspiring up in the midst of this created, living Garden, and in the midst of every plant therein, which is indeed, aspiring to be as God, or to be a Being of it selfe, equall to, yet distinct from God. . . . [A]s the purest water being let stand, does in time putrifie, so I say, God knew that the first fruit that this created Being would bring forth, would be an aspiring desire to be equall, or like God himself, which if the creature delighted in, and so ate, or satisfied himself in his own fruit, he should die; but if he forsook his own invention, and stuck close to God, acknowledging his [i.e., God's] Being to be his [i.e., Adam's] life, and all in all, then he should live. (2–3)[9]

In other words, God structured creation in such a way that the creature must know itself to be a creature utterly dependent on the Creator if it is to find true life. The temptation is to turn from God to our own fruit, our own self, for wisdom and life, but to do so is death. So "the ground of Adams fall, arises up first in Adams heart, as fruit growing up from a created Being" (4). Importantly, for Winstanley, the Serpent that guided humanity to sin was not a creature directly created by God, nor some eternal principle existing alongside God. Rather, the Serpent was the self-focused principle that arose within Adam himself, the inner corruption within humanity. In that sense, *we* originated it.[10] For "every action, or dispensation of God, is called a Spirit, or an Angel, and every action, or aspiring principle that rises up in *Adam*, which led him to disobedience, it pleased God that it should have a Being, and likewise be called a Spirit, but it is a dead Being, and a Spirit of darknesses" (21).[11] All this is the great "mystery of Iniquity."

But the great mystery of salvation, which is really the mystery of di-vine self-manifestation, is that God will not allow his creation, humanity,

---

9. The following in-text citations in this section on Winstanley are from *The Mys-terie of God*, unless otherwise stated.

10. So the Serpent was *indirectly* created by God. But it is not a creature in the sense of being a distinct substance, like humans are.

11. Unless otherwise specified, all italics in quotations are from the original sources.

to be forever ruined. If that were to happen, God himself would be dishonored, for his work would spoil in his hand and he would thus have failed to bring it to the fullness for which he intended it. "But the work of God shall be restored from this lost, dead, weedy, & enslaved condition, and the fruit of the created Being [i.e., the self-focused principle, the Serpent] shall utterly perish and be ashamed" (6). Thus God's work in creation is aimed "to destroy this Serpent out of the flesh, and all Beings, that is enmity against him, and to swallow up his Creature *Man* into himself, that so there may bee but onely pure, endlesse, and infinite Being, even God himself all in all, dwelling and walking in this garden, *Mankinde*, in which he will plant pleasant fruit trees, and pluck up weeds" (6–7). Here is Winstanley's expression of what other Christian traditions refer to as *thēosis* or deification—the profound eschatological union of God and humanity.[12]

In sum, Winstanley believed that God deliberately made creation in a fragile state, open to corruption if it curved in on itself, so that he might "destroy all the inventions and actings of the creature, that did spring up and arise from the creatures Being, as a creature, and not from God's acting in the creature" (20). The end result of the long pedagogical process is that in the end "every thing that is in, or about the Creature, that is of God, shall stand; but every thing that is in, or from the creature, that is not of God, shall fall and perish" (21).

The seven dispensations of the mystery of God

Now the mystery of God—which brings about the deliverance of humanity—does not take place all at once, but in stages. The seven dispensations of the mystery of God are as follows:

(1) The giving of the law to Adam (i.e., do not eat of the tree). Humanity is delivered over to two murderers: the law and the flesh. God's law—which is holy, just, and good—declares that there are two roads: God's road to life and the self's own road to death. But when combined with the flesh (i.e., our human aspiration to be as God and to be the source of our own life and being) the law becomes a killer, sentencing us

---

12. For Winstanley, even if God were to make sinful creatures pure again, if they were left to live according to God's holy law in their own created strength they would only fall into sin again. Deification is thus necessary to perfect creation.

to a state of death. In this condition, there can be no hope for us (apart from God).

(2) Immediately God steps in with a promise that encapsulates the core of the mystery: "And I will put enmity between thee [the Serpent] and the woman, and between thy seed and her seed; it shall bruise thy head, and thou shalt bruise his heel" (Gen 3:15, KJV). In Winstanley's interpretation, this means that the Serpent shall be uprooted from human nature, where it dwells, and be destroyed. And the one who will do this is the offspring of the woman—Jesus. So God makes clear from the start that he has no intention of destroying *us*, only the Serpent, to whom we have become enslaved. With his death comes our liberation.

(3) The promise of salvation becomes more specific in God's promise to Abraham that in his offspring the nations would find blessing (Gen 12:3).

(4) The fourth dispensation of the mystery is the period from Moses to Jesus—a time of increasing revelation in the form of types and shadows, anticipating the fullness in Christ.

(5) The critical fifth period runs from the appearance of God-in-the-flesh in the person of Jesus (who takes away the sin of the world) to the day of Pentecost, when God was manifest in the flesh of the saints by his Spirit. In redemption, God appears as the God of love, manifest in the flesh of Jesus Christ. God indwells the humanity of Jesus fully, bodily, which is unlike his relationship to the humanity of Adam. God battled the Serpent and "cast him out of heaven" (i.e., out of human nature) *in the humanity of Christ:*

> [F]or I beleeve that all temptations that Jesus Christ met withall, *(for in all things he was tempted like unto us)* they were but the strivings of the Serpent, as he did strive in *Adam* that fell, to maintain its being opposite to *God*; but Jesus Christ, or the anoynting in flesh, being not a created power, but the power of *God* in that created humanity, did not consent as the first *Adam* did, for he with strong hand resisted the whispering of the Serpent, and would acknowledge no other Being but *God*, and so prevailed, and cast the Serpent out of flesh, and hath obtained a legall power to quicken whom he will, or to cast the Serpent out of what man or woman he will. (25)

In Christ, *God himself* rules as King *in* humanity; in Jesus' humanity, God's wisdom becomes the wisdom of the creature; God's power, the power of the creature; God's joy, the joy of the creature; God's love, the love of the creature.

Thus redemption is *already* complete, both in the sense that God has *willed* from all eternity and *promised* from ancient times to do it (Gen 3:15; 12:3) and in the sense that the union of God and humanity is already achieved *in Jesus*. However, it is not yet completed in the creation as a whole. Christ serves as a firstfruit and a pledge of what God will one day do for the whole.

(6) The sixth dispensation is the period from Pentecost until the elect are gathered up on resurrection day for final judgment. This penultimate dispensation in which we now live is one in which only the elect participate in the divine life, and it continues "til the whole number of the elect be taken up to God" (44). Throughout this dispensation, "*God* is pleased to doe his worke in length of time, by degrees, calling some at one houre, and some at another, out of the Serpents bondage, and the times and seasons *God* hath reserved to himself" (29).

Winstanley's thinking seems to be akin to Calvinism here. The elect are those whom God chooses to call to salvation now, and when God calls they will come: "he will save under every dispensation whom he will, and bring them to *Sion* [a spiritual symbol for communal union with God]" (41); "Now for God to save some at one houre, and some at another, both when he will, and whom he will" (42). In Winstanley's view, this sixth period was fast drawing to a close, ushering in the final dispensation, the day of judgment.

(7) The coming dispensation completes and perfects the manifestation of God, and it has three phases: first, resurrection of the dead for both believers and unbelievers; second, final judgment, followed by a verdict of eternal life for believers and eternal condemnation for unbelievers (i.e., to be cast into the fire prepared for the devil and his angels); third, the salvation of all creation, including all those people in the lake of fire.[13]

The "day" of judgment, according to Winstanley, is not a literal day, but a season of unspecified length that endures as long as the work of

---

13. Winstanley sees the first death as the bondage to the Serpent brought about in Adam and the second death as the Serpent's death in the lake of fire. Those delivered from bondage to the Serpent in this life (the elect) take part in the first resurrection and the second death has no power over them. However, those still under the Serpent's power will enter the lake of fire with him until God finally casts the Serpent out of them too and they exit the fire, leaving the Serpent to his fate alone.

judgment lasts (only God knows how long that will be)—until all people are delivered from the second death.

The Serpent knows that he is destined to final destruction and nothing would make him happier than taking some of God's creatures down with him, "but the Serpent *only* shall perish, and God will not lose a hair that he made, he will redeeme his whole creation from death. . . . Therefore in the third part of this great day of judgment, after the City work is finished, and the trial over, then does the tree of life, God himself that dwells in the City, and is the light, and life, and glory of it, send forth dispensations, or Angels, bringing love to heale the Nations, and bring their glory into the City" (47, italics added).

Then God, in Christ, will "take up all his Creation, Mankind, into himself, and will become, the only, endless, pure, absolute, and infinite being, even infinitely for ever all in all, in every one, and in the whole, that no flesh may glory in it self, but in the Lord only" (13). This, in his view, is what Paul spoke of when he spoke of the Son having all things submitted to him and then he himself in his humanity submitting to the Father so that God will "*be* all . . . *in* all" (1 Cor 15:28). Creatures will no longer look to themselves for their life-source, but to God, who will be their life. In creation, humans were made "in a Being distinct from God," which is what made them susceptible to spiraling away from God, but, through Christ, in new creation humans will be "made spirituall, and swallowed up in life, or taken up into the Being of God" (18) such that the Serpent can never rear his head again.

Anticipating critics

To those who balk at the notion of being saved from hell, Winstanley argues that they already believe in it, for hell is the *present* condition of all those lost in sin. It seems that he saw the hell following the day of judgment as simply a climactic version of this same alienation. Thus, every elect person who is called by God to gospel-life in this age is someone delivered from hell. Those saved from the fire after the day of judgment are experiencing something of the same kind, albeit in an eschatologically enhanced form.

For those who say that if God will save all then they will eat, drink, and be merry, Winstanley warns, "thou shalt be cast into the everlasting fire . . . and while thou art in it, the worm of thy gnawing conscience shall never die, nor the fire of God's wrath, or the sense of his anger upon thee, shall never goe out" (20).[14] This, he insists, is not a theology for the morally lax.

For those who balk at the idea of their enemies being saved in the end, Winstanley comments,

> It is much for the glory of God for him to redeeme, not part onely, but all mankinde from death, which his own hands made, it is his revealed will so to do, therefore let it be your joy that the will of your Father is, and shall be fulfilled; and do not thinke the Saints are made unhappy, and God dishonored, if he heale them that were lost, and that did not enter into the City, in the beginning of the great day of judgment, for as he is honored in saving you of the Citie that were lost: so he will be honored in redeeming these that lye under the power of the second death. (Preface)

ON REFLECTION

Several features of Winstanley's theological outlook warrant comment. His account of evil in creation is interesting in that he seeks to offer a story that does not present evil (or Satan) as God's creation—that which God made was good and pure—while at the same time avoiding a Manichean dualism in which evil becomes an eternal principle alongside God. Evil and Satan have the potential to arise within humanity as a natural devolution of God's good creation should certain conditions not be met. And while God did not ordain the fall, he foresaw it and planned to use it to teach his creatures that life is found by looking to their Creator, not themselves. God's goal in creation was to indwell humanity, but this goal is not achieved until Jesus, who is an anticipation of the manifestation of God in the saints and ultimately in all creation.

Winstanley's focus on God's indwelling humanity as the *telos* of creation governs everything. It makes the incarnation central to his redemption narrative. What is striking and unusual is the lack of emphasis on the death of Jesus—he never spells out a theological role for this event in his universalist "system." One wonders whether he thought that the incarnation alone and the anointing of the Spirit are enough. Winstanley

14. For Winstanley, the biblical language of "eternal" fire and "eternal" punishment referred to punishment that endures for a dispensation, in this case that of the "day" of judgment.

does mention Christ's death in his works, and believed that it happened, but he has little interest in either Christ's death or resurrection as *past events*. What was most important about the resurrection, in his view, was its *contemporary* embodied meaning as an ongoing experience in the lives of individuals and the true community that they form (Christ rising and being present *within them*). The community *was* the body of Christ and Christ ought not to be thought of as "distant" or "apart from" his body. Thus, Winstanley's focus was on *the community inhabited by the risen Lord. In them* Christ was risen and *in them* the second coming was gradually manifesting in creation. But this is only the sixth dispensation; the time is coming when the earth will be filled with the knowledge of the glory of the Lord as the waters cover the sea (Hab 2:14). In *some* ways, he was a seventeenth-century precursor to Rudolph Bultmann's twentieth-century program of demythologizing theological language.

Indeed, in his last publication, *The Law of Freedom in a Platform*, addressed to Oliver Cromwell, he seems to take this "demythologizing" to the limit by claiming that it is beyond human knowledge to try to talk about what God is *in himself*, apart from and beyond creation, or to speak about what happens to the human soul *after death*. We have no access to such knowledge and it is fruitless to try to figure such things out.

> And if a man should go to imagine what God is beyond the creation, or what he will be in a spiritual demonstration after a man is dead, he doth (as the proverb saith) build castles in the air, or tells us of a world beyond the moon and beyond the sun, merely to blind the reason of man.
>
> I'll appeal to your self in this question, what other knowledge have you of God but what you have within the circle of the creation?
>
> For if the creation in all its dimensions be the fulness of him that fills all with himself, and if you yourself be part of this creation, where can you find God but in that line or station wherein you stand?[15]

This could indeed suggest that, in his mature thought at least, he had moved to understand talk of both hell and universal salvation as bringing out the spiritual dimension of *this-worldly* realities. He did not deny a further application to a heaven and hell after death, but he refused to speculate on it.

15. Winstanley, *Law of Freedom*, ch. 4.

His "spiritual" and "internal" reading of various aspects of biblical theology (Eden and heaven interpreted as human nature—God's dwelling place, the devil as human selfishness, hell as the experience of captivity to our own selfish and self-destructive desires, angels as divine actions/dispensations, etc.) is interesting and resonated with others in the period whose religion was focused on God within, rather than "outward religion." But while Winstanley was what we might call a demythologizer, it would be a mistake to see him as a seventeenth-century anti-realist, one who saw God as merely the symbol of the "divine" aspect of humanity (i.e., Reason).[16] Winstanley's theology is more nuanced than that, indeed looking to one's self as God is for him the very essence of sin. He certainly did emphasize the immanence of God and the centrality of experiential knowledge of God within (in understandable reaction against what he saw as a common view of God as distant and remote), but even in his later thought he does not abandon divine transcendence, and retains a distinction between Creator and creature, even in the final end-time union.[17] While it is true that he sees God as Reason, this association seems very similar to classical Christian Logos theology, grounded in John's Gospel (1:1–18) and developed by theologians since the second century. It is precisely a theology that holds in tension the transcendence and immanence of God—the Logos/Reason that cannot be reduced to human rationality, but which human rationality participates in. That his focus was on the presence of God/Reason within is not an indication that God was merely a religious symbol for an aspect of human nature. But it did mean that God could only be known as experienced in, by, and through creation. In his view, we need the humility not to try to press beyond that.

However, it was not universalism for which Winstanley is best remembered, but his theologically funded, proto-communist political activity. His musings on the wider hope do not appear to have made many waves, though later English universalists did look back to him as a precursor.

16. Contra David Boulton in *Gerrard Winstanley and the Republic of Heaven*.

17. That said, his later radical apophatic agnosticism about the transcendental referent of language about God, heaven, and hell is in real danger of losing his earlier balance of transcendence and immanence, a balance without which both transcendence and immanence lose their power. While he does not deny transcendence, he loses interest in it, which is a big step toward losing it altogether. Then all we are left with is evocative language. He did not get to that point, yet arguably the fine-tuning of his earlier thought is both more profound, theologically and philosophically, and more helpful to his cause.

3

Platonists and Puritans

THE SIXTEENTH-CENTURY PROTESTANT UNIVERSALISTS were, for the most part, not drawn from among the educated classes. However, that was to change in the seventeenth century. That century, in the period from 1658–62, witnessed a revival of interest in the works of Origen among certain scholars linked with Cambridge University, a small number of whom flirted with the theology of *apokatastasis* in one form or another. This was "an Origenist moment in English theology."[1] We also find some scholarly Puritans, with links to this same Cambridge movement, with distinctly Calvinist forms of universalism that are worthy of serious attention, not least because of the serious focus they place on the Bible. It is to the work of these Platonists and Puritans that we turn in this chapter.

ORIGENIAN UNIVERSALISM AND THE CAMBRIDGE PLATONISTS

During the Renaissance, Origen was read and defended by humanists of the caliber of Pico della Mirandola and Erasmus.[2] In 1486, in the twenty-ninth theological conclusion of his *900 Conclusions*, the former declared, "it is more reasonable to believe that Origen is saved rather than to believe that he is damned." From the second half of the seventeenth century, Origen's works began to enjoy a wider diffusion. His universalistic theories were sympathetically received by some thinkers such as the

---

1. Sarah Hutton, quoted in McClymond, *Devil's Redemption*, 405.
2. Crouzel, *Une controverse*; Schär, *Das Nachleben des Origenes*.

Cambridge Platonists[3]—a group of philosophical theologians working in Cambridge University.[4] They were based in Puritan colleges, but drew on both Puritan and Laudian[5] traditions, while subjecting both to critique and correction in the light of reason, understood as a gift from God.

The Cambridge Platonists were much interested in Origen, a Christian Platonist, and in the Platonic tradition, which they tended to see as a perennial philosophy (*philosophia perennis*), the idea of the continuity of Platonism through all the ages as the true philosophy (an idea typical of Italian humanism, for instance Marsilio Ficino, and of philosophers like Leibniz).

Like Origen, the Cambridge Platonists had both a theological and a philosophical formation; they did not deem philosophy and theology to conflict with one another, for they were convinced of the compatibility between biblically informed faith and reason.

Henry More, George Rust, and Ann Conway

Henry More (1614–87)

Henry More, a fellow of Christ's College, Cambridge, where he taught for many years, was raised as a Calvinist, though he could never come to terms with such theology. More wrote *An Explanation of the Grand Mystery of Godliness: or a True and Faithful Representation of the Everlasting Gospel of our Lord and Saviour Jesus Christ* (1660). Here he rejected Calvinistic predestination, just as Origen had rejected "gnostic"

---

3. The group did not acquire this name until the nineteenth century.

4. The most important were Henry More (1614–87) and Ralph Cudworth (1617–89), both fellows at Christ's College. Others were Benjamin Whichcote (1609–83); Peter Sterry (1613–72), who expounded universalistic tenets, including the restoration of the demons, in a manuscript that was not published; John Smith (1618–52); Nathaniel Culverwell (1619–51); and John Worthington (1618–71), all fellows at the Emmanuel College. Among the youngest are John Norris (1657–1711), George Rust, and Anne Conway, to whom we shall return. Cf. Cragg, *Cambridge Platonists*; Jones, *Cambridge Platonists*.

5. Laudianism was a reform movement within the early seventeenth-century Church of England. It affirmed the freewill of humans and the potential for all people to accept salvation, thereby rejecting Calvinistic predestination. Most of the Cambridge Platonists rejected Calvinistic views of freedom and predestination, though, as we shall see, Peter Sterry and Jeremiah White held on to the Puritan view, albeit with a universalist twist.

predestination, and insisted on the harmonization of justice and goodness in God, as Origen had done.

Among More's many literary works, there is one on the immortality of the soul dedicated to Lord Conway, his one-time student, and another dedicated to his wife, Lady Anne Conway.[6] Ann Conway was both an informal student and friend of More and, as we shall see, a convinced supporter of the doctrine of universal salvation.[7]

Belief in the preexistence of souls experienced a small revival in the seventeenth and eighteenth centuries, and More, along with some of the other Cambridge Platonists, accepted the Platonic and Plotinian doctrine of the preexistence of souls. For More, this doctrine played a helpful role in theodicy, explaining how God is not unjust in allowing people to begin and live life on earth in such difficult circumstances. (However, while this belief was considered at the time to be Origen's, it is not exactly in line with Origen's own thought, but rather with that of later Origenism.)[8] Furthermore, Henry More thought that the first human being was created as a pure spirit, and only because of the fall was it endowed with a body. (This too was considered at the time to be Origen's teaching, whereas in fact Origen actually thought that all rational beings had a "subtle body" from the beginning.)[9]

6. Respectively *An Antidote against Atheism: or, An Appeal to the Natural Faculties of the Mind of Man, Whether There Be Not a God* (1653; second edition with appendix 1655) and *The Immortality of the Soule, So Farre Forth as It Is Demonstrable from the Knowledge of Nature and the Light of Reason* (1659).

7. Both she and More shared many philosophical interests, including the publications of the Teutonic mystic, Jakob Böhme.

8. More expressed this doctrine in some poems, such as *A Platonick Song of the Soul, treating of the Life of the Soul, her Immortalitie, Sleep, Unitie, and Memorie after Death* (1647): "I would sing the Prae-existency / Of humane souls, and live once o'er again / By recollection and quick memory / All that is past since first we all began. / But all too shallow be my wits to scan / So deep a point and mind too dull to clear / So dark a matter. . . . Tell what we mortals are, tell what of old we were. / A spark or ray of the Divinity / Clouded in earthly fogs . . . / A precious drop sunk from Aeternitie, / Spilt on the ground, or rather slunk away."

9. See Ramelli, *Preexistence of Souls?*

More also insists on the importance of human free will and auto-determination ("autoexousy," a term also used by Ralph Cudworth). Here we see his Laudianism and his rejection of predestination at work, but these tendencies were reinforced by his Christian Platonism and easily grounded in the work of Origen. This affirmation of human freedom is, of course, not in contrast with universal salvation, as Origen's own work testifies.

Was More a universalist? Not as far as we can tell. His writings leave no *direct* testimony to that effect, though some have felt that his theology, especially in his *Divine Dialogues* (1668), which argue that God's wisdom and power cannot be separated from his goodness, pointed in that direction. Additionally, he did consider that spiritual progress after death was a reality. It is not accidental that Henry More, who betrays a strong Origenian influence, was close with some who very explicitly flirted with universal salvation—Bishop George Rust and Lady Ann Conway, both of whom were followers of More.

Bishop George Rust (d. 1670)

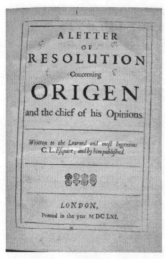

One endorsement of the Origenian doctrine of universal salvation is found in the anonymous *Letter of Resolution Concerning Origen and the Chief of His Opinions* (1661). This work is usually attributed to George Rust, a disciple of the Cambridge Platonist Henry More, and a fellow of Christ's College in Cambridge (1649–59). In 1660, Rust relocated to Ireland, where he was ordained a priest in 1661 (the year this work was published), later serving as Bishop of Dromore in Ireland, from 1667 until his death of a fever in 1670.

The letter explores Rust's understanding of Origen's ideas under six headings:[10] 1. the Trinity (14–21); 2. the preexistence of souls (embodied

---

10. Frustratingly, what is lacking in the book is any indication of where in Origen's corpus the author is getting his information. He has clearly read Origen and numerous other fathers, but for the most part he prefers to paraphrase what he takes their teachings to be, rather than to quote from them. (He does not have the same reticence

PLATONISTS AND PURITANS   39

in heavenly bodies) (21–46); 3. that *earthly*, material bodies were given to humans as punishment for sins committed in the "preexistent" state (46–55); 4. that in the resurrection we shall have heavenly bodies (a restoration of the kind of bodies we had before the fall) (55–71); 5. that after long periods of corrective punishment for the damned, they will be delivered to try their fortunes in regions of the world for which their present nature is fitted (71–81); 6. that the earth will become habitable again after being "destroyed" by fire (81–94). It will then be our eternal home. He then considers the objections to Origen from his opponents and offers what he sees as an Origenian response to each (95–135).[11]

While presented descriptively, presumably because of the incendiary nature of its content, there is no doubt that the author supports the doctrines being set forth. He certainly goes out of his way to offer a positive case for the truth of what he takes to be Origen's opinions (from reason and Scripture) and the problems with alternatives.

The argument put forward in this letter is that God created all beings out of love and for the sake of the happiness of these creatures. What are the implications for eternal torment in hell? Rust, with a touch of humor, attacks those who uphold the eternity of hell for "having easie wayes of assuring themselves that it shall not be their portion." In his view, punishments, both on earth and in the other world, are exclusively educative and purifying, inflicted out of love for creatures, with the end of perfecting them. According to the author, this makes it impossible to think that God created people who will eternally suffer merely retributive punishments, for such punishment would "have nothing in it of that end for which it was inflicted" (i.e., their perfection). The punishments of hell "are curative for the emendation of the party suffering; but this, if it be eternal in the scholastic sense of the word, leaves no place for the betterment of the sufferers, who are never to get out of this inexplicable labyrinth of woe and misery" (75).[12] If God created creatures that could

about quoting from Scripture.)

11. The following in-text citations in this section on Rust are from the *Letter of Resolution*, unless otherwise stated. The objections considered are that Origen's thought is proto-Arian (96–100), criticisms of the preexistence thesis (100–108), six objections to the spiritual nature of the resurrection body (108–30), and complaints about the salvation of demons and curative punishments (130–34). (He notes in 134–35 that Origen's thesis about new creation is not objected to.)

12. By the scholastic sense of eternal, Rust intends to distinguish the meaning of the Hebrew '*olām* and the Greek *aiōn*, both meaning an indefinite period of time, from the notion of eternal. They do not mean eternal in the scholastic sense "unless the

fall into a state beyond all hope of recovery, it reflects rather badly on his sovereign oversight of his creation. God would know whether certain creatures were beyond redemption and he would never have made them in the first place:

> That eternal minde therefore making all things out of a Principle of infinite love, and for the good and happiness of the things themselves, and seeing what he had made and how he had made them, and what was likely to be the lot of some of them from the necessary unperfectness of their Natures, if their future ill hap was likely to be more sharp and dolorous than all the good they should enjoy from him till that calamity befell them grateful and pleasant, his great compassion certainly would have persuaded him quickly to annihilate them; or rather his Wisdom would have judg'd it more decorous never to have made them. (72–73)

To those who object to the possibility of the salvation of fallen angels, he asks:

> what difference is there in the distance betwixt a *devil* made an *angel*, and an *angel* made a *devil*? I am sure the advantage is on the ascending part rather than on the descending; for the mercy and compassion of God to all the works of his hands may reasonably be supposed to help them up though undeserving, but there is nothing in his most righteous nature which would cast them down without their high demerit. (131)

Universal salvation, according to the author of the *Letter*, is not at odds with God's justice, which perfectly harmonizes with mercy. Like Origen, Macrina, and Gregory of Nyssa, Rust warns that purifying suffering will be long and harsh. Only in this way will even the worst sinners return to God. Those who do not respond to "the gentler smart" of divine correction in this age will experience "that day of vengeance" when the whole cosmos will be consumed with fire. This is the "Lake of slow-consuming fire and sulphureous stench that unreclamable Devils and obstinately-wicked men shall by the righteous hand of God participate. A sad pitiable Fate and torture unsufferable! but no doubt as just as great" (74). Yet this conflagration is the very same fire that consumes the earth prior to its rebirth in new creation. And this fire plays a role in the restoration of sinners to fit them for participation in new creation. This

---

nature of the thing then expressed require such an interminable duration" (132). The *pur aiōnion*, he argues, is not eternal in the scholastic sense (130–33).

notion of the length and harshness of otherworldly cathartic suffering was shared by other thinkers related to the Cambridge Platonists and by Jane Lead, to whom we shall return.

Lady Ann Conway (1631–79) and Francis Mercurius van Helmont (1614–98)

 Lady Anne Finch, viscountess of Conway (1630/31–79),[13] was a learned woman, well steeped in Greek, Latin, and Hebrew. She had read many theological, philosophical, and mystical/esoteric works and engaged them in critical and creative ways. Among the influences that shaped her thought was Origen, probably through the influence of Henry More, her unofficial mentor.[14] So perhaps her subsequent sympathy with universal salvation is unsurprising.

A severe headache afflicted Ann all her life from the age of twelve. From 1670, her physician, the Belgian Francis Mercurius van Helmont, moved in to Ragley Hall in Warwickshire, the Conway home, where he remained for nine years until her death in 1679.[15] His own intellectual development was interwoven with Ann's, and both became increasingly influenced by esoteric texts, such as the works of the mystic Jakob Böhme,[16] and especially the Jewish Kabbalism of Isaac Luria (1534–72).

---

13. Cf. Hutton, *Anne Conway*; Hutton, "Lady Anne Conway."

14. As a woman, Anne could not attend the University of Cambridge. However, More agreed to instruct her informally. Henry More also corresponded with her on Descartes's philosophy and considered her to be his intellectual equal. See Nicolson and Hutton, *Conway Letters*. She also influenced the philosopher Gottfried Wilhelm Leibniz, and actually anticipated his own work with her metaphysical theory of the monad. (Leibniz, incidentally, was impressed by the universalist theology of Johann Petersen and had read works by Jane Lead, both of whom we shall discuss later in this book.)

15. Francis van Helmont (fl. 1670–79), a friend of Henry More, supported universal salvation on the grounds that punishments decided by God are therapeutic and not retributive. In order to avoid encouraging immoral behavior, he insisted on the long duration and harshness of this suffering.

16. On Böhme, see the appendix.

Luria's system saw the transmigration of souls as essential to a theodicy aimed at explaining the suffering of the Jewish people—the Jews must be suffering for sins committed in previous lives. However, Luria also looked forward to a coming age in which all would be delivered from suffering. This intellectual system inspired both van Helmont and, through him, Ann Conway. Ann could not conceive of a good and loving God who should persecute her with constant headaches; the only explanation she found is that she must have sinned very gravely in a preceding life, and so needed a life of suffering as a purification.[17] She thus shared with the Kabbalist Luria and the Platonists More and Rust a belief in the preexistence of souls. Indeed, she not only believed in preexistence, but also the reincarnation of souls in numerous human lives, and indeed even in non-human lives: those who have lived brutish lives will be reborn as animals.[18] (In this conviction of hers, Lady Conway differed from Origen, who condemned the doctrine of the transmigration of souls.)[19]

Ann also shared with Rust—and Plato and Origen—the conviction that suffering is necessary for purification and salvation.[20] "All degrees and kinds of sin have their appropriate punishments, and all these punishments tend toward the good of creatures: under the influence of mercy and favour, judgment becomes a judgment in favour of the salvation and restoration of creatures."[21] That punishment aims at curing rather than crushing "is true even of the worst sinners."[22]

Ann Finch (Conway) supported the doctrine of universal salvation on the basis of two main principles, which were well delineated already in

17. However, she seems not to have considered that *innocent* suffering in a Christian perspective can also be a vicarious suffering, a participation in the cross of Christ, which is the vicarious suffering par excellence: the suffering of an innocent for the salvation of other sinful souls.

18. Her philosophical arguments for reincarnation can be found in Conway, *Principles*, ch. 6.

19. Origen was wrongly accused of having taught the transmigration of souls. However, his rejection of it is clear and unambiguous. See *Cels.* 3:75; 4:7.17; 5:29; 8:30; *Comm. Rom.* 5:1:392–406; 5:9:171–76; 6:8, 118–31; *Comm. Matt.* 13:1–2; *Comm. ser. Matt.* 38; *Comm. Jo.* 6:11:71 and 13:78. See also Pamphilus, *Apol.* 10.

20. The only literary work of her own was written in English between 1671 and 1675, but published posthumously in Latin in 1690, then in English in 1692 as a retranslation of the Latin version, since the original had been lost. See Conway, *Principia philosophiae antiquissimae*; see also Conway, *Principles*.

21. Conway, *Principles*, ch. 6, §8 (Bennett).

22. Conway, *Principles*, ch. 6, §10 (Bennett).

Gregory of Nyssa:[23] the infinity of the Good, who is God, and the finitude of evil, which is nonbeing and will eventually cease, so that every soul will return to adhering to the Good. Suffering is part and parcel of this process of spiritual restoration and indeed contributes to the fact that in the end restored creatures will never choose to sin again. The patristic influences are clear:

> But because there is no being, which is every way contrary to God, (*viz.* there is no being, which is infinitely and unchangeably evil, as God is infinitely and unchangeably Good; nothing infinitely dark, as God is infinitely Light . . .) hence it is manifest that . . . nothing can become infinitely more dark, though it may become infinitely more light: By the same reason nothing can be evil *ad infinitum*, although it may become more and more good *ad infinitum*: And so indeed, in the very nature of things, there are limits or bounds to evil; but none unto good. And after the same manner, every degree of sin or evil hath its punishment, grief, and chastisement annexed to it, in the very nature of the thing, by which the evil is again changed into good; which punishment or correction, though it be not presently perceived of the creature, when it sins, yet is reserved in those very sins which the same committeth, and in its due time will appear; . . . by that the creature will be again restored unto its former state of goodness, in which it was created, and from which it cannot fall or slide any more; because by its great chastisement it hath acquired a greater strength and perfection; and so is ascended so far above that indifferency of will, which before it had to good or evil, that it wills only that which is good, neither is any more capable to will any evil. See *Kabbal. denud.* Tom. 2. Tract. ult. p. 61, §. 9. p. 69., §. 21. and 70., §. 5. & *ibid.* Tract. 2. p. 157.
>
> And hence may be inferred, that all the creatures of God, which heretofore degenerated and fell from their primitive Goodness, must after certain periods be converted and restored, not only to as good, but unto a better state than that was in which they were created. . . . Now seeing a creature cannot proceed infinitely to evil, nor slide down into inactivity or silence, nor yet also into eternal passion, it uncontestably follows, that it must at length return unto Good; and by how much greater its sufferings are, so much the sooner shall it return and be restored.[24]

23. See Ramelli, "Good/Beauty."

24. Conway, *Principles*, ch. 7, §1 (Lopston).

Lady Conway explicitly rejected the eternity of hell, which would be an unlimited punishment for a limited sin, and therefore incompatible not only with God's mercy, but also with God's justice. "The common idea about God's justice—namely that *every* sin is punishable by endless hellfire—has given men a horrible idea of God, depicting him as a cruel tyrant rather than a benign father towards all his creatures."[25] Hell, she said, is reserved for the worst sins, and even then, like all punishment, it is aimed at the eventual healing of the sinner and is thus not everlasting.

Anne Finch's universalism saw Christ's incarnation, death, and resurrection as central to our return to God.[26] The patristic flavor of what follows should be clear:

> In taking on flesh and blood, Christ sanctified nature so that he could sanctify everything, analogous to fermenting a whole mass of stuff by fermenting one part of it. Then he descended into time and for a certain period voluntarily subjected himself to its laws, to such an extent that he suffered great torment and death itself. But death didn't hold him for long: on the third day he rose again, and the purpose of all his suffering, right up to his death and burial, was to heal, preserve, and restore creatures from the decay and death that had come upon them through the Fall. By doing this he brought time to an end, and raised creatures above time, raising them to the level where he dwells—he who is the same yesterday, today, and forever, without loss, decay, or death.[27]

Van Helmont too embraced universalism, seeing it as the climax of "a complex chronology of human existences leading to the final restoration

---

25. Conway, *Principles*, ch. 6, §9 (Bennett).

26. While Anne Conway was influenced by Jewish esotericism, one could not accuse her theology of pantheism or even panentheism (contra McClymond, *Devil's Redemption*, 416). In her ontology, the Creator/creation distinction is absolute—indeed, so absolute that Christ, the God-man, is needed to stand between them, ontologically speaking. (Under the influence of Kabbala, she sees Christ's humanity as a celestial humanity, eternally united to God, that precedes not only his incarnation in flesh, but also the creation of the cosmos itself.) See Conway, *Principles*, chs. 1–2, 4–5. Ann saw this view of Christ's ontological mediation as the basis for a kind of theological inclusivism. Those "Jews and Turks and other infidel nations" who recognize the necessity for "a medium" between God and human beings "can be said truly to believe in Jesus Christ even if they don't know that is what they believe in and haven't accepted that he has already come in the flesh" (ch. 6, §5; Bennett).

27. Conway, *Principles*, chs. 5 and 6.

of all at the millennium."[28] And he too considered punishment to be healing: "Is not the nature of all punishment Medicinal? And ought not every
Judge among Men sincerely to love those whom he condemns to punishment, and aim at their good thereby?"[29]

In November 1675, various Quakers, including George Fox himself,
had visited Anne and van Helmont, and they began attending Quaker
meetings. (Quakers were a Christian sect widely considered at the time
to be seditious.) In 1677, both of them converted to Quakerism, and
made her house a center for Quaker activity. She died two years later,
aged forty-seven.

The universalism of those within the orbit of Cambridge Platonism
was, as we have seen, somewhat heady, drawing on a curious and creative
blend of patristic, biblical, and esoteric sources, and would have appeared
rather suspicious from the standpoint of mainstream Protestant theological discourse. That was much less the case with the Puritan universalism
of Peter Sterry and Jeremiah White, even though Sterry was much influenced by Cambridge Platonism.

PURITAN UNIVERSALISM

Peter Sterry (1613–72), Puritan Universalist

Peter Sterry was born and raised in Southwark and went to study at Emmanuel College in Cambridge, aged sixteen. Emmanuel was a Puritan
college, but at the time was also becoming a center of Cambridge Platonism. Here Sterry studied under Benjamin Whichcote, one of the key
players in that movement. Sterry was a good student and became a very
learned man with a wide range of influences—Scripture, of course, but
also Plato, Plotinus, Proclus, the church fathers (Origen among them),
John Scotus Eriugena, the scholastics (including Aquinas), Renaissance
thinkers (such as Nicholas of Cusa), the mystics of the church (including

---

28. Almond, *Heaven and Hell*, 18. For a brief summary of van Helmont's complex
universalist system see, 18–20.

29. [Van Helmont], *Two Hundred Queries*, 114. Van Helmont also sponsored the
English translation of an anonymous Latin work published in 1693, *Seder Olam: or,
The Order of Ages: A Few Questions by Way of Exposition, on Each Chapter of the Revelation of St John* (ET 1694). This work takes a Christian theological and apocalyptic
framework and reshapes it in light of kabbalistic and Neoplatonic themes, in ways that
Conway and van Helmont themselves did. *Seder Olam*, like Conway and van Helmont,
also taught a universal salvation. See Almond, *Heaven and Hell*, 19–21.

Jakob Böhme), as well as rabbininc writings. It is little surprise that he was a Christian Platonist throughout his life as well as a devout Puritan.

In 1637, Sterry was elected to a fellowship at Emmanuel college, which still commemorates him in a stained glass window (seen above),[30]

but as the political tide turned at the university, he left Cambridge in 1640 and became a chaplain to Robert Grenville (Lord Brooke). After Grenville was killed in 1643, leading the fight against the Royalists in the Civil War, Sterry was nominated as one of the fourteen divines chosen by the House of Lords for the Westminster Assembly, with the commission to reorganize the church on a Puritan basis. It was this Assembly that drew up the famous Westminster Confession of Faith in 1646, which remains a Calvinistic doctrinal standard of faith among many Reformed churches to this day.

Sterry became a regular and well-known Independent preacher to the House of Commons at Westminster. In 1649, he became a chaplain and preacher to the Council of State, and in 1650 he became a chaplain and friend to Oliver Cromwell. "He belonged, in fact, to the group of Independent divines who really became the leaders of the Church under the Protectorate."[31]

Sterry was a great defender of toleration—his opposition, as an Independent Minister, to Catholicism and Presbyterianism was chiefly based on what he saw as their intolerant streak. His deep regard for tolerance and his respect for Jewish thought also made him a defender of Cromwell's 1655 proposal to allow the Jews to return to England. (The Jews were expelled from England in 1290.) Indeed, Sterry was one of those Cromwell brought into the consultations on the matter in order to break the deadlock. The Jews were allowed to return in 1657.

30. In this nineteenth-century window, Sterry is shown holding a scroll inscribed with "Ut Sit Deus Omnia in Omnibus," or "that God may be all in all" (1 Cor 15:28). In the background are depicted seventeenth-century Whitehall and St. Margaret's Church, Westminster.

31. Pinto, *Peter Sterry*, 20.

After Cromwell's death in 1658, the cause of the Independents col-
lapsed and the monarchy was restored. Sterry was lucky to get away, not
only with his life, but also with his freedom. He received a pardon from
the King in 1660 and became a chaplain to Philip Sidney, Viscount Lisle,
in London. In May 1672, Sterry became ill, and he died aged fifty-nine
in November.[32]

In many ways, Sterry is an anomaly—a Puritan who was a lover
of the arts and poetry, a Platonist who was a theological determinist, a
deeply rational mystic, and, most interesting from our perspective, a Calvinist universalist.

The heart of his theology was his doctrine of God. The only true
Being is God—creation has no subsistence of itself but derives its being
from God, who is utterly transcendent, yet profoundly immanent in all
things—"in All, thro' All, on every side, beneath, above, beyond All, ever,
every where the same, equally entire, equally undivided, . . . that Sacred
Circle of All Being, . . . whose Center is every where, . . . whose Circum-
ference is no where Bounded."[33] God is the artist, creation the artwork;
God is the poet; creation the poem; God is the composer and musician,
creation the music; God is the author, creation the story. (Interestingly,
given the fashions of the time, Sterry does not compare God to a mathematician or an artificer, nor creation to a mechanical artifact.) So God
alone is *real*; creation's being/becoming is only a shadow, but a shadow
that points beyond itself to its cause.

This cause, the triune God, is unity-in-diversity and the origin and
ground of all unity and diversity in creation. *And he is Love.* This comes
out very clearly at the start of the preface to *A Discourse on the Freedom
of the Will*. The first piece of advice to his readers is:

> 1. *Study the Love of God*, the *Nature* of God, as he is *Love*, the
> *Work* of God, as it is a *Work* of *Love*. . . . That *Love is the band
> of Perfection*. It is *Love* then, which runneth through the whole
> Work of God, which frameth, informeth, uniteth it all into one
> *Master-piece* of Divine Love.

32. Apart from a few sermons, all Sterry's publications were posthumous: *A Discourse on the Freedom of the Will* (1675), much admired by Richard Baxter (1615–91),
who was otherwise no fan of Sterry's theological method; *The Rise, Race, and Royalty
of the Kingdom of God in the Soul of Man* (1683), edited and with an introduction
by Jeremiah White, and *The Appearance of God to Man in the Gospel and the Gospel
Change* (1710).

33. Quoted in Pinto, *Peter Sterry*, 90.

> If God be Love, the Attributes of God are the attributes of
> this Love; the Purity, Simplicity, the Sovereignty, the Wisdom,
> the Almightiness, the Unchangeableness, the Infiniteness, the
> eternity of *Divine Love*. If God be Love, his Work is the Work of
> Love, of a Love unmixt, unconfined, supream, infinite in Wis-
> dom and Power, not limited in its workings by any pre-existent
> matter, but bringing forth freely and entirely from it self its
> whole work both matter and form, according to its own inclina-
> tion and complacency in it self.

And: "Our God, the God and Father of our Lord Jesus, is the God of
Love in the truest, the sweetest and best sense. He alone is Love it self . . .
an *infinite Love*, a sweet and clear *Sea*, which swalloweth up all bounds,
all shore and bottoms, into it self."[34] It is easy to see how such a theology of omnipotent divine love would lead one toward universalism. All
creation is birthed in divine love and determined in love toward its beautiful destination. The God of love is the source and *telos* of creation, its
alpha and omega. And, unlike most of the Cambridge Platonists, Sterry
the Puritan believer in predestination maintained that God determined
absolutely everything that happened, *including human free choices*.[35] "The
will of man then in every *motion*, *act*, and *determination* of it, is from
eternity *predetermined* in the Divine Understanding, as in its *first cause*
and *Original form*."[36] So not even creaturely freewill could derail God's
loving purposes for creation.

Of course, the story of creation is not monochrome, but has its disturbing and painful plot-twists, the fall into sin unleashing a world of
sorrow. It may be very hard to discern divine love if we focus only on the
present fallen world. However, we need to see the whole story to discern
the pattern of love, and to see that even the fall and consequent human
suffering—of which Sterry does not flinch from recognizing God as the
ultimate cause—play a role in bringing about the ultimate good of all.
God will make everything beautiful in his time.

Sterry's doctrine of atonement was more or less a standard Reformed one, save that he believed that it would extend to all.

---

34. Sterry, *Discourse*, 41.

35. Sterry's *Discourse* makes a philosophical-theological case against what we
would call libertarian notions of freedom. To him, non-determined freedom boiled
down to random action, which has no moral value. Freedom was, rather, the freedom
to act as we choose (even though what we choose is determined by our desires).

36. Sterry, *Discourse*, 40.

> *All men are redeemed by the same blood of the Lord Jesus, who*
> *hath given himself as a Ransom for all, to be testified,* ἐν <καὶ>ροῖς
> ἰδίοις, *in the proper times. Each person which hath his part in*
> *this Ransom, hath its proper time for its discovery to him. Thine*
> *may be now sooner. This person also now most of all lost in*
> *the depth of all evils, may have his proper time yet to come, for*
> *the taking off the disguise of these filthy Rags from him, for the*
> *discovery of the Glory, as a Son of God in him. . . . So look thou*
> *on every man as a brother to thee.*[37]

Sterry affirmed a doctrine of hell—it was, after all, the teaching of inspired Scripture. His fullest account is given in an unpublished manuscript entitled "That the State of Wicked Men After This Life Is Mixt of Evill, and Good Things." And he could make good sense of hell as one of the painful parts of the story of the world as it moved toward its final state, but a doctrine of *eternal* damnation for some creatures made no sense to him, being incompatible with divine goodness and the omnipotent love of God.

On Sterry's account, all the divine attributes "are the attributes of this Love," which means that divine justice, divine wrath, and divine punishment must be understood to be modes of God's love for sinners. "Love is the end [i.e., goal] of wrath."[38] If God "meets with opposition he rageth. He burns upon dark, unclear, intractable Hearts, as *Fire* in the *Ironworks*; till he hath poured them forth into the Temper, and Mold of his Spirit and Image."[39] As such, hell should be understood as reformative, aimed at the ultimate good of those condemned to it. So "no Individual Soul can be forever abandoned."[40] This includes fallen angels as well as humans. What God hates is sin, not sinners. Those in hell would look up and see heaven and be full of remorse, recognizing the incompatibility of their sinful lives with the glory of heaven. This realization is a fundamental step toward their restoration.[41] "Wrath is but for a moment; at longest the

---

37. Sterry, *Discourse*, preface.

38. Sterry, *Discourse*, 171.

39. Sterry, *Rise*, 52.

40. Sterry, *Rise*, 101.

41. Philip Almond considers this notion of ongoing transformation in the afterlife to be "perhaps the most significant development in conceptions of life after death in the seventeenth century" (*Heaven and Hell*, 76). However, we must remember that it was, in fact, a recovery of much earlier and quite widespread patristic notions.

moment of this Life, this Shadow, this short Dream of Lifes. The Truth of Life, the Perpetuity of Life, Eternity is for Love."[42]

Jeremiah White (1629–1707)

White's life

Jeremiah White, like Sterry, was also a Puritan with Independent convictions, a student at Cambridge University (Trinity College, 1646–53), then a preacher to the Council of State at Whitehall, and also a chaplain to Oliver Cromwell.[43] Sterry and White were colleagues and White edited and wrote the preface to Peter Sterry's book *The Rise, Race, and Royalty of the Kingdom of God in the Soul* in which we are left in no doubt that White was a great admirer of Sterry.

After Cromwell's death and the Restoration of the Monarchy, White was without a regular income.

> He lived privately . . . , preaching only occasionally. . . . He had, with great pains and charge, made a collection of the sufferings of the Dissenters by the penal laws after the Restoration [of the Monarchy in 1660], which contained an account of the ruin of many thousand families in the several parts of the kingdom. When James II came to the crown, and gave the Dissenters

42. Sterry, *Rise*, 385.

43. It seems that White had aspirations to marry one of Cromwell's daughters. "White allowed his ambition to go so far as to aspire to the hand of Cromwell's youngest daughter Frances. It is said that the lady did not look upon him with disfavour. The state of things came to Cromwell's knowledge. With the help of a household spy he managed to surprise the two at a moment when his chaplain was on his knees before his daughter kissing her hand. 'Jerry,' who was never at a loss for something to say, explained that for some time past he had been paying his addresses to the lady's waiting woman, but being unsuccessful in his endeavours, he had been driven to soliciting the Lady Frances's interest on his behalf. The opportunity thus offered was not neglected by Cromwell. Reproaching the waiting woman with her slight of his friend, and gaining her consent to the match, he sent for another chaplain and had them married at once" (Porter, "White, Jeremiah (1629–1707)").

liberty, he was much importuned to print it. Some agents of the king were with him, and made him very considerable offers, if he would comply: but as circumstances then stood, he was not to be prevailed with, for fear of serving and strengthening the Popish interest.[44]

Jeremiah White's posthumous publication *The Restoration of All Things* is, in my opinion, the most interesting statement of universal salvation to come out of the seventeenth century.[45] It was published anonymously in the first edition (1712) to protect White's reputation, but his name was added in a subsequent edition. Richard Roach, an Anglican priest and a member of Jane Lead's Philadelphians (see later discussion), edited and wrote the preface to the book's first edition,[46] and there he explains how White came to embrace the larger hope while at university:

> When he was at the University, and had studied all the schemes of Divinity, he could not find any, or from all of them together, that God was *Good*, that God was *Love*, as the Scriptures declared him. This put him into a great Dissatisfaction and Perplexity of Mind, from which he could no way extricate himself; but it grew upon him more and more, till it threw him into a Fit of Sickness, and that so dangerous [th]at there was no Hopes of his Recovery; but in it, at the worst, he had a Beam of Divine Grace darted upon his Intellect, with a sudden, warm, and lively *Impression*; which gave him immediately a New Set of Thoughts concerning God and his Works, and the Way of his dealing with his Offending creatures, which, as they became the Rule and Standard of all his Thoughts and Measures of Things afterwards, as I have heard him declare, so they gave in particular, the Ground and Occasion of this present Design. And upon this he presently Recovered.[47]

---

44. He preached occasionally at an Independent church in London. Calamy, *The Nonconformist's Memorial*, 162.

45. Even though its actual publication was not until the early eighteenth century.

46. The claim that the editor and author of the preface is Roach is made by D. P. Walker in *The Decline of Hell*, 121n4.

47. [Roach(?),] "Preface," iv–v.

White's thought

The book itself was written over a number of years, indeed he must have been thinking the issues through since his student days, but it was only completed soon before his death, aged seventy-eight in 1707. It offers a sustained set of competent expositions of various biblical texts, which allows White to set out a whole biblical theology that is at once both Calvinist and universalist.

It comes as something of a shock to some people to learn that Calvin himself, in his massive *Institutes of the Christian Religion*, never makes a single reference to the biblical assertion that "God is love" (1 John 4:8, 16), despite the fact that his work offers a comprehensive and thorough overview of Christian theology, as he saw it, engaging thousands of biblical passages. Clearly the idea was not central to Calvin's theology. What White offers is a glimpse of what Calvinism might look like if re-formed around the insight that "God is love." For, like Sterry, White *begins* with the doctrine of God's love and allows it to inform his entire theology.

God is indeed justice itself, wisdom itself, and power itself, but these and all other divine attributes find their unity in the triune love of God, he says. All divine attributes are subservient to and aim at divine love. Indeed, "Love is more than an Attribute, it is the very Name of God, it is God himself; an Attribute is an imperfect and a partial Expression of God to us; But Love is the full Expression of him, so far as God can be expressed and conceived by us. . . . God is Love, and therefore all his Attributes are the Attributes of Love" (178–79).[48] This has huge implications for how we think about God's justice and anger. "What must we conclude then? That his Severity is not without Goodness, nor contrary to it; not incompatible with it; his Goodness can admit Severity and yet remain Goodness notwithstanding" (58). White argues at some length that divine justice needs to be understood as a manifestation of love (186–90), as do holiness (190–92), faithfulness (192–93), wisdom, and power (193–97). So the common attempt to ground eternal punishment in God's holiness or justice utterly fails to grasp those very attributes, because it detaches them from love. "O then let us fear to set up a Wisdom, a Power, a Justice, a Holiness, a Greatness in God, without Love! Without Love as its Ground, its Root, its Essence, its Design, its Fruit, its Image, its End" (151). Love seeks the *good* of the other, not its eternal misery, and

---

48. The following in-text citations in this section on White are from *The Restoration of All Things*, unless otherwise stated.

love never fails. The same critique applies to Calvinist attempts to appeal to the sovereign *will* of God as the basis for everlasting hell, for that will is the will of the God *who is love* (199–210).

And the wrath of God, real as it is,[49] is his fierce opposition to sin and evil, and this too is motivated by his love for us (210–25). For "he can no more cease to be Love when he is angry, than he can cease to be God. . . . [T]he anger of God towards his own is the fruit of his Love" (213–14). Divine anger—which is in fact God's love actively opposing sin—will burn until it has consumed all that is evil in creation, then it will be gone forever. God's love is like the sun, permanent and shining, while wrath is akin to a cloud that temporarily passes across the sun, just "a Mist before his Face" (201).

Our salvation then is established in God's nature as love, which contains in itself *all* that is necessary to complete the restoration of the creature:

> God is *an Eternal act of Goodness, Love, and Sweetness, that carries his Effect and End Eternally in himself,* and tho' there be a process in the discovery of this Love to us, *yet in its first and Eternal emanation and motion,* (if we may so speak) he is in the term of his motion. For he hath and possesseth the term Eternally in himself, and whom he Loves, *he Loves to the end,* Loves fully, perfectly, furnishing and supplying all things to the End of his Love richly, freely, intirely, out of himself. (19)

The argument on the extent of salvation develops step by step, through the analysis of key texts. It launches with 1 Timothy 2:3, in which Paul exhorts the church to offer prayers for "all Men" on the ground that "this is acceptable in the Sight of God our Saviour, who will have all Men to be Saved and come to a knowledge of the Truth." God *wills* that *all* people (not only the elect) be saved and, argues White, God's will—which reflects his nature as love—is effective (Eph 1:11). God's will certainly *will* be done. God calls his church to pray for the salvation of all, which he would not do if it were not his intention to save all. "God wills that all Men be saved, this Will is the Will of an Omnipotent and Sincere Agent, an immanent and eternal Will, eternally in Act, that hath its end in its own Power, yea in his Arms and Embraces, and neither can, nor could it ever be resisted" (20).

---

49. White, being a classical theist, is well aware of the need to understand such language in a manner appropriate to God.

First Timothy 2 continues: "for there is one God, and one Mediator between God and Man, the Man Christ Jesus, who gave himself a Ransom for all, a Testimony, for its proper time." White thus proceeds to make a case for universal extent of redemption from (a) the unity of God (b) the unity of the mediator, Jesus, and (c) the extent of the ransom.

(a) God is one. There may seem to be contraries in God and in his works, but underlying this seeming tension, there is unity. So justice and mercy or election and reprobation, say, appear on the surface to represent a division in God's purposes and being, but not so. For running through all God's works is his goodness and love—all God's ways are aimed at the ultimate good of creation. Wrath and reprobation are not the end, but only part of the difficult and winding way toward the end. Both the elect and the reprobate have the same God and Father, for there is only one God. For "as he is *Alpha* and *Omega*; if his Love were the First, certain it shall be Last also: For who shall get the upper hand of that Love which is God himself?" (31).

(b) According to our text, we have "one Mediator between God and Man; not between God and the Elect, but between God and Men" (33). In the incarnation Christ took on human nature and so stands in place of all humanity. (c) And in his death he is a propitiation for the sins, not of the elect only, but of the *whole world* (1 John 2:2). For White it is inconceivable that any, let alone the majority, of those for whom Christ atoned will find themselves forever lost. Rather, Christ "shall see the travail of his soul, *and be satisfied*" (Isa 53:11). Although the global extent of Christ's atoning work is not yet evident, as the text says, it will be testified to *in its proper season.*

Now White does make a distinction between believers and unbelievers, the elect and the reprobate. God is the savior of all people, but *especially* of those who believe (1 Tim 4:10). In this text, White perceives an important distinction that allows him to see God as the universal savior while still maintaining that *currently* not all experience that salvation. It also opens a space for him to allow that many will indeed be cast into hell, which he paints in stark and terrible colors.[50] However, he warns, we

---

50. Like Rust—and like Origen, Macrina, Gregory of Nyssa, and other fathers—White too feared that the doctrine of universal salvation might encourage moral relaxation, at least among spiritually immature people. This is why his book includes a penultimate chapter entitled: "Being a Warning to Sinners" (225–38). Here it speaks in vivid terms of the burning wrath of God that his readers will face if they live sinful lives.

should not over-interpret the vivid rhetoric of hell. Such language needs to be read with care. As an example: "the Lord threatens, *That his Fury shall burn upon* Jerusalem, *and shall not be quenched. Jer. vii. 20.* Yet what sweet Promises were made to Jerusalem, and to that People afterwards; and after this long Rejection they are under the Promise of a glorious Return still, therefore these Terms [i.e., unquenchable fire] are to be understood in a limited or qualified sense" (44). So the day will come when hell will be empty and all will participate in the redemption paid for by Jesus. For "their Punishment, be it how long soever, how grievous soever, cannot extinguish *the Right and Claim of Christ's Blood for their Deliverance*, be it after Ages and Generations ever so many, Christ's Blood loseth not its Virtue, its Value, nor can be satisfied, but Cries till all for whom it was shed be delivered" (77).[51] White continues to build his case by exegeting various other texts (1 Pet 3:18–20; Rom 9–11; Eph 1:10; Col 1:20; Rom 8:19–23; 5:12–21, etc.) but we shall not consider them here.

Like Sterry, White takes the Calvinist line on human freedom and divine sovereignty. Humans do make free choices, but they are all under the oversight and rule of God. Ultimate power lies with God, not the human will, so the Arminians, he says, are mistaken to suppose that humans are able to ultimately thwart God's intentions for them. Sterry and White's determinism is alien to the patristic universalist tradition. However, exactly like Origen, and the Cambridge Platonists too, both Sterry and White identified freedom with the freedom to do good—whoever does evil is not free.

It is here, in the claim that God achieves all his purposes, that mainstream Calvinism runs into problems—for predestining some people to eternal life and others to eternal damnation is exceedingly hard to square with God's love. But White does not have this problem, for the doctrine of universal grace and the final deliverance of all takes the sting out of it. Universalism thus allows White to remove "all those false, barbarous and monstrous Representations of a God . . . which have hitherto hindered so many Minds" (8).

51. Those who object with the Anselmian argument that sin against an infinite Majesty requires a punishment of infinite duration in hell do not impress White: "this strikes at the Sufficiency of Christ's Satisfaction, in which God hath shewed there is a means of Satisfaction, without infinite Duration, and God is satisfied by that one Sacrifice for the Sin of the whole World, so that God wants not Satisfaction; besides that, if he did, he should by this Principle, be ever satisfying, but never Satisfied" (45). The irony is then that if divine justice requires everlasting torment in order to be satisfied, then justice will *never* be satisfied, *ever*, for that punishment will never be completed.

It is particularly interesting to see White's account of the doctrine of election, which is central to Calvinist theology. He considers election and reprobation to be "a clear Truth of the Gospel" (87). In his view:

> this Decree of Election is *definite, certain,* and *irrevocable;* so that they are known by Name and have great and certain *privileges* and Immunities; as not only certain and everlasting *Salvation,* presently *begun* at their calling and *perfected at Death,* and at the Resurrection of the Dead; but also certain preservation from all Damnable *Errors* of Seducing Spirits, and the contagious or deadly *touch,* or contagion of the *Evil one,* and the Sin *unto Death.*" (88)

So far so Calvinist. However, he develops the notion of the elect as the *firstfruits* of creation, the first part of the harvest to be gathered and offered up to God as an anticipation of the rest of the harvest being gathered in at the right time (Jas 1:18; Rev 14:4; Rom 11:16; 8:19–23). The elect are "*the First-Fruits of his Creatures,* and the pledge and assurance of their [i.e., all creatures'] Sanctification and Salvation" (88). For "the Harvest and the *full Crop* of it awaits Christ's *next coming*" (141). Thus, in White's hands election becomes not a doctrine by which people are forever divided into saints and sinners, but one that functions as a promise of universal salvation.

Another interesting argument used by White concerns human nature. Human beings, he maintains, are a microcosm of the whole created order: "For first in his Body he contains all *Vegetative and Sensitive Nature,* and in his Soul, or Spirit all *Rational and Intellectual Nature,* with all the Virtues, Excellencies, and Perfections of both" (145).[52] A human being—body and soul—forms a unity in which plants, animals, and rational beings converge in a point. In this way we dimly image God, the unified Creator of all things, from whom all things come and to whom all things are orientated. Each human person "is an entire World . . . worth more than the whole World of Inferior beings" (146), and so it makes no sense to suppose that God would eternally abandon such a precious creature made in his own image. Indeed, because of the unity of creation, when anyone suffers, the whole creation suffers in them:

---

52. The human being as microcosm dates from at least the fifth century BC and is a common theme in NeoPlatonic, kabbalistic (i.e., Jewish mystical), and alchemical thought.

> If so many millions of these intellectual Substances be never look'd upon, or visited with Redemption, not one Saint is *completely Saved*, for if each Spirit be an entire world, all Spirits are in each Spirit; as the Soul is in every part of the Body. And therefore it is said of the Body, through the *one Spirit* in all its members, that *whether one Member suffer, all the Members suffer with it . . .* : So it is with the *Mystical Body*, which is in Union . . . *with all Spirits*, and the whole Nature of things, and therefore those which have the First-fruits of the Spirit [i.e., the elect], do with the Creation groan within themselves, waiting for the Adoption, not Redemption of their own particular Bodies only, but the Redemption of the *Universal Body* [Rom 8:18–27]. (147)

In other words, given the metaphysical unity of creation, if all are not saved then *none* are fully saved: "the Saints are not fully glorified without the rest of Mankind" (148).

The Calvinistic universalism of Sterry and White had little impact on the Reformed tradition. Indeed, those universalists that followed in the Reformed tradition seem to have been unaware of their predecessors' work.[53] Yet the fact that this Calvinian tradition has continued to manifest a potential for periodically generating universalists—witness, for instance, Rev. James Huntington's *Calvinisim Improved* (1796)—is a matter that warrants further reflection. When combined with a view that God is love in God's being (and that divine wrath is a manifestation of divine love), Calvinism seems to find itself drawn in by the gravity of universal salvation, even if some struggle to stop it moving beyond the event horizon.

Sterry and White represent the intellectual end of the larger hope in the seventeenth-century Reformed world, but the universalist whose thought was to prove most influential on the wider world was neither an intellectual nor even a man, but an old woman in London by the name of Jane Lead, a devotee of the esoteric mystic, Jakob Böhme. The next chapter seeks to give her work some of the attention it merits.

---

53. For instance, James Relly, John Murray, Friedrich Schleiermacher, Karl Barth (to the extent to which one considers him a universalist), Jacques Ellul, Jürgen Moltmann, and Jan Bonda.

4

Mystic and Prophetess

Jane Lead, Böhmist Universalist

JANE LEAD (1624–1704), WHO has been neglected in scholarship until recently,[1] espoused a universalism strongly characterized by an esoteric and visionary element, but it also had clear echoes of philosophical and patristic theology as well. Even though scholarship has understandably focused on the former, we shall argue that Lead's thought concerning universal restoration was also nourished—like that of the Cambridge Platonists—by ideas that resonate with patristic thought.

Jane Lead was born and raised in Norfolk. She had a comfortable and conventional upbringing as an Anglican and led an unremarkable life until after the death of her husband in 1670, a merchant by trade, to whom she had been happily married for twenty-seven years.[2] She was forty-six when he died, leaving her destitute.

Jane had been living in London for twenty-five years at the time of her husband's death and a couple of months after that loss in 1670 she began having religious visions in which Lady Wisdom—a hypostasis of divine wisdom—appeared to her, disclosing various revelations: she saw "in the midst of a most bright Cloud, a Woman of a most Sweet and Majestick Countenance, her Face shining as the Sun, and her Vesture of

---

1. Smith, "Note on Jane Lead," 79–82; McDowell, *Women of Grub Street*; Hirst, *Jane Leade*; Hessayon, *Jane Lead and Her Transnational Legacy*. See also the chapter on Lead in Ramelli, *Gregorio di Nissa*.

2. Ariel Hessayon has recently challenged this conventional view, arguing that there are clues to indicate Lead was more radical in her earlier days than she lets on in her "Life of the Author." See Hessayon, *Jane Lead and Her Transnational Legacy*, ch. 1.

Transparent Gold, who said, 'Behold! I am God's Eternal Virgin Wisdom.'"[3] These visionary revelations of Sophia, God's own Wisdom, continued for the rest of her life.[4] She wrote them down and published them in at least fourteen books.

IOHANNES PORDAED SCHE.
Lond.   Anglus.

In 1668 Lead had joined a small group of spiritually minded believers in London, followers of Jakob Böhme's[5] esoteric theology, who were led by an ex-Anglican minister and mystic called John Poradge (1607–81).[6] Poradge distilled, simplified, and clarified Böhme's difficult writings into a form more easy to digest, and became the key channel for Böhmist teaching in the English-speaking world.[7] Poradge was a major influence on Lead, and Böhme's theology clearly played an important role thereafter in shaping her thinking. (Indeed, the figure of Sophia, Divine Wisdom, played a role in Böhme's thought, which Lead was already reading at the time of her first vision.) Lead, with all her prophetic revelations and visions, became a key member of the

3. Lead, *Laws of Paradise*, sig. A2r. Jane had undergone an earlier religious experience, aged sixteen (1640), which created inner spiritual turmoil.

4. Lady Wisdom appears in Proverbs 8 and in some Second Temple Jewish texts. By Lead's time, Sophia as a hypostasis of God's wisdom was a common motif in various strands of esotericism.

5. Jakob Böhme was a sixteenth-century Teutonic mystic whose mystical philosophy exerted widespread influence across all levels of society in Europe and America from the sixteenth to the nineteenth centuries. See the appendix of this book.

6. Poradge was ejected from ministry in 1654, freeing him up to pursue his more esoteric interests. Jane had met Poradge first in 1663 and considered him an enlightened man "who understood the deepest of God's secrets" (Lead, "Lebenslauff der Autorin," 421). It may also be worth noting that William Everard, the co-leader of the Diggers with Gerrard Winstanley, was at one time a part of Poradge's group (though see the appendix of this book).

7. His key publication was *Theologica Mystica*, published posthumously in 1683.

circle, which grew to over a hundred people, but when John Poradge died in 1681, the people slowly dispersed and the group faded away.

In the years 1694–96, the situation took a turn for the better. Lead began to hold meetings that were to become the foundations of the English Philadelphian Society, which emerged in 1697. The Philadelphian Society (named after the church of brotherly love in Revelation 3:7–13) seems to have had many similarities to the Poradge circle, though its size is unknown. Jane Lead was the founder and leader of the group, though she encouraged others, men and women, to exercise leadership roles and charismatic gifts. (During the seventeenth century, women were not normally considered eligible to lead, but the pneumatic authority of a prophetess could circumvent such conventions.)

The Philadelphians did not consider themselves a church, but a "society," as all the members belonged to other churches. Indeed, while they did not have formalistic worship themselves, they had no objection to "externals or rituals of the Christian religion"[8] and dreamed of the ecumenical unity of all true believers overcoming divisions in the body of Christ. The society sought connections with likeminded believers elsewhere—both in Europe and America. "Indeed, the Philadelphian Society believed in the gradual purification and unification of the Protestant churches through internal spiritual regeneration."[9] However, after her death in 1704 the society dwindled and faded away, part of it being absorbed by the French Prophet movement, some of whom arrived in London in 1706.[10] It finally flickered out in 1730 after the death of Richard Roach, Lead's successor.[11] Lead's legacy was not to be the legacy of a movement, but a legacy of ideas, which, as we shall see in the next

8. They thus contrast with many other so-called "spirituals," who opposed outward rituals.

9. Hirst, *Jane Leade*, 117.

10. The "French Prophets" were a radical charismatic and millenarian group of Protestant believers from France, preparing the way for the end of the world.

11. For instance, the Oxford-trained scholar Rev. Richard Roach (1662–1730), rector of St. Augustine's, Hackney, and a universalist, was a key member of the group. He may have edited and written the preface to Jeremiah White's universalist volume, as well as publishing his own universalist works. (The preface to the first edition of White's book is, alas, anonymous, but it is clear that its author knew him.) The preface to the third edition was written by John Denis the Elder (ca. 1735–85), who published it in 1779. Roach was author of the significant Philadelphian publication *The Imperial Standard of Messiah Triumphant* (1728). Michael McClymond describes it as "a literary milestone in English Philadelphian universalism" which "presents a full-orbed Philadelphian universalist theology" (*Devil's Redemption*, 506).

chapter, while they had little impact in England, wielded much more influence in both Continental Europe and America.[12]

Jane Lead was not always a universalist; she came to the belief later in life. We cannot be certain precisely when this was, but she first publically affirmed universal restoration in print in *The Enochian Walks with God* (1694),[13] when she was seventy-one years old, and further expanded it in *The Wonders of God's Creation: Manifest in the Variety of Eight Worlds* (1695) and *A Revelation of the Everlasting Gospel Message* (1697). When the vision first came to her she was skeptical, but was cautious not to dismiss it too quickly, and eventually found herself convinced, not least when she came to believe she found it taught in Scripture too. "For I myself was averse to the taking of this Universal Doctrine: But was always taught by Divine Wisdom, not to oppose, what I could not reach, or comprehend. So I did let it rest for some years after the *Vision* of it."[14] When she embraced it she did so with zeal and with more emphasis than the Cambridge Platonists, though, as she had expected, it brought her criticism ("some zealous angry flames")[15] and lost her some supporters.

Her newfound universalism marked one way in which she departed from Jakob Böhme's complex theology. Böhme had considered both light and darkness to have eternal roots in God, providing a metaphysical foundation for eternal hell. Lead came to reject this idea: "nothing of this evil could be said to be Everlastingly generated from God into the Angelical Principle."[16] Sin and evil began in time and will come to an end. Consequently, there can be no eternal dualism of light and darkness. Thus, she wrote in a letter, "I believe the torments of hell, and consequently all evil to be finite."[17] This too finds a striking resonance with the patristic belief in evil as a privation that will cease to exist when God prefects his creation.

Lead continued to regard Böhme's revelations as inspired, but as incomplete: "I must own that *Jacob Behmen* did open a deep Foundation

---

12. Including on Johann Georg Gichtel, Johann and Johanna Petersen, John Kelpius, William Law, George Stonehouse, and Elhanan Winchester, who described his own London church as "Philadelphian."

13. The version of this text quoted here is found at http://www.passtheword.org/jane-lead/enocwalk.htm.

14. Lead, *Revelation*, 15.

15. Lead, *Revelation*, 15.

16. Lead, *Revelation*, 27.

17. See Walton, *Notes and Materials*, 213. Quoted by Hirst, *Jane Leade*, 116.

of the Eternal Principles, and was a worthy Instrument in his Day. But it [i.e., the revelation of universal restoration] was not given to him, neither was it Time for the unsealing of this Deep."[18] Lead believed she was chosen by God to make known this fresh insight—present in Scripture, but previously "a mystery from the ages sealed up"—to the church for the fast-approaching last days.[19]

Her first relevant work on the issue of comprehensive salvation is *The Enochian Walks with God* (1694),[20] a book about making the difficult inner journey of mystical ascent into the presence of God and of some of the things she learned in that presence.[21] In the very subtitle, the restoration of the whole of creation is announced and grounded in the "Immense and Infinite Latitude of GOD's Love." Lead's work, she declares, will reveal the mechanism of universal restoration of all rational creatures to God, including those who have apostatized. The work uses a "biblical" style, with poetic insertions, but also echoes the kinds of arguments used by Origen and other patristic philosophers in support of universal salvation.

The premises of universal salvation, in Jane Lead, as in Origen and others, are God's infinite redemptive love, God's being the absolute Good, and a concept of otherworldly suffering as purifying and healing, rather than retributive. Her message is intended to "vindicate the Royal, and Generous Goodness, and Love of the Holy Trinity."[22]

Lead begins with announcing a message of "Glad-tidings to the whole creation, from the beginning of Time, to the final End and extension thereof," because—she avers—"God's bounteous Grace will thereto reach." God's love expresses itself by saving human beings, by means of Christ's sacrifice, *both* from the eternal punishment they deserved for their transgression, but *also* by manifesting in the soul the likeness to God, of which Genesis 1:26 speaks. The focus of her teaching is on this

18. Lead, *Revelation*, 25.

19. Lead, along with many others in the seventeenth century, was a committed pre-millennialist, convinced that the last days were at hand.

20. The first Italian translation of Lead's old English edition (1694) is offered by Ramelli, *Gregorio di Nissa*, Appendix 2, which also incorporates Lead's marginal notes.

21. The title refers to Genesis 5:24: "And Enoch walked with God, and was not [any longer], because God took him." Enoch was believed to have been granted amazing revelations by God into the cosmos and its future; Lead is claiming that the access Enoch had is open to others who will follow the right path, which she lays out in the book, drawing on her own Enochian experiences.

22. Lead, *Enochian Walks*, introduction.

transformative journey of "inward redemption" and deification. Origen and Gregory of Nyssa, too, thought that the final restoration would be a work of God's grace, depending on Christ's sacrifice. The very notion of the achievement of the likeness to God in the end (while the image of God is an initial datum) was typical of Origen, and Lead adopts it in several passages.

Soon after, Lead puts forward another notion that was dear to Origen and Gregory of Nyssa: the *holistic* idea of the resurrection. Not only the body is resurrected, but also the soul, whose faculties are restored to their original integrity.[23] Jane Lead precisely echoes this conception of the restoration of the faculties of the soul; she speaks of a spiritual reintegration and restoration as a complete renovation of every part of the soul. Furthermore, her references to the role of the Holy Spirit in this process of restoration correspond to the function that Origen ascribed to the Holy Spirit in the process of *apokatastasis*.

Like Origen, Lead also links the phrase "eternal gospel"—which, according to Revelation 14:6, will be proclaimed in the end times—with the restoration. She proclaims that the eternal gospel will reach both the free and the captives, be they in their bodies or out of them. This gospel will extend beyond the limits of time. Origen thought that the relationship that exists between the Old and the New Testament is the same that exists between the New Testament and the "eternal gospel" (more precisely, "gospel of the aeon," which will be revealed in the future aeon). In *On First Principles* 3.6.3 and 6.7 Origen links the "eternal gospel" to the acquisition of the likeness to God, the same connection that Lead draws in *The Enochian Walks with God*. Lead relates the "eternal gospel" to the eventual restoration in two further passages, making it possible, though undemonstrable, that Origen's work was one source that inspired her.[24]

Moreover, just like Origen, Gregory of Nyssa, and other early supporters of *apokatastasis* (including Diodore of Tarsus and Theodore of Mopsuestia), Lead wants to ground her doctrine of universal salvation in Scripture. She cites Christ's descent to hell in 1 Peter 3:19–21, which she, like many of the fathers, deems a salvific descent, and 1 Corinthians 3:14–15, concerning those who will be saved immediately and those who will be "saved through fire." She interprets this fire as purifying and can thus reconcile Christ's just judgment, based on each one's deeds, and the

23. See Ramelli, "Origen's Exegesis of Jeremiah," 59–78.
24. If not directly, then perhaps mediated through another source.

salvation of all. Lead also refers to Romans 5:14–16, to show that the healing provided by Christ is more abundant than the wound caused by sin: "for it is not to be the least doubted but the Efficacy of Christ, the second Adam, by the merit of his Blood-shed, and his Spirit given therein which will make all good again, which the first Adam had made evil."[25]

By stressing the universally salvific effect of Christ's cross, and specifically of his shed blood, Lead comes again close to Origen, who founded upon it one of his most important Christological arguments for universal salvation.[26] More generally, in many passages Lead, like Origen and Gregory Nyssen, bases universal salvation on Christ. For instance, she declares that Christ, out of love, wanted redemption for all, and this is why he manifested himself in flesh in order to destroy sin and purify sinners. She insists that, thanks to Christ's redeeming blood, sin is cancelled; Christ is the physician of souls, who restores them to health. This motif of Christ as physician was one of the main pillars in support of universal salvation in Clement of Alexandria and then Origen. For, as Origen says, "no being is incurable for the One who created it" (*Princ.* 3:6:5).

Lead, like the patristic supporters of *apokatastasis*, had to explain those biblical passages that might be interpreted as contradicting universal salvation. Therefore, she explains that "eternal punishment" in Scripture means a punishment that takes place beyond the temporal limits of the present world and can extend for several periods—Origen's aeons and Gregory of Nyssa's "periods"—but not beyond the end, when Christ will hand over the kingdom to the Father (1 Cor 15:28). The gospel is not for this age only, with death as a cut-off point for grace, but "will so far extend, beyond the Limits of time, to Creatures in ages yet confined."[27]

In Lead's scheme, human souls pass upon death out of this world into different "worlds," that are suited to their level of purity. These worlds are places in which God works for their purification and their advancement toward union with himself. Some of the worlds were places of fire and torment, though aimed at the ultimate good of those suffering. Thus, each creature journeys step-by-step back to God.

> Be it known there are provided several-Mansions, and Regions, by the wise foreseeing Gracious God, that knew how it would be, as to This matter, with the greater Number of His own

25. Lead, *Enochian Walks*, introduction.

26. For Origen see *Comm. Rom.* 4:11:73–75.

27. Lead, *Enochian Walks*, introduction.

Created brings; tho' he had proclaimed, a Love-Redemption, to
All by Christ manifested in Flesh, to destroy, and purge Sin out
of Flesh, which we see is very rarely done in the time of this
life; where One reacheth to This mark, a Thousand do miss it;
Therefore for such as were begotten by the Eternal Word, and
are going on, in all Good willingness in their spiritual progress;
(dying short of finishing it). They will be allowed to be in a
Paradisiacal Region, to Exercise their Spiritual Faculties, for the
effecting what they were prevented . . . and so go on to perfect
That State of Perfection, that shall make them meet, to make
the Higher removes, to reach the Mount-Sion-State, which is yet
more Glorious. . . . For all Souls must pass through the Refining,
and Calcining Regions, so prepared for their Purifying; and according to the measures, and degrees they do attain to Here in
this Life: Of this kind; the less they will have to do in the Life to
come, which will be much more easy.[28]

The Wonders of God's Creation elaborates on the eight worlds that were
revealed to her. Beyond those eight worlds is "the innermost Place of
Purity, which bears the Title of the *Still Eternity*; for that nothing but
Everlasting Rest, Stillness, and Silence is to be perceived here." That is
the final resting places of all humans, once they have "a Deified nature"
through mystical transformation and are united with God.[29]

Both Origen and Gregory of Nyssa, moreover, proclaimed the
eventual salvation not only of all human beings, but also of all rational
creatures. This is what Jane Lead, too, states in several passages, again
claiming that what she announces was revealed to her. Indeed, the title
page of *A Revelation of the Everlasting Gospel Message* makes the controversial notion very prominent: "Christ's Eternal Judgment shall come"
for the "Restoration of the Whole Lapsed Creation, Whether Human or
Angelical." She starts from the royal and generous goodness of the Holy
Trinity and declares that its end is the reconciliation and restoration to
itself of all rational creatures of every kind that are now dispersed and
separate from it. This "universal redemption" will take place at the end
of time, when all creatures will love, praise, and adore God. In another
passage, Lead proclaims God's "infinite and unsearchable love" for the
fallen angels. Their deceitful activity against humanity will come to an
end when all, including them, will be restored to their original condition.

28. Lead, *Enochian Walks*, introduction.

29. Lead, *Wonders of God's Creation*, 20–21. We shall find this notion of the "still
eternity" picked up from Lead by Stonehouse in the eighteenth century.

Lead refers to Ephesians 1:10, about the eventual universal recapitulation in Christ, and identifies it with this eventual universal restoration.[30]

Lead also shared with Origen the moral concern that overtly preaching universal salvation might contribute to moral relaxation. This was certainly a common objection in her day against anyone who wanted to "water down" the traditional teaching on hell. She overcomes this problem with the same expedient used by Macrina and Gregory of Nyssa and by Gerrard Winstanley and some Cambridge Platonists, namely a special insistence on the length and severity of otherworldly suffering for sinners who have neglected caring for their own salvation while still on earth. She warns those tempted to treat God's grace lightly that "Anguish and Terrour, of Soul, and Suffering, will be upon them here, and hereafter."[31] However, she also argued that preaching eternal torment was morally ineffective with most people; it "wrought little effect in frightening or terrifying 'em from their evil Courses." Rather, the message of divine love has its own transforming power: "if Love's Center were rightly and duly open, and made manifest, it would have worked far more naturally and kindly, to gain the Will of those who are Perverse and Obstinate."[32] The kindness of God leads us to repentance.

Lead allegorically identifies the final restoration with the Feast of Tabernacles, just as Gregory of Nyssa had done in his dialogue with Macrina, *On the Soul and the Resurrection*. Another allegory with patristic roots that was used often by Lead was that of the marital love between the soul (the bride) and Christ. Origen had especially deployed it in his *Commentary on the Song of Songs*. Also, Lead bases her announcement of the eventual universal salvation on 1 Corinthians 15:28, the biblical verse that was the favorite of Origen and Gregory of Nyssa in support of their own doctrine of *apokatastasis*. Lead expressly speaks of a general and universal restoration, when all rational creatures that had apostatized, after being purified to the extent needed, will enjoy again God's friendship. The universal redemption operated by Christ will then be achieved and Christ's mediating task as supreme high priest will cease. All that will be left for him to do is to hand the kingdom to God the Father; then, God will be "all in all."

In her vision, God says:

30. Lead, *Enochian Walks*, n.p.
31. Lead, *Enochian Walks*, introduction.
32. Lead, *Revelation*, 13.

> I will make all things new, the End shall return to its Original-Primary-Being; let none grudge that the Grace of God of this Latitude is, as to make a complete Restoration; for as there was neither Sin, nor Center to it, so it must be again, when the Hour of God's Judgment shall come, to pass a final Sentence thereupon, to cast all into That Lake, and Bottomless Pit, where all Sin, and Death, Sorrow, and Curse, shall become a Non-Entity: Then nothing of Diabolical Spirits, (any more God's Offenders, and his Creature disturbers or Tormenters) shall be. . . . [All this is] a forerunner of This Blissful Jubilee, the Trumpet of the Everlasting Gospel, of Love, Peace, and Reconciliation to every creature capable thereof, in Flesh, and out of Flesh, that are not yet fully redeemed.[33]

The Holy Trinity will thus be praised in perpetual joy and unity by all creatures. The motif that we see in the text quoted above of the restoration of the original unity of creation in the cosmic *telos* is clearly an Origenian and Evagrian heritage.

In conclusion, we can see that, while Lead's universalism is clearly grounded in her religious experiences and her reading of Scripture in that light, the many similarities with the Origenian tradition—which had experienced a mini-revival in the seventeenth century—suggest that it too was also a significant influence on the shape of her thought. She never directly references Origen so we cannot be certain that she had read him, but it is certainly possible that she had, and at very least his indirect influence on her work, mediated through the Origenian theology of others, seems highly likely.

While the Philadelphians were a small group, the mystical theology of Jane Lead was to have a wide and long-lasting impact through some of the radical Pietists, as we shall see in the next chapter.

EXCURSUS: A COMPARISON WITH A NON-ORIGENIAN AND NON-PATRISTIC NOTION OF UNIVERSAL SALVATION

The doctrine of universal salvation cherished by some Cambridge Platonists and Jane Lead and grounded in part in patristic philosophy is very different, in its theoretical presuppositions, from that of some contemporary preachers, who were much less steeped in the patristic tradition

33. Lead, *Enochian Walks*, n.p.

or even utterly ignorant of it. This is the case, for instance, with Thomas
Moor, a barber from London, who was active in the 1690s. Moor claimed
to be a prophet—Elijah, in fact. He was "a Man taught the Misteries of
the Scriptures, by the same Spirit that indited them."[34] (Such claims for
inspiration were not unusual among popular pneumatic preachers of the
period.)

Moor supported universal salvation in works such as *Clavis Aurea*
(*The Golden Key*, London 1695).[35] His claim was grounded mainly on the
Bible, especially Romans 11:11–33, where Paul announces the restoration
and salvation of all Israel and all the gentiles. Origen in his *Commentary
on Romans* (4:2–3) also understood this passage as a proclamation of
the final universal salvation. But Origen was at the same time one of the
strongest supporters of the idea of libertarian human free will, mainly
due to his anti-Valentinian polemic, whereas Moor definitely rejected it,
being a committed predestinarian, who denied that humans were responsible for their sins. Moor believed that God had created humans with a
flaw, an inclination to sin, to teach them the difference between good and
bad, right and wrong. God is thus responsible for sin, which is aimed at
the final good of creation. In this respect, his thought strongly differs
not only from Origen's, but also from that of Gregory of Nyssa, Evagrius,
and other fathers who supported universal salvation. His moral objection
to eternal hell, however, was more in tune with Origen's sentiments. He
argued that those who take all the Bible in a literal sense end up making
God the one who punishes us for our sins (which he caused us to commit) with eternal fire—"let them say worse of the Devil if they can."[36]
This resonates with Origen's pursuit of a theology *befitting* the deity.

Unlike Origen, Macrina, Gregory of Nyssa, Jane Lead, and others,
who denied the *eternity* of hell, but *not its reality*, Moor denied its very
existence. He interpreted all the references to it in the New Testament as
indications of suffering in *this* world (an idea to be reignited in the nineteenth century by Hosea Balou). What Jesus came to save us from was
not hell, but annihilation. Indeed, Moor is one of the few supporters of
the doctrine of universal restoration who denies any otherworldly punishment or purification. Unlike Origen, Macrina, and Gregory of Nyssa,
Moor was not worried about the moral consequences of such a denial.

---

34. Moor, *Second Addition*, iii.

35. See Burns, "London's Barber-Elijah," 277–90.

36. Moor, *Second Addition*, 28.

In his view, love for God encourages good behavior much more than the fear of hell does. Origen was also convinced of this, but he thought that this was the case only with people who are spiritually advanced; in the most immature, on the contrary, the principle of fear prevails. This is why Origen and many subsequent universalists were wary of overtly preaching universal salvation to all people.

There is no indication that Moor ever built up a group of followers, though it is likely his self-published works, which he sold from his house, had some admirers. They certainly generated a couple of published refutations. But Moor started no movement and left barely a ripple on the subsequent history of Christian universalism.

Part II

The Eighteenth Century
Toward a Universalist Movement

5

From Continental Europe to America
Radical Pietists and Universalism

On 14 September 1785, a small gathering of universalists met in Oxford, Massachusetts, at the invitation of Adams Streeter. Among them were Streeter himself, John Murray, Elhanan Winchester, Caleb Rich, and representatives from five of Rich's churches. The meeting had been gathered in response to a situation in which members of Murray's universalist society in Gloucester, Massachusetts, had their property confiscated by the local Congregational church for failure to pay tithes. Until this moment, the different strands of American universalism—Murray's, Winchester's, Streeter's, and Rich's—all functioned largely independently. Streeter argued that they would be stronger in the face of opposition to their Constitutional rights if they stood together. The gathering agreed a charter of compact and the temporary political alliance between the groups assisted in the legal victory Murray's society won against the Congregationalists. But the association only lasted until the immediate crisis was over and failed to produce any lasting union.

What is interesting for us is that the Oxford Association meeting represents the gathering together of streams of Christian universalism with very different roots that had converged in America and had now started to interact. In this section of the book, we will trace these streams from their sources to their intermingling and finally to their merging.

We can begin our story with the rise of Pietism in Europe. Pietism was a renewal movement within and without German Lutheranism, an attempt to reform the Reformation. Pietists felt that the Lutheran churches in Germany had fallen from the pure Reformation vision and its leaders were lacking in both spiritual and moral fiber. In the late seventeenth century, a scholar-pastor named Philipp Jakob Spener (1635–1705), the founding figure of Pietism, began to try to reform the German Lutheran Church. He started to gather small groups of people at his home for Bible reading and devotion in meetings he called *collegia pietatis*, from whence the name "Pietists" comes.

Pietism was a diverse movement, drawing on eclectic influences. It embraced those, like Spener, who continued to seek reform within the Lutheran Church, as well as those pursuing a more radical vision, who believed that the Lutheran Church was beyond rescue and had to be abandoned by true believers.

Pietists were characterized by an emphasis on the individual's inner regeneration by the Spirit, a new birth from above. They also prized the authority and centrality of Scripture, over and above church traditions and dogmas, and the capacity of laypeople, led by the Spirit, to study and understand Scripture. There was a growing tendency among the Radical Pietists, fueled by the emphasis on inner inspiration by the Spirit, toward mystical interpretations of the Bible, especially in the realm of eschatology. Many of the Pietists felt that the Last Days were upon them. There was a growing emphasis among the radicals upon chiliasm/millennialism, the belief that Christ will return soon, reign over a golden age for a thousand years on earth with his saints, and then resurrect all the dead for final judgment. (The more conservative Pietists, like Spener, always rejected such ideas.) This chiliastic emphasis on the destruction of the established churches was politically subversive and caused concern to some of the authorities. Some sought to suppress the new movement, though several princes took the radicals under their protective wings.

Another emphasis of many of the Radical Pietists was on what was known as Philadelphianism.[1] The Philadelphians believed, as their name suggests, that "brotherly love" should be the defining characteristic and priority of true believers. Denominational differences were of no matter. What counted was inner spirituality, not outward forms and ceremonies. They drew inspiration from Jane Lead's British Philadelphians,

---

1. The name comes from the letter to the church in Philadelphia from Revelation 3:7–13. If the seven churches are read as seven church ages, then the Philadelphian church, in the sixth church age, is the one that preserves the true spirit of Christian love until Christ's return.

who we met in the last chapter, and became a well-organized movement in Germany, far larger than its tiny, short-lived British counterpart.[2]

Radical Pietistic Philadelphianism, with its openness to charismatic insight from allegedly Spirit-inspired dreams and visions, was a wing of the movement that became open to universalism. Prophetic dreams of the salvation of all led some Radical Pietists to see the Scriptures in a fresh light, discovering there a teaching concerning universal restoration—a teaching to which they felt they had previously been blinded by church tradition, but which had in these last days been revealed afresh by the Spirit.[3] This message was not well received by all Pietists, especially in Halle, but it did gather an audience.

JOHANN WILHELM PETERSEN (1649–1726) AND JOHANNA ELEONORA PETERSEN (1644–1724)

Of particular importance for the story of universalism within Pietism are the Radical Pietists Johann Wilhelm Peterson (1649–1726) and his wife Johanna (1644–1724), both friends of Philipp Spener. (According to Johann, Spener himself, while not a universalist and while not speaking out publicly for or against universal restoration, privately confided that he hoped that it was so.[4])

Johanna herself could be said to have long had universalist inclinations. She writes, "Since my early youth, the faithful Lord has let me get into a great struggle when I could not grasp how God, who is essentially love, would condemn so many to eternal condemnation, as was believed

---

2. German translations of most of Lead's works were published in between 1694 and 1705, finding an immediate audience.

3. The turn toward universalism among the Philadelphians required a move beyond and modification of the teaching of Jacob Böhme, the German mystic who was (and remained) a major influence on parts of the movement (though not all were followers of Böhme's teaching). See the appendix of this book.

4. Johann Petersen, *Das Leben*, 330.

in those days everywhere."[5] The fate of the unevangelized in particular troubled her. Yet Scripture was clear that only believers were saved and so she wrestled her heart into submission. Then it was "revealed" to her that Christ preached the gospel to the sinners who died in Noah's flood (1 Pet 4:6), which gave her hope that perhaps there was a possibility of salvation beyond death. Nevertheless, certain biblical texts stopped her short of belief in universal salvation, "for at that time the return of all things had not been revealed to me."[6] Another step in more universalist directions came after a dream in 1664 in which the end-time conversion of the Jews and the heathens was revealed to her.[7] (The conversion of the Jews in the last days became a prominent feature of Radical Pietist millenarianism.) Furthermore, she had been in correspondence with Johann Georg Gich-

D. Joh. Wilhelm Petersen.

tel (1638–1710) about eternal damnation as early as January 1693 and seems to have been concerned with universal salvation in correspondence from the same year.[8]

The Petersens finally became full-blown universalists in 1694/95, when Johann was twenty-five and Johanna was thirty, under the influence of the English mystic Jane Lead (see previous chapter). Lead, as we have seen, believed that the Spirit had given a new revelation that "the everlasting gospel" preached by the angel to the nations in Revelation 14:6 was the gospel

5. Johanna Petersen, *Life*, 86.

6. Johanna Petersen, *Life*, 87.

7. Johanna Petersen, *Life*, 87–88.

8. On Johann Gichtel, his initial admiration of Lead and then his subsequent rejection of her work (and his fallout and break from with the Petersens in 1701), see Martin, "God's Strange Providence"; McClymond, *Devil's Redemption*, 487–91. Gichtel was initially open on the issue of universal salvation, but subsequently rejected it; perhaps it was too much of a departure from Böhme, and he always deferred to Böhme when in doubt. According to Martin, his rejection of Lead was driven by a mix of theological and psychological factors.

of the salvation of all men and angels. The Petersens were sent a pre-publication copy of the manuscript of one of her books, *The Wonders of God's Creation Manifested in the Variety of Eight Worlds* (London: 1695),[9] which they read with skepticism at first, but then suddenly "there was a stillness in both their spirits, as if someone had interrupted them and there came into their minds the words spoken in Revelation 21:5, 'Behold I make all things new.'"[10] Johann writes, "We came to understand that God is essentially love, and that his unending mercy would pour itself out on all his creation."[11]

Lead's universalism was based more on visions than on Scripture, so Johann and Johanna Peterson provided Lead's theology with a more solid biblical foundation. They appreciated the value of charismatic visions, but believed that everything must be tested against Scripture. Johanna Petersen—who, unusually for a woman in her day, was quite an amateur theologian—"corrected" some of the aspects of Lead's chronology of the restoration to bring it more into line with her own pneumatic interpretation of the book of Revelation (a modification that, she says, Lead herself appreciated).[12] Johann Petersen was able to modify aspects of Jane Lead's universalism in an attempt to fix other problems with it. For instance, Lead expected that the universal salvation would *precede* and induce the return of Christ. Johann denied this. He believed that at death souls were divided into the few who will await the millennium in a quiet place before being resurrected at Christ's return to reign with him a thousand years. The rest will be sent to a place of torment until the millennium is over. Then there would be a general resurrection of all the dead and the great day of final judgment. At the judgment, those who have been reformed in the postmortem torment will be sent into eternal happiness, significantly increasing the number of the saved, while the rest are cast into the lake of fire. They will suffer in the lake for thousands of years until they are humbled and receive the gift of faith. Then they too will be saved by Christ's merits. In the end, even Satan will be saved. Sin, lacking an

9. This particular volume was given to them by Baron Dodo von Knyphausen, a patron of various radical groups. Johann Petersen, *Das Leben*, 297. However, Martin has shown that they were already familiar with Lead and her work from at least 1694. Martin, "God's Strange Providence."

10. Walker, *Decline of Hell*, 234.

11. For Johann's account of their conversion to restorationism, see Johann Petersen, *Das Leben*, 297–307.

12. Johanna Petersen, *Life*, 92–94.

eternal root, cannot last forever—it must vanish from creation. When it does, God will be all in all.[13]

In addition to building a biblical case for universalism, he also gathered together earlier writings on universalism into a three-volume work called the *Mysterion Apokatastaseos Panton* (*The Mystery of the Restitution of All Things*; 1700, 1703, 1710).[14] Included in this work was a book by Paul Siegvolck entitled (in English) *The Everlasting Gospel*. We shall return to this text later.

Now convinced of the Restoration, Johann became an eager promoter of the message of *Wiederbringung aller Dinge* (God's restoration of all things) in both his preaching and his writing ministry: he travelled widely in German lands—having an extensive network of friends and acquaintances, and receiving many invitations to speak—and was a prolific author.[15] He also kept an account in his autobiography of where his Restorationist message was well received. Amongst those who accepted it was Eberhard Ludwig Gruber (1665–1728), the leader of the Inspirationists (a Radical Pietist sect), as well as various counts, barons, councilors, and other significant people.[16] It would be fair to say that much, though not all, of the universalism within German Pietism can trace its roots to the work of the Petersens, and through them to Jane Lead.

RADICAL PIETIST GROUPS

The universalists among the Radical Pietists came to gather in different interrelated groupings.[17] Of those that emigrated to Pennsylvania in the

13. Johann Petersen, *Mysterion Apokatastaseos*, 1.140–47.

14. A book that the philosopher G. W. Leibniz (1649–1716) read soon after it appeared and considerably appreciated.

15. Johann Peterson has about 150 works attributed to him. His wife Johanna published fifteen. Johann's most important Restorationist text was undoubtedly the *Mysterion Apokatastaseos Panton*. The most significant universalist text by Johanna is *Die Ewige Evangelium Der Allgemeinen Wiederbringung Aller Creaturen* (*The Eternal Gospel of the Universal Return of All Creatures*). This was published anonymously in 1698 and without a location or publisher listed, possibly because Philipp Spener had warned Johanna in 1695 against publishing such views. The tract went through three editions and stirred up a lot of responses, both pro and contra.

16. Johann Petersen, *Das Leben*, 290, 292.

17. There were also universalists among the Schwenkenfelders, yet another radical Reformation grouping that focused on inner spirituality over outward form, who similarly emigrated to America in the 1730s. The boundaries between radical groups

American colonies, we find three: the followers of Johannes Kelpius, the German Baptist Brethren (and a breakaway group, the German Seventh Day Baptists), and a miscellaneous group of other Separatists. Most or possibly all of these groups were influenced by the Petersens. In addition to them, we need to make mention of the Moravians (another Pietist group, some of whom were universalists) and the scholar Johann Albrecht Bengel.

Johannes Kelpius and his followers

The American colonies provided a "new world" free from corruption and oppression that was wide open for radical religious communities to prepare themselves for the millennium. The Frankfurt Land Company (of which Johanna Petersen was a member) bought up forty-three thousand acres in Pennsylvania, some of which was used to build Germantown (outside Philadelphia, which had been founded in 1682). The first group of German Pietists to sail for America was led by Johannes Kelpius (1667–1708) in 1693. We know that, later on, Kelpius embraced a belief in the restoration of all things, though we do not know when he first did so or under whose influence it happened (Jane Lead? Johann Petersen?). Kelpius's group settled briefly in Germantown before some moved off to form a celibate community called "The Woman in the Wilderness." The community, while it did not survive, represents the introduction of Pietist universalism into America.

were porous and influences ran between them. The works of Jane Lead and Johann Petersen were read by these groups too.

The German Baptist Brethren

The Bretheren were deeply influenced from their foundation by Ernst Christoph Hochman von Hochenau (1670–1721), a nobleman and a follower of Johann Petersen, whom he had first met while studying law at the University of Halle. Restorationism was a core doctrine to Hochmann, inherited from his mentor.[18]

Hochmann founded several Philadelphian communities in Wittgenstein.[19] In 1706 he was invited to Schriesheim, near Heidelburg, by a miller named Alexander Mack (1679–1735). Hochmann became Mack's mentor and the two men began evangelizing together, with Hochmann getting regularly imprisoned for the effort. Mack fled persecution to Scwarzenau in 1706 with a small group of followers. They decided, after the manner of the Anabaptists, that their infant baptism was invalid, and so in 1708 they (re)baptized each other.[20] This was the founding of the Pietist sect calling themselves the Church of the Brethren (also known as German Baptists, Taufers, or Dunkers).[21] Hochmann himself, on his release

---

18. It forms the basic theme of Heinz Renkewitz's biography of Hochmann (Renkewwitz, *Hochmann von Hochenau*).

19. The most significant of these, for our story, was that in Berleburg. Hochmann, a Swiss universalist Pietist called Samuel König (1671–1750), and Johann Reitz (1655–1720) founded the Philadelphian Society there in 1700, though Hochmann was banished by the Imperial Court at Wetzlar soon after, following reports of "charismatic" services held by Hochmann in the castle. However, the community remained and, after 1712, under the protection of pietistic Count Casimir, it became a thriving refuge for Philadelphians.

From 1720 on the community became a major publishing center for Radical Pietist literature, with their crowning glory being the eight-volume Berleburg Bible. This was a new translation and interpretation of the Bible according to Restorationist Philadelphian theology. It drew on an eclectic range of inspirations and could be somewhat disorientating and incoherent in its interpretative comment. The new community of Berleburg Pietists later built significant links with the Radical Pietists in Pennsylvania—sending people, publications, and even the printing press upon which the Berleburg Bible had been printed. This press was then used by Christopher Sauer/Sower in Germantown to publish many universalist books and pamphlets in America.

20. Most Radical Pietists retained the infant baptism of their Lutheran roots, but some, under Quaker influence, rejected all outward rituals, including baptism, while others, such as the Brethren, moved to believer's baptism, influenced by Anabaptists. This indicates just how eclectic and diverse Radical Pietism was.

21. Or perhaps it would be better to think of them as a sect with strong pietistic influences (especially via Hochmann). The community in Pennsylvania certainly had many links with Pietists and published many works by Pietists, but they were also quite distinctive.

from prison, was somewhat ambiguous about this development—he was not against such baptism, but strongly opposed the suggestion that it was a requirement, believing that this would be a step away from Philadelphianism. While Hochmann slowly drew away from the Brethren, who continued to formalize themselves as a distinct sect, they maintained his teachings.

Perhaps Hochmann's most influential statement of universalism, even if not his most profound, was made in 1702 when he was released from imprisonment in Detmold Castle. (He had been arrested for preaching.) He was asked to write out his creed as a condition of his release. The Detmold Confession, as it became known, was influential because it was later adopted by the German Baptist Brethren in Pennsylvania as their creed, showing the continued influence of Hochmann's teaching on the group. In the sixth article he wrote this:

> Concerning the restoration of damned men after death . . . : that just as all mankind are fallen in Adam, so must all men be reborn through Christ, the other Adam; if this was not true, it would necessarily follow that Christ was not mighty enough to restore the human race which was lost through Adam, and in this connection the whole fifth chapter of the Epistle to the Romans can be read, and from this it may be seen how the Restoration, through the mediatorship of Christ, is much stronger and more mighty than the power of sin through the fate of Adam. 1 Corinthians 15:22 states clearly that as in Adam all die, so in Christ shall all be made alive.[22]

Thus, the German Baptists in America made universalism a part of their communal confession. This was not, of course, to deny punishment for the unbelievers. Their main theological text was Mack's *Brief and Simple Exposition of the Outward But Yet Sacred Rights and Ordinances of the House of God* (1715), and this makes clear, on the basis of a range of biblical texts (Rev 1:7; 6:16; 14:9–11; 20:15; Matt 25:41; Mark 9:48; Isa 66:24) that "the torment of the condemned and unbelievers will be . . . inexpressible."

> Then the damned will see this [the blessing of the righteous] and stand in dreadful awe of such blessedness, and will say to one another with penitence, and sigh with anguish of the spirit: "This is the man we fools once laughed at. . . . We thought his life was madness. . . . How did he come to be reckoned among

22. Translation by Charlotte Irwin.

the sons of God, and why is his lot among the saints? Then we must have wandered from the true way. . . . What good did our arrogance do us? And what have wealth and ostentation done for us?" (Wisdom of Solomon 5:1, 4–8). They will ponder all of these things—how they spent their lives in sin, how they did not love God as the highest good, and lost through this folly all this great blessedness. Then they will experience torment, grief, and misery which no tongue can express, for they are banished from the presence of God and all the saints.

All that sounds very bleak and hardly universalist! However, things are not so simple. The *Rights and Ordinances* goes on:

Son: These things are most horrible to hear. Do tell me, are these torments and tortures to last for eternity, without end?

Father: According to the testimony of the Holy Scriptures, "the smoke of their torment goes up for ever and ever" (Revelation 14:11). *However, that it should last for eternity is not supported by Holy Scripture.* It is not necessary to talk much about it or speculate about it. The joyous blessedness is definitely forfeited by their folly. Even if at some time the torment should end after long eternities, they will never attain that which the believers have achieved in the time of grace through Jesus Christ if they obey Him.

Many who have heard about universal restoration commit the great folly not to deny themselves completely but rather hope for the restoration. This hope will most certainly come to naught when they enter the torment, and can see no end to it. Their pitiful comfort will vanish like smoke. Therefore, it is much better to practice this simple truth that one should try to become worthy in the time of grace to escape the wrath of God and the torments of hell, rather than deliberate how or when it would be possible to escape from it again. It is as if a thief were to console himself like this: "Oh, even if I am seized because of the theft, my punishment will have its end." Would not that be a miserable consolation!

Therefore, that is a much better and more blessed gospel which teaches how to escape the wrath of God than the gospel which teaches that eternal punishment has an end. *Even though this is true, it should not be preached as a gospel to the godless.* Unfortunately, in this day, everything is completely distorted by the great power of imagination of those people who teach and write books about restoration.[23]

Clearly the doctrine of universal restoration was *affirmed* but handled with *great caution* lest people abuse the teaching as license for laxity. It was thus reserved for internal consumption only, not for open declaration to "the godless." One is reminded here of the patristic pastoral hesitation about preaching *apokatastasis* to the spiritually immature.

The German Seventh Day Baptists

The first wave of German Baptists to move to Pennsylvania sailed in 1719, following persecution back home. Mack himself emigrated with some more in 1729. In the 1730s there was a split within the community in Pennsylvania, with the dissenters, led by Conrad Beissel (1691–1768), founding a community of celibates sixty-five miles away on the banks of the Cocalico River.[24] They were known as the Ephrata Community. Their theology seems to have been the same as that of the Brethren, universalism

23. Mack, "Rights and Ordinances," 113–15; Durnbaugh, *European Origins of the Brethren*, 398–400. Italics mine. My thanks to John Hopler for drawing my attention to this quotation. The passage can be found in context in Holsinger's translation of the whole text in Mack, "Rights and Ordinances," 115.

24. The site still exists as a museum: http://www.ephratacloister.org/.

included, with the exception that they practiced celibacy and celebrated the Sabbath on Saturday (hence, the German Seventh Day Baptists). Like the other Brethren, they remained under the influence of Böhme's mysticism and theosophy, German Pietism, and Philadelphianism.

The Separatists

From 1726 on, Separatists, influenced (like the Brethren) by the teachings of Hochmann and the Philadelphians, emigrated to various parts of Pennsylvania. These folk, however, were closer to the Quakers in their rejection of outward rituals like baptism in favor of "the internal revelation of the gospel."[25] They were "deeply religious personalities, keenly concerned for ethics in personal life and in the broader society, who, however, were antagonistic in principle to organized religion."[26] They too were universalists, and included among their number Christoph Sauer/ Christopher Sower (1695–1758) and, later, George de Benneville, to whom we shall return.

The Moravians

From 1735, another Continental pietistic stream that brought universalism to America was the Moravians.[27] It is likely that Count Nicolaus von Zinzendorf (1700–1760), the great man behind the Moravian mission movement of the third wave of Pietism, was a universalist. In his *Sixteen Discourses*, Zinzendorf writes, "By His [Christ's] Name, all can *and shall* obtain life and salvation."[28] Certainly some, albeit a minority, of the early Moravian missionaries believed in the salvation of all. One such was Peter

25. Rush, *Essays*, 241.

26. Durnbaugh, "Communication Networks," 46.

27. Thanks to Professor John Coffey for alerting me to universalism amongst the Moravians.

28. Zinzendorf, *Sixteen Discourses*, 30. Italics mine.

Böhler (1712–75), sent by Zinzendorf to the Americas, where he was active in spreading the gospel and was a key leader in the movement in both America and Britain. His universalism was clearly not something that dampened his missional passion.

The fact that Zinzendorf and Peter Böhler believed (and sometimes taught) a doctrine of universal restoration was one of the many idiosyncrasies that undid their relationship with George Whitefield, John Wesley, and Dutch and American Reformed Evangelicals. Wesley expressed concern to Zinzendorf about the universalism in the latter's *Sixteen Discourses*,[29] and the Dutch Reformed condemned Zinzendorf for it. Whitefield wrote to Wesley in 1740 that Peter Böhler, whom Wesley regarded highly, had told him that "all the damned souls would hereafter be brought out of hell" and advanced this "in order to make out universal redemption."[30]

Zinzendorf himself went to Pennsylvania in 1741 to try to establish a league of the different Pietist groupings, working together as "a church of God in the Spirit." He called the first of several convocations of all the groups at the start of 1742. According to Albert Bell, at the first convocation Zinzendorf proposed an article of faith that Jesus is "not only the Saviour of the faithful and the atonement for their sins, but also the atonement for the whole world and the Saviour of all men."[31] However, he was widely perceived to be seeking unity by means of imposing Moravian beliefs and practices on all the churches, which quickly generated considerable hostility. Relations between Zinzendorf's Moravians and the other Pietists broke down.

It is ironic that the different Philadelphian groups in Pennsylvania, with their commitment to brotherly love and their rejection of

29. Wesley, *Works of the Rev John Wesley*, 106.

30. Whitefield, *George Whitefield's Journals*, 587.

31. Bell, *Life and Times*, 32.

sectarianism, were unable to unify under a league due to certain differences in belief and practice, and because of a clash between strong personalities.

Johann Albrecht Bengel (1687–1752)

Johann Albrecht Bengel was a very important figure in Württembergian Pietism and an accomplished scholar with wide-ranging interests. He taught Latin, Greek, Hebrew, mathematics, and logic at a theological boarding school for fourteen- to eighteen-year-old boys in Denkendorf for twenty-eight years, preparing students for theology with an ultimate view to ministry, and he had a lasting impact through these students. After this he served in church and political posts in Württemberg. While Bengel had been influenced by the spirituality and theology of the Radical Pietists, he was unimpressed by their separatism. Refusing to separate from the Lutheran state church, he and the other Württemberg Pietists sought to renew it from within.

Bengel is best known for his publications, which included a critical edition of the Greek New Testament (1734), a publication that brought him much fame and established him as a father of textual criticism, and a commentary on the New Testament (1742), often considered Pietism's greatest exegetical achievement. John Wesley considered it so important that he translated it into English. However, Bengel is of interest to us because in his "Reich-Gottes Theologie" (Theology of God's Kingdom) he set forth a salvation-historical, millennialist scheme that climaxed in the universal restoration of the whole creation, with a place for aeons of purifying fire, but no place for an everlasting hell.

Bengel's universalism was developed by his pupil Friedrich Christoph Oetinger (1702–82) and shaped Württemberg Pietists for generations, especially through Bengel's Revelation commentary. While he was not a direct ancestor of the universalism that was transplanted to America by radical pietistic groups, his ideas are worth noting here because they ultimately informed Johann Christoph Blumhardt's (1805–80) growing inclinations to embrace the larger hope in the nineteenth century and, through him, Karl Barth and Jürgen Moltmann in the twentieth.

GEORGE DE BENNEVILLE (1703–93)

An interesting case study from the period is that of Dr. George de Benneville, a Separatist who came to Pennsylvania in 1741. De Benneville was born in London in 1703, the son of Aristocratic Huguenot (French Calvinist) refugees, fleeing Catholic persecution. He was brought up in the household of Queen Anne, who knew the family. As a boy, around 1716, he was sent to learn navigation on a boat bound for North Africa. His encounter with some pious and compassionate Muslims in Algiers convicted him of the shallowness of his own Christian devotion, yet on his return to London he fell back into a frivolous lifestyle. Nevertheless, the deep sense of his sin got the better of him: he became ill and experienced a vision of himself burning in hell. This sense of inner turmoil became chronic, until one day, fifteen months later, he found himself overwhelmed by an even deeper despair at his sinfulness than usual, and he simply let go, abandoning himself to the justice of God. Then:

> I discovered between Justice and me the criminal, one of the most majestic appearance, whose beauty, brightness, and grandeur cannot be described.—He cast a look of grace and mercy upon me, and regarded me with such love as penetrated my whole being, and animated my soul with so pure a flame, that I loved him again with a reciprocal love. He persuaded me in my heart that he was my Saviour, Mediator, and Reconciler.

De Benneville sensed Christ praying for him before the Father. He then heard the divine voice declare that his sins were forgiven. Unable to contain himself any longer, he wept with joy and gratitude.

This experience was life-changing for de Benneville, and so overwhelmed was he with the revelation of the depth and breath of God's saving love and the efficacy of the atonement that he became convinced— there and then, and for the rest of his life—that this atoning love extended to all humanity.[32] It also sealed in him a passion to preach the gospel to others so that they too could know this divine love.

---

32. De Benneville, *True and Most Remarkable Account*, 11–14.

The French Calvinist ministers in London became very concerned about George's new convictions and met with him to discuss matters, but agreement could not be reached: "for they held predestination, and I held the restoration of all souls. Having been the chief of sinners, I could not have a doubt but the whole world would be saved by the same power."[33] It is interesting that the very core of de Benneville's Evangelical conversion experience was understood by him to contain the seeds of restorationism. As far as we know, he was not aware of any others who taught universalism at this time.

George de Benneville was excommunicated and, aged seventeen, left for France to become a preacher for a couple of years. There he associated with various radical, pneumatic Protestants. They were often arrested and imprisoned, and on one occasion he got as far as the scaffold and was about to be beheaded when King Louis XV sent a messenger granting a reprieve. After release from prison in 1725 he went to Germany and Holland, associating with various radicals, including the Philadelphian community in Berleburg (see fn 19). He continued to travel and preach around Germany and the Lowlands for about eighteen years. Then he became seriously ill from stress caused by his concern over the plight of lost souls. In his near-death state he experienced a vision in which he was assured that he would soon "see" the "restoration of all the human species without exception."[34] His health continued to deteriorate to the point that he was thought to be dead—he himself felt his soul separate from his body. (He was presumably in some kind of coma.) In this state he experienced visions in which "the Most Holy Trinity" (de Benneville's favorite way of naming God) sent angels to guide him on a tour of seven zones of hell, where he saw the suffering of the damned and felt "great compassion towards the sufferers." After leaving hell, a messenger was sent to reassure him that "the Most Holy Trinity always works wonders in all times within his poor creatures, without exception. . . . [Y]ou shall return into your earthly tabernacle, to publish, and to proclaim to the people of the world an universal Gospel, that shall restore in its time all the human species, without exception, to its honour, and to the glory of the Most Holy Trinity." He then witnessed the multitudes of heavenly host worshipping the Triune God. He was next taken back to hell, and

33. De Benneville, *True and Most Remarkable Account*, 15.

34. The vision, which clearly had a big impact on de Benneville, is recounted in detail in de Benneville, *True and Remarkable Account*, 22–36. Quotations are from that section.

saw that there was no more darkness or pain—all was quiet. Suddenly the host of heaven shouted "An eternal and everlasting deliverance, an eternal and everlasting restoration, an universal and everlasting restitution of all things." Then the damned were delivered from their sin and clothed in white robes; they joined the heavenly host in worshipping God. At this point, he was taken on a tour of the five heavenly mansions. There he met Adam, who told him, "this love of God in Jesus Christ, by the power of the Holy Spirit, shall not only gain the victory over all the human species, but also surmount or overflow the kingdom of Satan entirely, with all the principalities of the fallen angels, and shall bring them back into their first glory, which they had in the beginning." He awoke from the vision and found himself in a coffin, having been assumed dead for about forty-one hours!

Receiving a call to preach in America, he emigrated in 1741, aged thirty-eight. By the time he arrived he was very ill, but was met at the wharf by Christopher Sower from Germantown (who apparently had received a dream from God to go and bring the sick man home).[35] Sower nursed him back to health, and thus began a fruitful relationship between the two men, especially in regard to various publishing projects. (Sower ran a printing press in Germantown.) The most significant of these was the publication of *The Everlasting Gospel* by Paul Siegvolck in 1753 (see next section).

De Benneville was eclectic and ecumenical in his influences and associations,[36] but radical in his instincts. He was of "spiritual" inclination, disliking formal creeds, religious hierarchies, and outward rituals, and eschewing social privilege (he fiercely repudiated any deference to himself on the grounds of his aristocratic lineage).

In addition to being a preacher, de Benneville was also a medical doctor, and his skills were in much demand in the colony. He became a respected figure in the community, and among the local Native American tribes,[37] and his time was spent in medicine, running an apothecary shop,

35. De Benneville himself moved to the Oley Valley in 1742, where he married, and then to Bristol township just outside Philadelphia in 1757, and finally to Philadelphia in 1787.

36. It is of interest to note that he was in correspondence with George Stonehouse (Bell, *Life and Times*, 59); see chapter 6.

37. He had a high regard for Native American peoples and worked among them as both a doctor and a preacher. He apparently contextualized his preaching to them by using religious symbols and categories with which they were already familiar.

as well as working as a schoolmaster, but always, until the end of his days at age ninety, preaching the "everlasting gospel" of God's universal saving love in Christ.

PAUL SIEGVOLK'S *THE EVERLASTING GOSPEL*

One of the influential Restorationist texts of the period was Paul Siegvolck's *The Everlasting Gospel*. The book was written under a pseudonym; the actual author was likely Georg Klein-Nicolai, a follower of Johann Petersen and a deposed pastor from Friessdorf, later pastor in Zeulenroda. It was originally published in German, being included as part of the first volume of Petersen's *Mysterion* in 1700. The book was translated into English and published by Christopher Sower in Germantown in 1753 at the instigation and expense of George de Benneville. (Elhanan Winchester also published an edition in London in 1792.) Given its wide circulation and influence, it is worth outlining the argument.

In good millenarian fashion, the work is presented as a gracious appeal of God to call sinners to repentance prior to the coming eschatological judgment (see its preface). What sets the book apart from some others is the theologically focused organization of the presentation of restorationism. The author builds his case step by step by highlighting key principles and defending them from the Bible.

Siegvolck begins with God (ch. 1).[38] God can only be known by divine self-revelation through the Spirit-inspired Scriptures. And what do we find there? That "all descriptions of the Divine Being, that we find in holy Scriptures, together with all that may be believed, thought, or uttered of God, center in this one word, *Love:* . . . GOD IS LOVE" (2). *Everything* God is and does comes from his love. God cannot hate himself and, consequently, cannot hate his creatures. It "necessarily follows hence, that even the most dreadful punishments which God, in the age or ages to come, will inflict on bad angels and men, as far as they proceed from him, are grounded in no other principle than that of Love" (4). We thus see that divine wrath and justice must also be understood to be "at the bottom nothing else but Love" (5). The biblical God will not inflict never-ending punishment on sinful creatures, for such punishment cannot be for their ultimate good (ch. 2).

38. The following in-text citations in this section on Siegvolck are from *The Everlasting Gospel*, unless otherwise stated.

The doctrine of God, as taught in Scripture, also teaches us that while sinners can resist God for a time, everything that God wills must be fulfilled *in the end* (ch. 3). And this divine will, according to the Bible, clearly includes the salvation of all people. So creaturely freedom can withstand the divine will for a time, but not for eternity, and God will even utilize such resistance for his ultimate purposes. (If a creature could resist God for eternity, then it would prove stronger than God, and evil stronger than the good!)

Creatures have their origin in God, and what God has made is good and can endure for eternity. However, sin and evil spring up from the will of the creature through choices made in this world, not from God (ch. 4). Such things cannot endure forever. To suggest otherwise yields an eternal cosmic dualism of good and evil. God loves *creatures*, with their good natures, which originate from him, and he hates *sin*, which seeks to corrupt those natures (ch. 5).

So it is not fallen creatures that are evil and worthy only of destruction, but their *perverted wills*. God in Christ works to undo the damage that sin has caused so as to restore creation to its primal goodness. Christ's atoning death on the cross was intended for all and is efficacious for all (ch. 6). If, per impossible, any remain unsaved in the end, then Christ's death for them was in vain and Satan has forever defeated Christ in regard to those creatures. If many or most remain in hell forever, then Satan far outstrips Christ in his triumph. This is unthinkable!

Chapter 7 moves on to consider that staple of all discussions of hell in this period—the word "eternal" (*aiōnios*). A few Scriptures describe the punishment of the wicked as "eternal" (Isa 33:14; Dan 12:2; Matt 18:8; 25:41, 46; Mark 3:29; 2 Thess 1:7–9), and such verses were foundational for traditional theology of hell. Siegvolck distinguishes different usages of the words before arguing, in chapter 8, that the punishment of the wicked is not never-ending, but endures for an age (i.e., a set period of time, with a beginning and end). Indeed, if it endured forever, the punishment would be disproportionate and unjust.

Damnation, like heavenly glory, comes in different kinds and in different degrees (chs. 9–10). Divine punishment of sin is "death." In this age, such "death" is a corrupt nature and an evil conscience with its accompanying spiritual and bodily torments. It is being enslaved to sin, reaping the harvest of the bad seeds we sow. The notion of "death" as punishment covers spiritual death, bodily death, and aiōnian death. We also need to distinguish the first death from the second death. Siegvolck believes that the "first death" covers not simply bodily death but the entire state of body and soul under the rule of sin and the wrath of God during (a) this life, (b) bodily death, and (c) confinement to Hades, with its torments (proportioned to one's sin). The second death is the lake of fire.

The books set out a grand view of history that breaks it down in the following fashion:

"This present age"			"The age to come"			The "still eternity"
Pre-flood	Post-flood WE ARE HERE	Christ returns	The millennium	Final Judgment	"the ages of ages"	"God will be all in all"
"the first death"					"the second death"	Death defeated

We currently live in the post-flood "age" of the present age, awaiting the soon-to-return Christ. When Christ returns at the end of this present age, those who have been faithful to him in this age will be raised to rule with him for a thousand years in the millennium (these are "the church of the first-born"). The rest will be confined to Hades, with its torments. At the end of the millennium, there is a general judgment. Then a second resurrection raises those who were not worthy to partake in the first, but who have come to Christ in Hades and had their names included in the Lamb's book of life (Siegvolck called them the "church of the *after-born*"). Yet, still many remain in sin and they are sentenced to the "second death"—confinement to the lake of fire for "the ages of ages" (i.e., a *very, very long* time). But, in the end, all will be saved through Christ from the lake of fire. The "church of the after-born" thus includes both those who are after-born from the first death *and* those who are eventually after-born from the second death (including those who blasphemed against the Holy Spirit).

At this point, "the future age . . . is changed into that still or silent eternity, wherein God is to be all in all, after Jesus Christ shall have subdued everything to himself, and brought all into order and harmony. I Cor xv.28" (85).[39] This return of all creatures to God does not, of course,

---

39. What Siegvolck calls "silent eternity" or "still eternity" is a phrase use by

destroy "the true difference between the being of the Creator and that of the creature" (108), but it speaks of all creatures "pervaded by God's Spirit, and, as one might say in a sort, *deified*, (or made partakers of the divine nature.) God with them, and they with God, in a manner will be but *one Spirit . . . joined unto the Lord. . . .* But this is impossible to be so long as the creatures remain in sin and death" (112). And in order to destroy all the works of the devil, Christ must annihilate sin in all fallen creatures.

Siegvolck ends the book with a defense of restorationism against the ever-present objection that it removes the motivation for godly living and thereby undermines civic order (ch. 13).

There are several interesting parallels between Siegvolck's theology and the patristic *apokatastasis* tradition. One thinks, for instance, of the restorative role of punishment, of an understanding of divine wrath that is "worthy of God," of the critical role played by the understanding of evil as a privation, of the necessity for sin's annihilation from the wills of sinful creatures, and of the distinction between "the age(s) to come" and the climax of creation beyond all ages in which God is "all in all" and the final restoration is complete. Siegvolck never makes explicit reference to any of his sources (Scripture excepted), but it seems very likely that he was aware of the patristic tradition. Yet Siegvolck is also clearly a Protestant with strong premillennialist convictions and a concern to demonstrate all his claims from the Bible in a way that the heirs of the Reformation would find acceptable. He was, in effect, rethinking and repackaging the patristic tradition for his own time and place.

Siegvolk's book was to become influential amongst those sympathetic to the universal restoration, especially in the "New World" of America. We shall be considering one of its most significant converts to the cause, Elhanan Winchester, in the next chapter. But before we reflect on Winchester we need to take a look at a few important British universalists in this period.

John Porradge and Jane Lead, adopted from Jakob Böhme. It manifests something of Böhme's and Lead's influence in Johann Petersen's circles. But see the appendix for qualifications on the nature and extent of this influence. The notion of the final stage of creation being beyond the end of *all* the ages is rooted in the church fathers (see esp. Ilaria Ramelli's first volume in *A Larger Hope?*).

6

Pietist Universalism in Britain and America

Law, Stonehouse, and Winchester

IN BRITAIN, UNIVERSALISM NEVER attained the status of a movement, with the brief exception of the small group of Philadelphians led by Jane Lead. Individuals such as Gerrard Winstanley, George Rust, Ann Conway, Peter Sterry, and Jeremiah White found their own ways into some version of universal restorationism. And while they took some actions aimed at passing along their new ideas—especially publishing them in books—there was no universalist denomination, or even a para-church movement, though the Philadelphians represented the embryo of one. This situation continued into the eighteenth century. Two somewhat different Christian believers will serve to illustrate this.

THE MYSTICAL UNIVERSALISM OF WILLIAM LAW
(1686–1761)

Life

William Law was, like Peter Sterry, a graduate of Emmanuel College in Cambridge.[1] He was ordained a deacon, but when he refused to swear an oath of allegiance to the new Hannoverian monarchy in 1716—for his sympathies lay with the deposed Stuart monarchy—his ecclesiastical career came to an end. He became chaplain to the family of Edward Gibbon

---

1. Also like Sterry, he is commemorated by a stained-glass window in the college chapel.

in Putney, London. There he wrote the two books that made him famous, both practical guides to Christian holiness and a critique of nominal Christianity.[2]

Sometime between 1733–37 Law was introduced to the work of Jakob Böhme, the sixteenth-century Teutonic mystical Lutheran, and after a little wrestling with Böhme's difficult texts, Law's own theology was transformed.[3] One can divide Law's books into pre- and post-exposure to Böhme. Needless to say, many who admired the pre-Böhme Law were unimpressed by the post-Böhme Law, among them John Wesley.[4] However, while the focus of the two periods is different—the former offers practical guidance while the latter offers speculative theology—they are not inconsistent with each other, and Law saw the later mystical theology as providing the theological frame within which to interpret the earlier practical advice. While Law was not influenced directly by Pietism, he shared with them (and Jane Lead and the Philadelphians) the influence of Jakob Böhme, which led to a certain degree of theological convergence. That is why he has been included in this chapter.

In 1740 Law returned to the town of his birth—King's Cliffe in Northamptonshire—and set up a "holy household" with Hester Gibbon

2. *A Practical Treatise upon Christian Perfection* (1726) and *A Serious Call to a Devout and Holy Life* (1729).

3. His first book in this new theological venture was *The Grounds and Reasons of Christian Regeneration* (1739).

4. Wesley was deeply impacted by these texts and recommended his Methodist leaders to read them, though he later came to see them as erring too much on the side of law rather than gospel, with a tendency to legalism. He considered the later works to be unintelligible nonsense (and published an open letter to Law in 1756 arguing this point). Alan Gregory argues that Wesley actually made little attempt to *understand* Law's later works, let alone offer to offer a substantive response to them (*Quenching Hell*, 8–9). On Law's appropriation of Böhme, see also Gregory, "No New Truths of Religion."

and Mrs. Hutchinson, a widow. Here they sought to live holy and generous lives, giving away about nine tenths of their income to endow local schools, almshouses, and a library, as well as caring for the sick and
needy in their parish. He also devoted much time to study and writing.
Universalist sympathies do not become overtly manifest until his later
publications.[5]

While conducting an audit of two schools in 1761, Law caught a
cold, which developed into a kidney infection and led to his death.

Theology

Law's post-Böhme theological system is complex and here we offer a very
basic sketch.[6] In essence, Law presents a sophisticated, albeit speculative,
story of creation, fall, and restoration, which is grounded in a vision of
God as love. God is:

> [A]n Infinity of mere Love, an unbeginning, never-ceasing,
> and forever overflowing Ocean of Meekness, Sweetness, De-
> light, Blessing, Goodness, Patience, and Mercy, and all this as
> so many blessed Streams breaking out of the Abyss of universal
> Love, Father, Son, and Holy Ghost, a Triune Infinity of Love and
> Goodness, for ever and ever giving forth nothing but the same
> Gifts of Light and Love, of Blessing and Joy, whether before or
> after the Fall, either of Angels or Men.[7]

Law will permit absolutely nothing into his theology that is seen in any
way to compromise this divine love. God "can be nothing else but all
Goodness toward it [i.e., creation], because he can be nothing toward the
Creature but that which he is, and was, and ever shall be in himself."[8]

---

5. *The Spirit of Prayer* (1749–50), *The Way to Divine Knowledge* (1752), and *The
Spirit of Love* (Part I in 1752 and Part II in 1754).

6. Law misunderstood the classical Christian doctrine of creation *ex nihilo*, taking
it to imply that the connection between God and creation was entirely arbitrary so that
creation was not a manifestation of God's glory in finite reality. The doctrine does not
in fact imply that, but given that Law thought it did one can understand his passionate
rejection of it. Böhme, who also rejected the doctrine, will have encouraged Law's
rejection of it. For a detailed outline and interpretation, see Alan Gregory's *Quenching
Hell*, which has been the main source for our own outline. Gregory is sympathetic to
Law, but unafraid to critique aspects of his theology.

7. Law, *Serious Call*, 423.

8. Law, *Serious Call*, 393.

This has implications for the controversial way in which Law came to think of wrath. Wrath is a passion that intends the harm of the other and so God *cannot* be wrathful toward creatures. When we speak of the wrath of God we speak about how a sinner experiences the self-destructive consequences of resisting God. It feels like experiencing divine anger. However, God is not inflicting those consequences—they are the inevitable outcome of turning away from the source of our being and happiness.

Now God is love in Godself—within the Trinity—and as such God does not need to create a world in order to have an object to love, which is to say that God does not need to create in order to be God. Consequently, creation is contingent, and has the nature of a gift. However, the act of creation is not arbitrary and unmotivated; rather, it is a natural outflow and opening out of the divine being to "the other."

> The Almighty brought forth all Nature for this only End, that boundless Love might have its *Infinity* of Height and Depth to dwell and work in, and all the striving and working Properties and Nature are only to give *Essence* and *Substance*, Life and Strength, to the *invisible hidden Spirit of Love*, that it may come forth in outward activity.[9]

Law's doctrine of creation is grounded in his notion of "Eternal Nature"—this is not an actual concrete world of nature, but rather a world of infinite possibilities (or an infinite multiplicity of possible worlds); all the many ways in which God's goodness, love, wisdom, power, and beauty might be manifested "beyond" the divine being in finite creaturely being. All these possible worlds have some mode of beginningless and endless "reality" in Eternal Nature (which Alan Gregory describes as "the beginning before the beginning"). The act of creation is God's actualizing one of these worlds. In Law's mind this was not creation out of nothing, but creation out of Eternal Nature.[10] And once God does this he commits himself to bring that created world and its particular history to its goal of manifesting his glory, come what may.[11]

9. Law, *Serious Call*, 366.

10. On creation out of nothing and Law's misinformed rejection of it, see Gregory, *Quenching Hell*, 112–15.

11. It is also worth saying that Eternal Nature (and consequently the actual created world) is a manifestation of the unity and triunity of God in the form of fire (corresponding to the Father), light (corresponding to the Son), and spirit (corresponding to Spirit). Fire is the life and cause of motion in creation; light is the love, beauty, understanding, and wisdom in creation; spirit is the unity in creation (allowing us to speak

According to Law, God first creates the angelic world. However, some of the angels began to adore themselves, rather than God, the source of their beauty. This led to the fall of the angels and the origin of Satan and his demons. However, the fate of the angels is their own *self*-destruction (not a punishment imposed from outside by God). The angelic desire for God is turned inward and is unable to find any satisfaction. They inevitably spiral inward and downward into despair and anger, for God never made the desires of creatures to be satisfied by finite creation. The "glassy sea" that was their heavenly environment is transformed into the formless waters of chaos that we find in Genesis 1:2.

However, God took this ruined angelic creation and set it within bounds, forming the material world we inhabit in the process, bringing good out of evil. (This is Law's interpretation of the Genesis 1 creation story.) In Law's view, our world is indeed good, but it is *not perfect*—there is within it the constrained potential for chaos and darkness. Resurgent evil is always a potential reality within material creation and, as we see in Genesis 3, when Adam and Eve divert their desire from God to themselves, as the angels before them had, it was indeed actualized.[12] Curving in on itself, humanity condemned itself to destruction, cut off from divine life.

"Nature" is structurally ordered by desire; it is part of the fabric of our very be-ing. The fall is a misdirection of our desire—a turning of the self in on itself and away from its true object (God), a process that ends up generating our own alienation and "death"—and salvation requires its reorientation.

---

of "nature" and a "uni-verse"), that which binds things into an environment. These three creaturely realities are not material, though they have material forms (e.g., Law associated electricity with fire). Every possible created reality manifests these three aspects in dynamic interplay and unity, none existing apart from the others. What he is reaching for is a vision of creation as in some way necessarily mirroring the glory of the Triune God. In this way, while avoiding pantheism, Law sees that "God is breaking forth into visibility." (Law, *Way to Divine Knowledge*, 145).

12. Law's theology of Adam and his embodiment is problematic in several ways. On which, see Gregory, *Quenching Hell*, 127ff, 139–41. Law sees sin start to appear when Adam, whom Law considers an androgynous individual rather than a male, starts to look away from God. God's response is to divide Adam into two creatures— one male and one female. This is actually an act of mercy, giving Adam a second chance. (The androgynous Adam interpretation of Genesis 2 is an ancient one, recurring especially in esoteric traditions like Jewish Kabbalah, alchemy, and, of course, Jakob Böhme, finding defenders today among Old Testament scholars such as Phyllis Trible. It remains, however, a minority report.)

Yet God does not leave us alone, even for a moment. Immediately following Adam and Eve's sin, God acts in grace and love for restoration. He not only promises salvation through Christ, the seed of the woman (Gen 3:15), but he actually *implants* God the Son within them at that point. According to Law, the divine Word is "breathed" or "inspoken" to them, and all human beings ever since have a divine seed within them. This divine seed within is the potential for recovery of the glory of God in us, the restoration of the image of God. This is our first explicit hint of Law's universalism. "See here the Beginning and glorious Extent of the *Catholic Church* of Christ, it takes in all the World. It is God's unlimited, universal Mercy to all Mankind."[13] This seed is "the hidden Treasure of every human soul . . . till it changes the Son of an earthly Adam into a Son of God."[14]

Of course, the inner Word can only bring about our eventual deliverance from sin because of the work of that same Word incarnate, Jesus Christ. It is those two aspects of the ministry of God the Son that "could *begin, carry on,* and *totally effect* Man's deliverance from the Evil of his own fallen Nature."[15] It is the work of the Word within that enables us to trust in the Word incarnate, and participate in his body through faith in Jesus and the sacraments of the church. It is the work of the Word incarnate that creates the environment in which the implanted seed of the Word can grow and form Christ-in-us. Indeed, Christ himself—the body of Christ, the church—is the environment in which the inner Word can grow. Law says that he "will assert no inward Redemption but what wholly proceeds from, and is effected by that Life-giving Redeemer, who died on the Cross for our Redemption."[16] Salvation thus requires the work of the Word *both* as incarnate *and* as within us, bringing us to new birth in the Spirit. Unless our will and desires are reoriented we remain locked in sin. (So we see that sanctification is, for Law, not an add-on to salvation, but integral to it. Christ has perfected our human nature in his own humanity and by the Spirit is able to conform our own humanity to his.)

How does Jesus save us? "God, the second person in the Holy Trinity, took our human nature upon him, became a suffering, dying man, that there might be found a man, whose sufferings, blood and death had

13. Law, "Spirit of Prayer," 27.

14. Law, *Serious Call*, 407.

15. Law, *Serious Call*, 445.

16. Law, "Spirit of Prayer," 23.

the power to extinguish the wrath and hell that sin brought forth, and to be the fountain of the first heavenly life to the whole race of mankind."[17] Jesus participates in our broken humanity and defeats both sin and death in our humanity. He lives a fully human life—with his desire directed Godward—and opens up such a human life for us.

Law had no time for penal substitution theories of the atonement, because these see the cross in terms of God's fury and punishment. The cross does make satisfaction for sin, he said, but not by pacifying an angry God. Rather, it satisfies God's love by working salvation and it satisfies sinners by restoring the divine image.

And Law, in his later work, was unflinching in his universalism and his condemnation of those who "blaspheme God" (his phrase) with a doctrine of double predestination and eternal hell. "[Christ] is the universal Remedy of *all* Evil broken forth in Nature and Creature. . . . He is the breathing forth of the Heart, Life, and Spirit of God, into *all* the dead race of Adam. He is the Seeker, the Finder, the Restorer, of *all* that was lost and dead to the Life of God. He is the Love, that, from Cain to the End of Time, prays for all its Murderers."[18]

Law reinterpreted the doctrine of election such that the objects of election and reprobation are not particular persons, some elected and other rejected, *but natures.* There are two natures that reside in all humans as seeds—a sinful nature and the divine Word, Adam and Christ, darkness and light. What God eternally elects to salvation is the heavenly seed implanted in everyone; and what God elects to reprobation is that which is "earthly, serpentine, and devilish"[19] in everyone. Thus, God has predestinated that the seed of the Word in each human will bring about life and the evil within each person will be destroyed. "Election therefore and Reprobation, as respecting Salvation, equally relate to every Man in the world; because every Man, as such, has *That* in him which *only* is elected, and that in him which only is reprobated."[20] (This is an interpretation of election that we will find repeated in some later universalists. It is, it ought to be said, somewhat implausible as an exposition of the plain sense of Scripture.)

---

17. Law, "Appeal to All That Doubt," 65.

18. Law, "Spirit of Prayer," 108. Italics ours.

19. Law, *Serious Call*, 463.

20. Law, "Spirit of Prayer," 264.

The achievement of God's ultimate purpose in creation may well take eons to come to pass, but come to pass it will, and for *all*, as the following quotation makes clear:

> God's Providence, from the *Fall* to the *Restitution* of all Things, is doing the *same Thing*, as when he said to the dark Chaos of fallen Nature, "Let there be light"; He still says, and will continue saying the same Thing, till there is no Evil of Darkness left in all that is Nature and Creature. . . . And if long and long Ages of fiery Pain, and tormenting Darkness, fall to the Share of many, or most of God's Apostate Creatures, they will last no longer, than till the great fire of God has melted *all Arrogance* into Humility, and all that is SELF has died in the long Agonies and Bloody Sweat of a lost God, which is that *all-saving* Cross of Christ, which will never give up its redeeming Power, till Sin and Sinners have no more a Name among the Creatures of God.[21]

William Law was well-known in the eighteenth century, but perhaps his biggest impact in the story of universal salvation came through the influence his work exerted in the nineteenth century on the thought of Thomas Erskine, who in turn mediated some of Law's key ideas to many others.

PIETIST UNIVERSALISM IN BRITAIN: GEORGE STONEHOUSE (1714–93)

The story

Before looking at the impact of Pietistic universalism in America we need to consider one more influential Pietistic Restorationist, George Stonehouse.[22] While a student at the University of Oxford, Stonehouse was possibly one of the members of the Holy Club at Christ Church College, set up by John and Charles Wesley and also attended by George Whitefield.[23] According to one source:

21. Law, *Address to the Clergy*, 64. According to Thomas Langcake, before he died, Law claimed that even fallen angels would be "delivered out of misery," because creation would be incomplete without them. See Gregory, *Quenching Hell*, 186.

22. Often confused with Rev. James Stonehouse.

23. Stonehouse matriculated from Pembroke College with a BA (1729) and an MA (1736). At least one source declares him a member of the Holy Club. Whatever the case on that score, he was certainly friends with Whitefield and the Wesleys in Oxford, as his subsequent relations with them demonstrates (see the diaries of John

Universal Restitution, considered as a Scripture doctrine, was first debated between the years 1729 and 1735, by a society of twelve young collegians of Oxford, emphatically called the Holy Club. John Wesley was tutor, and, of course, president of this society; and he, with his brother Charles, a Mr. Morgan, and one or two others, supported the merit of works. George Whitefield and James Hervey, (author of the Meditations,) adopted the Calvinistic side of the question; Messrs. Delamotte, Hall, Hutchins, and Ingram trimmed and became Moravians. The Rev. George Stonehouse of Hungerford Park (afterward Sir George Stonehouse, of East Brent, in the county of Somerset, Baronet,) had been labouring to reconcile the different opinions of his fellow-collegiaus, till he stood alone in support of his favourite tenet, viz. that Universal Restitution was a Scripture doctrine; and as the arguments he used with his different opponents had ever prevailed, they promised, that if he would collect his thoughts together in a discourse upon the subject, it should receive a candid answer.[24]

After Oxford, Rev. Stonehouse went to serve as priest at St. Mary's Church in Islington, London (1738–40). In 1738, he invited Charles Wesley to be his curate, though he had no license from the bishop to do this. Wesley and Whitefield preached there regularly, but their preaching proved unpopular with some of the congregation and the churchwardens had them banned. They and Stonehouse were told: "You have all the spirit of the devil."[25]

In June 1739, he had married Mary Crispe, a member of the gentry.[26] The disruption in Islington led to Stonehouse leaving the church in 1740 and associating with the Moravians. He moved to his wife's ancestral home in Darnford, near Woodstock in Oxfordshire, apparently turning away from the Church of England. This he used as his base for his own scholarly research, funded by his personal wealth. Stonehouse was an excellent linguist, fluent in several different languages, and much of

and Charles Wesley and Whitefield).

24. The source is a pamphlet called "Pre-existence of Souls and Universal Restitution, considered as Scripture Doctrines, extracted from the Minutes and Correspondence of Burnham Society, in the County of Somerset." It is quoted by Mr. G. S. Bromhead in *The Monthly Repository of Theology and General Literature* 13 (Jan 1, 1818).

25. Charles Wesley, diary entry for 27 April 1739.

26. Mary died in 1751, and Charles Wesley performed George's marriage to Molly Stafford in 1755.

his research was spent in the study of Syriac, culminating in the publication of a Syriac grammar. One source reports that he travelled Europe for twenty years in his academic researches, twelve of which he spent in Germany, especially with Count Zinzendorf.

It was not until 1761 that the first volume of Stonehouse's long-promised universalist work was published, entitled *Universal Restitution, a Scripture Doctrine*. The second part appeared in 1768 and was called *Universal Restitution Farther Defended* (*URFD* from hereon). One often-quoted source describes a later encounter with John Wesley:

> On a visit from Mr. Wesley, Mr. Stonehouse said, "Ah, John, there are only you and I living out of us all."
>
> W. "Better you had died too, George, before you had written your book."
>
> S. "I expected you had eaten up my book at a mouthful, John; but neither you nor any of the rest, though you all engaged to do it, have answered a single paragraph of it."
>
> W. "You must not think your book unanswerable on that account. I am able to answer it, but it would take up so much of my time, that I could not answer it to God."
>
> This declaration so stung the author, as to put him upon writing *Universal Restitution Vindicated*.[27]

The book referred to at the end was Stonehouse's third and final book on universalism, published in Bristol in 1773. However, the suggestion that this final book was inspired by the alleged conversation with Wesley, the arch-Arminian, is questionable because it is in fact five letters written in response to *Calvinist* critiques of *Universal Restitution*.

Stonehouse purchased an estate in East Brent in Somerset and lived there until his death in December 1793.

---

27. Quoted by Mr. G. S. Bromhead in *The Monthly Repository of Theology and General Literature* 13 (Jan 1, 1818) 565.

Stonehouse's theology

Universal Restitution, a Scripture Doctrine, is divided into two parts: an exploration of the kingdom of God and a study of the universal restoration of creatures.[28] Prior to that, he opens with a study of the Hebrew word *'olām* and the Greek *aiōn* and *aiōnios* (Letter I). These words, usually translated as eternal or everlasting, play a pivotal role in the case for an unending hell. Stonehouse argues that, for a host of reasons, they demonstrably mean no such thing.[29] Rather, they mean "a long tho' undetermined portion or period of time" (6). In the grand divine plan, there are many *aeōns* (ages) through which God works out his sovereign purposes.

This leads into his discussion of Christ's kingdom. This aiōnial kingdom of Jesus began with his earthly ministry and will endure for ages of ages. It contains many stages—his ministry, death, descent to Hades to liberate its captives,[30] resurrection, ascension, the conversion and return of Israel to the land, the millennium, the resurrection of the dead, final judgment, new creation and the lake of fire, and God's being all in all (Letter IV).

However, while the messianic kingdom is aiōnial, lasting "to the æons of the æons," *it is not everlasting* (Letter II)! His core text here is 1 Corinthians 15:24–28, in which Christ—once all creation has been subjected to him and his kingdom extends over the whole world—hands the kingdom over to the Father, so that God will be all in all. Christ's role *as Mediator* is no longer required from that point on. This, Stonehouse argues, clearly teaches an end to Christ's age-long (*aiōnios*) kingdom; albeit an end *far* in the future:

> after Christ's kingdom shall have lasted thro' several generations
> and æons, even to the utmost æon very far beyond the end of
> the world, and probably long after the new heavens and the new

---

28. All page numbers in this section on Stonehouse, unless otherwise stated, are from this book. A second shot at setting out a positive case for universal restitution is found in *URFD*, in which Stonehouse seeks to defend five key claims from Scripture: 1. It is Christ's avowed purpose to restore all people (Letter III); 2. Christ promises to restore all people (Letter IV). 3. Christ's death is efficacious for all (Letter V); 4. It is Christ's declared will to have all people restored (Letter VI); 5. Christ is *able* to effect the restitution of all (Letter VII).

29. For example, there are numerous biblical instances of things so designated that clearly have an end and are neither eternal nor everlasting.

30. On the descent, see Letter III.

earth. . . . [W]hen Christ shall have effected the general Restitution, by the reconciling of all things to God, and by the making
of all things new . . . [t]hen shall . . . even the son himself . . . deliver up his vicarial and æonian, or temporary power, together
with all the subjects of it, to GOD, even the father. (30)

Some qualification is in order here. The kingdom *itself* has no end
(Luke 1:33), but it will now be reigned over, not by the Messiah *as Messiah*—that messianic reign was aiōnial, not everlasting—but *by God*
(including God the Son). From this point onward "Christ will no longer reign as mediator, but as God, and one with his father" (28). This is
because Christ's kingdom is his, both in his capacity as *man* and in his
capacity as *the divine Logos* (58–61).[31] The first reign will one day cease;
the second will not. So we might say that, to Stonehouse, *the mediatorial
phase* of the everlasting kingdom is of temporal, albeit *incredibly* long,
duration.[32] This sets the theological background for Stonehouse's defense
of universal restitution, which occupies the rest of this book (Letters
VIII–XXIII) and *URFD*.

Stonehouse speaks of universal restoration or healing, but *not of
universal salvation*, arguing that the Greek word *sōzō* in the relevant contexts is a metaphor not of being delivered/saved from danger, but of being

31. Stonehouse's Christology was orthodox, but he appears, very idiosyncratically, to have been a *binitarian*, rather than a trinitarian. Letter V conflates the Spirit
and the Logos. The Spirit simply *is* God the Son, the Logos (80). Knowing that he was
consciously rejecting the faith of the church, he was a heretic on this matter.

32. Siegvolck had earlier offered similar qualifications:

> That economy, I say, will certainly have an end; namely, at the period when
> Christ's aim in obtained, and the Son himself shall be subject to Him that put
> all things under his feet. But hereby is not meant that the kingdom of Christ
> itself shall cease, which according to the word of God is to have no end. St.
> Luke i.33. But it will rather, through such subjection of Christ under God his
> Father, get an infinitely greater lustre. So that we must distinguish between
> the *particular government of Christ and his elect*, and *the kingdom of Christ
> and his believers* as one with the kingdom of his heavenly Father. The first will
> certainly cease, and consequently the eternities of eternities, or ages of ages,
> appointed for it will end; but the latter is to last for evermore, or to all eternity.
> (*Everlasting Gospel*, 63–64)

Siegvolck is clearly trying to find a way of distinguishing different aspects or modes
or phases of Christ's kingdom reign—one of which shall end and the other of which
shall not.

Elhanan Winchester was also careful to say that, while Christ's *mediatorial* kingdom, which is aionial, was completed once Christ handed it over to the Father, Christ
continues to reign, as a person in the Trinity, from the throne of God forever and ever.
See *Process and Empire*, poem 12, lines 264–71; *Restitution of All Things*, 7, 9.

restored to health. Many, in fact, are not delivered/saved from the threat of hell, but they will still be restored in the end. This notion is captured in Stonehouse's translation of 1 Timothy 4:10: "Christ is the *restorer* of all people, especially of those who believe." He takes this to mean that believers (the elect), through union with Christ, are regenerated and spared damnation, while the rest (the non-elect) are not—the former are saved; the latter are not. Their restoration *follows* end-time condemnation (Letter X). So all people are Christ's possession by purchase of his blood, and as such will be restored, but that does not require that they will all be saved from going to hell (Letters XI, XII). Thus, "it is the absolute purpose of God ultimately to restore the world from its present wretchedness, altho' he has no such purpose to save and preserve it from the wrath to come" (*URFD*, 87). This use of the words "saved" and "salvation" was not picked up by other universalists.

Stonehouse believed that God directly created souls and gave them an existence *before* they were embodied as humans. These preexistent souls became sinners through the misuse of their freewill *before* they were embodied, an idea he possibly inherited from seventeenth-century interpreters of Origen like the Cambridge Platonists.[33] Because they sinned, God appointed them to be born as the sons of fallen Adam. This sending into embodiment was actually for our good. The plan was that the Logos would then be born as a man so that, through the humanity of the Logos and his work in atoning for their guilt, they might be restored. Souls are ransomed by Christ as his own possession. So God assigned all humanity to share in the fate of Adam—enslavement to Satan, sin, and death—so that they might then also share in the fate of Christ—resurrection and union with God. And Christ performed this restorative work on behalf of *all* humanity, "For Christ has indeed exhausted the whole venom of sin in his own body, and is in himself singly both the cause and power of our recovery" (185). In Christ our debts are discharged and we stand innocent before God.[34] Thus, hell has no grip on those who are united to Christ.

33. Stonehouse was well aware of the works of Origen (he quotes from them) and there are numerous parallels (as well as some key differences) between his thought and Origen's.

34. In *URFD* (Letter V), Stonehouse argues for the very unusual view that Christ's death fully "disarms" the wrath of God for *all* sinners, so that none will ever have to face it, but that the wrath of *the Lamb* remains an issue for those who reject the gospel. For all people are now Christ's, bought with his blood, and he will deal with their sin.

> [A]ll creatures have a joint interest in *Christ*; and the life of all
> was offered up in *Christ's* sacrifice (*Luke* xix.10. *I John* iv.14.
> *Rom.* v.6. *Acts* iii.21. *Eph.* i.10. *Col.* i.20) from hence also is the
> apostle's reasoning (*ii Cor.* v.14) *If one* (that is *Christ*) *died for
> all, then all were dead*, i.e. dead virtually in *Christ* so dying for
> them. But *Christ* died for all men, (see *i John* ii.2. *i Tim.* ii.6. *i
> Cor.* xv.22, 49. *Rom.* v.6. *John* i.29) therefore are all men dead
> virtually in *Christ*. (316)

As Christ died for all, so too he rose for all. The resurrected Christ, says
Paul, is the firstfruits of the resurrection of all the dead (1 Cor 15:23).
This is a reference to the Israelite practice of offering the first part of the
gathered harvest to God as a symbol that all of the harvest comes from
him and belongs to him. "And as all the fruits of *Canaan* belonged to
Jehovah in the first fruits, so Christ being *the first fruits unto God* of all
the sons of *Adam*, all the sons of *Adam* are claim'd of God in his *Christ* as
property" (294).

Now the effects of Christ's sacrifice "do not immediately display
themselves universally" (193). Humans can, within limits, freely resist
God. But God can work with our human freedom to lead us to regeneration in Christ:

> For why may not the operations of the Holy Ghost upon the
> human soul, tho' resisted by that soul, be notwithstanding fi-
> nally effectual towards his restitution? Surely they may be partly
> resistable, and gradually effectual; the sacred influences gaining
> as it were in all their operations within us . . . giving us medi-
> ately . . . now a little light, now a devout desire, now a degree of
> liberty, now a dread of divine justice and a trembling like *Felix*,
> now a penitential sentiment, and so in other effects.
>
> For thus the Holy Ghost, accumulating his gracious lar-
> gesses by subsequent accessions thereof, abates our weaknesses,
> strengthens our native powers, and causes us to thrive by a kind
> of natural progress into a ripeness for, and condition adapted to
> receive, agreeably to the order and regulation of divine things,
> that last victorious regenerating gift. (*URFD*, 73)

The compatibility of human freewill and divine sovereignty only
seems a paradox to us because of our blindness (*URFD*, 105–6). In the
permissive will of Christ the principles of fallen nature are not as yet
abolished, but they cannot fail to be so in the end: "that as Christ is the
restorer of the world; the world must finally be restored; that as he draws
all men unto him, all men must finally come unto him" (200). Before that

day, many shall drink of the wine of the wrath of God to an age of ages
(Rev 14:10–11). However, some care must be taken when understanding
this language of divine wrath:

> Since mankind cannot judge of those things but by the sensa-
> tions which those things excite in us; and since these excited
> sensations bare no real resemblance with the objects that excite
> them; Our conceptions of GOD, founded upon those sensations
> which we call the perceptions of his wrath or anger, may also
> have nothing in them resembling any reality in the divine: In
> likeness of those sensations which we call pain, sickness, plea-
> sure, smells, colours, tastes, sounds, have nothing resembling
> them in the objects themselves that raise them in us, have no
> correspondent reality existing in the bodies felt, heard, or seen.
>
> By this way of thinking the sensations of God's wrath, re-
> venge or anger (excited in the minds of reprobates by the light
> of their reason and remonstrations of a dissatisfied conscience)
> are like the yellowness of objects to a jaundiced eye; which exists
> not in the objects of its vision . . . but is the mere effects of an
> inward distemper. (201)

We can speak about God's wrath, but such language expresses how sinners perceive the experience of being handed over by God to their own
sin—*how it feels to them*—rather than telling us about God's own inner
feelings or disposition. (This is very similar to William Law's view, and
indeed the view of many of the church fathers.) He later adds:

> Wherefore, althou' the LORD may seem to them that suffer to
> be an angry GOD, and a devouring fire; yet the blessed (whose
> eyes are clear and strong to see through the vail of wrath, into
> his real character) perceive with all joy and complacency that
> such anger and such fire are emergent from love only, and that
> it can only burn up what if heterogenial to true life, can only
> consume what ought to die; namely, that spirit in us which lives
> to the ruin of ourselves and others: and this done, all will be well
> again. (392)

Indeed, the pains of divine wrath experienced by the soul that rejects
God's gift of righteousness are in fact the pains that arise *from within* a
sinful soul when it is left alone to curve in on itself and experience its own
endarkened and empty self (410).[35]

---

35. In one of his many extensive footnotes, Stonehouse speculates something similar for Satan: "When satan's hatred of GOD is heightened to so exquisite a degree of it,

At death, all descend to Hades—but to different zones of it: some to zones of blessing and comfort, others to zones of punishment (including gehenna,[36] tartarus, and the abyss). Once the day of judgment arrives, all those not deemed worthy of the paradise of God go away to the lake of fire, the second death. But this is not the end of their story. According to Stonehouse, the promise that "there shall be no more death" (Rev 21:4), includes the lake of fire. This second death is that "which will destroy horribly all the enemies of our LORD, yet as a destroyer it is itself [styled] his enemy. I *Cor.* xv.26. The last enemy that is to be invalidated is death. And being our LORD's enemy, that is his last enemy, it must itself likewise lastly cease to be" (280; Letter XIV).

Death is a "strange work of God" that is "far from being agreeable to him" (290), yet in the providence of God it still serves a purpose in bringing about the gathering together in the fullness of time *all* things in Christ—"our LORD's severest dispensations of judgment, are only accessories to those of his benevolence and whether he brings evil or good upon us, still it all comes from the bowels of his love, and in his faithful provision for our truest happiness" (292).

The latter part of the first volume (Letters XVII–XXIII) and the beginning of the second volume are given over to a consideration of alleged "problem passages" in the Bible. We shall briefly consider three to give a flavor of his approach.

Regarding the aiōnial life of the sheep and the aiōnail punishment of the goats (in the aiōnial fire) in Matthew 25:46, Stonehouse predictably argues that neither the life nor the punishment and fire are described as eternal but as *age-long.* He then imagines the obvious response from his critic:

> But, you say, how then can you prove the eternal happiness of the saints? This is easy to be done (tho' not from the passage before us . . .) from the many other scripture passages where the immortality of christians is expressly declared.
>
> The æonian life of christians arises from the principle of immortality in them, which they derive from *Christ,* and which

as that he should hate even his own existence; dissolution may be at last his choice, and that wherein his desires may concenter. And in this situation his disease may possibly be advanced and ripen'd to its true, intended and necessary crisis or point of change" (335).

36. Slightly unusually, Stonehouse believes that gehenna is a part of Hades, rather than an equivalent to Revelation's lake of fire, and that it will come to an end after the judgment day when Hades is cast into the lake of fire (*URFD*, Letter II).

> will also carry them thro' all the æons into eternity: but the
> wicked, not having this principle in them for the power of their
> existence in the æonian periods, will be in a state of misery,
> whence will insue their corruption, and finally death. (359–61)

Regarding Judas, and Jesus' comment that "it had been good for
him, if that man had not been born" (Matt 26:24), Stonehouse argues that
it was a proverbial saying, containing allusions to sentiments expressed
by Jeremiah (20:11–18) and Job (3:2–9).

> But these words of our LORD, thus understood, import no more
> than that it had been better for that man that he had died in his
> mother's womb; that he had proved an abortive birth; that he
> had been carried from the womb to the grave. . . . If *Judas* had
> died in his mother's womb, he still would have been a man . . .
> and at the same time he would not have been the betrayer of
> his LORD and redeemer, and so would have escaped the curse
> which was the horrible issue of his treachery. (396–97)

On the threat of the fire of gehenna in Mark 9:43–48: the words
mean no more (or less) than that fire cannot be quenched nor the worms
die, but will most certainly continue their work unhindered *until it is
completed*. The italicized words, argues Stonehouse, are clearly intended
by Jesus to be supplied by his audience. He provides numerous biblical
parallels in which similar information is implicit but unstated. This is reinforced by the OT texts and phrases alluded to by Jesus in the saying (Jer
7:4; 17:27; Isa 66:24), in which we find "unquenchable fire" that is clearly
not fire that burns forever, but fire that burns *until its task is complete*
(*URFD*, Letter I).

Stonehouse, while one of the more scholarly proponents of universal restoration, was not its most influential teacher. He was not really
socially connected with fellow Restorationists and he exerted most of
his influence through his weighty publications. Nevertheless, his works
were read and admired by others with similar sentiments on both sides
of the Atlantic. Among his admirers was a young Baptist preacher named
Elhanan Winchester, and it is to Winchester that we now turn. It is time
to move the story back across the ocean to America.

ELHANAN WINCHESTER: AN AMERICAN
UNIVERSALIST IN THE PIETIST TRADITION

The story

Pietistic universalism, in both its German and British forms, proved to have a significant impact in America through, among other things, the conversion of Elhanan Winchester.

Elhanan Winchester Jr. was born in 1751 just outside Boston. Raised as a Congregationalist, at the age of nineteen (1769) he experienced "conviction and conversion" in a New Lights revival and made "a public profession of religion." His conversion followed the common Evangelical pattern of protracted anxiety over his sin followed by a revelation of divine grace:

> I had such a view of CHRIST, as to make me cry out, "Glory to God in the highest! This is salvation; I know this is salvation. . . . I saw the fullness, sufficiency, and willingness of Christ to save me and all men, in such a manner as constrained me to venture my soul into his arms; and if I had ten thousand souls, I could have trusted them all into his hands. And O how did I long, that every soul of Adam's race might come to know the love of God in Christ Jesus! And I thought I could not be willing to live any longer on earth, unless it might please God to make me useful to my fellow creatures. (*UR* III. A2)[37]

Note the universalist instincts inherent in his initial conversion experience (cf. de Benneville). He soon came to suppress these so as to conform to the Calvinist theology he had been raised with.

Winchester soon moved to join the Baptists and served as a revivalist preacher and minister at Reheboth (1771) and Bellingham in Massachusetts (1772–74), and Welsh Neck, South Carolina (1774/75–79).

---

37. To explain the in-text reference system: *UR* = *The Universal Restoration*; III = Dialogue III; A2 = The answer to the second question posed in the dialogue.

These churches served as bases from which he launched out on several itinerant preaching tours. He was also successful in evangelism back at his own church in Welsh Neck. In 1779, he was the key player in a local revival amongst both whites and local slaves (being a longtime vocal opponent of slavery). He led about a hundred slaves and 139 whites to Christ and baptized them, though this was not welcomed by all: "Many of the white people were exceedingly averse to the slaves being Christianized; many would not suffer those belonging to them to come and hear me, though the poor creatures begged it upon their knees. . . . My life was sometimes threatened, but, by the grace of God, I feared not the menaces of men, nor the rage of devils."[38] It was, he wrote, "a summer of great success, and I shall remember that happy season with pleasure while I live."[39]

In September 1779, Winchester left on another extended preaching trip up north, intending to return, but it was not to be. On his return from New England to South Carolina in October 1780, he stopped off in Philadelphia. There, the Baptist church, destitute of a pastor, sought to secure his services. In the end he was persuaded and never made it back to Welsh Neck.

It was not long after taking on the pastorate in Philadelphia that Winchester embraced belief in universal restoration. His journey from hyper-Calvinism to universalism took place over a two-year period and involved several elements. Central to it was Paul Siegvolk's *The Everlasting Gospel*. Winchester's first brief encounter with universalism was at the beginning of 1778 in Welsh Neck. He called to see a friend, who put a copy of Siegvolk's book into his hands. Winchester's friend did not know what to make of the book, so he asked Elhanan to explain it. Winchester dipped into it here and there for perhaps thirty minutes and quickly got a feel for what it was arguing. "I had never seen any thing of the sort before in my life; and I seemed struck with several ideas. . . . But, as I was only desired to tell what the author meant, when I had satisfied my friend in that respect, I laid the book down, and I believe we both concluded it to be a pleasant, ingenious hypothesis; but had no serious thoughts of its being true; and for my part, I determined not to trouble myself about it, or to think any more on the matter."[40]

---

38. Winchester, "Reigning Abominations," 27n.
39. Winchester, "Preface" to *UR*, x–xi.
40. Winchester, "Preface" to *UR*, iv.

Sometime later he was visited by an acquaintance from Virginia, and among his books Winchester found a copy of *The Everlasting Gospel*. He read a little more of it this time, but "as yet had not the least thought that ever I should embrace his sentiments; yet some of his arguments appeared very conclusive, and I could not wholly shake them off, but I concluded to let them alone, and not investigate the matter; and therefore I never gave the book even so much as one cursory reading."[41]

During his twelve-month preaching tour between South Carolina and Pennsylvania (1779–80), he would stay with friends, often fellow-ministers, and would sometimes engage them in discussions of Siegvolk's arguments. Winchester would play devil's advocate and defend the universal restoration to see what kind of responses and rebuttals they would propose. To his surprise, even the most able ministers were at a loss, not knowing what to say. And the defences of endless punishment that were offered served not to sooth Winchester's doubts about the traditional theology of hell, as he had hoped, but to *increase* them. Nevertheless, he continued to resist the doctrine with all his might and, he said, "sometimes preached publically against it with all the force I could muster."[42] Yet it had gotten under his skin. He describes himself as "half a convert" by the time he arrived in Philadelphia in 1780.[43]

Winchester's public ministry in Philadelphia was very successful, but his growing convictions with regard to universalism were about to create a crisis. A private discussion on the issue was leaked to a minister friend, who promptly cut off all links with him. Seeing the brewing storm, he determined to work out once and for all what he thought about the question. The deciding issue was this: was it *biblical*? He shut himself up in his room, read the Scriptures, and prayed for enlightenment, seeking to be open, as best he was able, to whatever he felt God revealing to him. The outcome of this was that "I became so well persuaded of the truth of the Universal Restoration, that I was determined never to deny it, let it cost me ever so much, though all my numerous friends should forsake me, as I expected they would, and though I should be driven from men."[44]

A second book that significantly shaped Winchester in his early explorations was George Stonehouse's *Universal Restitution*. A more

---

41. Winchester, "Preface" to *UR*, viii.
42. Winchester, "Preface" to *UR*, xii.
43. Winchester, "Preface" to *UR*, xv.
44. Winchester, "Preface" to *UR*, xviii.

personal influence was George de Benneville, who lived locally and whose acquaintance Winchester made soon after his conversion to universal restorationism, and the community of the Brethren eight miles away in Germantown. These people deeply impressed Elhanan with their piety. So Winchester was a home-grown American convert to the Pietist version of universalism, both in its German and its British versions. He in turn would promulgate and popularize this theology in the newly founded United States of America, and later in Britain.

The upshot of his full conversion to what was seen by many as a heterodox view was that the Baptist church split, with Winchester and his followers being forced out. They formed their own congregation, the Society of Universal Baptists, meeting in the University Hall in Philadelphia. Winchester led the church from 1780 to 1787. During this period, he and de Benneville went on several preaching tours together. However, in July 1787, Winchester announced to his congregation that he felt called by God to go and preach in England. Within forty-eight hours of the announcement, Elhanan had sailed!

In London, he preached in various nonconformist congregations while his "friends" grew in number. Eventually his supporters took the Chapel in Parliament Court to provide Winchester with his own preaching base. By all accounts, he would regularly receive four hundred to five hundred congregants. As in America, he went on preaching tours. In February 1790, he wrote of the many doors that were opening up for preaching the message—especially among Baptists and Presbyterians—across England. The subscribers that supported the publication of some of his books bear testimony to his widespread appeal beyond the bounds of the city. This was also where Winchester's publishing ministry took off, with numerous theological works coming to press. In 1788, the year after his arrival in London, he published his most celebrated book, *The Universal Restoration*.

One of the most striking aspects of Winchester's ministry was his unwavering insistence on considering all his "opponents" as siblings in Christ to be treated with humility, gentleness, and respect. By temperament Winchester hated controversy, and by religious conviction he believed that it was wrong to seek to win arguments while in the process failing to love those with whom one was in disagreement. "I have no great opinion of controversial writings in general; the combatants more commonly seek after victory than truth. . . . Writing on controversy is sometimes attended with many bad consequences, such as alienating the affections of Christians from one another."[45] He added, "For my own part, I by no means wish to contend with any man—and as far as I know my own heart, never yet did; and I hope I never shall write from any principle but love, and a desire to do good to mankind, within the very small circle of my acquaintance."[46]

He left London in May 1794 to sail back to America. No sooner had he landed than he began preaching again in various locations all over New England and surrounding areas. Writing to a friend in London, he wrote, "I have the greatest door open that I ever saw, insomuch that I am surprised at the alteration since I was here last. I have preached in a great many meeting-houses of different denominations, and to a great number of people, as often as eight or nine times a week, and with greater acceptance than I ever did."[47]

Winchester's health had never been good, and the more he exerted himself the worse it got, until in February 1796 he suffered a severe haemorrhage of the lungs. The doctor managed to stop the bleeding, and a few days later Winchester started preaching again! He preached regularly for several months until he was confined by disease to his deathbed, dying on April 18, 1797.

Theology

Winchester, like the Piestists who influenced him, was a premillennialist, fascinated with unfulfilled prophetic promises, a subject he preached and wrote on at great length.[48]

The heart of Winchester's universalist biblical hermeneutic is an attempt to find a way of holding firmly to all the diverse teachings of the Bible—not "in any wise to explain away or weaken, the force of either the threatenings or promises, set forth in this wondrous book" (*UR*.IV.A14). The Bible speaks *both* of some in hell *and* of universal restoration so, reasons Winchester, *both* those teachings must be true. Therefore any

---

45. Winchester, *Letter to De Coetlogon*, 3–4.

46. Winchester, *Letter to De Coetlogon*, 35.

47. Winchester, *Letter to De Coetlogon*, 216.

48. Winchester's beliefs about the future are spelled out in great detail in his *A Course of Lectures on the Prophesies That Remain to be Fulfilled* (1789), and more briefly, and in third-rate poetic form, in his *The Process and Empire of Christ* (1793).

understanding of hell that excludes the promise of universal salvation cannot be accepted.

Central to Winchester's case was what he took to be positive promises of universal salvation. For instance, Ephesians 1:9–10 pictures the goal of creation as the gathering together of "*all* things" in Christ; Colossians 1:19–20 speaks of Christ reconciling *all* created things to God through the cross;[49] Revelation pictures "every creature in heaven, on earth, and under the earth" worshipping the Father and the Son (Rev 5:13); Romans 5:18–20 claims that all those who died in Adam (i.e., every human being) will be made alive in Christ and that grace will undo all the damage that sin has done.

One slightly less conventional argument of Winchester's, which he deployed in several publications, is based on his reading of John's Gospel. It can be set out as follows:

1. *Major premise:* the Father has given all into the hands of the Son (John 13:3, cf. Matt 11:27; Luke 10:22).

2. *Minor premise:* all that the Father has given to the Son will come to him and will not be cast out (John 6:37), but will be raised up at the last day (John 6:39–40).

3. *Therefore*, all will come to the Son, will not be cast out, and will be raised up at the last day.

One aspect of this argument that is open to dispute is the interpretation of the texts in the minor premise *in the light of* the text in the major one. The texts in the minor premise had often, as Winchester was well aware, been used as an argument for a Calvinist theology. It is the major premise that allows one to suppose that those given by the Father to the Son are not a limited group, as Calvinists claimed, but *all* people (*UR.IV.A2*). Winchester saw his argument brought together in John 17:2–3: "For thou [the Father] hast given him [the Son] power over *all flesh*, that he should give eternal life to *all* that thou hast given him." He further reinforces his case by appeal to John 6: "If all shall be taught of God [John 6:45]; and all that are taught shall come to Christ [John 6:45]; and none that come to him shall be cast out or rejected [John 6:37]; if all these premises are true . . . how very naturally the conclusion follows, viz. that all shall be finally

---

49. Winchester discusses at some length whether "all" literally means "all" (*UR.I.A9*). He argues that "all" means "all without exception," except when the context indicates that it does not (e.g., 1 Cor 15:27).

brought home to God" (*UR.IV.A2*). As further support, he brings in John 12:32: "And I, if I be lifted up from the earth [on the cross], will draw *all* unto me." Christ will see the travail of his soul *and be satisfied* (Isa 53:11).

Winchester saw the positive case for universal restoration as founded on several theological principals (*UR.III.A1*). First, God is the universal and only *creator* of all—that all creatures are made by him and for him. Second, the universal *love* of God—he loves all that he has created (Wis 11:24). Third, Christ *died for all* (Heb 2:9; 1 John 2:1–2; 1 Tim 2:5–6; 2 Cor 5:14–15). Fourth, that God is *unchangeable* and so his love for his creatures cannot waver, no matter how heinous their sins may be and no matter how much he may hate that sin. Fifth, that God's *purposes* are unchanging and that those purposes are to gather all things together in Christ (Eph 1:8–11).

But what about the biblical teachings on hell? It is no surprise that in several publications Winchester engages in extended discussions of the Hebrew and Greek words translated as "eternal"/"everlasting" as applied to the eschatological punishment of the wicked. Winchester, like universalists before him, argued that the Hebrew and Greek words normally only indicate "an age"—a complete, albeit often long, period of time—and *not* eternal duration.

However, the traditional theology of hell was not simply founded on the use of the word "eternal," but also upon certain descriptions of judgment. For instance, gehenna is described as a place where the worm does not die and the fire is not quenched (Mark 9:43–49). Winchester drew attention to various fires in the Bible that are described in just as strong terms as the fire of gehenna but which went out long ago. For instance, Jeremiah 17:27 speaks of an unquenchable fire in the gates of Jerusalem (cf. Ezek 20:42–48); and Isaiah 34 speaks of Edom being consumed by an unquenchable fire that burns unceasingly, day and night, with smoke that rises forever. To take the texts *literally* would require us to say that the prophets were wrong, but this is to misunderstand the language. It indicates a fire that will not be quenched *until it has completed its task* rather than a fire that will not *ever* be quenched. We should, he believed, understand Jesus' words similarly.

Winchester's discussion of the Parable of the Rich Man and Lazarus in Luke 16—a classic text used to support traditional views of hell—is interesting. Here a great gulf separates Hades from paradise and no one can cross it. But Winchester deployed a theological trump card: *Christ* can pass the impassible chasm. "With man is it impossible; but with God all things are possible. And I believe, that Jesus Christ was not only able to pass, but that he actually did pass that gulph, which was impassable to all men, but not to him" (*UR*.II.A5). He went on to employ the theological motif of Christ's "descent into hell" to support this claim (discussing at length the biblical foundations of the motif along the way, e.g., 1 Pet 3:18–20; 4:5–6).

> For to this end Christ both died, rose, and revived, that he might be Lord, both of the dead and living." Rom xiv.9. . . . It seemed necessary, that our Saviour should visit men in all situations, that he might redeem them. . . . It was not only necessary that he should die, to vanquish death, and to redeem us from its power; but it was equally needful for him to go into those places, where spirits were confined in the regions of darkness, that he might gain universal dominion, spoil principalities, and redeem the captives whom he had bought with his blood (*UR*.II.A5).

So the gulf in Luke 16 can be crossed *through union with Christ*. It might indeed be "impossible" for the rich—like the man in Luke 16—to enter the kingdom; *but with God* nothing is impossible (Mark 10:27).

Winchester developed his theology of hell in light of the wider scriptural pattern of punishment followed by restoration—a motif that recurs across the Bible. He noted that "God frequently threatens the greatest judgements, and promises the greatest mercies, to the same people and persons" (*UR*.IV.A3). Indeed over and over again we see those who are living under divine wrath, in what seems a hopeless state, being redeemed. "I could justify this observation by hundreds of passages wherein God threatens his people with judgements the most severe, and declares—that his eyes shall not pity, nor his arm save; that he will visit their transgressions upon them, will utterly cast them off, and will not have compassion on them at all; and then such promises of mercy break out as are sufficient to astonish every one with their greatness" (*UR*.IV.A3). Even the judgment that serves as a paradigm of hell itself—Sodom, which was destroyed with eternal fire (Jude 7)—was to be restored (Ezek 16:44, 53–63). Punishment is indeed "a just retribution," but it is *also* intended as a corrective for the good of the one punished (*UR*.IV.A16).

For Winchester the theo-logic of the issue forces a choice between Calvinism, Arminianism, and Universal Restoration. "Either God created some to be miserable to endless ages [Calvinism], or must be frustrated eternally in his designs [Arminianism], or all must be restored at last [Universalism]." (*UR*.II.A3). One of the appeals of universalism to Winchester was that it offered a way to affirm and hold together key aspects of both the Calvinist and the Arminian systems—"to embrace them [both] in one grand system of benevolence." He articulates this most clearly in his sermon, *The Outcasts Comforted*. We can summarize his theological points in the table below.

Doctrine	Calvinists	Arminians	Universal Baptists
God loves all		☺	☺
The objects of God's love will come to salvation	☺		☺
God desires to save all		☺	☺
All God's purposes will be accomplished	☺		☺
Christ died for all		☺	☺
All for whom Christ died will be saved (his blood was not shed in vain)	☺		☺

We Universalist Baptists, he said, simply affirm beliefs that mainstream Protestants hold, so why are we considered heretical?

As Winchester saw it, the problems generated within both the Calvinist and Arminian systems stem from the conviction of those on both sides of that divide that eternal hell is a nonnegotiable first principle, requiring them to sacrifice other doctrines to accommodate it. Universalism, he believed, has the strengths of both sides but the weaknesses of neither.

One common eighteenth-century objection to universalism was that it encouraged licentiousness. Winchester denied the logic. The theological principles that undergird universalism—that God created all people to "glorify his name, and enjoy him forever," the love of God for his creatures, the death of Jesus for all, the *unwavering* love of God even in the face of our rebellion—in no way encourage sinful living (*UR.III.A1*). On the contrary, they encourage lives of holy devotion and gratitude. After all, *who* would reason as follows? "I know that God created me, seeks to do me good, sent his Son to die for me, and that he will always love me . . . so I must hate him!" Rather, the revelation of divine love solicits our loving response (1 John 4:19). Winchester claimed that his own experience over the years suggests that universalist belief "causes benevolence, meekness, humility, forbearance, forgiveness, charity, and all goodness to abound and increase" (*UR*.III.A2). In fact, belief in eternal torment does not seem to have restrained evil very well over the centuries. Indeed, it appears to be a chief reason that many *reject* Christianity (*UR*.III.A3).

Winchester represented an American, Evangelical version of universal restoration in the European Pietist tradition. But this was not the only version to appear in the second half of the eighteenth century in the British colonies in America. Alongside it we find a rather idiosyncratic Calvinist strain in the preaching of John Murray, who was a follower of the teachings of James Relly, a London-based minister. It is to them that we now turn, and in order to do that we need to look back to Britain.

7

Calvinist Universalism

Relly and Murray

WE HAVE ALREADY CONSIDERED how the mystical universalist thinking of Jane Lead was mediated to the American colonies through the influx of German Pietists. We have also seen how the English Moravian James Stonehouse's books were being read by some of the colonists. But it was not only mystical and Pietistic strands of Restorationist thought that made an impact. The Reformed tradition in Britain also generated its own version of universalism, which made its mark in America.

JAMES RELLY (1722–78)

The story

In the second half of the eighteenth century a new and unusual version of universalism appeared in the ministry of a Calvinistic Methodist preacher named James Relly.

Relly was born in the county of Pembroke, Southwest Wales, in 1722. He is described as a physically strong, "wild ungovernable youth, addicted to bad company."[1] In 1741, at the age of nineteen, he and his friends decided to attend a local religious service being conducted by George Whitefield, the Evangelical revivalist, with the intention of causing trouble and disrupting the gathering. However, Relly unexpectedly found himself entranced by the preaching and within a few days was

1. Wilson, *History and Antiquities*, 359.

converted. James and his brother John then took up vocations as evangelistic preachers in Wales, associated with Whitefield. Relly seems to have

been a hardworking and trusted preacher ministering on behalf of Whitefield over the next nine years in both Wales and England. Then, in 1750, the two parted company, apparently at Relly's initiative, and almost certainly over a theological difference that had arisen between them concerned the "Freeness, and Extent of Grace."[2] By this Relly meant that he had come to believe that salvation was *completely free* and not in any way conditional upon what we do, not even upon our repentance and faith. Furthermore, he now claimed that this saving grace extended not simply to a small group, the "elect," but to all mankind. He had become a universalist, but of a very distinctive and unusual kind. Despite this parting of the ways, Relly continued to regard Whitefield with "The love, the rev'rence, to a father due."[3] However, he seems not to have had such high regard for Whitefield's followers.

The divide between Relly and the mainstream of the Evangelical movement, in both its Calvinist and Arminian forms, caused considerable bad feeling.[4] He was accused by them of being antinomian, of various kinds of greed and immorality, and of encouraging treason.[5] In return, Relly accused them of teaching salvation by works—thereby undermining the gospel—and of doing the work of Antichrist.[6]

Relly continued travelling and preaching his gospel message in various cities around Britain until 1757, when he settled in London, renting various meetinghouses in which he would regularly preach (1757–78).

2. This phrase is from a poem Relly composed in 1770 upon hearing the news of Whitefield's death.

3. Wilson, *History and Antiquities*, 359.

4. The Arminian John Wesley, in a letter to the Rev. Mr. G——— (Letter CCIV, April 2, 1761), spoke of the mutual hostility, and how he had opposed Relly and others like him "privately and publicly for these twenty years."

5. A member of Whitefield's congregation, a Mr. William Mason, published a response to Relly's book *Union* (1759) entitled *Antinomian Heresy Exploded* (1760). Relly responded with his *Antichrist Resisted* (1761). The titles give a flavor of the tone of the debate.

6. This accusation is a theme running through all Relly's works.

While in London he also published a number of books and pamphlets, the most influential being *Union; Or a Treatise of the Consanguinity and Affinity between Christ and His Church* (1759). He died in 1778, at the age of fifty-six.

Without their inspirational preacher, the congregation petered out within three years, and with it Relly's message faded from the British scene.[7] However, as we shall see, it continued to exercise influence in America through one of Relly's converts, John Murray.

The "freeness and extent of grace" in Relly's Calvinist universalism

To understand Relly's idiosyncratic universalist views, we need to appreciate how he arrived at them. In the preface to *Union*, he explains how one day, in his work as an evangelist for Whitefield, he met with a man who challenged his account of the atoning work of Christ. Relly taught the mainstream Evangelical penal substitution theory of the atonement. According to this view, a holy and just God cannot simply overlook sin, but must punish it, as justice demands. However, the just punishment for sin is everlasting death, so how then can anyone be saved? The answer, given in the gospel, is that we can be saved because God sent Christ to take our place and God punished him in our stead. In this way justice is satisfied, because sin has been punished, yet sinners can go free. Such was the theory. Relly's interlocutor, however, was having none of it. How, he asked, can justice be satisfied if the one who commits the crime is not punished, but instead an innocent person is punished in his place? The Bible itself teaches that the innocent or righteous must not suffer for the sins of the guilty (Isa 3:10–11), and that the guilty should pay for their own sins (Exod 32:33; Deut 24:26). So the atonement, said the man, rather than satisfying justice, seems a prime instance of *injustice*.[8]

This simple observation deeply disturbed Relly, for he saw the problem and had no idea what the solution was. He went away and read around the subject, but found no help from any books. Thus, he says, "I applied myself more carefully to the reading and the study of

---

7. Though Thomas Whittemore claims that a Rellian congregation in the UK was still around when he was writing in 1830.

8. This objection was a common Socinian objection to Evangelical atonement theory in the period.

the scriptures, as without notes, or expositions: submitting in spirit, unto Him."[9] And in this way, setting aside the thoughts of others and simply reading the Bible, he found what he considered the solution to his problem—*the union of Christ and his church.*

The notion of the union Christ and his church was not new. Indeed, it was a staple of New Testament and Reformed theology. Relly, however, took it to a new level and made it the key to his entire theological system. Jesus had been joined with his church in such a way that what was true of him was true of them, and what was true of them was true of him. He was the head and they were his body (Rom 12:5; 1 Cor 12:27; Eph 1:22–23); he was the vine and they were the branches (John 15).[10] Because Christ and his church are, in the eyes of God, united as "one flesh" (Eph 5:29–32), he can be "made sin" for them (2 Cor 5:21), even though in himself he is personally sinless. By standing as the head of the human race he can rightly be punished on their behalf because, through his union with sinners, he is not an innocent bystander, but *genuinely shares in their guilt.* Thus, "[t]he *Union* and harmony of the Body, renders it equitable to punish, and chastise the whole Body, in one Member, for its offence in another: . . . As the *Union* of the body makes it equitable to punish the *head* for the offence of the other members; with like equity doth the members participate with the *head* in all its honours and glory."[11] Relly thus felt he had solved his core problem. When Christ dies for our sins, *we die in him.* And the reverse is true, in his resurrection we are raised with him (Col 3:1), in his ascension we are seated in heavenly places in him (Eph 2:6). *Through union with him* we are elect sons (Eph 1:4), beloved of God (John 17:23), righteous (2 Cor 5:21), and obedient. Christ is all these things and *in him* so are we. Only in this way, says Relly, can God's goodness and justice can be held in harmony.

Human history, for Relly, boils down to the story of just two people—Adam and Christ. Both stand as representatives for the whole race. In union with Adam, all sinned and all died; in union with Christ, all will be made alive (Rom 5:19).[12]

9. Relly, *Union*, xvi.

10. In *Union*, Relly explores multiple biblical images of union in addition to these, including Christ clothed with his people like Aaron clothed in his priestly robes, the church as a building with Christ as the foundation and capstone, and man and wife as one flesh.

11. Relly, *Union*, 88–89.

12. Relly, *Union*, 58–67.

> The free gift came upon *all men*, unto justification of life—Upon
> all on whom judgment came unto condemnation. Hence, it is
> true beyond all controversy, that, as all Adam's offspring, by
> means of his offence, were brought under judgment to condem-
> nation; so it is equally true, that, by means of Christ's righteous-
> ness, Adam and all his offspring were brought under the free gift
> of justification unto eternal life.[13]

As we were all "in Adam" before even we were born, so too we were all
"in Christ" before the foundation of the world. This is why Relly was a
universalist.[14] He saw Christ as "including mankind"[15] and having already accomplished redemption for all people, undoing the damnation
of all in Adam.

However, we need to appreciate that the universal reach of salvation
was not a primary interest to Relly; it was neither the foundation nor the
goal of his doctrine of union with Christ—after all, "[i]f there was but one
person in all the world to be saved, it would be no argument against the
truth of the doctrine of Union."[16] His real focus was the *method* of salvation, not its scope.[17] He saw a clear biblical teaching to be affirmed alongside others in the universality of salvation, and so he integrated it into his
understanding of union,[18] but while he affirmed universal salvation, he

13. Relly, *Epistles*, 44.

14. In *Antichrist Resisted*, his reply to Mason, Relly denies the accusation that he
was a universalist (15). However, in context, Relly's denial of universalism is clearly
not to be understood as a denial that all will be saved, but as a denial of the view
that affirms the universalist aspect of truth without also affirming the conditional
and particularist aspect. On these two aspects, see the discussion in the main text. He
thinks that the charge against him of universalism is false because he also affirms that
salvation is, *in one sense of the word*, limited to believers (16). Relly sees the apparent
conflicts between conditional and unconditional salvation, particular and universal
salvation, as false conflicts. In his system, each of these perspectives contains an aspect
of truth, and all are held together consistently in Christ (15–16; *Epistles*, Letter II).

15. Relly, *Union*, 130.

16. Relly, *Antichrist Resisted*, 17.

17. Relly, *Antichrist Resisted*, 17.

18. He infers it from various biblical texts, and from the revelation that "God is
love" and sent his Son to die for all people. He maintains that for God to create people
"with an unavoidable destiny to sin, and endless misery" (*Epistles*, 33) would conflict
with the divine nature and biblical teaching. See Relly, *Epistles*, Letters IV and V for a
consideration of a range of texts that he links to universal salvation.

said that he would not have been especially concerned to drop it should he be persuaded that it was wrong.[19]

According to Relly, salvation is *already completely accomplished* in Christ. Sin has been forever and finally dealt with. There is *absolutely nothing* for us to do, nothing that we can add to it. The shocking implication he drew from this is that repentance, faith, and obedience are not conditions placed on us in order to be saved. The world is *already* united to Christ and saved in Christ, *irrespective of its response to God.* "Your unbelief cannot make his grace of none effect."[20] We do not need to see good fruit in our lives or to feel an assurance in our hearts to know that we are saved, because our confidence of salvation should have *nothing* to do with what we do or how we feel. Our confidence is founded in Christ and his work alone.

This is the reason that Relly accused his fellow Evangelicals of trying to add to the finished work of Jesus and achieve salvation by human works—for they did look for appropriate human responses (faith, repentance, obedience) or feelings (inner assurance) as essential grounds for having confidence that we will be saved. It is also why they accused him of antinomianism, of teaching that it does not matter how we live, because we will all be saved regardless. Both sides in the dispute thought that the other taught a dangerous and false gospel, and arguably both sides were less than charitable in their interpretations of each other.

Relly was not, of course, against inward assurances from the Spirit or faith in Christ or good works. Rather, what he was desperate to make clear was that these things were not conditions of our salvation or the grounds of our confidence in our salvation.

But what about all those biblical texts that do appear to make salvation dependent on our response? Here Relly seeks to distinguish different biblical uses of the term "salvation."[21] There is "everlasting salvation," the state in which Christ has placed humanity before God in himself. This salvation, as we have seen, is completely independent of our knowledge of it or our response to it.

> [T]he elect, precious, the predestined to eternal life; and such are the people in him: . . . This is their election. Christ also sustained the reprobate character, when made sin for us, and when

19. Relly, *Epistles*, 7, 70.

20. Relly, *Union*, 163.

21. Relly explores this distinction in Letter II of *Epistles*, 12–19.

encompassed with the sorrows of death and the pains of hell. And as to universal salvation: He is also the truth of that. For, though we do see not yet all the individuals of Adam's race, as such, brought up, through the knowledge of Christ, to the great salvation: in him, all are taught of God [John 6:45]: in him, all know God, from the greatest to the least [Jer 31:34].[22]

But there is also a sense of "salvation" that concerns our *experience* of joy and peace and freedom from guilt and sin. This salvation is the fruit of conscious faith in the gospel and so *in this sense of the term* only believers are saved. Here salvation *does* depend on our faithful and obedient response to God, though we must recognize that even that response is a response that God himself, by his Spirit, graciously enables. Indeed, our repentance and faith and obedience are really an experiential participation in Christ's own vicarious repentance and faith and obedience.[23] "So truly through Faith we understand our *Union* with *Christ*; yet it is not our Faith that makes it."[24] "[B]y conditional salvation, I understand present salvation, or the salvation of Christ, enjoyed in this life: the conditions of obtaining and rejoicing in which, are undoubtedly faith and obedience."[25] This conditional salvation may come to us instantaneously or gradually, according to how God reveals himself to us.

Relly argues that for the time being God, according to his sovereign will, has chosen to reveal himself to a limited few. While all people are saved in the objective sense, only a few now experience the joy and freedom of that salvation. This is how Relly interprets talk of "the elect."

> [T]he elect are not a people chosen to be objects of God's love and salvation, to the final exclusion of others: but a people chosen to believe the truth, and to rejoice in the salvation of Jesus in time; while others remain in a state of ignorance, of what they are equally entitled to with the elect. The elect, who are predestinated to the present knowledge, and enjoyment of eternal life, can only attain this happiness through faith and obedience. . . . Election and Predestination, thus considered, are no denial to salvation finished for all, in the person of Christ; nor is it an objection to the future happiness of all; for whom Christ died: nay,

22. Relly, *Epistles*, 10–11.

23. The language of participation here is not Relly's, but it captures his meaning (*Epistles*, 14–15).

24. Relly, *Union*, 110.

25. Relly, *Epistles*, 25.

it rather supposes it; if the predestinate and elect are so called, from their being chosen to believe, and enjoy in time, what the residue neither know, nor enjoy but in eternity.[26]

What of hell? We have seen that Relly retained a belief that sin deserves to be punished with "eternal death."[27] However, given that Christ has now fully paid our debt, God, being just, will not punish the same sins a second time. Consequently, *nobody* will go to hell.

> All mankind, by means of transgression, had rendered themselves obnoxious to everlasting punishment; but Jesus gave himself as a ransom for all, by taking on him their condition, and exposing himself to all their woes: hence on the ransom's being found, they were delivered from going down to the pit. If Jesus gave himself as a ransom for all, then are all ransomed.[28]

However, Relly still retained a place in his system for sinners to face post-mortem torments. This is because, not having believed the gospel, they do not realize that they are saved and so suffer deep anguish with the sense of guilt and fear: "for men may, by unbelief, retain and hold fast to their guilt, and fear, and torment, the iniquities which the blood of Jesus hath expiated, and which God hath justified them from."[29] This "cannot be a state of punishment,"[30] but is rather *self-inflicted* mental torments, pictured in Scripture as undying fire and gnawing worms. This unbelieving condition may well last for a very long time, but in the end Christ will reveal himself to these sinners too, and they will be saved in both senses of the term. Then will be the end of the ages and God will be all in all.

It is clear that Relly was no liberal; his theology, while having a unique configuration, remained deeply Evangelical and indeed Calvinist.

---

26. Relly, *Epistles*, 27–28, 30.

27. Relly, *Union*, 48, 122. In fact, Relly's view is not so neat. Although speaking in such ways, in *Epistles*, Letter VII, he has a diatribe against eternal torments as an *actual* fate for anyone, claiming that such pains "pay no debt . . . cancel no offence . . . have no satisfaction to divine justice . . . are inconsistent with divine purity . . . are an absolute denial of Christ's dying for our offences" (97). It appears that Relly thinks that while sin is profoundly heinous, God would never inflict eternal torments, for his justice is concerned only with the annihilation of the sin, not the sinner. Torments, unless sent for the good of the sufferer, serve neither God's justice nor his love. It is unclear how this view is to be integrated with some of the other things he says.

28. Relly, *Epistles*, 59–60.

29. Relly, *Epistles*, 120.

30. Relly, *Epistles*, 146.

In his mind, all that he was doing was seeking to be a consistent Bible believer, finding a way to hold together divine justice and a penal substitutionary atonement. The theology by which he sought to do this was idiosyncratic and in certain aspects rather problematic, but it was profoundly Christocentric and arguably not without its insights.

JOHN MURRAY (1741–1816) AND JUDITH SARGENT MURRAY (1751–1820)

The story

REV. JOHN MURRAY.

James Relly's greatest influence was not through his own preaching and publications, but through the ministry of one of his converts, John Murray.

Murray was born in Hampshire in 1741 and baptized into the Church of England. His father was a rigid Calvinist, and John's very strict upbringing instilled "more *fear* than *affection* for my father" (8).[31] The Calvinism he learned at home caused him terror and extreme inner agonies concerning whether he was among the elect: "In fact, I believed that I had nothing to hope, but everything to fear, both from my Creator, and my [human] father" (12).

When John was eleven, the family moved to Cork in Ireland. Around this time, the Methodists appeared and John's father, eager for enthusiastic religion, got involved with them. John Wesley himself was "a great admirer of my father, and he distinguished him beyond any individual in the society" (18). John too was enamored by the Methodists, and was invited by Wesley to be the leader of a class of forty boys (18). This was a happier time in John's life, though doubts continued, and so did his emotional mountains and valleys. Wesley continued to pay him considerable attention and had great hopes for him, though was perturbed by the continuing

---

31. The following in-text citations in this section on Relly are from *Life of Christ*, unless otherwise stated.

commitment to Calvinism by John and his father (25–26). The hostility of the Methodists with whom he associated to his Calvinism was increasing, but an opportunity to spend time with the Calvinist evangelist George Whitefield in Cork in 1760 greatly encouraged him (60–61).

Murray left Ireland for London and joined Whitefield's congregation. He also fell in love with Miss Eliza Neale and they eventually got married. It was in London that he first heard of James Relly. He presents his conversion to Relly's teaching as akin to the conversion of St. Paul. He came across one of Relly's preachers speaking in the open air in Moorfields, and writes that on learning of the damnable doctrines being preached:

> My soul kindled with indignation . . . I could not forbear explaining: Merciful God! How is it that Thou wilt suffer this Demon to proceed?. . . . At this period, I should have considered my self highly favoured, to have been made an instrument, in the hand of God, for taking the life of a man, whom I had never heard, nor even seen; and in destroying him, I should have nothing doubted, that I had rendered essential service, both to the Creator and the created. (79)

Over the next few years, Murray heard and believed all sorts of horror stories spoken against Relly, and his hatred of the man grew (91). One significant incident for him was an occasion when he decided to try to win back a pious young woman from Whitefield's Tabernacle who had been ensnared by Relly's doctrine (90–93). He took some friends with him to converse with her. However, to his embarrassment, she very gently outfoxed him in theological debate. The issue under discussion was the role of unbelief in damnation. The woman's argument was that if Jesus is not the Savior of unbelievers before they come to believe then God cannot condemn them for not believing that Jesus is their Savior. "It appears to me, sir, that Jesus is the complete Saviour of *unbelievers*; and that unbelievers are called upon to believe the truth; and that by *believing they are saved, in their own apprehension, saved from all those dreadful fears*, which are consequent upon a state of conscious condemnation" (92). You yourself, she said, were once not a believer, and yet Christ died for you as Savior *before* you came to faith. Your faith did not turn Jesus from non-Savior to Savior. Faith, rather, is a response to salvation accomplished. Murray did not know how to reply and left humiliated and angry. He now "carefully avoided every Universalist, and most *cordially did I hate* them" (93).

The next significant event in his conversion was when Mr. Mason, a member of Whitefield's congregation, asked Murray to give feedback on the draft manuscript of an attempted rebuttal of Relly' *Union*. This Murray did, but at one point he found himself deeply unsatisfied with Mason's argument against Relly—something that he deeply lamented, because he still considered Mason to be on the side of truth. So he pointed out the problem in the argument. To his horror, Mason published the work as it stood and ignored Murray from that point on (95–97).

The final steps came when John happened across a copy of *Union* at the house of his wife's uncle and aunt. He borrowed it and began to read, very alert to its being a dangerous and poisonous book, but convinced that God would protect his elect (97). John and Eliza read it together, looking up all the biblical texts cited, and their perceptions of Relly and his views began to shift. The more he read of Relly's work, the more convinced he became that the man's detractors had significantly misrepresented him. An inner battle was being fought in Murray over the next few months as he wrestled with the new ideas. So John and Eliza decided to go and hear Relly, and the dam broke. He commented later that "I was constrained to believe, that I had never, until this moment, heard the Redeemer preached; . . . I attended with my whole soul. I was humbled, I was confounded." On the way home, he said to his wife, "I have never heard truth, unadulterated truth before. . . . It is the first consistent sermon I have ever heard" (100). From this moment on, Murray was an unflinching Rellyan. News of their attendance at Relly's meetings got out, and they were expelled from the Whitefield's Tabernacle (102–3).

A series of calamities followed John after this: those religious friends who once supported him now claimed back what they had given, forcing him into the hands of bailiffs. He was condemned to poverty. Then his one-year-old son died, after which his traumatized wife took ill and also died. His own health began to fail. There was nothing left "but the ghosts of my departed joys" (109). Now his creditors closed in and he was taken to a sponging-house (a place of temporary confinement for debtors), where he reached an all-time low, even contemplating suicide (113). His desire now was simply "to pass through life, *unheard, unseen, unknown to all, as though I ne'er had been*" (118). A chance meeting with a man from America led Murray to leave Britain for a new life of solitude and anonymity in the New World.

He set sail for New York in 1770, but the boat got lost in fog and a navigational mistake led them to run aground near Cranberry Inlet,

New Jersey. Disembarking, Murray wandered into the woods and met an old man called Thomas Potter (1689–1777), who gave him food and a bed for the night. Potter had been converted to universalism years earlier by some itinerants from the Ephrata Community, and had felt God tell him to build a meetinghouse for a preacher whom God would send. In spite of mockery from locals, Potter continued to trust that God would send the preacher. As soon as he saw the boat, he felt what seemed like an audible voice saying, "There, Potter, in that vessel, cast away on that shore, is the preacher, you have been long expecting" (127).

Being a public teacher of universalism was the last thing Murray had wanted to do in America, not least because he knew that his message would generate considerable opposition from established clergy, but he eventually came to see the hand of God in the events that had led him there and took up residence as the preacher (127–34), using his new home as a base for preaching tours into rural New Jersey, New York, Philadelphia, Newport, Providence, Boston, Newburyport, Portsmouth, East Greenwich, and New London, vowing not to ever take any fee for his ministry. Unsurprisingly, Murray's message was a polarizing one, and his autobiography records some of the incidents of welcome and strong opposition he faced over the years of his ministry.

In November 1774, he was invited to Gloucester, Massachusetts, and was delighted to find there a small group already committed to Relly's ideas (187–88). He was eventually persuaded to relocate to Gloucester as the preacher for the group, using the town and the base for his itinerant ministry. Murray and the Gloucester Rellyan group experienced considerable

opposition from the town. In 1782, members of the group had possessions seized in lieu of taxes not paid to the Congregational Church. The next year Universalists initiated a lawsuit against the Congregational Church, and in 1786 won their right to exist as an independent church. The Congregationalists responded the following year by legally challenging Murray's right to perform marriages (on the grounds that he was not a legitimate ordained minister). The Universalists eventually won that case as well.

In 1788, John married Judith Sargent, one of the Gloucester group, and their marriage was a happy one. Judith was an interesting figure in her own right, being well-educated, having proto-feminist views on the equality of women, and being a prolific author. Her most significant universalist publication was a catechism written to inculcate Rellyan theology in young believers (1782). It provides a succinct overview of this species of universalism in its American incarnation.

In 1793, he was invited to divide his time between the Gloucester and the Boston congregations, but in 1794, he, Judith, and their daughter relocated permanently to First Universalist Church Boston, where he served out the rest of his ministry.

John was incapacitated by a stroke in 1809, and used the next few years editing and publishing his *Letters and Sketches of Sermons* (1812). He died in 1816, after which Judith published *Records of the Life of the Rev. John Murray*.[32]

Theology

Murray did not publish theological books systematically defending his version of universalism. However, his three-volume *Letters and Sketches of Sermons* (totaling 1,261 pages) contain numerous extended theological and exegetical reflections—albeit, in the nature of the case, not systematically organized—and give a good flavor of his thought. Murray's theology was, he always insisted, unadulterated and unflinching Rellyanism. His assessment of mainstream Christian theology—in which Christ died for all, but that many will never be saved—was therefore blunt:

> To talk of Jesus as the Saviour of a people who are not saved; to affirm that he taketh away the sins of those, whose sins are not taken away; that he destroyed the works of the Devil, which are not destroyed; that the blood of Jesus cleanseth from all sin, yet we are *not cleansed from all sin*, but that our iniquities still remain before God, exciting both wrath and indignation; that Jesus came to make peace, yet peace is not made. . . . I say, thus to express ourselves, is more derogatory to the honour of God, than any language that is found in the mouth of the dissolute

32. John himself had completed the autobiography as far as 1784, but Judith had to complete the work (from 1785 to 1816) on his behalf, using her own knowledge of events as his wife and some of his own letters and writings.

publican. . . . Our Saviour, was not an equivocal or conditional
Saviour. (*Letters*, 1.191)[33]

All our redemption is *already complete* in Christ—what we need is illumination to increasingly see and live into this gracious redemption.

> [T]o know more and more of *this salvation*, is to grow in grace.
> We first learn we are saved from damnation due to our past sins,
> by his death, and immediately look for holiness in ourselves;
> but, being *in grace*, we soon grow strong enough to know that
> *He* who was our *death* is also our *life, by being our holiness*. Thus
> by little and little we grow into him, in all things, until we are
> enabled to believe we are *wise* in his *wisdom, righteous* in *his
> righteousness, holy* in his *holiness, strong in his strength*, suffering
> all things in his sufferings, doing all things commanded in the
> law, in his doings; and from hence we proceed to believe, that
> He who is *our* head, is the head of *every man*, that He, who by
> the grace of God tasted death *for us*, by the same grace tasted
> death for *every man*; that He who is *our* wisdom, is every man's
> wisdom; . . . that He who hath *accepted us*, hath accepted *every
> man, in the beloved*. (*Letters* 1.98–99)

As we have already articulated Relly's system of thought, we shall not
repeat Murray's version of it here. Two reflections are, however, in order.

Murray's interpretations of biblical texts vary from the level-headed
and sensible to the contrived and implausible.[34] Here are two interesting
examples. First, the Parable of the Rich Man and Lazarus from Luke 16:19–
31 (*Letters* 1.Letter I). Parables, says Murray, ought not to be read as if they
were literal history, but as allegories. On his interpretation, the rich man
symbolizes the Jewish nation (rich with all the covenant blessings of God).
The death of the rich man symbolizes the end of the Jewish dispensation;
the time when Israel rejected Jesus, and the apostles turned to the gentiles.
The Jewish nation is now in a state of death, of darkness, of loss, of torment. The impassable gulf between the rich man and Abraham shows that
God has blinded the eyes of the nation so that they *cannot* see the truth of
the gospel and be saved—for now at least. The poor man is the gentile nations. In the previous age, they were strangers to the covenant blessings of
Israel (Eph 2:11–12), and thus profoundly impoverished. But the coming

---

33. The following in-text citations in this section on Murray are from *Letters and
Sketches*, unless otherwise stated.

34. The far-fetched nature of some of his biblical interpretations was not lost on
the universalists who came after him.

of Christ led to the door closing on Israel (for a time) and opening on the gentiles. Now the poor man is brought into the light at Abraham's side, sharing in the covenant as a son. But at the end of this age, when the fullness of the gentiles has come in, Israel's temporary hardness will end and "all Israel will be saved" (Rom 11:25–26). So, reasons Murray, this parable is not even about the afterlife, let alone eternal torment.

Second, the Parable of the Sheep and the Goats (Matt 25:31–46). Murray argues that these don't represent two groups of people (the saved and the unsaved), but fallen human nature (the sheep) and fallen angelic nature (the goats). Christ died for the lost sheep, not the goats, so on the great day of separation, God will strip away the devil and his angels, casting them into eternal fire, and will redeem human nature, bringing all humans into eternal life (*Letters* 1.95–96, 134–38, 159–60, 268–69).[35] Then, human nature, free at last from the operations of evil spirits, will be liberated. This interpretation is very different from that of other universalists in America. Murray's Rellyanism could not contemplate any sinners for whom Christ had died being cast into the fire, even if only for an age. His solution was to cast demons, not humans, into the eternal fire.

This flags up what was the main disagreement between Murray and most of the other universalists in America—postmortem punishment. In Murray's mind, this teaching amounted to a denial of the efficacy of the atonement:

> The sufferings of Christ are supposed insufficient, and therefore there are a class, even of Universalists, who suppose that pain and sorrow must be extended to some unknown period, beyond the general judgment, in order that individuals may pay the mighty debt, which our Surety [Christ] left unpaid; while the advocate for eternal misery, pronounces positively that this debt *can never be paid.* . . . But, says the unbelieving Universalist, they *can* and *will pay to the utmost farthing,* and when they do God will be satisfied. Thus it is not the sufferings of the Saviour which are accepted as satisfactory, although never was sorrow like unto his sorrow, and it is therefore that the sorrows and the sufferings of the sinner must be added. (*Letters* 1.138–39)

Universalism in the eighteenth century was still wrestling with how to integrate its theology of Christ's death with its theology of global salvation.

---

35. Murray did not believe in the salvation of fallen angels. Judith incorporated this interpretation of the parable into her universalist catechism.

Alongside the presence of the distinctive Pietist and Calvinist universalisms, with their European roots, America in the eighteenth century also bred some apparently homegrown versions of universal salvation, which seemingly appeared independently of the influence the imported varieties. We shall consider these in the next chapter.

8

Homegrown American Universalism
Chauncy, Davis, Streeter, and Rich

CHARLES CHAUNCY (1705–87)—"OLD LIGHT"
UNIVERSALISM

IN ADDITION TO THE import of European universalists—both Pietist and Reformed—and their influence, there were various homegrown univer-

salists whose origins appear to be independent of the ministry of the European universalists. Most of these were radical separatists, but one stands apart as being a staunch defender of traditional New England Congregationalism— Charles Chauncy, the minister of the prestigious First Church in Boston for around sixty years.[1]

It seems that Chauncy dis- covered universal salvation all on his own through his reflection of Scripture. He tells us that his study of 1 Corinthians 15:21–28 (the text

1. Another Congregationalist minister with a unitarian bent, Jonathan Mayhew (1720–66)—the man who coined the revolutionary slogan "no taxation without rep- resentation"—had also come out against eternal torment and in favor of universalism, but an early death limited his impact on this score.

most cited by patristic universalists) opened his eyes to reconsider all of the Scriptures in a new light.[2] This he did with meticulous care. He was certainly not influenced by the universalists among the separatists of the Great Awakening (on whom see later discussion), being himself one of the so-called "Old Lights," a staunch opponent of revivalism. He was also not influenced by John Murray (of whom he was aware, but regarded with some disdain, considering his theology antinomian).[3] The theological view he ended up with was similar to that of the Pietists, but he shows no evidence of direct engagement with their work and his arguments are clearly the fruit of his own researches, even if he did draw some inspiration from the insights of others.

The first hint that Chauncy was inclined to universalism came in a sermon in 1762 entitled "All Nations Blessed in Christ." The issue was apparently one that concerned him throughout much of his ministry, but his mature thoughts were not finally revealed until the publication of a major study on the subject in 1784, when he was well advanced in years. Even then, his book, *The Salvation of All Men*, appeared without its author's name. Although accustomed to controversy, Chauncy was not looking for a fight.[4]

The Salvation of All Men contains two main sections: first, a positive biblical case for the final redemption of all, organized around six key propositions; second, a response to four standard objections. The book is by far the most scholarly of any universalist text published in the eighteenth century, eclipsing even Stonehouse's impressive work.

The text opens with a vision of God as the infinitely benevolent First Cause of all things, who intends his creatures to be finally happy and who has the wisdom and power to make it so (1–3).[5] Creation is moving toward the "happiness of all mankind," but it does not take a straight and short path to that goal. It is not hard to see the Enlightenment influence

---

2. "It was this [1 Cor 15:21–28] indeed that first opened to me the present scheme, serving as a *key* to unlock the meaning of many passages in the sacred writings" (*Salvation of All Men*, 197, cf. Chauncy's preface).

3. It is possible that he published the book when he did for fear that Murray would tarnish the reputation of universalism if a more "credible" version was not available.

4. It is perhaps no surprise that his work solicited a book-length response from Jonathan Edwards the Younger (1745–1801) entitled *The Salvation of All Men Strictly Examined* (New Haven: 1790).

5. The following in-text citations in this section on Chauncy are from *The Salvation of All Men*, unless otherwise stated.

on Chauncy's articulation of this vision in terms of human happiness.[6] While Chauncy clearly defers to the authority of Scripture, he does think that this universalist vision is *a priori* "more honorable to the Father of mercies, and comfortable to the creatures whom his hands have formed" (14), "a design eminently worthy of God's contriving, and of Christ's executing" (15), and we should all at least "be disposed to wish it might be well supported from Scripture" (13). Having set the scene, he moves to lay out his positive case—the six propositions, along with biblical defenses of them.

Proposition one: "From the time that sin entered into the world by the first man Adam, *Jesus Christ* is the person *through whom*, and *upon whose account*, happiness is attainable by any of the human race" (17–19).

Proposition two: "The *obedience* of *Christ*, and eminently his obedience to *death*, when he had assumed our flesh, in the fullness of time, is the *ground* or *reason* upon which it hath pleased God to make happiness attainable by any of the race of Adam" (19–20).

Proposition three: "Christ did not die for a select number of men only, but for mankind *universally*, and *without exception* or *limitation*" (20–22).

Proposition four: "It is the purpose of God, according to his good pleasure, that mankind *universally*, in consequence of the death of his Son Jesus Christ, shall *certainly* and *finally* be saved" (22–170). Here we find extensive exegetical analyses of universal justification in Romans 5:12–21 (22–91), universal liberation in Romans 8:19–24 (91–123),[7] universal reconciliation in Colossians 1:19–20 and related texts (123–46), plus the final unification of all things under Christ's headship in Ephesians and other texts (142–63). There is also a defense of the claim that if God desires to save all (1 Tim 2:4) then all *will* be saved, even though, according to Chauncy, people have libertarian freewill (163–70).

---

6. It seems to me that the influence of John Locke, whose biblical interpretations Relly cites on various occasions, may be felt here: "the highest perfection of intellectual nature lies in a careful and constant pursuit of true and solid happiness" (*Essay concerning Human Understanding*. 1689. Book 2, ch. 21). This sentiment found its way, via Thomas Jefferson, into the American Declaration of Independence in 1776 and was very much "in the air." But we should not overlook the more distant Aristotelian and Thomist roots to the notion.

7. Chauncy argues that the "all creation" in the passage primarily intends all rational creatures. But even if the reference is broader, embracing nonrational and inanimate created things, he maintains that it still includes rational creatures as well.

Proposition five: "As a mean in order to men's being made meet for salvation, God, by Jesus Christ, will, sooner or later, in THIS STATE OR ANOTHER, reduce them all under a WILLING and OBEDIENT SUB-JECTION to his moral government" (170–237). Chauncy's point is that human sinners are *not* incurable, and his focus is on texts concerning Christ's destruction of sin. Sin can only be subjected/destroyed by effecting a change in sinners so that they cease to rebel against God—this is their salvation. As long as sin remains in human hearts, even in hell, it remains undefeated: in the lake of fire sinners "will still continue [as] the *enemies of God*, and as much unsubjected to the government of Christ, as his *willing* and *obedient* servants, as ever" (183). A forced and unwilling submission to Christ is a mere display of superior power and does not constitute a defeat of the power of sin over the sinner. It is, at best, "a poor, low kind of submission" in comparison with the more glorious victory over sin represented by the submission of free obedience (192). Chauncy devotes considerable attention to 1 Corinthians 15:24–28 (197–226) in this section, a text he considers "*decisive* of itself" (197).

The sixth proposition: "The Scripture language, concerning the . . . RESTORED, in consequence of the mediatory interposition of Jesus Christ, is such as to lead us into the thought, that THEY are comprehensive of MANKIND UNIVERSALLY" (237–54). The vision of universal worship in Revelation 5:13 is Chauncy's springboard here into a discussion of a universalist interpretation of God's promise to Abram in Genesis 12 that "all nations" would be blessed in him, a promise fulfilled through Christ.

Having set forth his positive case, four objections are considered and refuted, the first of which receives the lion's share of attention. First, that the Bible teaches eternal torment (256–328). Second, that Jesus' declaration that it would be better for Judas never to have been born excludes his salvation (328–31). Third, that the unforgivable blasphemy against the Spirit suggests that some can never reach final bliss (332–40). Finally, the common fear that the loss of eternal hell will remove a key motivation for moral living (340–59). This last objection was an especially contentious issue in the new United States: "In a republic, fear of the sovereign could be replaced by fear of God, driving inherently depraved people to virtuous behavior in the effort to avoid future punishment."[8] So universalism was feared to be a civic threat to the fragile republic.

8. Lum, *Damned Nation*, 29.

It is clearly impossible to give anything other than a brief glimpse at this long and sophisticated work, but a few more details about some parts of the argument are in order.

Paul's two texts about Adam and Christ (1 Cor 15:12–21; Rom 5:12–21) receive a lot of attention. With regards to Romans 5, in which Adam and Christ are contrasted, Chauncy argues that the "all" who are the recipients of the grace of justification through Christ are the *same* "all" who find themselves condemned because of the sin of Adam (5:18); i.e., every human being. "The antithesis would otherwise be lost. For mankind universally are the object of condemnation; the same mankind must therefore be the object of the opposite justification. Besides, mankind generally are *the many* [οἱ πολλοί] in the foregoing 15th verse, who are expressly mentioned as the persons unto whom the gift by grace *hath abounded*" (60). Furthermore, the text contrasts the damage caused by Adam's sin with the super-abounding grace brought by Christ that more than resolves the problem (5:20). But if in the end many remain unsaved then "it will demonstrably follow, that Adam has done *more hurt* than Christ has done *good;* and consequently, that the race of men have more reason for complaint on behalf of his disobedience, than they have for thankfulness on account of Christ's obedience" (87–88). And this justification through Christ is spoken of in the text, not merely as an *offer* of justification or a *possible* justification, but as a justification that is *"certain* with respect to . . . actually coming into *effect"* (83).

1 Corinthians 15:21–28 is a key text for Chauncy. Here, in verses 21–22, Christ and Adam are compared: "the SAME ALL who suffer *death* though Adam, shall through Christ be *made alive.* The comparison between the *damage* by *Adam*, and the *advantage* by *Christ*, lies in this very thing" (201).

Chauncy's interpretations of parts of this passage were not in the mainstream, though they find many parallels with the way that Pietists like the Petersens, Siegvolck, and Winchester interpreted the text.

According to Chauncy, the sequence of events Paul depicts is as follows:

1. Christ is resurrected (15:23b).

2. Christ returns, and the saints (those who belong to Christ) are resurrected (15:23b).

3. [Next there comes a very long temporal gap, not explicitly mentioned by Paul, as his interest lies elsewhere. Chauncy posits this

unmentioned time period on the grounds that "the end" (stages 4–5) cannot come until all things are fully submitted to Christ, and this is not the case at the second coming, but only once death, which he believes has to include the second death (hell), is fully defeated.]

4. Then, all things are subjected to Christ. This event, says Chauncy, marks the end of Christ's aiōnial kingdom, for the *aiōn* of his mediatorial rule is over now that all creation is in submission (15:24–27).

5. Finally, Christ delivers his mediatorial kingdom over to the Father, subjecting himself to the Father (15:24). The final state of creation is now achieved: God is all, in all (15:28).

Now claims 3 and 4 are highly controversial. Chauncy defends at length his unmentioned timespan after Christ's return and before "the end," but many will remain unconvinced. His importing of the second death from the book Revelation into the exegesis will also strike many modern interpreters as eisegetical. However, we must remember that at the time interpreting one inspired Scripture in the light of another inspired Scripture was considered perfectly acceptable. And whatever we may think of his exegetical weaknesses now, his theo-logic is suggestive. Moreover, even those who reject his reading as an exposition of what Paul had in mind, may be sympathetic to it as a *legitimate extension* of Paul's thought. The second death, Chauncy argues, is as much an enemy to humanity as the first—both result from sin and both thwart the human hope of eternal life with God. Indeed, the second death is a better candidate for "the *last* enemy" that needs defeating (15:26), for the first death is over and done with by judgment day, while the second death only begins at that point. The Pauline logic that makes death an enemy requiring defeat, arguably makes the second death *even more* of an enemy that must be vanquished. Furthermore, in a similar theological extension of Paul's logic, Chauncy argues that the kind of resurrection life Paul speaks of in the chapter is not a bare return to life, but an immortal, imperishable, glorious, spiritual life that comes through union with Christ. It is this life that constitutes the swallowing up of death in victory and until all share in it, death has not been *fully* vanquished. This, thinks Chauncy, is where Paul's ideas inexorably lead. Even if Paul did not think through the implications of his teachings here, and Chauncy's comments "go beyond" what Paul says, perhaps we may still think his insights valid.

The claim that Christ's "eternal" kingdom will come to an end once all creation is subject and its purpose is fulfilled is also found in millenarian Pietist writings, as we have seen. Indeed, its origins are much earlier, reaching back into the fourth century in the work of Marcellus of Ancyra. The church rejected Marcellus's interpretation of 1 Corinthians 15, adding the words "of whose kingdom there will be no end" to the Nicene Creed as a result. So strictly speaking, this view, left unqualified, is formal heresy. However, Siegvolk, Stonehouse, and Winchester *did* qualify it, being committed to orthodox Christology; Chauncy, whose Christology was Arian, did not.[9]

With regard to human freedom, Chauncy is an Arminian and readily affirms "that men, as they are *free agents*, have the power of *resisting*, or *opposing*, those *means*, which God, from his desire of their salvation, may see fit to use with them" (166). Nevertheless, he believes that God in his infinite wisdom, goodness, and power is capable of devising "a scheme, with reference to *all men*, which shall, in *event*, without breaking in upon their *liberty*, or using any *means* but such as are *moral* and *rational*, and therefore adjusted to their character as *moral agents*, infallibly issue in their salvation" (166–67). God is capable of soliciting a *free* response from all in the end, even if the road to this destination be long and twisting. "Now, if God *desires the salvation of all*, and Christ died that this *desire* of God might be complied with, is it credible that a *small portion* of men only should be saved in *event*?" (168).

Chauncy argues that none of the hell texts say that hell will be endless. It will certainly be painful and of long duration—being *aiōnios* (i.e., age-long), but the age to which it belongs will come to a completion when all things have been submitted to Christ and God is all in all. The aiōnial life of the righteous is indeed everlasting, but we know this not because it is described as *aiōnios* (which does not mean everlasting), but because it is *life*, a participation in Christ's own indestructible, immortal, resurrection life. The aiōnial punishment and death of the wicked is precisely *not* this. The wicked in hell are mortal, corruptible, and captive to death (286–88).

Chauncy never associated with the growing universalist movement, which he seemed to regard with some disdain,[10] but they were certainly

---

9. Arian Christology was experiencing something of a resurgence in mainstream churches in both Britain and America in this period.

10. One suspects that there was a certain social and intellectual snobbery to this, with Chauncy being a part of the establishment (his father was a prosperous merchant, his grandfather a London minister, his great grandfather was the second president of Harvard; and his mother was the daughter of a supreme court judge in Massachusetts)

aware of his book and, with the exception of the John Murray, generally appreciated the support it provided for their cause.

ISAAC DAVIS, ADAMS STREETER, CALEB RICH—
SEPARATIST UNIVERSALISTS

Chauncy was something of an oddity. The majority of the homegrown universalists were separatists who had been deeply affected by revivalism and who felt called to pursue their agendas beyond the bounds of Congregationalism.

The Great Awakening (1736–45), America's first mass revival, generated very diverse responses. Some, the so-called "Old Lights," like Charles Chauncy, vocally opposed it; others embraced it wholeheartedly, though in different ways. The born-again saints of the revival were divided between those—the so-called "New Lights," like Jonathan Edwards—who sought to renew New England Congregationalism from within and those individuals and whole congregations who sought a more radical solution, breaking away from Congregationalism (though still deeply influenced by it), and setting up new groups in which they could pursue their own "pure" revivalist faith.

The Great Awakening began to unsettle the Congregationalist hegemony, with dissenting groups like Baptists growing significantly as a result, yet Congregationalism remained resilient well into the 1770s. The crack in the dam came with the dual impact of the American Revolutionary War (1775–83), which took a toll on Congregationalism's parish system, and the mass migrations of the 1770s and 1780s to the hill country as the northern and western frontier opened up. The established church simply did not have the resources to minister to a population spread so far and so thinly, and this new fluid context created space for frontier folk to develop their Christian faith in "unauthorized" directions. Most of those who migrated to the rural hinterland had been impacted by the Evangelical revival and the conditions were ripe for the rise of radical charismatic sectarian groups led by inspired leaders.

One of these radical revivalist groups, or loose network of groups, was universalist in orientation, beginning in the early 1770s and focused in the rural hill country. Its leaders included Isaac Davis (ca. 1700–1777),

---

and well-educated, while most of the universalists were on the social margins and uneducated.

Adams Streeter (1735–86), and Caleb Rich (1750–1821). This strand of universalism is often underestimated or completely ignored, with all the attention given to Murray and Winchester. However, "the numerical and cultural center of New England Universalism was in the hill country. There Streeter, Davis, and especially Rich developed an independent form of Universalism that was embraced by thousands of rural folk."[11]

Isaac Davis was a physician from Somers, Connecticut, with radical revivalist influences. As an old man, in the 1770s, he published a universalist treatise entitled *What Love Jesus Christ Has for Sinners* (n.d.), and gathered a small, short-lived community around him, known as Davisonians.

Davis maintained that Adam's sin had brought eternal death for all humans—we all deserve to suffer in hell forever. However, Christ became sin for us and his death paid the full price for our sin, thereby providing full pardon for all the children of Adam. The Calvinist background to this system is clear. We do not know how he moved to his new theological position. It has similarities to that of John Murray, but it seems likely that he arrived at it independently of Murray.

Adams Streeter, a fellow Separatist and later a Baptist elder, was converted to universalism in 1777, perhaps under Isaac Davis. Streeter was an important preacher and shaper of the early movement, ministering in Milford and Oxford, Massachusetts, and Providence, Rhode Island, also making connections with John Murray in Boston.

More important, however, was Caleb Rich, a Massachusetts man with deep Calvinistic Baptist roots, who was led through a series of visions in 1772 to affirm the annihilation at death (rather than the eternal torment) of those predestined not to be saved. As a result, he was expelled from Warwick Baptist Church for heresy and set up his own "religious society" in 1773. This grew into several flourishing congregations in Massachusetts and New Hampshire. A further charismatic episode—a visitation from a celestial visitor in 1778—corrected the error of Rich's annihilationism and turned him toward an all-encompassing salvation. From the vision he perceived that

> [t]he atonement of Jesus Christ the Second Adam guaranteed that "the first Adam and every individual of his posterity from the beginning of this world to the end" would "truly and positively" pass "from death unto life." . . . [T]he Second Coming was

11. Marini, *Radical Sects*, 68.

fast approaching, to "sweep and cleanse . . . sin, death, hell, pain, sorrow, or evil" from the universe. On this apocalyptic note, the visitor assured Rich that he had a call "to proclaim the same gospel" and then he disappeared.[12]

What would be destroyed at death was not the sinner, but the *sinful part* of the sinner. The following day, the vision was confirmed to Rich when what felt like electricity charged through his body, causing a trembling that lasted for days. Soon after, Jesus himself appeared in a vision, clinching the authenticity of the experience to Rich.

Rich then began to fearlessly proclaim a universalist gospel, which he considered to have been directly revealed to him by God. He was ordained as minister of the general society of universalists in Richmond, Jaffrey, and Warwick in New Hampshire by Adams Streeter.

Rich was not a great preacher, but his ministry was effective in rural communities. Indeed, it was through Rich's preaching that the Baptist Hosea Ballou (1771–1852), the most influential theologian and leader in the nineteenth-century Universalist denomination, was led to embrace salvation for all. We shall return to Ballou in the next chapter.

THE RISE OF UNIVERSALISM AS A DENOMINATION

John Murray and Elhanan Winchester ministered universalism in the towns and cities, but the rural hinterland belonged to the likes of Davis, Streeter, and Rich. However, the three streams—Rellyan, Pietist, and indigenousness—discovered each other and sought to work together from early on.[13] There was friction and problems because of some of the large personalities involved,[14] because their different versions of the faith were not fully compatible, and because the universalists, especially in the rural hinterland, tended to be fierce individualists, resistant to being told what to think or do, preferring minimalism when it came to doctrinal

---

12. Marini, *Radical Sects*, 74. Rich's account is found in Rich, "Narrative of Elder Caleb Rich."

13. While the Brethren (German Baptists) remained as a distinct group (and still exist), many of them moved to join Universalist Societies.

14. Murray in particular could sometimes get tetchy about those who differed from him theologically. For instance, he regarded Rich's theology as "impious" and "blasphemous," and his preaching careless. Murray's initially warm response to Winchester too cooled somewhat when Winchester remained stuck in his non-Rellyan ways.

and ecclesial conformity. There were several abortive attempts to create a more formal coalition, one of which was the historic gathering in 1885 in Oxford, Massachusetts, with which we opened this chapter. However, each of these attempts was a step along the road to union, and by the end of the century a fledgling universalist denomination finally emerged.[15]

One can gauge the basic shape of American universalist belief at the end of the century in the carefully worded Articles of Faith (Philadelphia, 1790), penned by Dr. Benjamin Rush (1746–1813), one of the signatories of the Declaration of Independence.[16] The articles attempted to find a way of holding together Rellyan and Winchesterian universalism (notice the absence of any reference to the contentious issue of postmortem punishment). While this creed carried no authority, it does indicate where the movement was theologically located at the time.

> Section 1. OF THE HOLY SCRIPTURES. We believe the Scriptures of the Old and New Testaments to contain a revelation of the perfections and will of God, and the rule of faith and practice.
>
> Section 2. OF THE SUPREME BEING. We believe in One God, infinite in all his perfections; and that these perfections are all modifications of infinite, adorable, incomprehensible and unchangeable Love.
>
> Section 3. OF THE MEDIATOR. We believe that there is One Mediator between God and man, the man Jesus Christ, in whom dwelleth all the fulness of the Godhead bodily; who, by giving himself a ransom for all, hath redeemed them to God by his blood; and who, by the merit of his death, and the efficacy of his Spirit, will finally restore the whole human race to happiness.
>
> Section 4. OF THE HOLY GHOST. We believe in the Holy Ghost, whose office it is to make known to sinners the truth of this salvation, through the medium of the Holy Scriptures, and to reconcile the hearts of the children of men to God, and thereby dispose them to genuine holiness.
>
> Section 5. OF GOOD WORK. We believe in the obligation of the moral law, as to the rule of life; and we hold that the love

---

15. Following Russell Miller, we might see 1785 as the first official appearance of universalists as a "sect" and 1794 as the start of universalism as a denomination. Miller, *Larger Hope*, ch. 4. See too Bressler, *Universalist Movement in America*.

16. Rush, an eminent member of Philadelphia society, had moved from Calvinism to universalism under the influence of Winchester (who was a friend), Stonehouse, Siegvolck, and Chauncy.

of God manifest to man in a Redeemer, is the best means of producing obedience to that law, and promoting a holy, active and useful life.

In light of subsequent developments, the explicit trinitarian shape of the Articles is worth noting.[17] The majority of the universalists at this time were (or thought they were) trinitarian, but that had already started to change by the mid-1790s and, as we shall see, the nineteenth century saw a very rapid shift in denominational universalism toward theological unitarianism.

ADDENDUM: CATHOLIC UNIVERSALISM IN THE EIGHTEEN AND NINETEENTH CENTURIES

While belief in a final restitution slowly increased among Protestants, it remained very marginal within Catholicism until the twentieth century, when a form of "hopeful universalism" became acceptable. What we do find before this shift is individual Catholics who express hope for a wider mercy. However, such views gained nothing of the traction they began to gain in sections of Protestantism.

In the eighteenth century, for instance, Andrew Michael Ramsey (1686–1743), known as the Chevalier Ramsey, espoused universal salvation. Ramsey was a Scottish convert to Catholicism who lived the majority of his life in France and was a learned and celebrated author. He had studied under François Fénelon (Catholic archbishop and theologian) for six months and was linked to the influential Catholic mystic Madame Jeanne Guyon (1648–1717), herself sympathetic to the idea of universal

---

17. However, the Articles do not explicitly rule out unitarian interpretations of their content. This may have been a deliberate fudge, given some of the friendly relations between the universalists and various unitarian thinkers, such as J. B. Priestly.

salvation.[18] He also became interested in the Philadelphians during a visit to London around 1708.[19]

Despite his mystical bent, Ramsey also had very logical and mathematical inclinations and sought to present a rationally acceptable case for the faith. In *The Philosophical Principles of Natural and Revealed Religion* (1748/49),[20] he makes a case for (among other things) the larger hope.[21] His proposition LVIII states that "God's ultimate design in creating finite intelligences could only be to make them eternally happy in the knowledge and love of his boundless perfections (a); almighty power, wisdom and love cannot be eternally frustrated in his absolute and ultimate designs (b): therefore, God will at last pardon and re-establish in happiness all lapsed beings" (1.430).[22] He proceeds to defend this proposition at some length. Again:

18. As evidenced throughout her commentary on Revelation. See her discussions on texts in Revelation about judgment, hell, and the ever-open gates in the new Jerusalem, in Guyon, *Jeanne Guyon's Apocalyptic Universe*. Guyon believes that divine punishment/destruction/annihilation is *restorative* and not God's *final* word. Of those in the lake of fire (Rev 21:8) she writes: "Jesus Christ places the cowardly and the faithless in the ranks of the worst criminals that are excluded from his grace, at least *as long as their crimes remain*. The worst sinner can *convert* and become the greatest saint. But those with these vices are not in God's interior kingdom without *leaving the vice*" (161, italics mine). One can thus exit from the lake. She sees those once excluded as as entering into the new Jerusalem, having been transformed by Christ: "The *pearls which are the twelve gates* show the purity of the interior voice that gives entry to all and receives the different persons. The exterior of the church has uniformity of faith and sentiments in *one wall*. Through the gates will come Jews, Turks, barbarians, infidels, heretics, schismatic, bad Christians, false Catholics, impious, and atheists. All will come from different countries and laws and religions without the doors changing for their reception. They will be received not only in the wall, which is the exterior of the church, and therefore the same devotees of today. But they enter into the same city, that is to say, they participate in his Spirit, they become all *interiors*. All will be led by the Holy Spirit and all will be placed in the truth" (167). Her vision of God's ultimate triumph requires the salvation and deification of all people: "All must be reduced to unity, so that Jesus Christ reigns throughout the universe and that he consummates the divine marriage with human nature. Then there will only be the will of God" (139).

19. McClymond, *Devil's Redemption*, 423.

20. The book sets out to argue that natural reason leads us to embrace a version of classical theism and that this is fully consistent with revealed Christian religion, which is also most reasonable.

21. His works were read and appreciated by Protestant universalists, despite their anti-Catholic sentiments.

22. The following in-text citations in this section on Ramsey are from *Philosophical Principles*, unless otherwise stated.

As God however, cannot be eternally frustrated in his designs; as finite impotence, folly, and malice cannot for ever surmount infinite power, wisdom, and goodness; as the sacrifice of the Lamb slain cannot be for ever void and of no effect; reprobate souls and angels cannot be ever inconvertible, nor God unappeaseable, nor moral and physical evil undestructible. All stains, blots, and imperfections in the work of infinite power, wisdom, and goodness must be for ever washed out; otherwise God would not have an absolute empire over the heart; he would not act according to the laws of eternal wisdom; he would not love essential wisdom, goodness, and justice. Wherefore infernal punishments must at last cease, and all lapsed beings be at length pardoned and re-established in a permanent state of happiness and glory, never to fall again. This is the end and consummation of all things, and the design of all God's promises and punishments. If he does not accomplish this end sooner by converting all lapsed beings, it is not because he will not; but because he cannot do it in a permanent and efficacious manner without doing violence to their liberty, destroying their free natures, and thereby frustrating for ever the eternal designs of his wisdom, which were to make intellectual beings happy by love and by free love, their supreme felicity. (1.491–92)

The reference above to God's soliciting a free response raises a standard objection. What if we choose to resist God forever? But, argues Ramey, God can win us over without violating our freedom. How? Because we are created to desire happiness and that happiness is only found in rightly relating with God, who made us for himself. To resist God leads to our unhappiness and no creature can continue to choose against its own deepest created nature and desires. Indeed, hell is the natural consequence of our choosing to defy God, who is in reality our own deepest inclination. However, finite creatures cannot resist the infinite God and their own created desires, buried as they may be under sin, forever (1.430–31). Even those in hell will be released as soon as they turn back to the divine source (1.435).

God will be all in all so God's providential plan "cannot be bounded and partial, it must be extensive and universal; it must embrace all beings, all times, and all places" (2.325). Ramsey explicitly endorses Origen's theology, though he seeks to purge the Origenian heritage by arguing that Origen never endorsed the preexistence of souls decried by the fifth ecumenical council. On this matter, Ramsey was arguably a more nuanced interpreter of Origen than some of the Cambridge Platonists (of whose work he was aware).

As McClymond observes, Ramsey's case for universalism is *a priori*, arguing from first principles to theological conclusions, and it bypasses a discussion of Scripture and de-emphasizes Christology.[23] This does not invalidate his arguments for universal salvation, which may still be effective and have a continuing place in a universalist apologetic, but it would make them inadequate for a Christian theology of universal salvation.

In the nineteenth-century Catholic Church, the possibility of universal salvation was discussed more by philosophers and poets than by theologians.[24] However, there were some exceptions. For example, Saint Thérèse of Lisieux, Doctor of the Catholic Church, seems to have flirted with a hope for universal salvation. In a Christmas comedy for her fellow nuns, *Les anges à la crèche de Jésus* (*The Angels at Jesus' Crib*, 1894), she imagines a debate between the infant Jesus and the angel of the final judgment. The latter obviously insists on the necessity of the punishment of sinners ("Oublies–tu donc, Jésus, beauté suprême! / Que le pécheur doit être enfin puni?"), but Jesus remarks that it is not the angel who will judge everybody, but Jesus himself, whose blood purifies sinners ("Celui qui jugera le monde / C'est moi, que l'on nomme Jésus. / De mon sang la rosée féconde / Purifiera tous mes élus"). Jesus adds that he loves all souls very deeply and that in the end *every soul will be forgiven* ("j'aime les âmes / Je les aime d'un grand amour . . . toute âme obtiendra son pardon").

Given the minimal amount of work on universalism among Catholics before the twentieth century, and the fact that scholarship has yet to devote much attention to what little interest there was, our focus for the rest of this book will be on Protestantism.

---

23. McClymond, *Devil's Redemption*, 422–27. Though McClymond overstates his case when he says that the "universal return to God, as Ramsey envisages it, will take place by human initiative and is not dependent on a divine-human mediator or savior figure" (424); again, Christ "seemingly played no role in his understanding of human salvation" (426). The passage quoted above uses the following argument for universalism: "the sacrifice of the Lamb slain cannot be for ever void and of no effect." So the accusation of Ramsey's bypassing the savior is at least something of an exaggeration. That said, he does develop his case for universalism in a way that merely glances in the direction of Jesus. This contrasts with Jeanne Guyon, one of his inspirations, whose vision of universal salvation was deeply biblical and Christ-centered.

24. See Müller, "Die Idee," 12–14 (on France); 15–16 (on Italy).

Part III

The Nineteenth Century
Enlightenment, Romanticism,
and Universal Salvation

9

The Enlightenment, Hosea Ballou, and Denominational Universalism in America

THE UNIVERSALIST MOVEMENT OF the eighteenth century was, for the most part, trinitarian in its view of God. There were deviations from this—John Murray was a modalist (though he may not have been aware, and probably wouldn't have cared that his views deviated from Christian orthodoxy),[1] George Stonehouse seems (idiosyncratically) to have been binitarian, and Charles Chauncy was a unitarian, with an Arian Christology (as were more than a few Congregationalists). But, while their works were read, Chauncy and Stonehouse were never part of the movement in America and their views on the Trinity were unusual for universalists. More representative was Elhanan Winchester, whose doctrine of God and of Jesus was that of mainstream Christian orthodoxy. Yet, by the end of the first decade of the nineteenth century, the new Universalist denomination was almost entirely unitarian in its theology.[2] How did this happen?

It is not easy to trace the shift in any detail, but the most important factors seem to have been the New England (and New York) context within

---

1. E.g., Murray, *Letters and Sketches of Sermons*, 1.254.

2. There were few exceptions. "After Murray's death in 1815 the only clergy known to be preaching trinitarian universalism were Paul Dean in Boston and [Edward] Mitchell in New York—and he was never in formal fellowship" (Miller, *Larger Hope*, 1.105). In fact, Dean was actually a modalist, like his mentor John Murray. A more unusual exception is First Universalist Church in Providence, Rhode Island (founded in 1821). To this day it is trinitarian and publicly affirms both the Apostles' Creed and the Nicene Creed.

which the movement grew and the influence of Hosea Ballou.[3] Regarding the former, unitarian theology was already gaining traction within the established churches in Massachusetts, Maine, and New Hampshire, and at Harvard, the oldest college in the area. The idea was out there and had some respectability. Regarding the latter, Ballou was a very popular preacher in the movement and in 1795 he preached his first unitarian sermon, making a break from the trinitarianism of his youth. He now considered the doctrine of the Trinity to be contrary to both reason and Scripture and had no qualms about ridiculing it and developing a unitarian alternative. Ballou's influence in the denomination—especially after the publication of his most important work, *A Treatise on Atonement*, in 1805—was huge, and very quickly other preachers and churches fell into line with this new theology. Some, like John and Judith Murray, fiercely kicked against this change of theological direction, but to no avail.[4]

Interestingly, a similar shift took place back in England.[5] In 1794, Elhanan Winchester had left his church in London in the pastoral care of William Vidler (1758–1816), a Calvinistic Baptist minister from Sussex, who had converted to universalism through reading Winchester's work. Vidler, like Winchester, had been trinitarian. However, he was converted to a unitarian view of God by Richard Wright[6] some time between 1798 and 1802, and he enthusiastically led the Parliament Court congregation down that road. The move was very divisive and split the congregation, resulting in the trinitarians leaving. Vidler brought the church into the General (i.e., Arminian) Baptist network in 1802. That entire branch of Baptists was shifting in universalist and unitarian directions, and by 1815 its General Assembly reported on "the success of Unitarianism which,

3. See Miller, *Larger Hope*, vol. 1, chap. 6.

4. In one awkward incident in 1798, Ballou was filling the pulpit in Boston for John Murray while Murray was away. He preached a subordinationist Christology from 1 Corinthians 15:26–28. Judith Murray was incensed and sent a message to be read out after the closing prayer declaring, "I wish to give notice that the doctrine preached here this afternoon is not the doctrine which is usually preached in this house." (This was seen as a very rude thing to do and the parish committee later apologized to Ballou.) John Murray was candid in his appreciation of Ballou, but also in his disagreement. Murray did not invite Ballou to the installation of Edward Mitchell as Murray's (brief) successor in Boston in 1810. He expressed his joy at the absence of "a Socinian, Deistical, Sadducean Universalist"—presumably Ballou! (This is as reported in a letter by George Richards to Edwin Turner of Salem.)

5. McClymond, *Devil's Redemption*, 595–98.

6. Richard Wright was the minister of the General Baptist Church in Wisbech, East Anglia.

with the exception of Baptism, may surely be called the cause of the General Baptists."[7] This strand of the British Baptist tradition gradually faded and died away.[8]

Thus it was that universalism, which in Christian circles had almost always been trinitarian before this point, became associated in the minds of many with unitarian theology. The ground for the theological shift was prepared by the movement's focus on individual Spirit-filled believers interpreting Scripture for themselves and its ultra-reformational hostility to the authority of church tradition. This did not automatically lead to unitarian theology, but it opened people up to unconventional interpretations of the Bible and an indifference toward—even a mischievous delight in—denying orthodox doctrine in the pursuit of a "pure" Christianity.

Parallel with this anti-traditional mode of Christianity was the anti-traditionalism of the eighteenth-century Enlightenment, which extoled the authority of reason as the route to truth. The Enlightenment's focus on reason had impacted earlier universalists,[9] as it had Evangelicals more generally, but with Hosea Ballou there came a notable shift in emphasis from a focus on Scripture and spiritual experiences to one on Scripture *and reason*. Ballou held fast to the inspiration and authority of the Bible to his dying day, but he also placed a great stress on rational argument. The Bible must be interpreted, he said, in the light of reason. And to him the doctrine of the Trinity was patently irrational.

This focus on the importance of reason had a major impact on denominational universalism and was to shape its direction from the very start, and not merely in relation to the Trinity. More than anyone else, it was Ballou who directed the movement in this way.

Given the huge importance of Hosea Ballou, we shall use his story and theology as a convenient window through which to view changes within the wider Universalist denomination.

7. Quoted in Brown, *English Baptists*, 108.

8. The drift toward heterodoxy among the General Baptists led Dan Taylor to break away and set up the New Connexion of General Baptists. This orthodox strand of Arminian Baptists later merged with the Calvinistic Baptists to form the Baptist Union.

9. See, for instance, Elhanan Winchester's *Defence of Revelation* (1796), a published response to Thomas Paine's infamous *Age of Reason* (1794).

HOSEA BALLOU (1771–1852)

Hosea Ballou was born into the family of a poor Baptist preacher in Richmond, rural New Hampshire, in 1771.[10] Hosea's mother died before he was two, so Maturin, his father, raised his eleven children alone. The home was a strict Calvinist household, but not one that lacked love.

Hosea had no formal education as a child as there was no school, so he had to teach himself to read and write. From his youth he was very inquisitive and possessed a sharp mind. In particular, he was fascinated with theological issues and was constantly questioning the "givens" of the Calvinist theology he had inherited.

When Hosea was seven or eight, Caleb Rich began preaching the universalist message around Richmond, and after winning some converts he became the minister of a universalist society spread across Warwick (his home base), Richmond, and Jaffrey. So Hosea would have become aware of this religious opinion as a child, not least because some of his distant relatives were among Rich's converts.

Ballou had long struggled with the Calvinist doctrine of reprobation and so the universalist alternative intrigued him, though his instinct was to treat it as suspect. He spent many hours in his late teenage years debating the issue with Caleb Rich, seeking to expose its flaws, yet the issue would not let his mind rest.

In 1789, when Ballou was nineteen, he was converted by two Baptist evangelists and baptized, yet his doubts about Calvinism persisted. He decided to look more closely at the Bible in relation to the issue of the scope of salvation and eventually found himself more and more persuaded that

---

10. Sources on Ballou include Ballou, *Biography of Rev. Hosea Ballou* (though this was written from the perspective of a devoted son immediately upon the death of his father); Whittemore, *Life of Rev. Hosea Ballou* (which is tedious and suffers from not knowing what to leave out); Safford, *Hosea Ballou*; Cassara, *Hosea Ballou* (far and away the best biography); Miller, *Larger Hope*, vol. 1, ch. 6 (with a focus on theology).

God would indeed save all people. For this he was excommunicated by the Baptist church in Richmond.

He enrolled himself in school to catch up on the education missed in his childhood and then set off to become an itinerant universalist preacher.[11] He had already started to receive a good reputation as a preacher by 1794, when, aged twenty, Hosea attended the General Convention of Universalists in Oxford, Massachusetts. Here he was unexpectedly ordained. Elhanan Winchester, in his sermon on the last day of the convention, grabbed a Bible and pressed it against Ballou's chest, declaring, "Brother Ballou, I press to your heart the written Jehovah!" Ballou was then charged to serve as an ordained minister, much to his surprise. From that point on, the Rev. Ballou devoted himself totally to the ministry of itinerant preaching, with his reputation growing year by year.

His first pastorate was over three churches in Vermont (1803–9), followed by Portsmouth, New Hampshire (1809–15), Salem, Massachusetts (1815–17), and finally Boston's newly formed Second Society of Universalists (1817–52), where he ministered for almost thirty-five years.[12] Though he now worked from fixed church bases, he still travelled widely on preached tours. He was also involved in various denominational matters: playing a key role in the annual General Convention (from 1791 onward); helping to draw up the Winchester Profession of Faith (1803), the closest the universalists got to a formal creed;[13] helping compile a new hymn book (1808);[14] publishing numerous influential books; co-launching, editing, and writing for *The Universalist Magazine* (1819–20), which became an important means of propagating the faith, and other universalist magazines;[15] and, most importantly, drawing thousands to universalism through his preaching ministry over the decades. He was a fearless apologist for the universalist faith and he loved to debate—in print and face-to-face—with ministers who took traditional positions.

11. Ballou always prepared his sermons, but delivered them extempore, without any notes.

12. There were always somewhat awkward relations with Paul Dean, John Murray's successor at the First Society of Universalists.

13. Formal creeds were regarded with great suspicion by the universalists, but the pragmatic situation made it prudent. The Winchester Profession, accepted at Winchester, New Hampshire, was a modification of the 1790 Philadelphia Articles. It was the "profession" of the denomination throughout the nineteenth century.

14. A complete flop.

15. *The Universalist Expositor* (1830–31) and *Expositor and Universalist Review* (1833–40).

Ballou was always his own man when it came to theological matters. He did not replicate the theological systems of any of the "founding fathers" of American universalism, but drew on eclectic influences to craft his own system. And his thought was not static, but continued to develop, such that on several issues one can trace shifts—some gradual, some sudden; most early, but some late. The major period of theological reconfiguring took place between 1790 and 1805 when his seminal *A Treatise on Atonement* was published.

One can easily see the influences of universalists like Rich, Winchester, and perhaps especially Chauncy,[16] and unitarians like Joseph Priestly, on Ballou's thought, but one of the more surprising inspirations was the work of deists like Ethan Allen, whose *Reason: The Only Oracle of Man* (1784) was a blistering attack on Christianity in the name of reason. This book deeply impacted Ballou—one can see, for instance, Allen's arguments against the Trinity replicated in Ballou's work. Of course, Hosea never embraced Allen's deism nor his rejection of the Bible, but the book forged his lifelong commitment to the authority of reason. Ernest Cassara considers Allen's book to be Ballou's likely introduction to unitarianism and the spark that forced him to rethink the atonement.[17]

A Treatise on the Atonement (1805, 1832)

Ballou's most influential publication was *A Treatise on the Atonement*, which was the culmination of the main phase of his theological rethinking. Its divergences from previous universalist books and its widespread impact justify us outlining his argument. The discussion proceeds in three stages from an analysis of sin (the illness), through atonement (the cure), to universal salvation (the effects of the cure).[18]

Part 1. Sin (15–70)

The first section considers the nature, the causes, and the effects of sin.

16. In, for instance, his unitarianism, his Arian Christology, his focus on God's commitment to "happify" human beings, his notion that sin causes misery to the sinner.

17. Cassara, *Hosea Ballou*, ch. 5.

18. The page numbers in this section come from the 1812 reprint edition of the *Treatise on the Atonement*.

The nature of sin (15–24). Intention plays a critical role in Ballou's understanding of sin—it is an evil intention that constitutes an evil action. Sin is a deliberate violation by an agent of what that agent believes is a moral law. Now, we are finite creatures so, of course, our understanding of the moral good is limited, as well as our understanding of the particulars of any specific situation in which we choose to act or of the consequences of our actions. Our evil intentions are finite as are the consequences of our actions. For sin to be infinite would require us to violate an infinite moral law, but such a law would be beyond our comprehension, and thus beyond our ability to violate. Sin is as finite as the agents that cause it.

Now the mainstream Western tradition in Ballou's day saw sin as infinite on the grounds that it is committed again the infinite law of the infinite God. As such it is infinitely bad and deserves an infinite punishment (i.e., everlasting hell). This view Ballou sets out to expose as irrational by means of a fleet of arguments.

Sin is usually declared infinite on the grounds that it violates God's infinite will for creation. However, says Ballou, this argument won't work. If God is infinite in power and wisdom, then *nothing violates his will—not even sin*. If it did, God would only have finite power and wisdom, and violating his will would incur only *finite* demerit. Ballou's God is so ultra-sovereign that even human sin is part of God's predetermined will, a temporary part of the overall plan leading to final salvation. God's intentions for the events that happen are for the ultimate good of creatures and as such those events are not evil acts of God, but good acts, even if they are painful and even if God often works through the acts of human agents whose intentions, and thus whose acts, are evil.[19]

The doctrine of infinite sin has a series of unpalatable consequences. If sin is infinite then nothing is greater than it, not even divine goodness or love or power or God himself. If sin is infinite it has infinite consequences that will torment not only creatures, but also God, forever. If every sin is infinite and every sin is as bad as every other, "the smallest

---

19. One theme that remained constant throughout his life was the conviction inherited from his Calvinist roots and reinforced by Ferdinand Olivier Petitpierre's book *Thoughts on the Divine Goodness* (Amsterdam, 1786) that God was *completely* sovereign over every single event in the history of creation. *Nothing* happens that has not been ordained by God. In this he found common ground with Relly and Murray, and disagreed with Stonehouse, Chauncy, and Winchester, among others. To his mind, theological determinism was the guarantee that God would achieve his purpose to save all people.

offence against the good of society, is equal to *blasphemy* against the Holy Ghost" (19). Against this is the clear teaching of Scripture that some sins are worse than others (Matt 12:31; 1 John 5:16).

The causes of sin (24–56). Ballou dismisses the traditional Christian story that the origins of sin are found in the fall of rebel angels. This, he says, simply knocks the problem back a level, rather than explaining anything—we now have to explain Lucifer's sin and find ourselves tied in knots when we attempt to. (In fact, Ballou does not even believe in the existence of the devil, except as a symbol of the carnal mind, not unlike Gerrard Winstanley.)

Ballou develops his own theological anthropology in which *Christ* was the image of God granted rule over creation. In Genesis 1, humanity was created in the image of God in that humanity was created in Christ, the heavenly man. This, however, was *before* man was formed from the dust of the ground. So here we have a version of the preexistence of human souls prior to their enfleshment. When God sends humans to be embodied, they are thereby constituted as mortal creatures with natural passions and limited self-knowledge. Thus, humans have a dual nature: a heavenly nature (after Christ) and an earthly nature. The latter is the origin of our natural appetites, the satisfaction of which can never satisfy "the heavenly stranger within" (32). The earthly mind of humans can only dimly grasp the moral law impressed on it in a shadow-like way by the heavenly self. Our dual existence is one of conflict between the passions arising from our embodied nature and the heavenly self.

The story of the garden of Eden is not literal history, but a figurative story to communicate the ideas explained above. There the carnal human mind (symbolized by the serpent) is hostile to God and cannot submit to God's law and deceives us from the law of the spirit of life in Christ (the tree of life) to indulge the fleshly nature (the tree of knowledge). Notice that for Ballou, this situation of human conflict with sin is *not* a result of a fall from a state of perfection, but is *the condition in which we exist by virtue of being embodied beings.* God, in his wisdom and for the ultimate good of his creatures, formed Adam from the dust subject to struggle and frustration and death. The struggle and the sin were all part of the bigger plan. Ballou-the-determinist does not flinch from seeing God as the ultimate cause of human sin. Though "the immediate causes of sin are found in our natural constitutions" (41), the appetites and passions and confusions that arise from embodiment. *We are not mortal because we sin, but sin because we are mortal.*

The effects of sin (56–70). For Ballou, the consequences of sin are experienced by sinners in *this life* in the wounded conscience: "There gnaws the worm that never dies, there burns the fire that is never quenched. A consciousness of guilt destroys all the *expected* comforts, and pleasures of sin" (56). He rejected the notion that sin can bring happiness in the short term, but will bring disaster in the afterlife. Sin brings disaster *now*. It only offers false promise, for *by its very nature* it torments the soul. We desire to sin, but only because we have been deceived into thinking it will make us happy. For as long as a soul sins, it remains in spiritual death.

Now our dual-natured humanity is such that in our earthly nature, formed in Adam, we *cannot* obey the law of God, but in our heavenly nature, created in Christ, we are in perfect conformity to the divine law. Both of these claims are true of human beings now.

Part 2. Atonement (71–123)

Three false views of atonement (71–104). Ballou begins with an attempt to pull apart some of the main Protestant atonement theories of the day in order to set his own account up as an alternative. The first "false" view of atonement is the Calvinist view of penal substitution, the mainstream Evangelical view (71–87). Ballou argues that we must reject any suggestion that God punished Jesus for our sins in order to clear our debt. His rejection of penal substitution—a view he tries to demonstrate as irrational and offensive—marks another shift within American universalist theology, which previously had been largely sympathetic to the view; indeed, in its Rellyan versions it had made the view *pivotal* to its universalism.

The second "false" view is that of Hugo Grotius, which was held in New England by the followers of Samuel Hopkins (1721–1803) (87–97). Here the death of Jesus is simply a display of the justice of God in the punishment of sin. Christ suffers the alleged infinite penalty of the law, satisfying justice. In the atonement, God acts for the display of his own glory, rather than for the good of the creature as such.

The third "false" view is that Christ's death dealt with the original sin of all humans forever, but not the actual sins (97–104). This was a view held by some of the Arminians in New England. Thus, no one will ever suffer for the sin inherited from Adam; but this simply places humanity in the position of being on probation, and if people commit actual sins of their own they will be judged and condemned for them, unless they repent. So the atonement put all people into a position in which they may *possibly* be saved (if they avoid sin or be sure to repent of it all), but there are no guarantees for anyone.

The necessity of atonement (104–16). A key move Ballou makes in setting out his own account of atonement is to argue that atonement is not made in order to change God's orientation to us, but our orientation to God. It is not *God* that needs to be reconciled to us; *we* need to be reconciled to God. Sin made Adam mistakenly think of God as his enemy (so he hides from God) and that good works could reconcile God back to him (he covers himself with self-made leaf garments). But God's attitude to Adam has not changed: God calls to him, clothes him, and promises that the woman's seed will crush the cursed serpent's head. God still cares for humanity as a father. "As God was not the unreconciled party, no atonement was necessary for his reconciliation" (106). Rather, the atonement is necessary *to change us*—to renew humanity's love for God. The atoning work of Christ therefore "was the *effect*, and not the *cause* of God's love to man" (106). God needs no blood sacrifice to reconcile himself to humanity. Such a notion is horrific and tends to breed Christians who imitate their God by hating and persecuting "sinners."

Humans sold in slavery to sin cannot see clearly and are dissatisfied with God. Consciousness of sin and distorted knowledge of God make God appear to us as angry. Atonement helps us to see God as he really is toward us. The death of Christ is, in other words, an attestation of God's unchanging love for sinners. It is a revelation of divine love aimed at changing our perceptions of the divine and overcoming the enmity against God lodged in the human heart. "[T]he manifestation of God's love to us, causes us to love him, and brings us to a renewal of love" (124).

Ballou insists that "[w]ithout atonement, God's glorious design, in the everlasting welfare of his offspring, man, could never be effected" (112), but he does not make clear why God could not have achieved his goal of revealing his true self to humanity and renewing our love for him apart from Christ's death. He does claim that God has not given to anyone bar Christ the ability to effect reconciliation, but his argument for this is simply that if God had done so he would not have needed to send Christ (121–22).

Jesus, the Mediator who atones (116–23). As a unitarian, Ballou does not believe that Christ is the second person of the Trinity. Christ is the supreme created being—"the first human soul which was *created*, as Adam was the first man that was formed" (119). He is the original image of God, and like an ambassador he represents God in his words and actions. As such he is able to perform atonement by functioning—in his official role (not in his being)—in the place of God.

The Nature of Atonement (123–40). Jesus has the power to remove the veil of darkness from our hearts and to enable us to properly perceive both God and the world, thereby causing us to love God and to hate sin. (Christians who think God is an enemy who needs pacifying and who should be served out of duty have clearly not yet received the enlightening atoning work of Christ, but remain in darkness.)

Part 3. The consequences of atonement: universal salvation (140–236)

Atonement will eventually produce "the *universal holiness* and *happiness* of mankind" (141). God created humanity in Christ then formed them in flesh and blood in Adam. This phase of human existence in which spirit and flesh battle and in which sin makes us captives is overcome in atonement. God's grand plan is to restore humanity "back from his *formed* state . . . to his original *created* state" (141). And *nothing* can even threaten, let alone thwart, God's sovereign purposes.

Ballou seeks to dismantle a range of theological defenses of hell and of limited salvation. To take an example, in response to those who say that God creates hell so that those in heaven can better appreciate the blessings they have, Ballou asks us to imagine a father with enough provisions to keep his ten children all alive and happy. "Which way would good sense and parental affection chuse, either to feed five to the full, and starve the rest to death, that their *dying groans* might give the others a *better appetite*, and *their food* a *good relish*, or to let them all be hungry enough to relish their food well, and all alike partake of it?" (145).

Ballou also makes some positive arguments against eternal hell. For instance, Ballou's view is that misery is parasitic upon sin. If sin ceased to exist, then misery would cease to exist. So, for God to perpetuate sorrow and pain for eternity in hell would require him not to defeat sin, but to perpetuate it for eternity by having people sin endlessly. Such a view, he says, is absurd.

Furthermore, Christ's happiness will not be complete until "he see the travail of his soul and be satisfied" (Isa 53:11). That is to say, Christ remains unsatisfied until all for whom he died come to share in salvation; and if hell is forever then he will never have his happiness complete. Nor will the redeemed enjoy complete happiness if their fellow human beings remain in everlasting misery. Eternal hell thus forever takes the shine off the final joy of Christ and the redeemed.

To those who believe that the saints will rejoice in the justice of hell, he replies, "If perfect reconciliation to God will effect complete happiness at the sight of human misery, the more we are reconciled to God, the more satisfaction we should take in seeing our fellow creatures miserable! Then, those, who can look on men in distress, with the least sorrow, are the most reconciled to divine goodness; and those who feel the most sorrow at the afflictions of their fellow men, are the most perverse and wicked!" (183). Even if hell was divine justice, we do not need eternal misery to appreciate divine justice. Indeed, what kind of judge would take *delight* in sentencing sinners to death! Only a disgusting one. "I had rather be possessed of that *sympathy* which causes me to *feel* for *another*, than to enjoy an *unsocial pleasure* in a *frosty heaven* of *misanthropy!*" (189).

Ballou tries to show that many of the biblical texts about the fires of hell are aimed at salvation. His hermeneutical key for understanding all texts about the fire that causes suffering to the wicked is 1 Corinthians 3:15: "If any man's works shall be burnt, he shall suffer loss, but he himself shall be saved, yet so as by fire." This fire has the power of salvation, and it is this fire that Ballou sees whenever Scripture speaks of the fire of divine judgment (154). Ballou's biblical exegesis, while clearly very much his own, bears similarities to the allegorical exegesis of John Murray. Ultimately, what is destroyed is the sinful Adamic nature (the hay, wood, and stubble), not the sinner.

Hell is the state in which the human sinful condition meets the fire of divine revelation. He likens it to a traveler who rests in a dark cave for the night, unaware that it is filled with poisonous snakes. He is unperturbed by the snakes until the sun rises in the morning, and by its light he sees the serpents and is deeply distressed. But it is not the light of heaven that torments him; it is the snakes. The light simply enables him to see them as they are. So too, God's divine fire reveals to us the nature of our sin and fills us with torment (161). *This* is hell.

He seeks to build a positive biblical case for universalism from the by-now familiar proof texts. Some of his key texts, however, are a little more unusual. For instance, Psalm 72:11, which says "Yea, all kings shall fall down before him; all nations shall serve him." Such submission and service, he argues, cannot take place if most kings and nations exist in endless rebellion in hell. On the contrary, Scripture teaches that all people come from God, that God wills all to be saved, that Christ died to save everyone, and that God "works all things after the council of his own will" (Eph 1:11). So we know God has revealed his will on this matter—that all should be "holy and happy" in the end—and we know that he will accomplish all of his purposes. QED.

> If the servants of Christ here on earth desire the *increase* in *holiness*, and the *decrease* of *sin*, which would be most agreeable to such a desire, the belief, that the greatest part of mankind will grow *more* and *more sinful* to *all eternity;* or, to believe, that *sin* will continually *decrease*, and *righteousness increase*, until the former is wholly *destroyed*, and the latter becomes *universal?* (218)

In 1832, Ballou published a revision of the *Treatise*. By this time his thinking had moved on, so he cut various passages and rewrote others in some significant ways. Ernest Cassara identifies the following changes:[20]

1. Ballou moves away from the somewhat fanciful claim that God first created humans in Christ (spirit) and then formed them in Adam (flesh), though he still affirms that humans are both of heaven and of the dust, and he still sees the cause of sin as linked with the conditions of embodiment.

2. He now denies Christ's preexistence, perhaps under the influence of the writings of Joseph Priestly, though he still believes that God invested Christ with the power necessary to make atonement.

3. On the issue of hell texts, he now interprets them as references to the destruction of Jerusalem in 70 AD, rather than to the destruction of the Adamic nature.

So even though Ballou's major theological reconfiguration was complete by 1805, he continued to develop his thought, sometimes in significant ways.

The Restorationist controversy (1817–31)

One of the issues that had divided the movement from the start was the matter of punishment in the afterlife. This issue was to raise its head again and became a significant controversy within the young denomination.

20. Cassara, *Hosea Ballou*, 134–35.

Ballou was somewhat undecided on the issue for some years. In some correspondence from 1797 he denied future punishment, then later changed his mind and affirmed it. Very unusually for a universalist book, his *Atonement* volume in 1805 did not even raise, let alone seek to answer, the question, reflecting his ambivalence. A key turning point came with a series of letters between Ballou and his friend Edward Turner, published in *The Gospel Visitant* from 1817–18. The aim of the letters was to show both sides of the question so readers could better appreciate the issues. Ballou let Turner pick which side to defend. Turner picked the view that the wicked would be punished in the afterlife and Ballou therefore argued against it. This exercise forced Hosea to think through his own position more carefully, and as a result he became forever convinced that there would indeed be no suffering for anyone after death.

The traditional universalist view, defended by Turner, became known as restorationism, while Ballou's view became known as ultra-universalism. Ballou had stumbled his way toward ultra-universalism over a period of years, but it was really the logical outworking of the perspectives he defended in his *Treatise* in 1805, as we shall see.

After the published debate, Ballou then started preaching ultra-universalism at his Boston church, though he was much more restrained in *The Universalist Magazine*. However, when he stepped down from editing the magazine in 1820, his successor encouraged regular discussion on the restorationist issue, first in the main articles and then in the letters pages. Thus, the temperate debate sparked by Ballou and Turner's original correspondence was fanned into flame and then a forest fire within the denomination, with key pastors lining up on both sides. The whole discussion became very hot-tempered, with personalities playing as strong a role as theology in the disputes. In the end, after several twists and turns, a small group of eight restorationist pastors left and set up their own short-lived society in 1831. Most of the restorationists chose to stay, wounds were healed, and things settled down.

There is some irony in the fact that, while Ballou's ultra-universalism had come to dominate within the denomination in the 1830s, its triumph was short-lived, and even before he died in 1852 restorationism had become the dominant view again; by the end of the century, ultra-universalism was virtually extinct among the Universalists. But Ballou never gave up his ultra-universalism and published his mature thoughts on the matter in *An Examination of the Doctrine of Future Retribution* in 1834.

In understanding Ballou's view, we need to make clear that while it may seem superficially similar to Relly's and Murray's, it was, in fact, very different. First of all, it was different in that Rellyans were prepared to see some suffering for people after death—albeit self-inflicted mental wounds resulting from their ignorance of the fact that God has redeemed them, rather than punishments from God. Ballou saw no suffering of any kind after death, which earned his position the name "death and glory." Second of all, it was different because the rationale behind the view was completely unlike that of the Rellyans. They denied punishment after death because of their view of the atonement as a universal penal substitution. We have seen, however, that Ballou vigorously rejected this model of atonement. His reason for denying postmortem pains was very different.

Ballou argued that teaching about future rewards and punishments is actually ineffective as a motivation for good living. Time and time again people show that they will act in a way that they believe will bring them pleasure in this life, even if it is something that they are told will bring them misery in the next. So threatening hell is morally *ineffective*. Threats of hell also fail to generate love for the good, creating, at best, fear. They are also are *pernicious*, for they present us a view of God that is "unlovely and unworthy of being loved."[21]

Ballou believed that sin generates misery *here and now* and that righteousness brings joy *here and now*. If people are to be motivated to live well, they need to learn to appreciate that sin only falsely promises a joy that it cannot really deliver, that sin is in fact inherently horrible. When people grasp this, they will be sufficiently motivated to live godly lives.

Ballou sought to show that the Bible only speaks of suffering for sin in this life. Beginning in Eden, he argues that Adam was not threatened with afterlife punishment. Continuing through the Old Testament, he seeks to show that it cannot be found there either. Jesus is then interpreted against the background of OT prophetic discourse, speaking symbolically of punishment in this world, with gehenna referring not to hell, but to the destruction of Jerusalem. The warnings of coming judgment in the Epistles are also seen in this way.

The reason why suffering ends at death is fundamentally tied up with Ballou's anthropology and his understanding of sin. Suffering for sin only exists for as long as one is sinning. Once one ceases to sin and asks

---

21. Ballou, *Examination of the Doctrine of Future Retribution*, 24.

for forgiveness, suffering vanishes too. Now sin arises from the human condition of embodiment. But once the body is dissolved in death, then all carnal desire ceases and all sin ceases. Consequently, all suffering for sin is banished. Ballou's theological system cannot find a place for suffering in the afterlife. For it to continue would require sin to continue, which would create all sorts of theological problems for him.

Ballou's end

Ballou was a revered and loved patriarch within the denomination by the time he died in 1852. When he began his ministry, the Universalists were a small and despised group, but that changed dramatically.

> By 1840 the faith was prospering in all the states and territories of the young nation. There were almost seven hundred societies, with 311 preachers—and these figures were to almost double in the remaining dozen years of Ballou's life. At his death there would be more than 800,000 adherents to the faith. How things had changed since his young manhood, when a handful of preachers served the faithful.[22]

One of the changes within the movement was already beginning to make itself felt before Ballou's death: from the late 1840s, the impact of German higher critical approaches to the Bible was seen among the younger preachers. Ballou and many in the older generation were unhappy about such skepticism toward Gospel miracles and undermining of biblical authority. He felt that the faith would be damaged by such views, and for a while the new thinking was held at bay.

THE UNIVERSALIST DENOMINATION IN THE SECOND HALF OF THE NINETEENTH CENTURY

The history of the Universalist denomination is recounted in numerous studies, and there is a lot that could be said.[23] Our focus in this book, however, is on the theology of key individuals, with a particular focus

---

22. Cassara, *Hosea Ballou*, 151.

23. Far and away the most thorough study is Miller, *Larger Hope*; but see also Cassara, *Universalism in America*; Williams, *American Universalism*; Eddy, *Universalism in America*; Bressler, *Universalist Movement in America, 1770–1880* and the numerous helpful articles on the Online Dictionary of Unitarian and Universalist Biography.

on mainstream Christian orthodoxy. Thus, having considered the transitional figure of Ballou, we shall take our leave of the denomination, given that it placed itself outside Christian orthodoxy and that its history is already easily available. Nevertheless, it would be negligent not to gesture at some of the significant themes and trends among the Universalists over the rest of the nineteenth century and on into the twentieth.

Universalists were very active in various social and political causes. "The emphasis in the 1840s and 1850s and for many decades to follow was placed not so much on theological speculation as on the practical and moral side of Universalism, and the translation of its principles into social action."[24] Their belief in the radical equality of all people before God had implications beyond the doctrine of hell. For instance, they were strongly democratic and Republican in their politics and saw Universalism as the version of Christianity that most naturally resonated with the ethos of the newly formed United States of America. Their radical egalitarian theology also served to motivate advocacy for further social change. One such cause from the start was that of the abolition of slavery. Elhanan Winchester and Benjamin Rush had been outspoken opponents of slavery, and in 1790 the Philadelphia convention issued a statement that:

> We believe it to be inconsistent with the union of the human race in a common Savior, and the obligations to mutual and universal love, which flow from that union, to hold any part of our fellow creatures in bondage. We therefore recommend a total refraining from the African trade and the adoption of prudent measures for the gradual abolition of slavery of the negroes in our country, and for the education of their children in English literature, and the principles of the Gospel.[25]

Their ethical and political stance here arose from the theological, and Universalists remained consistently abolitionist throughout the nineteenth century.

Another common concern among Universalists was the rights of women. They admitted women into their colleges on the same basis as men and were the first denomination to officially ordain women to the ministry (starting with Olympia Brown in 1863). Thereafter they had many female leaders, many of whom were also active in the women's suffrage movement or other causes (e.g., Clara Barton, who founded the

24. Miller, *Larger Hope*, 1.132.
25. Quoted in Williams, *American Universalism*, 45.

American Red Cross). Further causes championed by Universalists included temperance, penal reform, and abolition of the death penalty (all following directly upon their rethinking the penal theology of hell), fair labor arrangements, humane treatment of animals, dignified treatment of children, and so on.[26]

Universalists were also very busy in printing and disseminating their newspapers, pamphlets, and books. Indeed, Richard Eddy notes 2,013 universalist publications between 1750 and 1889, with the low point being 1750–59 and 1760–69 (with only four publications in each decade), and the height of activity being 1830–39 (378 publications) and 1840–49 (351 publications). A rapid rise indeed in the number of universalist books! This dropped off during the Civil War (only 159 publications between 1860–69), and only picked up slightly thereafter.

German higher criticism of the Bible and Darwin's theory of evolution by natural selection (1859) began to stir discussion within the denomination, as it did in the Christian mainstream. The eventual result of those contentious debates was a general assimilation of and accommodation to the new ideas. While the Universalists had always been a Bible-based denomination, they had also stressed the importance of reason. Now reason was calling for a rethink of the Bible itself, and so the Universalist's theology of the Bible became increasingly liberal, perceiving God as revealing himself in Scripture through imperfect men and their fallible writings. Similarly, evolutionary theory was not some road to atheism, but pointed to the work of the great Designer. Some of the denomination's intellectuals who helped midwife the new thinking were Orello Cone (1835–1905), a well-known biblical scholar, and Thomas B. Thayer (1812–86), a leading theologian.

Darwinian thinking, along with the general cultural optimism of the nineteenth century, led Universalist theology—with its stress on rationality—in new directions. For instance, toward the end of the century there was a growing discomfort with the notion of a fall from grace into sin. The Darwinian trajectory was one of gradual ascent to higher forms, not a depressing descent. This transformation of Universalist theology continued on into the twentieth century with a trend away from emphasizing the uniqueness of Jesus and Christianity and a growing inclination toward humanism and religious pluralism. This change, which was gradual and contested, marked a stark departure from the earlier

26. On all these issues, see especially Miller, *Larger Hope*, which explores them all in great detail.

theology of the movement. In 1870 a pluralist understanding of the church and salvation was very much a minority position, but by 1946 it was the dominant view among Universalists. Indeed, some looked for an evolution of religion *beyond* Christianity. The Humiliati, a fellowship based at Tufts University from 1945 onward, adopted a symbol with the cross demoted from the center. Their rationale was that "Christianity is not central or even necessary to Universalism. . . . The important feature of the symbol is the circle, not the cross."[27] Christianity has been a signifi-

cant step along the road, but universalism can be found in all religions and *it*, not Christian faith, is the higher form into which religion is evolving.

The patterns in growth changed significantly. The hostility of the mainstream churches to the idea of universalism subsided and, as a consequence, those who would have otherwise been drawn out of the traditional churches into the Univer-

salist denomination by the idea found that they could embrace it where they were. In addition, the increasing movement of Universalism away from its biblical roots and Christian orthodoxy would not have endeared it to most Christians exploring the wider hope. "Whereas in 1888 Universalism was claimed to be the sixth largest denomination in the United States, by the second quarter of the twentieth century it was on its way to becoming one of the smallest."[28]

In the late nineteenth and twentieth century, there were various discussions of mergers with other likeminded bodies. Eventually, after many decades of on-and-off negotiations, the longstanding love-hate relationship between the Universalists and the Unitarians came to an end and the two bodies merged to form the Unitarian Universalist Association in 1961.

It is time to take our leave of the organized Universalist movement of nineteenth- and twentieth-century America and move on to consider universalists within mainstream Christianity. We shall begin our explorations in Continental Europe with two outstanding men: the celebrated Reformed theologian Friedrich Schleiermacher and the influential Lutheran pastor Johann Christoph Blumhardt.

---

27. Quoted in Williams, *American Universalism*, 77.

28. Cassara, *Universalism in America*, 39.

Romantic Universalism in the Continental Mainstream

Schleiermacher and Blumhardt

IT IS TIME TO consider the continuing story of universalism outside of the Universalist denomination. It would be true to say that there was no such thing as Christian universalism as a distinct *movement* within the mainstream churches. In contrast to the eighteenth century, what we find is individuals within various denominations reaching universalist conclusions and making them public in some way or other, but not seeking to set up some distinctively universalist church outside the established churches. Rather, they were content to remain where they were, even if they sought in various ways to broaden the traditions within which they resided by arguing for the permissibility of belief in—or at least the tentative hope for—the salvation of all people.

There is a very distinctive "feel" to the versions of universalism espoused in the nineteenth century that sets them apart somewhat from their predecessors, especially in their British manifestations (as we shall see in subsequent chapters). This change seems to reflect wider cultural shifts, and a more "liberal" approach to religion. Its contours should become clear by the end of the section.

To begin, we shall move back from America to Continental Europe, and consider the significant theological work of Friedrich Schleiermacher.

FRIEDRICH SCHLEIERMACHER (1768–1834)

Friedrich Schleiermacher was a hugely important Christian theologian, albeit a controversial one, and is generally regarded as the father of modern liberal theology.[1] For the purposes of our story, he is perhaps the first significantly influential scholarly theologian to embrace universalism since the time of the church fathers.

Schleiermacher was born and raised in Prussia, the son of a Reformed pastor, and was educated at a Moravian Pietistic school, and then at the more liberal University of Halle. While he moved away from the conservative Calvinism of his upbringing, he always remained deeply influenced by the Augustinian and Reformed traditions within which he continued to locate himself.

Schleiermacher was a New Testament exegete, a translator, a philosopher (doing groundbreaking work in hermeneutical theory), and a theologian at the Universities of Halle (1804–7) and then Berlin (1808–34), as well as being a full-time pastor for nearly forty years and a leading player in attempts to unify Lutheran and Reformed churches in Prussia. He published many works, but the most important was his systematic theology, *The Christian Faith* (1820–21). It is here, and in his essay *On the Doctrine of Election*, published in 1819, that he develops his thoughts on universal salvation.[2]

It is interesting to observe that Schleiermacher seems to have come to universalist conclusions through his own reflections on the mainstream Reformed tradition, rather than through having read or conversed with other universalist theologians. Thus, we shall see that Schleiermacher's

---

1. On Schleiermacher, see his autobiography, *Life of Schleiermacher*.

2. The essay *On the Doctrine of Election* was written as a response to the work of a leading Lutheran theologian, Karl Gottlieb Bretschneider (1776–1848), who had offered a sharp critique of the Reformed doctrine of election. *The Christian Faith* was his textbook on Christian doctrine that arose from his lectures at the University of Berlin.

universalism has its own distinctive shape—with certain features that are possibly unprecedented in universalist history.[3]

The feeling of absolute dependence

The striking innovation of Schleiermacher's approach to theology is that he grounded human piety and theology not in reason, as some of his contemporaries were trying to do, but in "feeling," in self-consciousness. Simply by virtue of being human, we find themselves with an innate sense of the divine, what Schleiermacher refers to as a feeling of "absolute dependence" on a transcendent Other: "The common element in all howsoever diverse expressions of piety . . . is this: the consciousness of being absolutely dependent, or, which is the same thing, of being in relation with God."[4] This is the seed from which all human rational reflection on God grows. It is also the seed from which religious community grows, for such a "God-consciousness" inevitably tends toward community-formation as people recognize in others that same sense of the divine that they themselves have. This is the basis for the formation of the church. It is also, as we shall see, one of the bases of his universalism. *All* human beings are created with a sense of absolute dependence on the divine Other—created, as Augustine may say, with a heart that is restless until it finds rest in God. Even those blinded to this by sin are not beyond the divine enlightenment that reawakens the heart to God.

Sin, understood in these generic terms, is that which stops or diverts the healthy development of our God-consciousness. Sin is, in effect, a "God-forgetfulness."[5] According to Schleiermacher, redemption is then to be understood in terms of the divine rekindling in darkened humans of this inner awareness of God. God does this through Christ, whose own perfect God-consciousness becomes the means by which we recover our own *sensus divinitatis* through fellowship with him.

---

3. For a careful study of Schleiermacher's doctrine of election in its historical context, see especially Hagan, *Eternal Blessedness for All?*

4. Schleiermacher, *Christian Faith*, 12.

5. Schleiermacher, *Christian Faith*, 54.

Church and world

This divine enlightenment, however, does not occur instantaneously (for any individual) nor simultaneously (for humanity as a whole). Schleiermacher makes a sharp distinction between the church and the world, between those who are redeemed and those who are perishing. The church, a subset of humanity, is the community of the redeemed, those who have been regenerated through Christ. But the church is located in the context of a wider world that does not participate in salvation in Christ.

He speaks of the world/church relationship as that of two circles: the world is the outer circle—the set of all human beings—while the church is the inner circle, the set of regenerated human beings. The inner circle enjoys sanctification and salvation, while the outer circle enjoys preparatory grace as God works within it, bringing people to the point of embracing the gospel. Unbelievers are "called," when they hear the gospel preached, but not thereby "chosen" (in one sense at least). The chosen, or elect, are those that God *enables to believe* the gospel. (We shall return to this notion soon in order to qualify it.)

The relationship between the two circles, the inner and the outer, is thus dynamic. The inner circle of the church grows as people enter it from the outer circle.[6] Schleiermacher's eschatological hope, as we shall see, was that it would one day expand to the size of the outer circle—at that point, *all humans* would be part of the church, the redeemed.

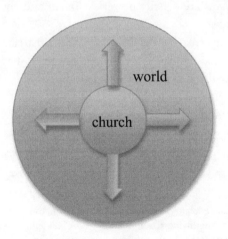

6. Schleiermacher, *Christian Faith*, 525.

Providence and election

In accordance with his tradition, Schleiermacher is committed to a very strong view of divine providence, the notion that *everything* that happens in history happens as a result of God's sovereign will. (This even includes the fall of Adam and Eve into sin and death.)[7] Unlike some universalists, Schleiermacher had no time for views in which humans could mess up God's plans, even slightly. God's will is done—*always*.

This view of sovereignty has implications for redemption. Schleiermacher is a fierce opponent of the idea that we can do anything to *merit* our salvation; indeed, because of our sin, we cannot even generate faith in our hearts. In other words, apart from God's action in us we cannot even believe the gospel and we cannot be saved. The flip-side of that is that God's saving grace in us is *irresistible*—if God enables faith in us then we *will* believe. This means that for Schleiermacher, as for the mainstream Reformed tradition, those currently outside the church and salvation are there because God has not yet enabled them to believe. Those in the church are those that God has chosen to believe the gospel now.

Why does God discriminate between people in this way? We do not (and cannot) know, he says, and it is not our place to question it. It is simply part of the wisdom of God's governance of the world.[8] But one thing that we can know is that this division between people has *no basis in the persons themselves*, as if some have more merit or are worthier than others. All humans are equally powerless in sin and equally lost, apart from divine grace.

Where Schleiermacher departs from the mainstream Reformed tradition is that he does not see this division between lost and saved as *permanent*. It is one thing to recognize that God does not save everyone all at once—this seems an undeniable state of affairs; but it is quite another to propose that God plans to leave things that way for eternity.

> While Christian sympathy is not disquieted by the earlier and later adoption of one and another individual into the fellowship of redemption, yet on the other hand there does remain an insoluble

---

7. Annette Hagan explains his thinking: "Original sin, too, is then an integral part of the all-encompassing divine act of creation. . . . Adam fell precisely because of the ordination of humankind to both sinfulness and redemption. He, and in his wake the human race, had to sin so that they could be redeemed" (*Eternal Blessedness for All?* 112).

8. Schleiermacher, *Christian Faith*, 534.

> *discord if, on the assumption of survival after death, we are to*
> *think of a part of the human race as entirely excluded from fel-*
> *lowship....* [I]f only everyone who has lagged behind us is some
> time or another taken up into living fellowship with Christ,
> our sympathetic concern can accept the fact with perfect sat-
> isfaction without any contradiction arising between it and our
> God-consciousness.[9]

All human beings stand in solidarity in that they are all equally
created to be conscious of God, are all are equally lost in sin and undeserving of salvation, and are all redeemed in Christ, for redemption is
"universally and completely accomplished by Jesus of Nazareth."[10] There
is no basis for an *eternal* discrimination between the two circles. After all,
on what grounds would one postulate such an *eternal* distinction within
the human race? Perhaps something of merit among the elect? But that
is Pelagianism! As a Reformed theologian, Schleiermacher insisted that
if there is eternal perdition then it *must* be grounded in God's decree,
but such a decree would be sheer caprice! And, writes Schleiermacher,
"I know of no way in which [the doctrine of eternal damnation] can be
reconciled with the universal love of God."[11]

So what of the doctrine of election? Schleiermacher rejects the idea
popular with many Calvinists that God elects some to salvation and
elects others to damnation (the so-called double decree). He also argues
that the claim popular among Lutherans of his day that God elects some
to salvation but simply passes over the rest (rather than electing them for
damnation) really amounts to the same thing as the double-decree. After
all, on that latter view God is still *actively choosing* to let someone go to
hell forever, rather than redeeming them, so the problem with election
remains.

Schleiermacher's alternative view is that there is *a single decree to*
salvation for all humanity. God foreordains the redemption of humanity:
this single decree concerns *the human race*, rather than individuals as
such, but the race cannot be saved without all its component parts (the
universal and the particular are, according to Schleiermacher, inseparable in God's thought).[12] "The truth of the matter . . . is that only *one*

9. Schleiermacher, *Christian Faith*, 539, 542.

10. Schleiermacher, *Christian Faith*, 56.

11. Schleiermacher, *On the Doctrine of Election*, 77. Universalism, in addition,
surmounts any conflict between divine love and justice (78).

12. Schleiermacher, *On the Doctrine of Election*, 55.

divine decree can be assumed, one that embraces all, namely the decree concerning the arrangement within which those of the mass [of humanity] who are capable of individual spiritual life are gradually quickened."[13]

> Only once we have let go of the particular . . . and have, instead of this, broken into contemplating things as a whole, are we convinced . . . that one cannot speak, in particular, of a divine decree concerning each individual person. Rather, we can say that there is *one* divine decree by which God determines what will become of each and every human being and thus that this is not at all different from the order according to which the dead mass is quickened by the divine Spirit.[14]

This single degree covers everything, including the staggered entry of the human race into life.

We can still speak of God rejecting or passing over people, distinguishing between elect and non-elect, but we can only do so in a *limited* sense, i.e., that *at this present moment* God is choosing to pass over this person rather than to bring them into the church.[15] We need to grasp that for Schleiermacher "election and rejection of any individual are the two contrasting, yet correlated, aspects of the one single divine decree, 'whereby through divine power, yet in a natural way, the human race is to be transformed into the spiritual body of Christ.'"[16] So the reprobate are simply the *not-yet*-saved, those *currently* passed-over by grace. But they remain loved by God, who has eternally and unconditionally decreed their redemption, their participation in the fellowship of Christ.

Given that many are clearly unredeemed at the time of their deaths, that their foreordination to salvation has not been fulfilled, one can postulate that death is not the end of the journey: "the state in which he [the unrepentant] dies is only an intermediate state."[17] Death and damnation is a step along the road, not the end of it: "because damnation is taken to be a necessary stage, it must also be a stage of development. . . . [T]he

---

13. Schleiermacher, *On the Doctrine of Election*, 65. As all humans are created with the potential for God-consciousness, all fall into this category. Note, however, that they are *gradually*, not simultaneously, quickened.

14. Schleiermacher, *On the Doctrine of Election*, 73.

15. Schleiermacher, *Christian Faith*, 548; Schleiermacher, *On the Doctrine of Election*, 75–76.

16. Hagan, *Eternal Blessedness for All?* 112, quoting Schleiermacher, *On the Doctrine of Election*, 76.

17. Schleiermacher, *Christian Faith*, 549.

damned likewise cannot be excluded from being objects of the divine love since everything that belongs to the ordered world of human life must be an object of the divine attributes."[18]

This view, Schleiermacher thinks, elevates the work of Christ higher than the mainstream tradition is able to. Here Christ works for the salvation of all, rather than just some (contra Calvinism), and his work is efficacious for all, rather than just for some (contra Lutheranism).[19]

Schleiermacher's view of the final consummation is necessarily *corporate*—the final perfection of humanity as the church, the body of Christ, in an eternal indissoluble fellowship with Christ and with each other. Here God-consciousness, which is necessarily consciousness of others who share that same consciousness, is complete. "[W]hen human development has reached its *telos*, and the human race is the body of Christ, these differentiated human levels [i.e., the differences between the world and the church] will have been resolved as the plentitude of humanity existent as the singularity of the body of Christ, joined to the head."[20]

Schleiermacher's understanding of the corporate solidarity of humanity also raised a serious problem for the traditional notion of hell. For Schleiermacher, humans who become more conscious of God are actually recovering something fundamental to their humanity, and as their personal consciousness draws closer to what he calls their "race-consciousness" they become more aware of their solidarity with other humans. So a growing God-consciousness inevitably leads to a growing sense of sympathy and fellow-feeling for other humans, even the reprobate. The consequence of this is that the misery of the damned diminishes the blessedness of the redeemed, and if some people are damned forever then the redeemed can *never* achieve complete happiness.[21] This is perhaps the most influential of Schleiermacher's arguments for universalism.[22]

18. Schleiermacher, *On the Doctrine of Election*, 77–78.

19. Schleiermacher, *Christian Faith*, 560.

20. Nicol and Jorgenson's "Introduction" to Schleiermacher, *On the Doctrine of Election*, 19.

21. Schleiermacher, *Christian Faith*, 543. The argument is expanded in the appendix to §163.

22. It was anticipated by Origen (*Hom. Lev.* 7.2.10) and Hosea Ballou, and a version of this argument has been most recently and influentially defended by philosopher Thomas Talbott.

Conclusion

Schleiermacher, as Murray Rae explains, "refused to give doctrinal status to his universalist claims. [His] refusal was based on the insufficiency of the evidence of Scripture, or in the contents of consciousness. It is clear, however, that Schleiermacher favored a universalist view."[23]

Friedrich Schleiermacher was a goliath in the history of modern theology, casting a shadow up to the present day, yet it is interesting to note that his universalist theology of election had very little impact on his contemporaries or on subsequent generations. It was more or less passed over in silence from day one and is only now beginning to attract more attention.[24]

However, universalist hope did not vanish from the German lands. It is found among some philosophers,[25] some of the more liberal theologians,[26] and was maintained among some of the Pietists who had not relocated to America. Prominent among these were the Württemburg Pietists, who had been deeply influenced by Albrecht Bengel, his student Friedrich Oetinger, and Count Nicholas von Zinzendorf, all of whom were universalists, as we have already seen. Christian Collins Winn describes the distinctive constellation of emphases of Württemberg Pietism as follows:

> The key motifs of this form of Pietism were centered on the question of the in-breaking of the kingdom of God in history. They include: 1) the belief that the kingdom of God was already

23. Rae, "Salvation-in-Community," 195.

24. Alexander Schweizer (1808–88), one of Schleiermacher's students, was almost the only theologian to develop the universalist theology of his teacher. Another was Augustus Tholuck (1799–1877), also a student of Schleiermacher. The reviews of Schleiermacher's essay on election almost universally ignored the issue, and with two exceptions, those that did mention it condemned it. The exceptions were the reviews of Wilhelm de Wette (1780–1849), the important Lutheran pioneer of the historical criticism of the Old Testament, and Ernst Wilhelm Christian Sartorius (1797–1859). Both in their own ways affirmed Schleiermacher's proposal of universal salvation. (On the reception of the essay, see Hagan, *Eternal Blessedness for All?* 119–37.)

25. Friedrich Schelling (1775–1854) defended a version of universalism. He considered 1 Corinthians 15:28 to contain the "most profound" words in the New Testament. See McClymond, *Devil's Redemption*, 657–64.

26. For example, Blanchard argues that Albrecht Ritschl (1822–89) "had universalist leanings," though he never explicitly endorsed universalism. See Blanchard, *Will All Be Saved?* 100–101. Another liberal theologian of note who defended universalism was Adolf von Harnack (1851–1930).

related to history in a very intimate fashion, so that God was active in the world not only as the reviver of souls, but also as the transformer of the world; 2) that when the kingdom came in its fullness, it would consist in the universal outpouring of the Holy Spirit, which, for some, implied a universal restoration of all things or "apokatastasis"; 3) because God was so intimately at work in history, many within this tradition sought to overcome the perceived dualism of classical Pietism between the soul and body, thus making space for healing and the miraculous; 4) God's work in the world and history also constituted a call to missions, which included a definite concern for the political and social issues of the day; and 5) a nascent critique of some of the motifs of classical Pietism, especially the subjectivist orientation of the practice of piety (i.e., the concern over one's own salvation).[27]

The most significant Christian theologian and minister to arise from the midst of Württemburg Pietism, as far as our focus is concerned, was Johann Christoph Blumhardt. Blumhardt grew up among them and was deeply affected by the tradition, even as he innovated within it. We shall consider his life and thought before returning to Britain.

JOHANN CHRISTOPH BLUMHARDT (1805–80)

Life

Johann Blumhardt was born the son of a poor laborer in Stuttgart at the time of the Napoleonic Wars, a time of conflict, trouble, and famine for the city.[28] "I know what I'm talking about when I talk of misery and poverty," he later wrote.[29]

His father was a follower of the theology of Bengel, with its millenarian focus, and even believed that Christ would return to inaugurate the millennium in 1836. The family tended to view the great trials shaking their world through the lens of this theology, interpreting them as the

---

27. Winn, *Jesus Is Victor*, 67–68.

28. Helpful biographies of Blumhardt are Ising, *Johann Christoph Blumhardt* and Macchia, *Spirituality and Social Liberation*. On Blumhardt's sympathy with universalism, see Groth, "Chiliasmus und Apokatastasishoffnung"; Macchia, *Spirituality and Social Liberation*; and Winn, *Jesus Is Victor*, 106–8. For Blumhardt's healing ministry in the wider context of healing movements, see Robinson, *Divine Healing*, ch. 2.

29. Blumhardt, *Täglich Brod* (Meditation on 16th July 1879).

tribulations preceding the millennium. Such predicting of dates for Christ's return was something that Johann would later come to strongly

repudiate for its extreme naivety. Nevertheless, he always retained Bengel's stress on the importance of eschatology as a means for better understanding the significance of events in this age. Blumhardt read his world through the glasses of eschatology and the strong expectation that Christ was coming soon.

Johann was also influenced by a "commune" in Württemberg of separatist Pietists known as the Kornthaler movement.[30] Their emphasis was on the impact that the kingdom of God makes in *this* world. That teaching was forever formative for him, even though he never accepted their desire for distancing themselves from the state church.

After studying theology at Tübingen (1824–29), Johann moved to serve as a pastor for a year and then as a teacher at the Basel Mission House (1830–37). In 1837 he became a Lutheran pastor in Iptingen, and then in 1838 he took on the parish pastor's mantle in Möttlingen. It was his ministry in Möttlingen that changed everything.

The congregation in Möttlingen was spiritually apathetic, and he seemed unable to break through to them. Then, in 1841, a twenty-six-year-old woman known at Gottliebin Dittus came to him to speak of her spiritual troubles. Various paranormal activities had been going on around her and her house. After some investigation, Blumhardt came to believe that demonic forces were at work. The breakthrough came when she was in an unconscious state and convulsing and he was praying over her. He was seized with indignation at what the devil was doing to the woman and grabbed her hands, encouraging her to pray, "Lord Jesus, help me!" She ceased convulsing and awoke, repeating the words of the prayer. This was the start of a protracted ministry of deliverance for Gottlieben over the next eighteen months, fighting with the weapons

---

30. Johann was a very close friend with the son of the leader of the community.

of Scripture, prayer, and fasting. Things got worse before they got better, but he refused to give up. His focus was ever on Jesus' triumph and its implications for her deliverance. Then, at the end of December 1843, the demon's power was broken—it roared from the possessed girl and left, shouting "Jesus is Victor! Jesus is Victor!" Gottliebin was free.

This event was transformative for the community, who were awakened from their spiritual lethargy as a revival broke out, but also for Johann Blumhardt, who spent many years rethinking his theology in the light of what had happened. He came to see healing as integral to the ministry of the coming kingdom of God, alongside forgiveness, a sign of its already-in-breaking power. His theology came to emphasize inaugurated eschatology, without ever losing sight of the fuller reality to come, and was holistic, teaching salvation for the *whole* person, body and soul.

Johann's healing ministry became controversial with the church authorities, and he was ordered to stop laying on hands for healing and absolution from sin. However, he felt that this holistic ministry was essential, so with the help of a benefactor he purchased Bad Boll, a large house and spa about seventy miles from Möttlingen, where he could continue his ministry. People came from far and wide to stay at Bad Boll, which could accommodate up to 150 guests, and to receive Blumhardt's spiritual guidance and healing prayer. The expectation among those at the house was for God's kingdom to come and impact the situations of those who sought it. Johann ministered here from 1852 until his death in 1880.[31]

Theology

Johann divided history into three periods:[32] that of the Father (the period from Moses to Christ), that of the Son (the period of Christ and the age of the church), and that of the Spirit (a coming period in which the Spirit

31. Johann's son, Christoph Blumhardt (1842–1919), took over the work at Bad Boll after his father's death. He too gained a reputation for his divine healing and deliverance ministry. He also took his father's kingdom theology and worked it out in the socioeconomic and political sphere, becoming one of the founders of Christian Socialism in Germany and Switzerland, serving in parliament. He was also a pacifist strongly opposed to the First World War. On Christoph Blumhardt's theology, see Zahl, *Pneumatology and Theology of the Cross*, and Winn, *Jesus Is Victor*, ch. 3.

32. This was not an uncommon move in some circles. The most famous name associated with it is the medieval Sicilian millennialist and mystic Joachim of Fiore (ca. 1135–1202).

would be poured out on all flesh, and the church would be restored and would work preparing the world so that it was ready to receive Christ at his return). This age of the Spirit would climax with the fullness of the coming of the kingdom. It was, for Blumhardt, a "time of universal conversion":[33]

> Great changes take place as soon as God sends forth his Spirit: great things start to come to life again among those who believe in a childlike way. "This one will say, 'I am the Lord's,' another will be called by the name of Jacob, yet another will write on the hand, 'The Lord's,' and adopt the name of Israel" . . . *All the generations of people* will be renewed with God's divine nature. We will be astonished by how quickly the Spirit of God can work among us *all*. People from all over the earth will gather from all sides, saying, "I also want to belong to the Lord! . . ." *Nobody* will want to stay behind and be excluded from the blessings that flow to the people of God. Then the servants of God will receive the authority to say, "Yes, you belong to the Lord, you will also belong to God's Israel; it is also given to you. Just come!" Oh, what a wonderful time that will be when *everyone, even those who are now involved in foolishness and perversity,* are filled with only one thought. "How can we enter the realm of grace with the blessings of God and be called by the name of Israel and Jacob!"[34]

> Because this feast has not yet been proclaimed everywhere, and not everyone can participate in it, we still wait for the prophecy [Isa 25:6–9] to be fulfilled. But a great awakening is promised to all nations, and will be experienced wherever the gospel is preached. There is a special power of God that belongs to the gospel—the Holy Spirit. It is through the Holy Spirit that the gospel will come to rich fruition; it will renew *every heart— everyone and everywhere*—and the world will be refreshed and happy, because through this *humankind* will have received a new life from God.[35]

Living in the space between the inauguration of the kingdom and its coming fullness, we do not always see healing and deliverance, but

33. See "The New Heart" in Blumhardt, *Gospel Sermons*, 220.

34. See "The Great Flood of the Spirit" in Blumhardt, *Gospel Sermons*, 72. Italics added.

35. See "The People's Feast and Its Effect" in Blumhardt, *Gospel Sermons*, 277. Italics added.

Blumhardt believed that Christians should seek it, reach for it, pray to the Lord to pour out his Spirit to bring more. "Blumhardt's hope revolves around two poles, a hope for the in-breaking kingdom of God and for the universal outpouring of the Holy Spirit."[36] In this time, we must battle the work of the devil, proclaiming the victory that Jesus won on the cross, but the day is coming when God will "be all in all," throughout the cosmos.

Blumhardt came to believe that the signs of the kingdom breaking into the present in the lives of particular people—in healing, deliverance, reconciliation, and forgiveness—were signs of the full salvation that was coming in the future to *all* people. They were thus signs of the future *of the whole world*, not merely the church; they had cosmic signification. As such, Blumhardt blurred the hard-and-fast distinction between believers (the elect) and unbelievers (the non-elect). The believers were simply those who were experiencing now the saving grace that would eventually come to all. So, while Johann believed in the salvation of the individual soul, his focus was much wider, on the coming kingdom and its restorative work across the whole cosmos.

We see his universalism come out as "the confession of hope."[37]

> [H]ere at the cross the possibility opened up that some time it will happen, that *all* knees must bow in heaven, as well as on earth and *under the earth*, and *all* tongues confess, that Jesus Christ is Lord to the glory of God the Father. This is so great that we cannot express it, and hardly dare to conceive it. But Good Friday proclaims a general pardon *over the entire world*, and this general pardon will yet be revealed, for *Jesus did not hang in vain on the cross*.[38]

> The hope of the New Testament refers to the expectation of the end of all things when all will again be brought into harmony, when all pain ceases, all mysteries are revealed, and the fullness of God's mercy in Christ Jesus will unfold over all creation, and this shall be revealed to the children of God when the groans of all creation are quieted. And when it says here "hope of salvation," it is not meant in the sense that we hope for salvation after death; the Holy Scripture means by this salvation the final

---

36. Winn, *Jesus Is Victor*, 95.

37. Johann was not always a universalist, but his later theology had a clear shift in that direction. See especially Groth, "Chiliasmus und Apokatastasishoffnung."

38. Blumhardt, *Evangelienpredigten auf alle Sonn*, 190. Quoted in Groth, "Chiliasmus und Apokatastasishoffnung," 91. Italics added.

deliverance of all groaning creation from its torments and need, its misery and distress.[39]

Jesus, our deliverer and Savior—who burns with longing to deliver everyone from the evil under which we still groan. Christ has already appointed a day in which he *will* accomplish this.[40]

By sending Jesus Christ His Son, our Lord, to us, He became not the Father or God of judgment but the Father and God of mercies, the God of all comfort. Nothing but mercy pours down from above, nothing but comfort awaits us! And gleaming brightly before us is mercy and comfort for poor, sinful, suffering mankind.[41]

[T]his judgment by the disciples [Matt 19:27–30] is no judgment toward damnation; rather it is a preparation for submission and for acceptance of salvation. . . . Even in the Old Testament the word "judging" (*richten*) is sometimes used in the sense of "setting right," as for instance when it says "Zion must be judged by right and justice." . . . The "judgment" shall be the means to bring as many as possible back into the fold. Finally, all knees shall be bent and all tongues confess that Jesus Christ is Lord. In order to make this possible there will have to be a lot of judgment-work done.[42]

Blumhardt was unsympathetic to those who believed that "Wrath and nothing but wrath is approaching" for unbelievers; that all those beyond the church "he will let go to hell, not caring to do anything

---

39. Blumhardt, *Die Verkündigung*, 102–3. Quoted in Winn, *Jesus Is Victor*, 105–6.

40. Blumhardt, "Do Not Worry!" in *Gospel Sermons*, 53. Italics added.

41. Blumhardt, *Die Verkündigung*, 102–3. Quoted in Winn, *Jesus Is Victor*, 105–6.

42. Blumhardt, *Blätter aus Bad Boll*, 218–19 (unpublished translation by the Brüderhof). Blumhardt's *Gospel Sermons* reveal clear universalist rhetoric in a number of the sermons: "When Will the Kingdom of God Come?" (on Luke 17:20–25; pp. 258, 260–61); "The Legacy of the Departing Savior" (on Luke 24:49–53; pp. 23–24); "Into the Kingdom of Life" (on Col 1:12–14; p. 33); "Do Not Worry!" (on Ps 55:22; p. 53); "The Little Flock" (on Luke 12:32; p. 77); "The Great Flood of the Spirit" (on Isa 44:1–5; p. 72); "The Peoples' Feast and Its Effects" (on Isa 25:6–9; p. 277); "Without Ceasing" (on 1 Thess 5:17; p. 138); "The Wise Men's Star" (on Matt 2:1–12; pp. 228–30); "The Fight for the Kingdom" (on Matt 6:13; p. 274); "The New Heart" (on Jer 24:7; p. 220). He clearly believes that the judgment day will bring disaster for the impenitent, but he sees the judgment as aiming at their ultimate salvation. And while he is open to the theoretical possibility of annihilation for the super-hardened (260–61), he speaks mostly as though he does not expect such a possibility to be realized. Rather, he seems cautiously confident that all will be saved.

extraordinary out of love for them." Judgment is restorative. Winn sums up as follows:

> He simply affirms the reality of judgment, while at the same time emphasizing that hell was not originally created for humanity, but rather for the devil, that it does not have an eternal character, and that "even in judgment he [God] cannot deny his mercy." Though it would be wrong to say that Blumhardt held to a systematic doctrine of the *apokatastasis ton panton*, it is clear that his hope for creation was sympathetic with it. It is also clear that he believed that, "the Lord Jesus is nevertheless the compassionate and gracious One, even if the whole world is not so clearly aware of it and able to experience it. At last, however, His countenance will shine upon all men."[43]

According to Dieter Iser, "Blumhardt has great sympathy for the idea of *apokatastasis*, the restoration of all things, but refrains from any more specific doctrine of restoration due to the absence of a univocal drift in the biblical materials. . . . God has the final word; a universal demonstration of grace cannot be a statement of doctrine, but an object of hope."[44]

Not many people today have heard of Johann Blumhardt, or of his son Christoph (1842–1919), who followed in his father's footsteps, but their influence continues to be felt, albeit indirectly.[45] Their Jesus-centered kingdom theology, with its cosmic hopeful *telos*, was to be an important influence on two highly significant twentieth-century theologians, both of whom play a significant role in the subsequent story of universalism— Karl Barth[46] and Jürgen Moltmann.[47] In recent years, however, there has been a small but growing interest among theologians in recovering the

43. Winn, *Jesus Is Victor*, 108.

44. Ising, *Johann Christoph Blumhardt*, 406.

45. Christoph, like his father, embraced universalism. He wrote, "There can be no question of God's giving up anything or anyone in the whole world, either today or in all eternity. The end has to be: Behold, everything is God's!" Quoted in Moltmann, "Logic of Hell," 47.

46. On which see especially Winn, *Jesus Is Victor*, which is a study specifically about the influence of the Blumhardts on Barth.

47. Consider: "My 'Theology of Hope' has two roots: Christoph Blumhardt and Ernst Bloch" (Moltmann, "Hope for the Kingdom of God," 4). Of these two, Blumhardt was the most important. On Blumhardt's influence on Moltmann, see Winn, "Before Bloch."

Blumhardts for the contemporary church. So perhaps their voice will be heard once again.

For now, we need to return to Britain and turn the clock back a little as we continue our story. Friedrich Schleiermacher reflected the influence of contemporary Romantic sensibilities in his Christian theology. One of the pioneers in Britain of theology under the influence of the Romantic Movement was the well-connected Scottish lay theologian Thomas Erskine. It is his story we will consider in the next chapter.

Universalism in Great Britain I

Thomas Erskine, Romantic Pioneer

THE LIFE OF THOMAS ERSKINE (1788–1870)

THE NAME OF THOMAS Erskine is not well-known in contemporary theology, but in his day he was much discussed and was certainly among the most significant British theologians of the nineteenth century.[1] Tübingen theologian Otto Pfleiderer (1839–1908), writing in 1890, said that Erskine, along with John McLeod Campbell (1800–1872), represented "the best contribution to dogmatics which British theology has produced in the present century."[2] Erskine was a pioneer, anticipating several theological themes and ideas that came to dominate subsequent theology.

---

1. On Erskine see Foster, "Representation and Substitution in Thomas Erskine of Linlathen"; Needham, *Thomas Erskine of Linlathen*; Horrocks, *Laws of the Spiritual Order*; Horrocks, "Postmortem Education."

2. Pfleiderer, *Development of Theology*, 382.

He was also a lightning rod for controversy, most especially in his native Scotland, where conservative Calvinism ruled supreme.

Erskine was born near Dundee, Scotland, son of a Church of Scotland father and an Episcopalian mother. After the death of his father, his maternal grandmother raised Thomas in Airth Castle. While having both Presbyterian and Anglican influences growing up, Erskine was never especially interested in denominationalism and never fully accommodated himself to any one form of Christian worship. He attended Episcopalian, Presbyterian, and Congregational churches.

Unusually for such an influential theologian, Erskine was not a Christian minister of any sort, nor did even he have any formal theological training. (Indeed, it was his lay status that exempted him from some of the ecclesiastical control that could otherwise have sought to constrain his more radical ideas.) Erskine went to Edinburgh University, where he studied law and was admitted to the Faculty of Advocates in 1810. However, in 1816 he inherited a family estate in Linlathen, near Dundee, and retired from the legal world, giving himself to the study of theology and the pursuit of holiness. Although lacking a theology degree, he had a sharp, inquisitive mind, as well as a voracious appetite for learning and for rethinking the theological tradition in ways more relevant to the modern world, influenced as it was by the mood of Romanticism.

Erskine was very well-connected in the Christian world of his day, and was regarded as a good and pious man, even by his outspoken opponents. He knew many of the key ministers in his native Scotland and in England, and he went on three extended tours of Europe to observe and support Protestant missionaries (1822–25, 1826–27, 1837–39), especially in France, Italy, and Switzerland, where he made friends with numerous ministers, theologians, and philosophers. He was also friends with various novelists, poets, and other influential figures. As we shall see, many of the subsequent nineteenth-century universalists owed an intellectual debt of one kind or another to Thomas Erskine, both through his publications and through personal contact.

Erskine's publications cluster in the period of 1820–37. After that he published no more books prior to his death in 1870, though he did authorize the posthumous publication of some essays and short fragments in *The Spiritual Order* in 1871. This is where we find perhaps his most overt extended statement of universal salvation in the essay entitled "The Purpose of God."

THEOLOGY

Erskine lived in a rapidly chang-ing world, a world that posed various difficult challenges to traditional Christianity, and he self-consciously set out to con-struct a theology that he felt was true to Scripture and the tradi-tion, but that also resonated in the cultural climate of his day.

One of the cultural shifts at work during the late eighteenth and early nineteenth centuries was a move toward emphasizing the *subjec-tive* side of reality—the conscience of the individual, and the importance of moral and spiritual transformation, ethics, personal experience, and human feelings. Schleiermacher's theological project was a Continental attempt to reconstruct theology around such a subjective center; Erskine did something very similar in Britain. (Interestingly, Erskine never refers to Schleiermacher or his work, which is surprising given the number of similarities between them, but there is no question that he knew of it.[3])

The theological tradition that Erskine had inherited was that of Scottish Federal Calvinism, which was very much constructed in terms of legal categories: God the Lawgiver and Judge gives and enforces laws, but humans break the laws and thus incur righteous penalties from the Judge. God's justice demands that the infringements of his holy law be punished by everlasting damnation. The problem is that God cannot simply forgive people without at the same time denying his own justice. This is the dilemma that the gospel provides the solution for: Christ was punished by God for human law-breaking, exhausting his wrath, thereby satisfying the requirement of justice that such violations be punished. Thus, God is now able to forgive us and to legally impute Christ's own righteous status to us, so that although we are still sinners we are now legally righteous before God (i.e., we are justified). To this it should be

---

3. See Horrocks, *Laws of the Spiritual Order*, 235–37. Erskine was friends with one of Schleiermacher's students, Augustus Tholuck (1799–1877), Pietist revivalist, a professor of theology in Berlin, and apparently a universalist (Horrocks, *Laws of the Spiritual Order*, 238–39).

added that, according to Calvinism, God only sent Christ to represent and die for the elect, the chosen few, *not* for all people.

Erskine *hated* this whole approach to theology, even though his training was in law. He thought that it misrepresented God and misunderstood the real problem of sin and the divine answer found in the gospel. Indeed, as we shall see, he thought it actively *stopped* people from experiencing the salvation available through Christ. So his mission became that of providing what he considered a more authentically Christian alternative.

Before outlining Erskine's theology, we need to step back for a moment to appreciate his theological method, for it was different from that of his Calvinist opponents. Critical to Erskine was the authority of our "reason and conscience." Authentic religion needs to resonate with our inner self, to "ring true," to witness in our spirits. If I *merely* accept some theological claim as true on the basis of some *external* authority (such as the Bible or tradition) then I do not adequately believe it. It is the affirmative response of my reason and my conscience—the *inner* authorities— that enables me to affirm the teachings of Scripture and tradition and to grasp their truth. Religion, he claims, must be able to make sense of my human experience—my spiritual awareness of divine transcendence, my innate moral sense and my acute awareness of moral failure (both confirmed by my conscience), and human suffering—if it can make any claims to truth. His whole theological method works by taking the importance of subjectivity and its inner authority as core; not as a substitute for Scripture and tradition, but as a way of engaging them.[4]

God as Father

As a central theological move, Erskine switched the key metaphor for God from Judge to *Father*, a move he thought justified by the New Testament and one that resonated with his conscience. This switch had far-reaching effects, allowing him to reconfigure theology around an intimate relational image, rather than a forensic and cold one. For Erskine, the *unselfish love of God* takes center stage. God created all people as his children with the intention of perfecting them in righteousness. *Everything* that God does in his relation with humans is, according to Erskine, governed by his Fatherly love. Consequently, any theology that proposes unfatherly

4. See Erskine, "Bible in Relation to Faith."

behavior by God toward humans is anathema. For instance, God is not some indignant King who looks at us with rage for snubbing his authority, nor a Judge who must dispassionately ensure we pay the price for our transgressions; he is *a Father* who desires to transform us and perfect us.

It is not easy for us to appreciate how novel this approach was in his day, for such was his influence that by the end of the nineteenth century the themes of the Fatherhood of God and the brotherhood of man had become mainstream, at least in the liberal tradition. But he, along with his friend John McLeod Campbell, was one of the key pioneers who pointed theology in that direction.

In Erskine's hands, the doctrines of creation, sin, salvation, election, and judgment are all reconstructed around God's Fatherhood.

Creation

All humans are created "in the Son" so that they may share in the Son's eternal relationship with his Father. *All* human beings are made in the image of God, as children of God. This proposal was novel in the 1820s, and flew in the face of the more common view that we *become* children of God through faith in Christ (John 1:12). Erskine claimed that, in creation, Christ is the head of humanity, and humanity is his body—a relationship traditionally reserved for the church and Christ.[5] In addition, and also very controversially, Erskine claimed that Jesus indwells *all human beings* by virtue of their creation in Christ. This innate "Jesus light," which draws us Godward, is what underlies our reason and conscience, and is what Christ seeks to awaken within us by his Spirit through the gospel. Divine revelation will thus resonate with us at the deepest levels of our created being, even if we resist it for a time because of sin. The influence of William Law is clear here and elsewhere.[6]

Creation itself is not merely ordered according to physical laws, described by the blossoming sciences, but also by spiritual laws, laws of love directed to our spiritual perfection in holiness.[7]

5. Though sometimes Erskine does speak of being united with Christ in his body through faith in the gospel.

6. Inspired by Law, Erskine also read Jakob Böhme in German, though Law provided the interpretative framework for his reading of Böhme.

7. This emphasis led Julia Wedgewood (1833–1913) to write that in Erskine's theological reading of Paul, "the apostle [Paul] took the place of Newton of the spiritual world, declaring to us the one mighty principle corresponding to gravitation in the

At the core of his theology of creation lies Erskine's conviction that God "must create only for good" and that the moral intelligences he creates must be "created to be good" with a goodness that can come only from God's Son himself, the source of all goodness. So we are created to indwell the Son and to share in his overflowing goodness.[8]

Sin

But all is not well with creation. Sin diverts humans away from God and their creational purpose in Christ. Sin is not first and foremost the infringement of a law, but the spurning of divine love and the separation of oneself from God and from the human calling to living together in relationship with God. Sin leads to a self-imposed condition of suffering, misery, and death, but it does not lead God to hate us, to spurn us, nor to seek to crush us. He hates *sin*, because sin damages us. Indeed, his absolute hatred of sin underlies his unwavering commitment to deliver us from it. So *we* reject God; he does not reject us. God's "holy love . . . is the union of an infinite abhorrence towards sin, and an infinite love towards the sinner."[9]

Salvation and forgiveness

Salvation is not some legal fiction, an "imputed righteousness" that is nothing more than a legal status before God in which God regards us as righteous, even though we are not. Indeed, salvation is not even deliverance from punishment, but is instead a deliverance *from sin itself*: "Salvation is not forgiveness of sin; it is not the remission of penalty; it is not safety. No, it is the blessed and holy purpose of God's love accomplished in the fallen creature's restoration to the divine image."[10] As such, salvation is not a once-and-for-all granting of a legal status, but an ongoing transformation into the image of Christ. As Don Horrocks puts it:

> Salvation . . . was not an external forensic fact but existential deliverance from within, a transforming condition of the human

---

visible universe, which kept all things in order" (Wedgewood, *Nineteenth-Century Teachers*, 71).

8. Erskine, "Divine Son," 39–40.

9. Erskine, *Unconditional Freeness*, 16.

10. Letter to Monsieur Gaussen, Dec. 7, 1832, *Letters*, 1.294.

> soul resulting from the innate, creative power of the gospel to reveal "righteousness," defined relationally by Erskine as "the loving fatherly purpose of God." When this was believed . . . the gospel automatically regenerated and justified those appropriating it, resulting in the truth itself becoming personalized within the individual.[11]

Christ is the agent of salvation. The second person of the Trinity came as a human being and lived as the perfect Son of the Father—totally dependent on him in filial trust. He was the model human with true faith in God, and we are called to enter into his faith-full relationship with the Father. Reassuringly, the "revelation of the Son . . . gives the fullest and most absolute demonstration that our sin had not made God cease to be our Father, or abandon His purpose of training us into a participation of the Son's character and blessedness."[12]

The death of Christ was not a mechanism to rescue us from punishment or to change God's attitude toward us. God's attitude toward us is that of unchanging and unconditional love. The cross *displays* God's love for us and, when we inwardly grasp this truth, makes it possible for that divine love to transform us and be formed in us. Our own lives become cross-shaped. Christ thus dies *for* us as our representative head (but not *instead* of us as our substitute)—we are then united by the Spirit with him in his death, surrendering our lives to the Father with him, and thereby joining him in his resurrection. In this way, Christ is the one who opens the path for the restoration of human nature. This atonement model is a significant shift away from the penal substitution theory that characterizes Calvinism (and several versions of earlier post-Reformation universalism) and it sets the agenda for nineteenth-century universalism.[13]

Importantly and controversially, according to Erskine in *The Unconditional Freeness of the Gospel* (1828), our forgiveness does *not* depend on our faith in the gospel. Rather, God, in his love, has *already* forgiven *all* people through the finished work of Christ.[14] This message *is* the gospel.

11. Horrocks, *Laws of the Spiritual Order*, 60–61.

12. Erskine, "Father Revealed in the Son," 244.

13. Erskine's friend John McLeod Campbell later developed a similar, but much fuller, doctrine of the cross in his controversial classic *The Nature of the Atonement* (1856).

14. Don Horrocks explains: "Christ's death historically had uniquely achieved full *pardon* for a new humanity by representing them as its Head and accepting the righteous divine condemnation of death for the old fallen flesh" (*Laws of the Spiritual Order*, 107). This forgiveness, however, does *not* mean that the *penalty* for sin

So forgiveness does not depend on our believing the gospel; instead, we believe the gospel because the fact that God has already forgiven us is revealed to us. Faith is our holistic existential response to that revelation—a joyful and transformative trust in the forgiving Father. The gospel declares our forgiveness and our faith in it changes us: "it is the enlightened belief in this pardon which heals, and purifies."[15] While forgiveness is already the objective truth for all people, it is only effective to salvation in our lives when we subjectively grasp hold of the fact in faith. Thus, all people are currently forgiven, but not all people are currently saved.

Election

Election was an issue that could not be ignored in Calvinist Scotland, but Erskine's radical reconfiguration of it in *The Doctrine of Election* (1837) proved highly contentious. According to Erskine, the subject of election is Christ's sinless humanity and the subject of reprobation is Adam's sinful humanity. So God elects *a way of being human*—i.e., Christ's way of filial trust and submission to the Father. Each one of us finds our hearts pulled in two directions: toward the old reprobate humanity in Adam and toward the new elect humanity in Christ. Faced with this inner conflict we must choose Christ, not Adam; the Spirit, not the flesh. Whether we share in Christ's election or Adam's reprobation depends on *our* choices.[16]

Educative punishment and universalism

Judgment there is, but it is corrective, not retributive. God's primary aim in punishment is *education*, training in goodness and holiness. "The purpose of God in sending affliction is not to *destroy* but to *correct*,—that is, to educate."[17] And knowing us completely, he knows exactly what kind of training we each need: "He meets my need, according to His full under-

---

is removed. We must still face the penalties for we need them as part of God's loving educative process of refinement.

15. Erskine, *Essay on Faith*, 139.

16. Erskine's doctrine of election is strikingly similar to the one William Law sets forth in *The Spirit of Love* (1752/54). Law was a major influence on Erskine. Another theologian with universalist inclinations who influenced Erskine's work was the Baptist John Foster (1770–1843), a fierce critic of the doctrine of eternal punishment.

17. Erskine, "Purpose of God," 71.

standing of me, by a course of circumstances chosen for my own personal education by His fatherly love and wisdom."[18] This idea, of course, flows out of his core belief that God is our Father and his purpose in creation is to form us in his image. "Man being the chief work of God . . . , his education—his moral and rational development—is the highest purpose of God that we can conceive."[19] Again, "education must have been the purpose of creation."[20] And: "I contend that the revelation of God as the Father necessarily involves the belief that education is the purpose with which he created us . . . [Contrary to those who see God as a Judge who puts us on probation,] *we are tried that we may be educated, not educated that we may be tried.*"[21]

For Erskine, it is the case that:

> in God mercy and justice are one and the same thing,—that His justice never demands punishment for its own sake, and can be satisfied with nothing but righteousness and that His mercy seeks the highest good of man which certainly is righteousness, and will therefore use any means, however painful, to produce it in him. If men could understand that God's purpose in rendering to them according to their works is to instruct them in the true nature and character of their works, that so they may apprehend the eternal connexion between sin and misery, between righteousness and blessedness, and thus be led from sin and take hold of righteousness, they would also understand that it is in mercy that He deals thus with them, and that in fact the purposes of mercy can in no other way be accomplished.[22]

It is in this context that Erskine's universalism comes into focus. His early works hint in the direction of universal salvation with their doctrine of God's universal Fatherhood, Christ's universal indwelling of humanity, universal election in Christ, Christ's universal atonement, universal pardon for sin, and so on. As early as 1830, some had begun to express the opinion that Erskine was on a road that led inevitably toward the "heresy" of universalism. Erskine himself seemed to fumble his way toward this wider hope.[23] It was his notion of educational punishment,

18. Erskine, "Purpose of God," 50.

19. Erskine, "Divine Son," 28.

20. Erskine, "Purpose of God," 51.

21. Erskine, "Purpose of God," 59.

22. Erskine, "Purpose of God," 72–73.

23. According to Don Horrocks, his first unambiguous statement of it was in a

extending beyond this life into the postmortem state, that allowed him to affirm total salvation without requiring that God ignore human freewill. Instead, God teaches us *until* we see the truth of sin and its consequences and grasp the unconditional grace of God offered in the gospel.

> The assurance that the righteous Creator can *never cease* to desire and urge the righteousness of His creature is the eternal hope for man, and the secure rest for the soul that apprehends it. For if this be His purpose for one, it must be His purpose for all. *I believe that it is His purpose for all, and that He will persevere in it until it is accomplished in all.*[24]

> God's purpose of unchanging love, which will *never cease* its striving *till* it has engaged *every* child of man to take Him in this contest [against sin].
>
>   In coming to this conclusion, it is manifest that I am constrained to adopt the assurance that the purpose follows man out from his present life, through all stages of being that lie before him, *unto its full accomplishment.* . . . [T]he ruling power in the universe, the only absolute Power . . . is a Being whose nature is righteous love, who is therefore the enemy of all sin, and who will *never cease* His endeavours to extinguish it, and to establish righteousness throughout His moral creation.[25]

Punishment for sin is motivated by the purpose of education, not retribution. This confidence is important, for then "I cannot but trust Him, and feel myself safe in His hands, eternally safe." But if I think that I am on probation now with a final judgment after death and my eternal destiny then forever fixed, "I should say that trust in Him becomes impossible."[26] Any confidence I have before God would then be self-confidence—confidence in my goodness or my faith—rather than God-confidence. But I am not good enough—so I face God in terror. I may call God Father, but how can I trust in his love or feel secure in his hands if I see him primarily as an impartial retributive Judge?

Contemporary developments in geological sciences impressed on Erskine God's very great patience in shaping his creation and informed his understanding of the ways of the Father: "We are evidently in the midst of a process, and the slowness of God's process in the material

letter to his cousin, dated 2 January 1827 (*Letters*, 1.92).

24. Erskine, "Purpose of God," 54–55. Italics mine.

25. Erskine, "Purpose of God," 69–70. Italics mine.

26. Erskine, "Purpose of God," 59, 60.

world prepares us . . . for something analogous in the moral world; so that at least we may be allowed to trust that He who has taken untold ages for the formation of a bit of old red sandstone may not be limited to three-score years and ten for the perfecting of a human spirit."[27] In other words, why imagine that death is the point at which God ceases to educate us?

The notion that God deals sin a final blow by punishing it in hell forever or annihilating sinners did not impress Erskine: "that is not the victory of good over evil, but the victory of strength over weakness. The victory of good over evil is the conversion of all evil beings into good beings."[28] This is what necessitated an eschatological universalism, for anything less would amount to the failure of God's purpose in creation.

Right theology and spiritual formation

Erskine's focus on spiritual and ethical transformation, which proved to be one of the tributaries that fed the later holiness movement in Britain, gave an important place to right theology. For in order to make any progress in moral or spiritual life "I must have . . . a confidence in His purpose to make me and all men LIKE HIMSELF. This is the confidence I must have in God if I am not to fear Him, or hate Him, or despise Him."[29] It is our childlike trust in the gospel that saves, because the revelation of God's Fatherhood and his loving purposes (which witnesses with our spirits) melts our hard hearts and leads to transformation in us. Salvation is the name for that transformation away from sinful living and toward righteous, God-related living. Thus he could speak of "the dynamic efficiency of the doctrines [of Christianity] in producing spontaneous obedience."[30] This effect is not the result of our increased effort, which will get us nowhere, but the awakening by God of "a principle of love" within us.[31] The reverse side of this is that if our conceptions of God and his purposes are warped, as he believed they were in the Calvinism of his day, then the right kind of faith will not be awakened in us, hampering God's work of salvation in us. "We cannot love a law or an abstraction,

27. Erskine, "Purpose of God," 53. Cf. Letter to Mr. Craig (1863?), *Letters*, 2.242.

28. Letter to an unknown correspondent, n.d., *Letters*, 2.237.

29. Erskine, letter to Professor Lorimer, 5 August 1858, *Letters*, 2.215.

30. Erskine, "Spiritual Order," 15. This transformed life, says Erskine, is the real evidence of the truth of Christianity.

31. Erskine, "Spiritual Order," 18.

nor can we love a Being whose mind and purpose towards ourselves we cannot apprehend and trust."[32] Instead of filial trust, we will look at God with terror and insecurity as the one who will torment us forever if we are not among his chosen few (and how can we ever be sure that we are?). Such are the laws of the spiritual order—we need a true and inner revelation of the Father, through Christ, by the Spirit if we are to be rescued from the power of sin.

Erskine's radical and eclectic theology was unsurprisingly treated with great suspicion and outright hostility in his homeland of Scotland. As his universalism became more overt, even some of his friends expressed disquiet. Nevertheless, he was to impact the thought others who came to have universalist sympathies, whether implicit or overt, both those who knew him personally (such as F. D. Maurice, George MacDonald, Charles Kingsley, Edward Pumptree, Julia Wedgewood, and Emelia Gurney) and those who only knew his works (such as Samuel Cox and Thomas Allin). The next chapters will explore the thought of some of those who came under his influence, beginning with those in the Church of England.

32. Erskine, "Spiritual Order," 23–24.

12

Universalism in Great Britain II

Romantic Explorers in the Church of England

UNIVERSALISM AND THE CHURCH OF ENGLAND

THE DOCTRINE OF ETERNAL torment had been coming under increasing pressure since the seventeenth century, and in the nineteenth century the tide of popular and theological opinion turned increasingly against it. Several factors were at work here.

First of all, the growth of the British Empire in the eighteenth and nineteenth centuries, combined with regular reports from the rapidly increasing number of Protestant missionaries across the world, made Christians back in Britain more aware than at any previous time in history just how many non-Christians there were in the world. Given that traditional theology consigned most or all such people to eternal torment, many began to feel increasing discomfort with the notion that God would send *so many* people to hell. In addition to this, there was a growing body of evidence, from the accumulated experiences of many of these missionaries, that preaching hell was not only ineffective in bringing about conversions, it was often positively counterproductive.

Second, the nineteenth century witnessed changing views on punishment. Since the seventeenth century, there had been various significant modifications in British law to the kinds of punishment that were deemed appropriate and the kinds of crimes for which they were applicable. In 1689, the English Bill of Rights had excluded "cruel and unusual punishments," meaning torture, and this trajectory continued through the eighteenth and nineteenth centuries. The number of crimes for which one could in theory be executed dropped dramatically, from 220 at the start of the nineteenth century to five by 1861; public executions were stopped in 1868, in spite of their popularity. Some notable Victorians, such as Charles Dickens and Elizabeth Fry, made the public more aware of the terrible conditions in prisons and applied pressure for prison reform. There was also the growing influence of Jeremy Bentham's utilitarianism. Bentham had argued that the punishment of criminals needed to be justified in terms of its utility—its ability to serve a desirable goal. This led to growing pressure to consider punishment not merely as retributive or a deterrent, but also in terms of how well it helped to *rehabilitate* criminals. Once people started thinking in such ways, questions about hell were immediately raised. Clearly eternal torment with no hope of deliverance was useless in terms of rehabilitation. Indeed, it seemed to be very "cruel and unusual." Furthermore, on reflection, it even seemed to violate the most basic instinct of retribution itself, the very theory on which it was based. The retributive theory of punishment asserted that the punishment should be proportioned to the crime. But how could an infinite punishment be a proportionate response to a finite set of sins?

Third, the nineteenth century was a period of growing religious doubt: the fast-advancing sciences and developments in Germany in the critical study of the Bible served to make old sureties less secure. There was also a growing religious agnosticism, especially amongst certain intellectuals.[1] The doctrine of hell was an obvious target for such critics of religion, and this too set believers on the back foot. The secularist Austin Holyoake, for instance, argued that the doctrine of hell "brutalises all who believe in it"[2] and that it was useless as a tool of moral improvement. Christianity was being accused of being immoral, and some were rejecting the church because of its theology of hell. This provoked some Christians to feel that rethinking hell was a matter of missional urgency.

Some of the growing disquiet over the doctrine of hell is captured in the following words from the highly regarded Florence Nightingale (note the clear universalist direction of her thought):

1. Though there is evidence that disquiet over hell was deeply felt among the working classes too. See Rowell, *Hell and the Victorians*, 147–49.

2. Holyoake, *Heaven and Hell*, 8. Quoted in Wheeler, *Heaven, Hell, and the Victorians*, 185.

I can't love because I am ordered. Least of all can I love One who seems only to make me miserable here to torture me hereafter. Show me that He is good, that He is loveable, and I shall love Him without being told.

But does any preacher show this? He may say that God is good, but he shows Him to be very bad; he may say that God is "Love," but he shows him to be hate, worse than any hate of man. As the Persian poet says; "If God punishes me for doing evil by doing me evil, how is he better than I?" And it is hard to answer, for certainly the worst man would hardly torture his enemy, if he could, for ever. And *unless God has a scheme that every man is to be saved for ever, it is hard to say in what He is not worse than man; for all good men would save others if they could.* . . .

How, then, is it possible to teach either that God is 'Love' or that God commands any duty—unless God has *a plan for bringing each and all of us to perfection?* . . .

It is of no use saying that God is just, unless we define what justice is. In all Christian times people have said that "God is just" and have credited him with an injustice such as transcends all human injustice that it is possible to conceive.[3]

This is the context within which we should try to understand the series of debates on hell and the scope of salvation that the Church of England found itself embroiled in from the middle of the nineteenth century. We shall briefly sketch these debates to indicate the gradual growing openness on the question of a wider hope.

Frederick Denison Maurice (1805–72) and the *Theological Essays* (1853) controversy

F. D. Maurice was an Anglican priest and Christian Socialist leader who occupied two professorships at King's College London. He had been brought up Unitarian, but converted to Anglicanism and was a significant and influential theologian within the Broad Church movement.

A controversy was stirred up over the publication of Maurice's *Theological Essays* (1853).[4] *Theological Essays* was written to address Unitarian objections to orthodox Christianity, and it was the final essay on "Eternal Life and Eternal Death"—his response to those who object to Christian

---

3. Nightingale, "A 'Note' of Interrogation"; italics mine.

4. On the Maurice controversy, see Rowell, *Hell and the Victorians*, 76–89; Laufer, *Hell's Destruction*, 119–24.

orthodoxy because of the doctrine of eternal torment—that was to prove the cause of much controversy.

Maurice concedes to the critic that many mainstream Christians did indeed embrace such a doctrine, and he laments the fact that some of them, like the Evangelical Alliance, felt the need to make it a nonnegotiable doctrine of the faith on par with the doctrine of the Trinity. He fears that the traditional doctrine of hell plays a key role in bringing the church and its gospel into disrepute, and so he seeks to show that orthodoxy is broad enough to encompass alternative views of eternal punishment.

Maurice focuses his response on the notion of eternity. The core of his argument is the claim that, in the New Testament, *aiōnios* ("eternal") is first and foremost a descriptor of *God* and his own "eternal" life. It has no *temporal* connotations; no sense of duration. So it does not mean "everlasting" or "without beginning and end."[5] Indeed, it is not even a negation of time (i.e., *a*temporal), but is something positive—God's own life, righteousness, and love.

In Maurice's view, this divine usage should determine how we understand the other usages—both eternal life and eternal punishment. *Aiōnios* is a term denoting the *quality*, not the *quantity*, of life (or punishment). Thus, eternal life means a sharing in God's own life. "The eternal life is the righteousness, and truth, and love of God which are manifest in Christ Jesus" (449).[6] Eternal death, on the other hand, is a separation from that life; it is the "punishment of being without the knowledge of God, who is love" (455). Being separated from all God's attributes, the lost are indeed in hell because all that remains to them is to be locked

5. After all, he says, even on the traditional view, eternal life and punishment cannot be life and punishment "without beginning" (449–50). It is worth noting that Maurice's understanding of *aiōnios* is different from the interpretations found in previous universalists. They did not deny an important temporal aspect to *aiōnios*, indeed they relied upon it.

6. The following in-text citations in this section on Maurice are from *Theological Essays*, unless otherwise stated.

in their own sinful ways. So "the eternal punishment is the punishment of being without the knowledge of God, who is love, and of Jesus Christ who has manifest it" (450). "What is Perdition but a loss? What is eternal damnation but the loss of a good which God had revealed to His creatures. . . . They did not believe that Love was at the root of all things, and that to lose Love, was to lose all things" (454).[7] This view, he believes, if rightly understood, is "a more distinct and awful idea of eternal death and eternal punishment than we [currently] have. . . . The thought of [God] . . . letting them alone, of His leaving them to themselves, is the real unutterable horror" (473). And this looming horror of being totally God-less is already becoming a reality in the existential experience of many people. They can relate to it in ways that they cannot relate to material images of torture in hell. "Every man who knows what it is to have been in a state of sin, knows what it is to have been in a state of death" (475). "If they fall into it, it is because they choose it, because they embrace it, because they resist a power which is always at work to save them from it" (474). (Note that God's power is said to be *always* at work to save—Maurice, like Erskine, whom he held in high regard, rejected the idea that death brings to an end all opportunities for salvation.)[8]

It is from this fate of sinking into sin that Christ came to rescue us. (Maurice, again like Erskine, argued that salvation should not be thought of as salvation from punishment in hell, but as salvation from *sin*.)

On the issue of universalism, of whether all the damned may one day be reached by God's love, Maurice expresses a pious agnosticism, but a deep hope.

> I ask no one to pronounce, for I dare not pronounce myself, what are the possibilities of resistance in a human will to the loving will of God. There are times when they seem to me—thinking of myself more than others—almost infinite. But I know that there is something which must be infinite. I am obliged to believe in

7. It is of some interest that when Maurice considers Jesus' warning to his disciples to "fear him which, after he hath killed, hath power to cast into hell" (Matt 10:28), he argues that it makes no sense to suppose "that this enemy is—not the devil, not the spirit who is going about seeking who he may devour, not him who was a murderer from the beginning,—but that God who cares for the sparrows! They are to be afraid lest He who numbers the hairs of their head should be plotting their ruin" (469). This interpretation was revived more recently by New Testament scholar N. T. Wright, though it remains uncommon.

8. Maurice was very open about the enormous theological debt that he owed to his friend Thomas Erskine.

> an abyss of love which is deeper than the abyss of death: I dare
> not lose faith in that love. I sink into death, eternal death, if I
> do. I must feel that this love is compassing the universe. More
> about it I cannot know. But God knows. I leave myself and all
> to Him. (476)

So while Maurice was not a universalist, he was certainly open to the
real possibility that universal salvation *may* be the outcome of creation.
We should certainly hope that it will be, with a hope grounded in God's
infinite love, a love more infinite than the human resistance to it.

The traditional view of hell laid great store in the word *aiōnois*, and
Maurice's revisionary understanding threatened one of the planks upon
which this theology was built. It was therefore no surprise that the publication of the book led to complaints to R. W. Jelf, the principal of King's
College, and the setting up by Jelf of what amounted to an inquisition
against Maurice. Jelf was simply unable to understand the position being
advocated by Maurice, and despite Maurice's regular insistence that he
was not teaching that all would be saved and that his views were fully
consistent with everything required of Anglican orthodoxy, Jelf and the
council thought that Maurice was deliberately fudging the issue, and that
in reality he was a universalist. He was therefore dismissed from his position at the college, making him what Rev. Edward Plumptre referred to as
"the proto-martyr of the wider hope."[9] In spite of this, the issue did not
go away and, as we shall see, some of Maurice's colleagues, friends, and
relatives took up the cause, stirring trouble as they did.

H. B. Wilson (1803–88) and the *Essays and Reviews* (1860) controversy

A massive controversy erupted after the publication of the seven Broad
Church essays in the landmark volume *Essays and Reviews* (1860), edited
by John William Parker.[10] One of the two most controversial was Rev.
Henry Bristow Wilson's essay on "The National Church," which argued
that Anglicanism should be less rigidly attached to the Thirty-Nine Articles.[11] In his essay, Wilson touched on eternal punishment. He believed

---

9. Plumptre, *Spirits in Prison*, viii.

10. On the debate about *Essays and Reviews*, see Rowell, *Hell and the Victorians*,
116–23; Laufer, *Hell's Destruction*, 124–26.

11. H. B. Wilson was a professor of Anglo-Saxon at Oxford (1839–44) and vicar

that few people died in a state ready for God's presence in heaven. But this, he claimed, does not mean that the majority are doomed to hell. Rather, there is room for spiritual progress in the afterlife after the great day of judgment. The dead are like seeds sent to "nurseries as it were and seed-grounds, where the undeveloped may grow up under new conditions—the stunted may become strong, and the perverted restored." He went on to say that when Christ "shall have surrendered His kingdom to the Great Father [an allusion to 1 Corinthians 15:28]—all, both small and great, shall find refuge in the bosom of the Universal Parent, to repose, or be quickened into higher life, in ages to come, according to His Will."[12] This certainly sounds like some version of hope for universal salvation.

His liberal views on hell were challenged in the church courts. In 1862, the judgment was delivered that Wilson's view was incompatible with the plain sense of the Athanasian Creed (with its comments on "everlasting fire"), to which all Anglican clergy had to subscribe. He was also guilty of making one's future fate depend wholly on moral conduct, irrespective of one's religious belief. Wilson was given a year's suspension of his living. He appealed the judgment, and in 1864 the appeal was allowed. The judgment declared

> We are not at liberty to express any opinion upon the mysterious question of the final punishment, further than to say that we do not find in the [Anglican] Formularies . . . any such distinct declaration of our Church upon the subject as to require us to condemn as penal the expression of hope by a clergyman, that even the ultimate pardon of the wicked, who are condemned in the day of judgment may be consistent with the will of Almighty God.[13]

This judgment started a firestorm of protest, especially from Evangelicals and Anglo-Catholics. They feared that this level of latitude over the interpretation of creeds opened the door to any and every heresy. They also thought that a weakening of the doctrine of hell removed a key motivator for moral behavior and set society on a road to moral perdition. The Oxford declaration against the essayists, organized by the Anglo-Catholics, was signed by almost 11,000 clergy. It proclaimed the historic Anglican belief in everlasting hell. The Archbishops of Canterbury and

---

of Great Staughton in Cambridgeshire from 1850 to 1888.

12 . Wilson, "National Church," 205–6.

13   Quoted in Rowell, *Hell and the Victorians*, 119.

York also expressed sympathy with the Oxford declaration. However, within a decade, when the subject of hell was again a matter of intense controversy, "not only was the argument conducted against a background of a more decided agnosticism, the general tone of the debate was much calmer. A growing appreciation of the results of biblical criticism did much to weaken the simple appeal to the authority of texts, which had been so frequently employed by the defenders of eternal punishment."[14]

Frederic W. Farrar (1831–1903) and the *Eternal Hope* (1878) controversy

At the end of 1877, the archdeacon of Westminster, F. W. Farrar, who had been a student of F. D. Maurice and continued to consider Maurice a mentor, preached a series of sermons on eternal punishment, published the following year as *Eternal Hope*, an "epoch-making book."[15] The book was perhaps clearer in what it denied than in what it affirmed.

Farrar sets out four views on hell: endless torment, annihilation, purgatory, and universalism. He then proceeds to deny the first three. The doctrine of endless hell he believes to be a view that is "to the utter detriment of all noble thoughts of God, and to all joy and peace in believing" (xiv). It is both unbiblical and abhorrent. Thus, "we . . . do in the high name of the outraged conscience of humanity,—nay, in the far higher names of the God who loves, of the Saviour who died for, of the Spirit who enlightens us,—hurl from us representations so cruel, of a doctrine so horrible, with every nerve and fibre of our intellectual, moral,

14. Rowell, *Hell and the Victorians*, 122–23.

15. Edward Plumptre's assessment in *Spirits in Prison*, viii. Farrar says in the preface that he had not intended to publish the sermons, but so many misleading accounts of what he said were circulating, he was forced into it. He denies that his intention was to cause any controversy. On the Farrar/Pusey debate, see Rowell, *Hell and the Victorians*, 139–52; Laufer, *Hell's Destruction*, 137–39.

and spiritual life" (71).[16] It's safe to say that he was not keen on the traditional doctrine. If not eternal hell, then what? He did not opt for annihilation (which he considers "ghastly") or purgatory (in its Roman Catholic version, at least).[17] On his own scheme, this leaves only universalism. So he was he a universalist?

Farrar certainly recognized the strengths of universalism—its affirmation of God's infinite love, its careful attention to biblical texts concerning universal restoration and Christ's universal atonement, and its presence in the works of some great teachers in the early church and those he calls modern-day saints, such as Thomas Erskine and Bishop Ewing of Argyll. Farrar has a lot of time for universalism, and considers it an "open question" for Anglicans (85). Indeed, "[e]very man must long with all his heart that this belief were true" (xv). Nevertheless, in spite of its strong appeal, he declares, "I dare not lay down any dogma of Universalism; partly because it is not clearly revealed to us, and partly because it is impossible for us to estimate the hardening effect of obstinate persistence in evil, and the power of human will to resist the law and reject the love of God" (xvi). What we do know is that God is love, a merciful Father, not a "remorseless Avenger," a God who desires none to perish, that sent Christ to redeem all. "[B]ut how long, even after death,

---

16. We shall not rehearse his arguments (contained in the preface, the third sermon, "Hell—What It Is Not," and Excursus II and III) as many of them will be familiar by now. He considers the traditional doctrine of hell to be based on what he stresses are *demonstrably false* translations of gehenna as "hell," krisis as "damnation," aiōnios as "everlasting," and *asbeston pur* as "fire that shall never be quenched." He argues that, upon inspection, these translations have no sound foundations and, on a closer inspection of key texts, the doctrine of everlasting torment has no solid basis in Scripture. Furthermore, the doctrine is ethically monstrous and theologically catastrophic. It may be worth taking one example, because it is a little unusual, of his response to proof texts for eternal torment. Let's consider his comments on Jesus' words about Judas that "it had been good for that man if he had not been born." Farrar observes how Jesus says nothing about torments and their endlessness. He maintains that the restoration of Judas does not mean his admittance into perfect bliss. "A man's sin may be ultimately forgiven him; he may even attain to a certain degree of peace; and yet, while the memory of his sin remains, he may be the first to acquiesce in the sorrowful decision that it had been well for him if he had not been born. A cessation of agonizing remorse is not the same thing as perfect peace, nor are the alleviations of deserved punishment identical with the beatific vision" (xxxix).

17. While critical of the Catholic version of purgatory, he does grant that it is a more merciful doctrine than the traditional Protestant one, offering at least some mitigation to the doctrine of hell, as we can see in Dante's *Divine Comedy* (58–59).

man may continue to resist his will;— . . . that is one of the secret things which God has not revealed" (86).

This is a little confusing for readers, who may wonder what will happen to those who might resist God's love forever. If they do not face eternal torment or annihilation or purgatory and will not be saved . . . what will happen to them? Part of the answer may be found in Farrar's modified version of "purgatory."

Farrar clearly affirmed that "the fate of man is not finally and irreversibly sealed at death" (86). He takes the descent of Christ into Hades to preach to the "spirits in prison" as evidence of this. (As we have seen, such a view had been gaining traction in certain circles through the nineteenth century, perhaps because it "fitted better with a dynamic, evolutionary picture of the universe, than the conception of fixed and unalterable states into which men entered at death.")[18] While rejecting the term "purgatory," he does support the notion that God continues working for the salvation of souls who die out of a state of grace. This was a "condition in which . . . imperfect souls who die in a state unfit for heaven may yet have perfected in them until the day of Christ, that good work of God which has been in this world begun" (xix). This purification takes place "in that Gehenna of aeonian fire beyond the grave" (88), a "remedial fire" (112). Such teaching regarding the fires of gehenna serving for purification he considers to be found in many of the church fathers. Will God punish us? "Yes, punish us, *because* he pities us" that we "would be melted by the heat of love" (97). That said, when Farrar speaks more carefully in Sermon V, he explains that the pains of the afterlife are all self-inflicted, the inevitable consequence of our actions, and not directly inflicted by God. God creates a law-governed universe in which certain courses of life bring about certain painful results. He will work in and through those consequences to teach us and correct and purify us, but God does not directly punish us. According to Farrar, the fires of gehenna are the enlightening yet horrible pains of conscience after our misdeeds—"the glare of illumination which the conscience flings over a soul after a deed of darkness" (148). Thus, salvation is "not from Him and His wrath, but from yourself and your own self-destruction" (151–52).

Nevertheless, the problem remains: one may still wonder at the fate of those dead souls who continue to defy God right up "until the day of

18. Rowell, *Hell and the Victorians*, 216. In this regard, it is perhaps of interest to note that it was Farrar who arranged for Darwin to be buried at Westminster Abbey, and at the funeral served as a pallbearer and preached the sermon.

Christ." What happens to them? Farrar does not venture to say, taking his cue from Jesus' answer to the question of whether only few will be saved—Jesus refused to answer the question and warns to questioner to make sure that *they* themselves are saved (Luke 13:23–24, Sermon IV). Farrar does likewise.

So, Farrar took the stance, as Maurice before him, of pious agnosticism, while affirming "a distinct *hope*" (xxi) in the final victory of the love of God.[19] He said, presumably if the end should fall short of universal salvation, "my hope is that the vast majority, at any rate, of the lost, may at length be *found*" (88). This is because God will save "all who do not utterly extinguish within their own souls the glimmering wick of love to God" (116). Yet protest as he might, many mistakenly believed that he was in fact a full-blown universalist.

Farrar's work generated some hostility, as one would expect, but also a lot of sympathy. *The Contemporary Review* commissioned a series of reflections on it by thinking churchmen who took differing views on the subject. The most important response, however, came from Edward Pusey, the celebrated Oxford Anglo-Catholic. Pusey was deeply concerned by Farrar's abandoning hell, fearing that it would open the floodgates of immorality by removing an important incentive to avoid sin. In 1880, he published his reply in a scholarly work entitled *What Is of Faith as to Everlasting Punishment?* Unlike many defenses of eternal hell, this one took the more unusual line of arguing that much of the perceived problem with hell was generated by the Protestant two-destiny view of the afterlife. The idea that everyone was destined for heaven or hell did not seem to match our experience of real people with all their shades of grey. Purgatory as a preparation ground for heaven helped deal with this. Pusey also expressed his view that we have no solid grounds for supposing that the majority of humanity would be damned, so we can reasonably hope for the salvation of the bulk of the human race. However, he did see our choices in this life as the only opportunity we have to avoid eternal damnation.

19. Farrar claims that the views set forth in the sermons were ones that "I have never since my early youth had the slightest doubt" (xii). He also claims Andrew Jukes's universalist text *The Restitution of All Things* among the influences in his preparation of the work—"a singularly calm, devout, and thoughtful treatise" (xii)—and Samuel Cox's universalist text, *Salvator Mundi* (xxxii). On Jukes and Cox see chapter 13 of this book.

Farrar was pushed into writing a much more scholarly book in response to Pusey, entitled *Mercy and Judgment* (1881). He still denied being a universalist, arguing that his and Pusey's views were not as far apart as Pusey thought, and continued to assert that all but the most reprobate would make spiritual progress in the intermediate state.

Edward Plumptre (1821–91) and *The Spirits in Prison* (1884)

Rev. Edward Hayes Plumptre had links with several of those we have already examined. He was the brother-in-law of F. D. Maurice and, like Maurice, was for many years a theological professor at King's College London. He was also a friend with F. W. Farrar, who had dedicated his book *Eternal Hope* to Plumptre. In addition, it is worth knowing that

Plumptre, like Maurice, knew Thomas Erskine and George MacDonald. It is perhaps no coincidence then that Plumptre also published in the area of eschatology and the wider hope, nor that he dedicated his book to Maurice.

Plumptre's book, *The Spirits in Prison and Other Studies on Life After Death*, was published in 1884, while he was serving as the Dean of Wells Cathedral in Somerset. Plumptre was, like Maurice and Farrar, open to the *possibility* of universal salvation, though reverently agnostic as to its truth or falsity.

The Spirits in Prison was in fact a collection of various studies written over a number of years on issues concerning the afterlife. The central essay, after which the book is named, is a sermon preached in 1871 at St. Paul's Cathedral. It is an examination of the idea that Christ "descended into hades" (as the Creed declares) and "preached unto the spirits in prison" (1 Pet 3:19). This hopeful doctrine had a high profile in the early church yet in post-Reformation England was almost lost. In Hades, Christ gathered the righteous dead around him, while "others, worthy of but a lower place, had yet found mercy. They had perished in God's great judgment, when the flood came upon the world of the ungodly, but they had not hardened themselves against His righteousness and love, and therefore were not shut out utterly from hope" (5).

This doctrine has always served as a beacon of a wider hope for ordinary Christians in the church, even in periods when official teachings said that "change and progress are excluded altogether from the state into which men pass at death" (10). "We may thank God, even though the protest has come in the form of wild dreams and fantastic speculations, that the natural instincts of men have risen up in revolt, and protested against conclusions so irreconcilably at variance with all belief in the love of Christ and the Fatherhood of God" (11). Purgatory, despite its many errors, provided at least a hope for progressive purification after death for some, and hence some spiritual consolation, which Protestants have looked at with envy.

With regard to universalism, Plumptre is eager to point out that it has deep roots in the tradition—including Origen (the "noblest, loftiest, most loving of the teachers of the ancient Church") and Gregory of Nyssa ("to whom we owe the fullest defence of the Nicene Confession of our faith") and many others in the East. The Church of England now even considers it "compatible with her dogmatic teaching" (13). "It has had many individual witnesses, some in the high places of the Church, some among her noblest thinkers and most loving hearts" (13) . . . and so on. So, he is certainly very sympathetic. However, there are problems with it, in particular human freedom, which we know from daily experience can frustrate God's purpose, and biblical teachings on final exclusion from the divine presence. There are indeed biblical texts that support universalism, but there are also others that point the opposite direction and "[w]e must be content to leave this seeming contradiction as part of the great mystery of evil from which the veil has never yet been lifted" (15). We must teach that final punishment of evil is everlasting, and that while if received "as the chastisement of a righteous Father, may lead men to repentance," it can also harden rebels against God.

So must we be agnostic about hope? "Has no glimpse behind the veil been given us?" It is here that the "lost" article of the Creed, the teaching on Christ's descent, comes into its own. Plumptre exegetes the text as teaching that Jesus went to the dead spirits in Hades who had been "unbelieving, disobedient, corrupt, ungodly; but who yet had not hardened themselves in the one irremediable antagonism to good which has never forgiveness" (18). Jesus, who had only just prayed, "Father forgive them, for they know not what they do," was not there to gloat and to tell them of the kingdom that could never be theirs. He preached the gospel to them. "And it was published to them, not to exempt them from all penalty, but that having been judged, in all that belonged to the relations of their human life with a true and righteous judgment, should yet, in all that affected their relation to God, 'live in the spirit'" (19). These sinful spirits in Hades repented and entered the gate of life. While Peter speaks of Christ preaching to those who disobeyed in Noah's time, "[w]e have no sufficient grounds for limiting the work on which [the apostles] dwell to the representative instance or time-boundaries of which they speak" (21).

Plumptre clearly believes that we cannot exclude the possibility that some people may harden themselves against God to the point that they are beyond recovery, so he is not a universalist. However, he is confident that, at the very least, this is not the case with the *vast* majority of people. And given God's continuing work in our lives after death, we have solid grounds for hope.

Thus, Plumptre calls for a recovery of the neglected creedal clause and the hopeful early church practice of prayer for the souls of the dead. "In every form, from the solemn liturgies which embodied the belief of her profoundest thinkers and truest worshippers, to the simple words of hope and love which were traced over the graves of the poor, her voice went up, without a doubt or misgiving, in prayers for the souls of the departed" (25). In chapter 9, Plumptre traces more carefully the ancient Christian practice of prayer for the progress of the dead in the afterlife and advocates its contemporary use. "The prayers of the faithful might hasten their progress upwards, or make them more capable of Divine compassion, or help them to a higher or earlier place in the first resurrection, or mitigate, in some mysterious way, the keenness of their pain" (26). (The problem, as Plumptre sees it, was that such prayer eventually became linked in the West with purgatory and thus, when Protestants rightly rejected purgatory, they also rejected prayer for the dead.) What is interesting about this call is that wider-hope books prior to Plumptre, perhaps because of their Protestant origins, had not made the connection with common early church activity of prayer for the dead.

The rest of the book is a series of academic studies on issues such as life after death in the OT and NT (considering the need to maintain the tension in its teaching on the scope of salvation),[20] a much more de-

20. "I do not attempt to formulate a reconciliation of the two contrasted views. . . . We seem landed, as in other questions, God's fore-knowledge and man's free-will,

tailed study on Christ's descent into hell in the tradition and its biblical roots, the variety of early church eschatologies (in which Augustine does not come out well),[21] the salvation of the heathen (in which he defends a version of inclusivism), the wider hope in English theology from the sixteenth to the nineteenth centuries (including a defense of Maurice against the charge of dogmatic universalism), eschatology in modern German theology,[22] prayers for the dead (an ancient and appropriate Christian practice), purgatory (a Catholic distortion of a genuine insight into the healing and purifying fire of divine correction),[23] conditional immortality (which he rejects), *aiōnios* (in which he maintains that, with the exception of John's Gospel, "eternal" *is* concerned with duration, contra Maurice), the damnatory clauses in the Athanasian Creed, and the intermediate state (defended as a mode of disembodied and conscious existence in which there can be progress toward God, even for one like Judas). Plumptre's work was the most scholarly of the nineteenth-century hopeful universalists. He had read widely in contemporary scholarship on Scripture, patristics, historical theology, and modern theology.

That Farrar and Plumptre's books did not generate the level of furious controversy witnessed in the 1850s through to the 1870s and that, unlike Maurice, they did not lose their jobs (indeed, Farrar later became dean of Canterbury and Plumptre remained dean of Wells until his death) shows something of the changing temperature of Victorian Anglicanism.

God's predestination and man's responsibility, in the paradox of seemingly contradictory conclusions. I do not say that such reconciliation is for our faculties and under our conditions of thought, possible. We must, it may be, be content to rest in the belief that each presents a partial aspect of the truth which may one day be revealed in its completeness. We may at least tolerate, as the Church of the third and fourth centuries tolerated, those who hold either to the exclusion of the other. We may endeavor to appropriate to ourselves whatever is profitable in the way of encouragement or warning, of hope or fear, in each" (73).

21. "And so the dark shadow of Augustine fell on the theology of the Western church, and condemned its thoughts of the love of God to so many centuries of disastrous twilight" (152).

22. He considers the work of Protestants: Carl Nitzsch, H. Martensen (Danish), Dorner, Julius Müller, and Franz Delitzsche, who all saw the possibility of ongoing grace and forgiveness beyond death, even if they were not universalists.

23. "Our purgatory, if we may venture to rehabilitate that abused and dishonoured word, will not be confined to the baptized or to those who have known historically and through human teachers the revelation of God, but will include all who have lived according to the light they had, and have, in however feeble a manner, repented of their sins and followed after righteousness" (309–10). This healing, purging fire will not exclude those who got sucked into heresy, nor consist in material fire.

Thomas Allin (1838–1909) and *Universalism Asserted* (1885)

The most unflinching and overt Anglican defense of universalism came from Rev. Thomas Allin. Allin was an Anglican priest from Ireland and an amateur botanist, and trained at Trinity College, Dublin. He moved to Somerset in England in 1877 and there published a significant and staunch defense of universal restoration, appropriately entitled *Universalism Asserted as the Hope of the Gospel on the Authority of Reason, the Fathers, and Holy Scripture.*[24] The book went through nine different editions between 1885 and 1905 as Allin kept modifying it.

One observation of relevance regarding Allin's book was how Anglican it was. Indeed, the very structure of this book is shaped by his Anglican instinct that theological reflection needs to take seriously the so-called the "three-legged stool" of Scripture, tradition, and reason. The title makes this clear. Allin begins with reason, works through tradition, and ends with Scripture. But his burden all along is to show that these three witnesses are deeply interrelated, mutually reinforcing, and are in complete harmony in asserting the truth of a universal restoration. He also works hard to wheel in lots of names among the great and the good within the Anglican Church to support his cause. Furthermore, he is keen to suggest that universalism is actually more in tune with themes at the heart of the Anglican Prayer Book and the Nicene Creed than is eternal hell.

It was not uncommon to hear universalists accused of believing heresy, but Allin was as concerned to avoid heresy as any nineteenth-century Anglican. Indeed, one could see the whole of his argument in *Universalism Asserted* as an attempt to turn this accusation back against the believers in hell. It is *they*, not the universalists, who are in the greatest danger of heresy!

Now at first blush this suggestion sounds absurd. Clearly belief in hell is not formally heretical, as most of the great orthodox theologians in the past fifteen hundred years have been believers in an eternal perdition. So how could belief in hell possibly be flirting with heresy!?

---

24. In fact, the 1885 edition was entitled *The Question of Questions: Is Christ Indeed the Saviour of the World?* But the second edition, published in 1887, took on the title that the book retained thereafter, *Universalism Asserted*. The definitive edition is now the new Annotated Edition (2015), edited, annotated, and with an introduction by Robin A. Parry and entitled *Christ Triumphant*.

Perhaps an example from Allin's arguments will help us to see what he is getting at. Allin argues that if hell continues to all eternity, then sinners continue in their resistance to God for all eternity, sin continues forever, evil continues forever. As such, we end up with an everlasting cosmic dualism in which good and evil are co-eternal. Even if God can imprison sin in an eternal chamber in some corner of creation, he has merely contained it, not undone and defeated it. Yet such an idea threatens to undermine some central Christian convictions about God and evil.

Allin also argues that a hell from which there is no ultimate restoration—whether that hell be eternal torment or annihilation—would undermine the doctrine of God (his love, his justice, his goodness, his omnipotence), the victory of Christ, the power of the atonement, and so on and so forth. Indeed, Satan would seem to achieve a good part of his purposes for the world!

Of course, those who believe in hell also affirm God's love and justice, omnipotence, the atonement, divine victory, etc. But Allin's point is that when they do so they either (a) have to add in qualifications that serve to undermine the very beliefs that they affirm or (b) they have to simply ignore the contradictions in their belief set and talk out of both sides of their mouth at the same time.

So the doctrine of hell, in Allin's view, is perhaps a little like a cuckoo in the nest of Christian theology: it is a real and present danger to the genuine chicks. Given the oft-heard, though in my view incorrect, assertion that universalism is formally heretical, what is interesting is that the heart of Allin's case, though he does not put it in these words, is that to maintain a consistent and healthy Christian orthodoxy we ought to jettison belief in eternal hell. *Hell*, in other words, *is bad for orthodoxy*.

Anglican as he was, Allin was very critical of Western theology, and this very much included his own tradition. He believes that Augustine effected a seismic shift in the shape of Western Christian theology, twisting it almost out of recognition—a claim his subsequent two volumes attempted to substantiate.[25] The dominance of the "traditional" teaching on hell owes a massive debt to this Augustinian de-formation in the tradition. So Allin was Anglican who opposed the legal-shaped "Latin" theology of his own church and embraced Eastern, "Greek" thought. But such Greek theology was, he believed, true to the heart of Angli-

25. *Race and Religion: Hellenistic Theology: Its Place in Christian Thought* (1899) and the posthumously published *The Augustinian Revolution in Theology* (1911).

canism, and resonated well with some of the "modern" theology being taught by some Victorian theologians, even if most Anglicans have not yet perceived this.[26]

The most interesting part of Allin's book is the first section (chapters 1–3) in which he argues that the popular belief about hell is wholly untenable, clashing with conscience, ethics, and reason, and undermining the church's task of mission. All attempts to defend it, he argues, fall apart under inspection. However, the most significant advance that Allin's book made was its discussion of patristic material in the second section (chapters 4–5, and parts of chapter 6). Plenty of earlier books had discussed the question of hell and universalism in the early church, but none had done so with the breadth and depth of Allin's book. While his work has now been long superseded, it contains much of continuing value and remains an often-overlooked landmark in the recovery of teaching on *apokatastasis* in the early church. He seeks to demonstrate that belief in universal restoration "prevailed very widely in the primitive church," was taught by those who "were among the most eminent and most holy of the Christian Fathers," and that it was never condemned by the church and is consistent with the catholic creeds (85). He does this by surveying a mass of material from the second century to the start of the fourth century, from the early-fourth to the mid-fifth century, then on to the twelfth century. As topping on the cake, he finally does a survey of numerous universalist sympathizers since the Reformation, with various notable Anglican clergy thrown in for good luck.

The final section of the book is an overview of biblical doctrines (creation, incarnation, atonement, sacraments, resurrection, eschatological death, judgment and fire, election, covenant) and texts (OT and NT), seeking to show that the larger hope is firmly rooted in Scripture. At times, Allin turns again to the church fathers to show that they often interpreted the biblical texts and doctrines under inspection in universalist ways.

We do not know how or when Allin embraced universalism, but we do know that he read widely on the subject and his published work, coming after many of the other nineteenth-century publications mentioned in this section, was able to draw on them (e.g., Foster, Erskine, Maurice, Farrar, Plumptre, Jukes, and Cox). In some ways, his work represents a culmination of universalist arguments throughout the

---

26. He considered his way of being Anglican to be liberal, rationalist, evangelical, and catholic (no caps).

century, though he went much further than the very cautious hope of fellow Anglicans Maurice, Farrar, and Plumptre. What is also of interest is that, so far as we can tell, his book generated far less heat and controversy than those of his predecessors, further indicating the continuing change in theological climate.

Taking stock of nineteenth-century developments in the Church of England

Tracing the decreasing heat in the various hell debates from 1853 to 1887, one can detect a broadening out of Anglicanism over the second half of the nineteenth century. This is perhaps seen most clearly in the "resolution" to the debates over the Athanasian Creed.

In the 1870s, controversy raged within the Church of England over the damnation clauses in the Athanasian Creed.[27] The Creed not only ends with a declaration that at the judgment those who have done evil will depart "into everlasting fire," but it also condemns all who do not affirm the faith as set out in the Creed to "perish everlastingly." The Book of Common Prayer required the use of the Athanasian Creed on certain important feast days. In practice, this often did not happen, but the Oxford Movement led to a tightening up on such laxity. Increasing numbers of worshippers thus found themselves confronted with and disturbed by this text. In 1867, a Royal Commission looked into the rituals of the Church of England, and the issue of this creed became a focus, setting off a wider debate. The fate of those who had never heard the gospel was a particular sticking point. The debate about the merits and demerits of using the Athanasian Creed rumbled on among the clergy through the 1870s. Should it be dropped from the Prayer Book? Should some explanatory clause be added to qualify its damnation clauses? Passions were high. For some, it was an authoritative statement of the catholic faith; for others, it was a stumbling block. In the end, no clear resolution was reached, but considerable latitude on its interpretation was allowed. In 1873, a convocation agreed on a statement that the Church of England affirms the necessity of the saved holding fast to the catholic faith, and the peril of not doing so. But this allowed plenty of room to maneuver on hell. By the 1890s, the Archbishop of Canter-

---

27. On the debate about the Athanasian Creed, see Wheeler, *Heaven, Hell, and the Victorians*, 192–94; Laufer, *Hell's Destruction*, 128–30.

bury declared, perhaps a little hyperbolically, that no one in the Church of England took the hell clauses in the Athanasian Creed literally any longer.

Thomas Allin clearly saw various eminent figures in the Anglican establishment of his day as sympathetic to the wider hope. In addition to some of those already mentioned, he claims B. F. Wescott; the eminent NT scholar and Bishop of Durham, Canon Charles Kingsley; the famous novelist, social reformer, priest, and theologian, Canon Basil Wilberforce (grandson of William); and a number of other named clergy.

By the 1890s, ex-Prime Minister William Gladstone could comment, albeit with some concern for the impact on morality, that hell had been banished "to the far-off corners of the Christian mind . . . there to sleep in deep shadow as a thing needless in our enlightened and progressive age."[28]

28. Gladstone, *Studies Subsidiary to the Works*, 206.

13

Universalism in Great Britain III
George MacDonald among the Poets

THE LITERARY WORLD AND HELL

NUMEROUS POETS AND NOVELISTS in the nineteenth century felt distinctly uncomfortable with the traditional doctrine of hell. Many of the major literary figures of the century were at least agnostic about the outcome of the final judgment, and several expressed open hostility to the idea of eternal torment, and even showed universalist tendencies. One thinks, for instance, of the novelists Charlotte, Emily, and Anne Brontë, James Anthony Froude, Charles Kingsley, Edna Lyall, Margaret Oliphant, and William Thackeray, or the poets Robert and Elizabeth Browning, Samuel Taylor Coleridge, Philip Bailey, and Alfred Tennyson.[1]

---

1. And the list should certainly include some of the great American poets and novelists of the period too: John Greenleaf Whittier, Oliver Wendell Holmes, Ralph Waldo Emerson, and Harriet Beecher Stowe (whose brother, the theologian Edward Beecher, challenged traditional hell in his *History of Opinions on the Scriptural Doctrine of Retribution* [1878]). It is worth noting that, when George MacDonald went on a literary tour of America, he met all of those mentioned here.

Consider Tennyson, the Poet Laureate, who expressed his disdain for eternal torment by refusing to recite the Athanasian Creed in church, a creed Charlotte Brontë called "profane."[2] Tennyson's poem *In Memoriam* (1849), which has been described as "the most important poem of the Victorian period on the subject of death and the future life,"[3] expresses a yearning and a tentative hope that after the many griefs of this life, "all will be well." Here is the key section:

Oh yet we trust that somehow good
Will be the final goal of ill,
To pangs of nature, sins of will,
Defects of doubt, and taints of blood

That nothing walks with aimless feet,
That not one life shall be destroyed,
Or cast as rubble to the void,
When God has made the pile complete.

Behold, we know not anything,
I can but trust that good shall fall.
At last—far off—at last, to all,
And every winter change to spring.

The wish, that of the living whole,
No life may fail beyond the grave,
Derives it not from what we have,
The likest God within the soul?

I stretch lame hands of faith, and grope
And gather dust and chaff, and call,
To what I feel is Lord of all,
And faintly trust the larger hope.

The "larger hope" of which he speaks and for which he can only "grope" and "faintly trust" became the term of choice for many when referring to views leaning in universalist directions. It is worth noting that F. D.

2. Wheeler, *Heaven, Hell & the Victorians*, 194.
3. Wheeler, *Heaven, Hell & the Victorians*, 2.

Maurice dedicated his *Theological Essays* to Tennyson (in turn, Tennyson wrote a poem for Maurice when the latter lost his job at King's College), and F. W. Farrar dedicated his *Mercy and Judgment* to him, referring to him as "the poet of the larger hope." George MacDonald described *In Memoriam* as "*the* poem of hoping doubters, *the* poem of our age . . . the cry of the bereaved Psyche into the dark infinite after the vanished love."[4] His poem certainly caught something of the spirit of the age.

Consider too the following from a lesser-known poem, *Festus* (1839), by Philip James Bailey (1816–1902).

> All men have sinned: and all have died,
> All men are saved. Oh! Not a single soul
> Less than the countless all can satisfy
> The infinite triumph which belongs to me.[5]

After all, "To whom shall mercy hope deny?"[6] Even Lucifer, after the first edition of the poem, has hope: "This day art thou / Redeemed to archangelic state."[7]

The nineteenth-century novelist who is perhaps best remembered today as embracing "the larger hope" is the Scottish author George Mac-Donald, and he deserves closer attention.

GEORGE MACDONALD (1824–1905)

Life

George MacDonald was born and grew up in a farming household in Huntley, rural Aberdeenshire.[8] He had been brought up Congregational-ist, hence Calvinist, but from childhood had struggled with the idea that God elects some people and not others for salvation. "I well remember feeling as a child that I did not care for God to love me if he did not love everybody."[9] This distaste for the Calvinist vision of the deity followed him like a shadow throughout his life.

4. MacDonald, *England's Antiphon*, 329.

5. Bailey, *Festus: A Poem*, 578. On Bailey, see Wheeler, *Heaven, Hell, & the Victorians*, 98–101.

6. Bailey, *Festus: A Poem*, 65.

7. Bailey, *Festus: A Poem*, 582.

8. Two excellent biographies are Hein, *George MacDonald: Victorian Myth-maker*, and Raeper, *George MacDonald*.

9. MacDonald, *Weighed and Wanting*, 47.

MacDonald attended King's College, at the University of Aberdeen, before moving to London to work as a private tutor in 1845. While studying as an undergraduate he found his faith in some turmoil as it went through a chrysalis phase; he was unlearning much that he had been taught in his youth and looking to God and Scripture for new directions. What he desired was a wholehearted, passionate love for God, and this he gradually found: "I love my bible more. I am always finding out something new in it. I seem to have had everything to learn over again from the beginning—All my teaching in youth seems useless to me—I must get it all from the bible again."[10]

In 1848, he attended Highbury Theological College in London to train for the ministry before moving in 1850 to Trinity Congregational Church in Arundel to serve as minister. However, things did not go well there, and in 1852 the congregation cut his salary because of "heresy" (in particular, the idea that "with the Heathen the time of trial does not . . . cease at their death") with the intention of forcing him out. George and his wife Louisa were unable to support their family (they had just had their first baby, Lilia), so George was forced to resign the pulpit in mid-1853, leaving behind any ambitions of a future in ordained ministry. The family moved to Manchester and then in 1859 back to London.

George's true gift turned out to be as a poet and novelist, rather than as a minister. This was not a new love. His first published poem had appeared in 1846, and his first book of poetry, *Within and Without*, in 1855. Other notable publications included *Phantastes* (1859), the fantasy novel that famously baptized the imagination of C. S. Lewis; *David Elginbrod* (1863); *Robert Falconer* (1868); *At the Back of the North Wind* (1871); *The Princess and the Goblin* (1872); *The Princess and Curdie* (1882); and *Lilith* (1895). The first and last of these publications were pioneering works in the genre of fantasy literature and continue to be influential today.[11] His

10. Quoted in Raeper, *George MacDonald*, 56.

11. Those novelists who name him as a significant influence include C. S. Lewis, W. H. Auden, G. K. Chesterton, J. R. R. Tolkein, E. Nesbit, and Madaleine L'Engle (who

sensibilities were Romantic, and he had immersed himself in the works of German and English Romantics like Goethe and Schiller, Wordsworth, and Coleridge. His theology too reflected the same Romantic dispositions, as we shall see.

Slowly but surely, MacDonald's work began to gain an audience. He was never an A-list author, but he became well-known and respected by many. Indeed, in 1868 the University of Aberdeen conferred an honorary LLD degree on him for "high literary eminence as a poet and author."

MacDonald's patron, Lady Byron, introduced him to numerous key people to help establish the young unknown writer, and MacDonald became increasingly well-connected with the great and the good in his day. His friends and acquaintances included Charles Dodson (who wrote under the name Lewis Carroll); John Ruskin; Arthur Hughes (the Pre-Raphaelite artist); Mark Twain; Charles Kingsley; Alfred Tennyson; Charles Dickens; Wilkie Collins; Walt Whitman; Harriet Beecher Stowe; Oliver Wendell Holmes; Octavia Hill; Josephine Butler;[12] and numerous others.

In 1879, the MacDonald family moved to Bordighera in Italy, where they spent many happy years. But tragedy was never far away. Throughout his life, George had known the loss of many people close to him—his mother when he was eight (1832), his brother and father (1858), and his patron, Lady Byron (1860)—but the loss of several of his children— Mary Josephine (1878), Maurice (1879), Grace (1884), and especially his beloved Lilia (1891)—was a very profound blow. The death of Lilia, his firstborn, cut especially deep and shaped the novel *Lilith*, which he was writing at the time. Death was always an important theme that MacDonald wrestled with in his works, but in none more so than *Lilith*, his final work.

In terms of universalist-related connections, we should note that George was a good friend with F. D. Maurice, whom he regarded as a mentor. MacDonald attended St. Peter's Church in Vere Street, London, where Maurice was vicar (1860–69), so that he could sit under his preaching. Indeed, Maurice managed to lure MacDonald to become an Anglican, in part because it allowed him more freedom for theological exploration. He found a likeminded soul in Maurice, and George even

---

was herself a Christian universalist).

12. Josephine Butler (1828–1906), the Christian social reformer, best known for her work with and for prostitutes, also believed in universal salvation.

named one of his sons Maurice in his honor (with F. D. serving as godfather to the boy).[13] MacDonald wrote the following verse about Maurice and hell:

> He taught that hell itself is yet within
> The confines of thy kingdom; and its fires
> The endless conflict of thy love with sin,
> That even by horror works its pure desires.[14]

Both Maurice and MacDonald looked for inspiration to, among others, Samuel Taylor Coleridge (the Romantic poet and philosopher-theologian); Schleiermacher; the Cambridge Platonists; Origen; Jakob Böhme; F. W. Robertson;[15] William Law; and Thomas Erskine. In reading MacDonald's work, one cannot but be aware of the strong parallels between his thought and that of Erskine. MacDonald was not friends with Erskine, but he did visit him in Linlathen in 1865 and corresponded with him.[16] William Raeper sums up the emphasis of Erskine, Maurice, and MacDonald very simply as follows: "the rediscovery of the Father."[17]

The larger hope in George MacDonald

As a matter of fact, universal salvation was not one of the key issues addressed by MacDonald and he rarely spoke directly about it. Nevertheless, it is not hard to see that universalism was a natural outcome of his core theological convictions. We shall briefly outline some of those core convictions and indicate how they relate to the breadth of salvation.[18]

As with Erskine before him, the starting point was MacDonald's rejection of the Calvinist understanding of God. MacDonald had been

13. George also knew Edward Plumptre, who worked at King's College, London.

14. MacDonald, "Thanksgiving for F. D. Maurice." This verse was omitted from the published version. It is reproduced in Raeper, *George MacDonald*, 408n52.

15. Frederick William Robertson (1816–53) was a celebrated Anglican preacher with Evangelical roots, best known for his ministry in Brighton. He had criticized the traditional doctrine of hell.

16. MacDonald's interest in Erskine may have been sparked by A. J. Scott, a close friend of Erskine's and another important influence on MacDonald.

17. Raeper, *George MacDonald*, 241.

18. Perhaps the key outlet for MacDonald's universalist-inclined theology is found in the three volumes of his *Unspoken Sermons* (series 1 [1867], series 2 [1885], series 3 [1889]). As so many editions of these sermons exist, in the citations that follow we shall indicate the sermon, but not the page number.

instinctively repulsed by this vision of the deity from his childhood days, which made growing up in a church context dominated by Calvinism existentially troubling for him. Gradually he discarded Calvinist theology and embraced a new vision of God—one that renewed his dead faith, turning it into a burning, passionate love for God.

MacDonald came to believe that the *person* of Christ himself has to be the heart of the Christian understanding of the revelation of God—and the God revealed in Christ is *the loving Father of all humanity*. All of MacDonald's theology is oriented around this center.

And what is the very core of the truth about God, as made known in Jesus? "In one word, God is Love. Love is the deepest depth, the essence of his nature, at the root of all his being. . . . His perfection is his love. All his divine rights rest upon his love."[19] *Nothing* true that we ever say about God will contradict this central truth—God is love. And any assertions about God incompatible with divine love are necessarily falsehoods.

Furthermore, God is seen to be kenotic, not despotic. "How terribly, then, have the theologians misrepresented God. . . . Nearly all of them represent him as a great King on a grand throne, thinking how grand he is, and making it the business of his being and the end of the universe to keep up his glory, wielding bolts of a Jupiter against them that take his name in vain." However, God's glory was not the manifestation of his power, said MacDonald, but his humility. "Brothers, have you found our king? There he is, kissing little children and saying they are like God. There he is at table with the head of a fisherman lying on his bosom."[20]

In light of the divine self-revelation in Christ, MacDonald's understanding of creation, sin, and salvation were all recrafted. God's purpose in creation was to have children in a loving relationship with him. Sin was to be understood primarily in relational, not legal, terms. Salvation too was relational—God's purpose is that of restoring his children to himself.[21]

19. MacDonald, "Creation in Christ."

20. MacDonald, "Child in the Midst."

21. MacDonald loved the Bible, not for its own sake, but because it pointed him to Jesus. "The Bible is to me the most precious thing in the world, because it tells me his story." However, he was very aware of the dangers of idolizing the Bible and of treating *it*, rather than Jesus, as the prime locus of divine revelation. His focus was thus always on Christ: Scripture points not to itself, but to him, and must be read not according to the letter, but according to the Spirit—it must be read in the light of Christ. The way he handled difficult texts in the Bible manifests this hermeneutic. If a biblical text appears to present God behaving in what seems to be a wicked way incompatible with

MacDonald's new vision required a distancing from the existing theology. Thus, he denounced the Calvinist understanding of salvation as rescue from God's wrath, he denied the theory of justice that it presupposed (i.e., retributive), he loathed the understanding of the cross by which this salvation was thought to be achieved (i.e., penal substitution), he repudiated the common doctrine-focused understanding of justification by faith and the idea of imputed righteousness, and he rejected the traditional doctrine of hell.

Rejecting Calvinist theology: no to retributive justice

Underpinning the Calvinist understanding of salvation from sin is a theory of justice that MacDonald thought flawed. According to this theory, justice requires God to punish sin "for the sake of punishing."[22] However, "[s]uffering weighs nothing at all against sin"[23] and does *nothing* to compensate or make right what is wrong. As Thomas Talbott explains: "In and of itself, MacDonald contended, punishment does nothing to make up for the slightest of our sins; it 'is *nowise* an *offset* to sin.' It neither atones for our sin, nor 'balances the scales of justice,' nor justifies God's decision to permit sin in the first place, nor somehow restores God's stolen glory. . . . So why is God prepared to punish sin? . . . [T]o deliver us from evil."[24]

Divine justice, says MacDonald, is not retribution, but a work of divine love, and God punishes not as an end in itself, but as a means to an end—our purification. "Primarily, God is not bound to *punish* sin; He is bound to *destroy* sin."[25]

---

the revelation in Jesus then we must say that we are not certain how to understand the text, but that whatever it is saying about God it *cannot* be what it appears to say. One must keep looking for what it is God is saying through the text, but one must *never* accept that God acts wickedly, nor that what seems to you to be wicked is really good. You must never "receive any word as light because another calls it light, while it looks to you dark. Say either the thing is not what it seems, or God never said or did it. But of all evils, to misinterpret what God does, and then say the thing as interpreted must be right because God does it, is of the devil" ("Light"). This role for conscience in the hermeneutic reminds one of Erskine and Coleridge.

22. MacDonald, "Justice."

23. MacDonald, "Justice."

24. Talbott, "Just Mercy of God," 234. He quotes from MacDonald, "Justice."

25. MacDonald, "Justice."

> I believe that justice and mercy are simply one and the same
> thing: without justice to the full there can be no mercy, and
> without mercy to the full there can be no justice; that such is the
> mercy of God that he will hold his children in the consuming
> fire of his distance until they pay the uttermost farthing, until
> they drop the purse of selfishness with all the dross that is in it,
> and rush home to the Father and the Son, and the many breth-
> ren—rush inside the centre of the life-giving fire whose outer
> circles burn. I believe that no hell will be lacking which would
> help the just mercy of God to redeem his children.[26]

MacDonald was concerned too that retributive justice acts independently of love. As presented in traditional theology, God is torn between
wanting to forgive sinners in his love but *having* to punish them in his
justice. In positing an inner divine conflict between justice and love, traditional theology threatens the divine unity. "God is one; and the depth
of foolishness is reached by that theology which talks of God as if he held
different offices, and differed in each. It sets a contradiction in the very
nature of God himself. It represents him, for instance, as having to do
that as a magistrate which as a father he would not do."[27]

Rejecting Calvinist theology: no to penal substitution

The Calvinist saw the cross as the means by which God was able to resolve
his inner conflict between his justice and love and thereby save the elect.
MacDonald, however, thought penal substitution flawed at several levels. First, it construes God's relationship to us in mechanical rather than
relational ways. Second, it requires God to employ some legal trickery
in order to forgive us, thus failing to appreciate the very nature of God's
forgiveness. Forgiveness is freely given and requires no fancy footwork
on God's part to enable him to grant it. Third, it actually extinguishes
the possibility of forgiveness of sin, for if God insists on exacting the full
penalty for our sins by punishing them in Christ then he has not *forgiven*
the sin at all. Fourth, even if it made sense, all that penal substitution
could accomplish would be to provide an escape hatch from punishment
in hell, leaving us unchanged, still enslaved to sin. Fifth, it is incoherent
even on its own terms, for on a retributive theory of justice, the punishment of an innocent man (Jesus) and the failure to punish the guilty (us)

26. MacDonald, "Justice."
27. MacDonald, "Justice."

could not be the fulfillment of divine justice. "Justice *could not* treat a righteous man as an unrighteous. Neither, if justice required the punishment of sin, *could* justice let the sinner go unpunished."[28] MacDonald considered the teaching that Jesus was a sacrifice to pacify God's wrath to be pure paganism: "Believe in Moloch if you will, but call him Moloch, not Justice."[29]

According to MacDonald, this notion of justice and atonement, understood as a mechanism to divert God's wrath from us, gets atonement back-to-front. Christ's atoning work was not to reconcile God to us, but to reconcile *us to God*. God unwaveringly loves us. It is not *God's* attitude that needs changing through atonement, but *ours*.

> He came to satisfy God's justice by giving him back his children; by making them see that God is just. . . . And there isn't a word of reconciling God to us in all the Testament, for there was no need of that; it was us that needed to be reconciled to him. And so he bore our sins and carried our sorrows, for those sins . . . caused him no end of grief of mind and pain of body, as everyone knows. It wasn't his own sins, for he had none, but ours, that caused him suffering; and he took them away. . . . He took our sins upon him, for he came into the middle of them and took them up—by no sleight of hand, by no quibbling of the lawyers about imputing his righteousness to us, and such like, which is not to be found in the Bible at all, though I don't say that there's no possible meaning in the phrase, but he took them and took them away, and here am I, . . . growing out of my sins in consequence.[30]

Thus he cries, "Away with your salvation from the 'justice' of a God whom it is a horror to imagine! Away with your iron cages of false metaphysics! I am saved—for God is light!"[31]

Rejecting Calvinist theology: no to salvation through right doctrine

MacDonald was very critical of the idea of salvation by faith in Christ when it was understood to mean salvation through believing in the right

28. MacDonald, "Righteousness."

29. MacDonald, "Righteousness."

30. MacDonald, *Robert Falconer*, vol. 3, ch. 5. English translation from Scots by David Jack (2016 edition, 326–27).

31. MacDonald, "Light."

doctrines. Believing that certain teachings and theories are true is not saving faith. Saving faith, he said, is believing *in* a person—Christ. "Even

if your plan, your theories, were absolutely true, the holding of them with sincerity, the trusting in this or that about Christ, or in anything he did or could do—the trusting in anything but himself, his own living self—is still a delusion. . . . [W]e must believe in the atoning Christ, and cannot possibly believe *in* any theory concerning the atonement."[32]

And belief in Christ means *childlike obedience* to Christ. If you don't obey then you don't believe. Consequently, in MacDonald's view, there are plenty of Christians out there who are no more "saved" than many unbelievers, for although they believe the "right" doctrine, they lack childlike trust in and obedience to Christ. "It is better to be an atheist who does the will of God, than a so-called Christian who does not."[33]

The doctrine of "imputed righteousness," by which God looks at sinners but considers them—by means of a legal fiction—to be righteous, even though they have not become righteous was "the poorest of legal cobwebs spun by spiritual spiders."[34]

Salvation, rather, is a long journey of sanctification, of self-denial and obedience to our loving Father, not a single moment in our lives. It is deliverance from sin, not deliverance from God's wrath.

> He came to deliver us from the evil in our being. . . . He came to deliver us, not from the things we have done, but the possibility of doing such things anymore. . . . Jesus was born to deliver us from all such and other sin—not primarily from the punishment of any of them. When all are gone, the holy punishment will have departed also. He came to make us good, and therein blessed children.[35]

32. MacDonald, "Truth in Jesus."
33. MacDonald, "Truth in Jesus."
34. MacDonald, "Last Farthing."
35. MacDonald, "Salvation from Sin."

Christ made the way back to the Father open for us, he showed us the path, and he enables us to walk in it. He walked the route of the cross, but not so that we don't have to; he did it to show us *how*, so that we can take up our cross and follow him. "I believe that he died that I might die like him—die to any ruling power in me but the will of God."[36]

Rejecting Calvinist theology: no to traditional hell

The traditional doctrine of hell was anathema to MacDonald. Not only was it unjust and unloving, thus incompatible with the truth revealed in Jesus, but it also represented the perpetuation of evil forever in God's good creation, and thus a permanent failure on God's part to achieve his purposes. Speaking of Dante's inferno, MacDonald writes, "Such justice as Dante's keeps wickedness alive in its most terrible forms. The life of God goes forth to inform, or at least give a home to victorious evil."[37] This is not the defeat of evil, but its triumph! Traditional hell makes no sense in light of MacDonald's understanding of justice: "The justice of God is the love of what is right, and the doing of what is right. Eternal misery in the name of justice could satisfy none but a demon whose bad laws had been broken."[38]

MacDonald resisted the traditional idea that death was a point of no return, fixing our fates in eternal heaven or eternal hell. God cannot be less merciful than a human parent. "No amount of wrongdoing in a child can ever free a parent from the divine necessity of doing all he can to deliver his child."[39] Therefore, the claim that God would one day give up seeking the salvation of his children "is false as hell."[40]

Nevertheless, MacDonald did teach a postmortem punishment from God, a version of hell. God's love refuses to leave us in sin and will burn with painful but purifying fire. This fire is actually the presence of *God himself*, for our God is, in his purity, a consuming fire.

> It is the nature of God, so terribly pure that it destroys all that is
> not pure as fire, which demands like purity in our worshipping.
> It is not that the fire will burn us if we do not worship thus; but

36. MacDonald, "Justice."
37. MacDonald, "Justice."
38. MacDonald, *Alec Forbes of Howglen*, ch. 28.
39. MacDonald, "Voice of Job."
40. MacDonald, "Voice of Job."

that the fire will burn us *until* we worship thus; yea, will go on burning within us after all that is foreign to it has yielded to its force, no longer with pain and consuming, but as the highest consciousness of life, the presence of God. Yea, the fear of God will cause a man to flee, not from God, but from himself; not *from* God, but *to* him. . . . The wrath will consume what they call "themselves"; so that the selves God made shall appear. . . . That which they *thought* themselves shall have vanished.[41]

MacDonald was under no illusions about the resistance of sinners to God's work in them, even when experiencing the painful flames of love. But "[i]f still he cling to that which can be burned, the burning goes deeper and deeper into his bosom, till it reaches the roots of the false-hood that enslaves him."[42] However, if the self-deceived rebel *still* resists the truth then there is God's last resort—"He shall be cast into the outer darkness who hates the fire of God."[43] This is to grant the sinner what they mistakenly think they want—to be apart from God.

> But when God withdraws from a man as far as that can be with-out the man's ceasing to be; when the man feels himself aban-doned, hanging in a ceaseless vertigo of existence upon the verge of the gulf of his being, without support, without refuge, without aim, without end, . . . then will he listen in agony for the faintest sound of life from the closed door; and if the moan of suffering humanity ever reaches the ear of the outcast of darkness, he will be ready to rush into the very heart of the Consuming Fire to know life once more.[44]

This outer darkness "is but the most dreadful form of the consuming fire—the fire without light—the darkness visible, the black flame. God has withdrawn himself, but not lost his hold. His face is turned away, but his hand is laid upon him still."[45] In this state, all one's illusions of oneself and God shatter and that which prompted one's flight from God is gone, opening the door to restoration.

MacDonald did contemplate the possibility that God would an-nihilate sinners who resist him to the end—if the only alternative was eternal torment (which it is not). He was clear that such an annihilation

41. MacDonald, "Consuming Fire."
42. MacDonald, "Consuming Fire."
43. MacDonald, "Consuming Fire."
44. MacDonald, "Consuming Fire."
45. MacDonald, "Consuming Fire."

of sinners would not in any way make up for the wrongs they have done and it would constitute a failure for God. "Annihilation itself is no death to evil. Only good where evil was, is evil dead. An evil must live with its evil until it chooses to be good. That alone is the slaying of evil."[46] In the end, however, MacDonald did not believe that annihilation of sinners would be necessary. "Escape is hopeless, for Love is inexorable. Our God is a consuming fire."[47] Sinners *cannot* resist God forever. It is part of the very essence of humanity that we are created with an orientation to God, so as long as a human being, an image of God, exists there is *always* a way for the Creator to reach him or her.

> Those who believe God will thus be defeated by many souls, must surely be of those who do not believe He cares enough to do His very best for them. He *is* their Father; he had power to make them out of Himself, and capable of being one with Him: surely He will somehow save and keep them! Not the power of sin itself can close *all* the channels between creating and created.[48]

> But at length, O God, will you not cast Death and Hell into the lake of fire—even into your own consuming self? . . . Then indeed will you be all in all. For then our poor brothers and sisters, *every one*—O God, we trust in you, the Consuming Fire—shall have been burnt clean and brought home.[49]

> "Every creature must one night yield himself and lie down," answered Adam: "he was made for liberty, and must not be left a slave!"[50]

The only victory of God that makes any sense in MacDonald's view is the victory of divine love, which is the destruction of sin from all

---

46. MacDonald, *Lilith*, ch. 30.

47. MacDonald, "Consuming Fire."

48. MacDonald, "Justice."

49. MacDonald, "Consuming Fire." Italics mine.

50. MacDonald, *Lilith*, ch. 42. The lying down in question concerns lying down in death in the house in which dreamers sleep until the end of the world. In the novel, this death is a good death in which life is found. However, not all the dead are ready to embrace this peaceful and healing death. The book follows the journey of Mr. Vane as he is prepared to sleep in the house. Lilith too, having escaped the outer darkness, falls asleep into this healing sleep. Adam's point to Vane here then is not the truism that all people die, but that all creatures must eventually yield to the mode of death that is restorative, life-giving sleep. Even *Lilith* yielded and lay down, finding life.

sinners. If, *per impossible*, God were not to achieve this goal, then love would lose and so would justice. This universal victory is declared in the resurrection itself—Christ is risen and this means that all humanity will rise too: "If Christ be risen, then is the grave of humanity itself empty. We have risen with him, and death has henceforth no dominion over us. Of every dead man and woman it may be said: He—she—is not here, but is risen and gone before us."[51]

The salvation of Lilith

MacDonald's most powerful literary presentation of God's reconciling to himself even the most hardened of sinners is found in the redemption to Lilith.[52] Lilith, a figure from Jewish mythology, was Adam's first wife. MacDonald presents her as an erotic, angelic creature obsessed with power, and unable to bear the thought of being married to Adam and populating the world with humans. After bearing a child, a daughter, she fled, sold her soul to "the great Shadow," and became the queen of the city of Bulika, where she rules as a tyrant over her subjects. Fearing that her child would be the cause of her downfall, Lilith made her great mission that of finding and killing her own daughter. Lilith has become a wicked creature that can only steal, kill, and destroy, and she absolutely resists with every fiber of her being all offers of forgiveness and attempts at reconciliation.

In the story, Mr. Vane, the central character, takes Lilith prisoner and brings her to Mara, the daughter of Adam and Eve. Mara then seeks to help Lilith to see the truth about herself and to repent. The account of Lilith's fierce and sustained resistance to Mara's work is insightful and revealing. Lilith refuses to turn away from her wickedness and insists that she, Lilith, is her own ruler and that she acts according to the desires of her self. "I will be myself and not another!" Mara counter-claims that in fact Lilith does not know her true self; that her true nature is good, but that the Shadow inclines her to act against who she is in her core. "You are not the Self you imagine." Lilith seems not to care, so long as she *feels* like she is doing what she wants then she considers herself to be self-made. As Alvin Kimel explains, "Lilith must learn one necessary truth—she did

51. MacDonald, *Miracles of Our Lord*, 268.

52. All the quotations are from *Lilith*, ch. 39. A contemporary afterlife fiction deeply inspired by MacDonald is Michael Phillips's *Hell and Beyond* (2013).

not create herself and cannot will her nonexistence. As long as she believes that she is an autonomous, independent, self-sufficient being, she remains a slave to the Shadow."[53]

Lilith, living under a delusion, sees God as a threat to her liberty. To obey him is slavery and she refuses to abandon her "freedom," even if she is tortured. Mara has no intention of torturing Lilith into submission to God—"Such compulsion would be of no value. But there is a light that goes deeper than the will, a light that lights up the darkness behind it: that light can change your will, can make it truly yours and not another's—not the Shadow's. Into the created can pour itself the creating will, and so redeem it!" The slave is not the one who obeys God, says Mara, but the one who resists God and becomes enslaved to sin.

Kimel explains that Lilith's redemption takes place in four stages. First, the fire of God—taking the form of a white-hot worm from the hearth—enters her heart, revealing her true created self. This revelation is profound torment for her, for now she "sees at last the good she is not, the evil she is. She knows that she is herself the fire in which she is burning." But, says Mara to Vane, "she is not forsaken. No gentler way to help her was left." Lilith, however, still refuses to turn from her false self.

In the second stage, Lilith cries tears of self-loathing. This is not sorrow, but it is a step in the right direction. However, Lilith still resists.

In the third stage, God grants her what she thinks she seeks—oblivion, nothingness, the outer darkness. Vane tries to explain it:

> The source of life had withdrawn itself; all that was left of her conscious being was the dregs of her dead and corrupt life. . . . I gazed on the face of one who knew existence but not love—knew nor life, nor joy, nor good. . . . It was not merely that life had ceased in her, but that she was consciously a dead thing. . . . She now saw what she had made, and behold, it was not good! She was a conscious corpse. . . . Her bodily eyes stood wide open, as if gazing into the heart of horror essential—her own indestructible evil. . . . But with God all things are possible! He can save even the rich.

At this moment, Lilith cries out, "I cannot hold out! I am defeated." She cannot deceive herself any more. Mara comforts her and assures her that while she is a slave she is on a journey to being again God's free child, filled with the life of God.

---

53. Kimel, "Salvation of Lilith."

The fourth and final stage is that Lilith must open her hand and sur-render that which it contains—something unnamed that will bring life to the wasteland. She struggles to do this and begs Adam to sever her hand so that she can surrender the object. This he does, and Lilith falls asleep into healing peace.

MacDonald's son Grenville wrote: "[*Lilith*] was written, I do think, in view of the increasingly easy tendencies in universalists, who, because they had now discarded everlasting retribution as a popular superstition, were dismissing hell-fire altogether, and with it the need for repentance as the way back into the Kingdom."[54] This seems entirely plausible. The story very beautifully illustrates how MacDonald imagined the consum-ing fire of God burning within a recalcitrant sinner in order to redeem them and bring them back to themselves, to God, to eternal life.

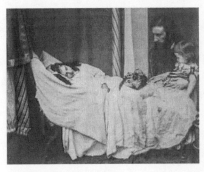

George MacDonald is today perhaps the best known of the nineteenth century's universalists, though he himself would never have used the term "universalist" to describe himself. His mature theology, while very much his own, rooted in his own child-hood intuitions and early spiritual awakening, clearly resonates with the Romanic sensibilities of the era and bears notable similarities to the theology of Thomas Erskine, F. D. Maurice, and others with whom Mac-Donald was familiar. And as with those thinkers, his ideas have multiple echoes of themes found in the Origenian tradition. Whether these echoes were intentional or not, indeed, whether MacDonald was even aware of them or not, is hard to say. What we might say, however, is that his theol-ogy represents those themes in a very nineteenth-century, poetic mode.

It is time, as this stage of our investigation draws to a close, to con-sider some of the universalists of the nineteenth century who remained more Evangelical in their Romantic theology. In the next chapter, we shall consider an Independent, a Baptist, and a Holiness preacher.

54. MacDonald, *George MacDonald and His Wife*, 551–52.

14

Universalism in Great Britain IV

Independents, Baptists, and the Holiness Movement

THE NINETEENTH-CENTURY BOUNDARY-PUSHERS WERE not confined to the state church, but included those on the fringes of Anglicanism, nonconformists, and others. Three of the most influential in Britain in the later nineteenth century were Andrew Jukes, Samuel Cox, and Hannah Whitall Smith.

ANDREW JUKES (1815–1901)

Life

Andrew Jukes was born in Bombay in 1815, his father having worked for the East India Company. He moved to England in 1820 after the death of his father. After leaving Harrow School in 1832, where he had been close friends with F. W. Faber, later to become a famous hymn writer, he joined the army in India and then in 1837 went to study at Cambridge University, where he was deeply influenced by the Evangelical Anglican minister Charles Simeon. Jukes was a capable theologian and biblical scholar; his Cambridge thesis on the interpretation of prophetic texts even won the Hulsean Prize in 1840.

Andrew Jukes started and ended his life as an Anglican. After training at Cambridge University, he went to St. John's Church in Hull, for which he was ordained a deacon in 1842. However, as an Evangelical, he had various problems with what he was expected to believe and teach: he could not reconcile himself with the matter of baptismal regeneration, he had problems with certain of the Thirty-Nine Articles (including Article 2, the declaration that Christ died to reconcile the Father to us, rather than vice versa), and he did not think that the Athanasian Creed was correct to claim that one's salvation depends on getting one's trinitarian theology correct. In addition, some controversy had arisen over a sermon he preached and then published on Christian unity, which was seen by some in authority in the Anglican church as too open to communion with dissenters. Thus, Jukes reluctantly seceded from the Church of England in 1842, never becoming ordained as a priest.[1]

Jukes and his family soon got rebaptized by a local Baptist minister, though he never became a Baptist. Instead he became an independent Evangelical minister in Hull. His church has been compared to the Plymouth Brethren in its informality and its dependence on the inspiration of the Spirit, though while there were many informal links with Brethren assemblies, and Jukes's theology had many convergences with Brethren (and Baptist) theology, it was not ever formally linked with that or any network.[2] Perhaps the best-known member of Jukes's Hull congregation was Hudson Taylor, who later founded the China Inland Mission. Taylor was deeply inspired in his faith during his time there.

Jukes continued to study Scripture, the church fathers (having a special love for Origen), and more recent mystical writers like Jacob Böhme and William Law. He was also in correspondence with F. D. Maurice. Jukes preached and published a lot, bringing out a whole string of biblical and theological studies from 1847 until 1893. His biblical interpretation gave a lot of space to the typological interpretation of Old Testament texts, which was fairly typical of Evangelicals in his day. The publication

---

1. For biographical information on Jukes, especially his later years, see Jeaffreson, *Letters of Andrew Jukes*. On Jukes's secession from the Church of England, his expansive ecclesiology, and his links with the Brethren, see Randall, "I Felt Bound."

2. On this, see esp. Randall, "I Felt Bound."

for which he is best known is his book-length defense of universal salvation—*The Second Death and the Restitution of All Things*.[3]

Jukes's initial ponderings about universalism went back to his undergraduate days, when he had realized that *ōlām* and *aiōnios* do not mean "everlasting." He mused privately on the issues for many years, then gathered some letters that he had sent over a period of years to a friend on the subject of eternal punishment and collected them into a book manuscript, which he circulated among friends, but refused to publish. In 1867, he relented under the advice of his friends and the book appeared as *The Second Death and the Restitution of All Things*. It was one of the seminal nineteenth-century defenses of universal salvation.

Unsurprisingly, his book generated controversy and some fierce dissent from many of his friends and associates in the ministry, who distanced themselves from him.[4] The stress and hurt of this, combined with various stresses from his twenty-five-year ministry, especially the strain of raising funds for a massive new building for the church (pictured here), led to a physical and mental breakdown. He left Hull and took a tour of Greece, Egypt, and the Holy Land in 1867–68.

On returning to England in 1868, he moved to London, and determined to rejoin the Church of England, moving away from his Brethren connections. He was not ordained a priest, but he was granted permission by the Bishop of London to officiate at the Anglican Eucharist, though he was still unwell and did not take up ministry again immediately, and never again was employed fulltime in ministry. However, Jukes continued to serve the church with his gifts in numerous ways, and became acquainted with other universalists at this time—including George MacDonald and Hannah Whitall Smith, through whom he became involved

3. This book included a postscript of quotes from William Law on universal restoration. The rest of the book was given almost entirely to biblical interpretation.

4. John Nelson Darby (1800–1882), for instance, wrote a strong critique of Jukes in his "Examination of the Book." Darby argued that Jukes taught we are saved through our own suffering and death, rather than through Christ's.

in the Broadlands Conferences. Jukes would speak at the conferences, and in Broadlands circles he became known as "Saint Andrew."

Andrew Jukes died in 1901 and was buried beside his wife in Hull.

Thought

The Second Death and the Restitution of All Things begins with the problem to be resolved: how can we make sense of biblical teaching on the final destiny of humanity when its witness seems to be contradictory, with various texts seeming to indicate that some people will be forever lost, while others appearing to teach that all will be saved. Unusually in such discussions, his answer to this question begins with some groundwork on the doctrine of Scripture and its interpretation.

Scripture—its nature and interpretation

To understand the divine revelation in the Bible, we must start with the revelation of God par excellence: the incarnation of the Logos in Christ. This is the key to understanding the structure of all the lesser divine revelations, including Scripture, nature, and providence. Jesus is "the Word of God made flesh . . . not partly man and partly God. . . . So exactly is Holy Scripture the Word of God; not half human and half divine, but thoroughly human, yet no less thoroughly divine" (5).[5] Thus, "Scripture is pre-eminent, and differs from other books exactly as the flesh of Christ differs from the flesh of other men. . . . I see it is human; I see that it has grown; I see that it can be judged and wounded. . . . But it is like Christ's body, the peculiar tabernacle of God's truth" (9). Like the flesh of Christ, the letter of Scripture "is a veil quite as much as a revelation, hiding while it reveals, and yet revealing while it hides; presenting to the eye something very different from that which is within, even as the veil of the Tabernacle, with its inwoven cherubim, hid the glory within the veil, of which nevertheless it was the witness; and that therefore, as seen by sense, it is and must be apparently inconsistent and self-contradictory" (9). In other words, the reason why Scripture *seems on the surface* to contradict itself is a result of the very nature of the self-manifestation of God to creatures. God, in love, has to accommodate himself and reveal him-

---

5. The following in-text citations in this section on Jukes are from *Second Death*, unless otherwise stated.

self to creation through the created order itself and this involved paradox and a measure of "hiding quite as much as it reveals" (10). How many saw Christ as a mere man, failing to discern the glory of God made known in and through him! So too the humanity of Scripture both veils and reveals God's word.

Now, Jukes is insistent that the Bible is the supreme authority for guiding Christian belief and practice, trumping every other authority, including tradition, reason, and conscience. However, Scripture must be interpreted aright, in accordance with the mind of the Spirit. Individual texts must therefore be read in the context of the *whole* canon. He thinks that the traditional teaching on hell affirms one set of biblical texts (those that seem to limit the final number of the saved), but is forced to ignore or deny another set (those that seem to teach universal salvation) and to "represent God in a character absolutely opposed to that in which the gospel exhibits Him" (26). Jukes sees his book as offering a way that allows both sides of the biblical tension to stand, clarifying how the contradictions are only apparent.

The key to the puzzle, claims Jukes, is found in three insights into the ways of God.

1. The truth of the firstborn and firstfruits (28–41)

The basic idea here is that *God works out his purposes for the whole of humanity through a select subsection of that whole.* Indeed, this is the gospel itself! For Paul, the gospel, first declared to Abraham, is that "in your seed [descendants] shall all the families of the earth be blessed" (Gen 12:3; Gal 3:8). The seed of Abraham (Israel) are the means by which God will restore blessing to all families in creation. That is the good news, fulfilled in Christ. The idea of the few blessing the many comes out in numerous Old Testament ideas, in particular teachings on firstfruits and firstborn.

We shall consider Jukes's teaching on the firstfruits (and set aside his teaching on the firstborn for reasons of space). The notion of firstfruits comes from Old Testament law. There were in fact two firstfruits offerings. The first was the first sheaf or ears of corn to appear from the earth. These were offered to God in sacrifice at the Feast of Unleavened Bread, during Passover (Lev 23:10–11). The second firstfruits were leavened cakes offered fifty days later at Pentecost (Lev 23:17).

For Jukes, a lover of typology, Christ in his resurrection fulfills the firstfruits of the Passover. The firstfruits were, after all, offered on the day after the Passover Sabbath (Lev 23:11), the very day on which Jesus was raised. St. Paul makes this same connection, speaking of the risen Christ as "the firstfruits of those who have fallen asleep" (1 Cor 15:20). Jesus' resurrection was chronologically first—preceding the general resurrection—but was also the promise that the rest of the dead would follow, though each in his own order (15:22–24). Christ was not resurrected *instead of* us, but *on our behalf*, the means by which our resurrection will come and the guarantee that it will.

In the same way, Paul says that the few Jews who currently believe in Jesus as Messiah (including himself) are a firstfruits offering on behalf of the whole of Israel, consecrating the whole of the harvest (the nation of Israel) to God—"for if the firstfruit be holy, the lump is also holy" (Rom 11:16). The fact that the number of the saved within Israel is small—a mere remnant—does not mean that God has abandoned the rest of the nation. His calling and election are irrevocable and the time is coming when "all Israel will be saved" (Rom 11:26).

Now the church is that which is foreshadowed in the firstfruits of Pentecost—the day on which the church was birthed as God poured out his Spirit. Thus, James speaks of believers as "a kind of firstfruits of all he has created" (Jas 1:18) and Revelation talks of those "redeemed from mankind as firstfruits for God and the Lamb" (Rev 14:4). Again, the idea is that the elect are not chosen *instead of* the non-elect, but *on behalf of* them, to be a means of ministering blessing to them and as a promise of the fuller harvest to come. Jukes thinks that God has blessed the church in Christ (v. 3) "that in the dispensation of the fulness of time He might gather together in one all things in Christ, both which are in heaven and which are in earth, even in Him" (1:10, KJV)

To Jukes, the church will serve as priests into the age to come, ministering to "the spirits in prison." But there is always hope for the damned: "the first-fruits [the church], being safe, the harvest [the rest of humanity], already sanctified by the first-fruits, shall also be gathered in" (37).

Being one of the firstfruits is not easy, but a narrow way that few find. It is to be offered as a sacrifice, to take up one's cross, to give oneself for the service of others in service to God.

> Here then is the key to one part of the apparent contradiction between "mercy upon all," and yet "the election" of a "little flock"; between "all the kindreds of the earth blessed in Christ,"

and yet "a straight and narrow way" and "few finding it." . . . The
first-born and first-fruits are the "few" and "little flock"; but
these, though first delivered from the curse, have a relation to
the whole creation, which shall be saved in the appointed times
by the first-born seed, that is by Christ and His Body, through
those appointed baptisms, whether fire or water, which are required to bring about "the restitution of all things." (38)

Thus does the microcosm foretell the fate of the macro-
cosm. (48)

All this contrasts with the traditional view in which Jesus saves and
blesses the firstfruits and "leaves the rest to torments endless and most
agonizing" (39).

2. The truth that God works for redemption across successive ages (41–55)

God's purposes in Scripture are worked out across numerous ages, both
past and future. And those who enter into the life of God do not do so
all at the same time, but over an extended period of time. He sees these
ages figured in the Old Testament in the division of time into periods of
seven days, seven weeks, seven months, seven years (when debts among
Israelites were forgiven), seven-times-seven years, the latter climaxing in
the Jubilee Year in which all debts (Israelite and non-Israelite) within the
land are cancelled. Jukes sees the different periods here as types of the
different ages in the divine plan of blessing, with the final being the "ages
of ages" after which all debts are wiped out.

Jukes illustrates the differences in the ages from the biblical teaching on Ammon and Moab. These nations were under a curse, cut off
from the congregation of Israel: "No Ammonite or Moabite may enter
the assembly of the LORD. Even to the tenth generation, none of them
may enter the assembly of the LORD forever. . . . You shall not seek their
peace or their prosperity all your days forever" (Deut 23:3, 6). Thus, Ezra
and Nehemiah forced any Jews with Ammonite wives to put away those
wives and any children they had with them (Ezra 10:2–3, 44; Neh 13:1,
23, 25, 30)! In addition, the prophets speak of the coming *utter destruction* of Moab and Ammon (Jer 48; 49:1–5; Ezek 21:28, 32). Yet, they then
promise the post-annihilation restoration of those decimated nations
(Jer 48:47; 49:6). The same pattern, says Jukes, can be found in God's

dispensations with Egypt, Assyria, Elam, and Sodom. God "works, not in one act, but by degrees, through successive days or seasons" (47).

All the ages (*aeons*) of which the Bible speaks, both past and present, are periods of time, none of which are eternal and all of which come to an end.[6] By analogy with all previous ages, we cannot presume that the ages to come will be everlasting. Indeed, Jukes revives a teaching we found in various church fathers and eighteenth-century universalists, i.e., that the handing over of the aionial kingdom by Christ to the Father so that God will be all in all (1 Cor 15:24) marks the end of *all* the ages. Throughout these ages, God is working out his redemptive purposes; once he has completed his battle with sin and evil, the ages will come to a close. This is the Jubilee Year.[7]

3. The truth that the way to life is through judgment and death (55–73)

According to Jukes, one central error in common Protestant views on the cross of Christ is the belief that Christ died *instead of* us—sparing us from dying. This, he thinks, is to miss the meaning of the atonement. Rather than being delivered *from* death, Christ delivers us *by* death and *out of* death. Christ does not die instead of us, but on our behalf, as our representative. His followers do not—indeed, must not—avoid death, but instead should take up their crosses: "for whoever will lose his life for my sake will find it" (Matt 16:25). Death is now the way to life. In baptism, we are united with Christ in his death (Rom 6:3–4). We are crucified with Christ (Gal 2:20), and if we die with him we shall live with him (2 Tim 2:11–12). So Christ enters into our human condition, as prisoners of sin and death, and embraces it to the full. Then God raises him from the dead, breaking the prison open, and enabling us, in the Spirit, to turn our deaths from a prison into a gateway to life. Death—Christ's death and our deaths in Christ—becomes the way back to God.

In addition to dying with Christ to the power of sin, restoration to our human destiny requires that we also share in Christ's resurrection

6. Jukes also seeks to show that the adjective *aiōnios* does not mean "eternal" or "everlasting," even when applied to God, the covenant, or redemption. As we have already looked at such arguments, we shall not repeat them here.

7. Jukes is keen to stress that the fact that the ages to come are not everlasting in no way undermines "the true eternity of bliss of God's elect" (55), for this life is a participation in the divine nature and the indestructibility of the resurrection body.

life. In Christ, crucified and risen, humanity is remade and restored. "But whether in Christ, or in us, the work is only wrought through death. Man to be saved must die to that which keeps him far from God. And the way to bring about this death is God's judgment, who, because He loves us, kills to make alive" (61). Thus, "Christ is and must be the one and only way, by which any have been, or are, or can be saved" (77).

The condemnation of God's holy law slays us, but it is a necessary part of God's redemptive work in us. God judges us so that he can save us, because our salvation requires the condemnation and destruction of that which is evil in us. Then God brings new creation. We can accept God's judgment in this life, allowing our sinful selves to be slain, and thus enter into new life now. Alternatively, we can resist divine judgment here and now, but then we "have to meet it in a more awful form in the coming world" (63). As Jesus said, "*everyone* will be salted with fire" (Mark 9:49, italics added), there is no avoiding it. This purificatory salting will either take place in this life as we die to ourselves, or in the fires of gehenna. But this second death is also a means to an end, and that end is the restoration of those experiencing it.[8]

In some ways, Jukes's universalism seems different from some of the other universalisms that we have considered. His argument for it certainly has a distinctive shape, and he is more concerned with explaining the teaching of Scripture than many of the other nineteenth-century universalists. Yet, his mystical bent and his rejection of penal substitutionary atonement as missing the life-transforming point of the gospel make his work resonate in many ways with Erskine, Maurice, MacDonald, and others.

SAMUEL COX (1826–93), UNIVERSALISM, AND THE BAPTISTS

Baptists were, for the most part, Evangelicals who maintained the traditional view of hell. In 1812, the New Connexion of General Baptists (Arminian)[9] and the Particular Baptists (Calvinist) decided to join

---

8. Jukes then has the obligatory chapter in which he seeks to respond to critics of his view. He considers criticisms under the categories of tradition, reason (which is mostly theological objections), and Scripture.

9. The New Connexion of Dan Taylor had broken away from the earlier General Baptists, who had become increasingly deviant from Christian orthodoxy in their theology.

together for the gospel cause, and in 1813 the Baptist Union's constitution was published. Among its resolutions was the following: "That this Society of ministers and churches . . . maintaining the important doctrines of . . . the eternal misery of such as die in impenitence." However, Baptist ecclesiology—which insisted on the autonomy of individual congregations—opened up space for diversity. The Baptist Union could provide guidelines "but never laid out concrete statements of belief that demanded assent from its members."[10] Nevertheless, it would be true to say that Baptist churches and publications were dominated by the theology of eternal conscious torment in hell, and dissent was not welcomed.

Nonetheless, dissenters started to arise, the first being the Rev. John Foster (1770–1843), who argued against the eternal duration of hell, maintaining that the punishment must be proportioned to the severity of the offences.[11] (It is of interest to note that John Foster had been an influence on the early Thomas Erskine.) Further dissent arose with the defense of annihilation by Rev. Henry Hamlet Dobney and of salvific inclusivism with an article in *The Baptist Magazine* (1866) by a C. Carter. But it was Rev. Samuel Cox who went the extra mile and embraced a full-throated universalism.

Life

Samuel Cox was a Londoner and apprenticed at the London docks, where his father worked, before training for the Baptist ministry at Stepney Academy, as John Foster before him, and being ordained in 1852.[12] He ministered at various churches before settling down in 1863 as the pastor at Mansfield Road Baptist Church in Nottingham. Cox was minister in Nottingham for twenty-five years, until 1888.

Samuel Cox was a high-profile leader in the Baptist Union and President of the Baptist Association in 1873, and served as the founder and editor of *The Expositor* from volume 1 to volume 20 (1875–84), a respected and academically informed theological journal aimed at ministers and lay people. Cox himself also wrote thirty books and edited another twenty. His services to scholarship were recognized by the awarding of a

10. Heap, "Baptists and the Afterlife," 4.

11. Foster, *Letter of the Celebrated John Foster*.

12. Most of this information on Cox comes from the *Dictionary of National Biography*, 1901 supplement.

DD degree from the University of St. Andrews in 1882 (with Aberdeen and Edinburgh also offering to confer DDs on him).

In 1869, Cox published *The Resurrection*, in which he took a similar approach to the notion of the "firstfruits" as Andrew Jukes had.[13] Cox's debt to Jukes is explicit in his later work, and it is certainly possible that he was already under Jukes's influence at this point. Whether or not that was the case, this publication certainly makes very clear hints in universalist directions. Further expressions of his dissenting views were published under a pseudonym (Carpus) in *The Expositor* in 1875, an article on heaven that he republished in 1877 in his *Expository Essays and Discourses*. Here he challenged the notion of death as a radical break and presented the idea of purifying divine judgments.[14] The notion of "the larger hope" was also introduced in *Expository Essays* (Cox, as others, had been influenced by Tennyson). However, amazingly, this book did not attract criticism. That brief calm preceded the storm created by his next book, published in the same year—*Salvator Mundi, Or, Is Christ the Saviour of All Men?* This was an in-your-face argument for a confident belief in universal salvation. The preface opens with the words, "The main object of this book is to encourage those who 'faintly trust the larger hope' to commit themselves to it wholly and fearlessly" (vii). Cox's fellow-Baptists were less than enthusiastic about his new book, and from 1878 various negative reviews appeared in Baptist periodicals. Cox responded to his critics in some expositions in *The Expositor* in 1881 on "The Sin unto Death—I John 5:16" and "The Sin against the Spirit" and in his subsequent book *The Larger Hope*, published in 1883. However, Cox's views were simply too far out of step with the mainstream of Baptist thought and Cox's "heretical" theology led to his forced resignation from his role at *The Expositor* in 1884, though his own church in Nottingham kept him on.[15]

Cox was not, however, without his sympathizers and admirers (like John Clifford, editor of the *General Baptist Magazine*, F. W. Farrar, and Thomas Allin) and *Salvator Mundi* remains one of the classics of nineteenth-century universalism.

---

13. See sermon 3 on the Adam and the Christ (*Resurrection*, 60–84).

14. Carpus, "Heaven," *The Expositor* 1 (1875) 268–74.

15. His resignation in 1888 was due to failing health.

Thought

Salvator Mundi opens with an extended discussion of an issue raised by Jesus' comment that Tyre, Sidon, and even Sodom *would have* repented *if* they had witnessed the miracles that the unresponsive Galilean towns of Jesus' day had witnessed (Matt 21:20–24). Jesus was emphasizing just how blind and stubborn his contemporaries were, but Cox's question is this: why did God not provide those ancient cities with the circumstances in which their repentance would have come about? That is a theological problem—one repeated for every one of the millions of people who die never having had a chance to hear the gospel presented adequately, or even at all. Surely God will do *all he can* to save people, so why withhold that which he knows will prove effective?

> For myself I can only say that I see no way out of the difficulty, no single loophole of escape, so long as we assume what the Bible does not teach, that there is no probation beyond the grave, that no moral change is possible in that world towards which all the children of time are travelling. I, at least, am so sure that the Father of all men will do the most and best which can be done for every man's salvation as to entertain no doubt that long ere this the men of Sodom and of Tyre and Sidon have heard the words of Christ and seen his mighty works—seen and heard Him, perchance, when He stood and shone among the spirits in the Hadean prison, and preached the gospel to them that were dead, in order that, while still judged by men according to the flesh, they might live according to God in the spirit [1 Pet 3:19–20; 4:6]. (17)

Cox asserts that "a man's salvation should not depend on the age, or on the moral conditions of the age, into which he is born, and which he has done nothing to determine" (21). He makes no apology for his appeal to "Reason and Conscience" alongside Scripture in his theological musings here. "Doubtless we hear the voice of God in Scripture, and in Scripture hear it most distinctly; but that voice also speaks within us, in our reason and in our moral sense. And he who has drawn a conclusion from Scripture which Reason and Conscience imperatively condemn should need no other proof that he has misinterpreted the Word of God" (24). This hermeneutic, which in some ways echoes that of Origen, albeit in modern Victorian dress, is something that sets interpreters like Cox, Erskine, MacDonald, and Allin apart from the more conservative theologians in their day.

Traditionalists, says Cox, take only one of the threads of teaching found in Scripture (to the exclusion of the more hopeful thread), and even then the texts to which they appeal are capable of being interpreted differently. He argues that, on the one hand, "the Scriptures, when fairly interpreted, do not sustain that theory of the future state which has long found general acceptance" (34). And "on the other hand, we may hope to find that there are great principles, principles that run through the Bible from end to end, which point conclusively to a very different theory. . . . No such words are to be found in the Greek . . . nor any words which convey . . . the conception of a final and ever-during place of torment" (34).

Cox begins by working through texts in which the KJV uses the words "damnation" and "hell." His argument is that "*neither of these words is to be found in any part of the New Testament*, or, indeed, in any part of the whole Bible; nor even any word which at all answers to the conception which they quicken in our minds" (39). Contrary to the KJV, there are *no* instances in the NT in which *krinein* (to judge), *krisis* (the act of deciding/judging), and *krima* (the sentence of judgment) should be translated as "to damn," "damning," or "damned." Similarly neither tartarus, Hades, nor gehenna ought ever to be translated as "hell." All three, he argues, refer to the intermediate state, not one's final destiny. Tartarus only occurs in 2 Peter 2:4, and there it is a place in which wicked angels are kept imprisoned prior to the day of judgment. Hades is the world of the human dead to which all go prior to the day of judgment. Hades is divided into paradise and gehenna, in which the righteous and the wicked anticipate the time of reckoning. The valley of Ge-Hinnom beside Jerusalem, with all its associations of wickedness and destruction, became an illustration and symbol of the fate of the unrighteous. A study of Second Temple Jewish uses of gehenna, contends Cox, "positively discountenance" using "hell" as the English translation—"That is to say, the uninspired Jewish writings for the six centuries nearest to Christ know nothing, absolutely nothing, of 'hell'" (72). Some gehenna texts envisage annihilation, while others envisage salvation from gehenna; some envisaged the duration of gehenna as twelve months; some for a day; some for as long as the righteous wanted it to endure. So "'the propositions which they contain are so variable and unstable' that 'no firm and unshifting dogma may be deduced from them' as to the future punishment of the guilty" (74). However, we can conclude, he believes, that the rabbis did not believe in a material fire, and that they thought this fire would one day be extinguished.

Cox prefers to translate gehenna in the NT more literally as "Valley of Hinnom," understanding the phrase as a symbol—after all, "how should *our* whole body, the bodies of English men and women, be cast into a Palestinian valley?" (83). Jesus' teaching on the punishment of the Valley of Hinnom is harsh and full of figures of speech that need to be read aright. Jesus is "teaching an Oriental people, in the Oriental forms with which they are familiar" (81). If we over-literally interpret the concrete imagery and idioms, we end up with nonsense. If we read them with sensitivity to the cultural context, we end up with the notion of everlasting hell disappearing out of the picture. He concludes:

> We have now examined every passage in the New Testament in which the word Gehenna occurs. We have found that for the most part it is used in a purely figurative sense; that, so often as it is used in a literal sense, it denotes the punishments executed on criminal Jews in this present world: and that, in the one or two cases, in which it veils a reference to the punishments of the world to come, it would be understood by those who heard it as denoting that brief agony which, as they thought, would precede the entire destruction of the wicked. (87–88)

Lest readers fear that Cox has gone soft on sin, he adds:

> But do not too hastily assume that, by getting rid of the word "hell," you also get rid of the doctrine of retribution. To sin is to suffer even here and now, and will be to suffer hereafter. . . . And if any man abide in sin to the very last moment, we may well believe that he will then enter into suffering so intense and so protracted as that he may feel it had been better for him had he never been born.

However, there is an important qualifier: "The merciful God, simply because He is merciful, does not shrink from inflicting any pain on us which is necessary to our welfare." (89). The afterlife sufferings are "sufferings imposed by Love for our deliverance from evil" (90). This, believes Cox, is a world away from the God who sends people to everlasting suffering, with no prospect of relief, for committing brief finite sins—an action that is neither just nor loving.

Having finished undermining the biblical basis for the classical doctrine of hell, Cox moves on to present his alternative vision. He calls it "The Christian Doctrine of the Aeons." The Greek *aiōn* means "an age" or a "period of time" (not "an eternity"), whether long or short, and the adjective *aiōnios* means "age-long" (not everlasting). Scripture does not see time as a single aeon, but divides it up into numerous aeons or ages. Each of these ages has a start and an end. Looking backward, the past is composed of numerous ages, but so too is the future. The NT will often speak of "the *age* to come," but can also speak in the plural of "the coming *ages*" (Eph 2:7), which can be grouped together as "the ages of ages" (Rev 5:13; 14:11). These ages "are epochs or periods of time in which God is gradually working out a gracious purpose which He purposed in Christ Jesus long ere man fell from his first estate, long before those 'age-times' . . . in and through which men are being recovered from the fall" (107). God's purpose for creation reaches back "before the ages," but "binds the ages together in a sacred unity" (110) and reaches forward to a final destiny beyond the ages when "the successions of time pass away" and God will be all in all (110).

Even when the words *aiōn* and *aiōnios* are applied to God, Cox does not think that the translation "eternal" is appropriate. Rather, he says, they describe God's relation to the aeons of time. God is the "King of the Aeons" (1 Tim 1:17), the aeonial God (Rom 16:25–26), who rules over all the aeons. The Spirit is the aeonial Spirit (Heb 9:14), *the Zeitgeist* (Time Spirit), "animating and informing these ages with a Divine intention and significance" (113).

Similarly, all aspects of God's redemptive work are described as aeonial—aeonial judgment, aeonial life, aeonial punishments, aeonial fire, aeonial inheritance—for, according to Cox, they belong to God's purpose being worked out through the Christian aeons. But on no occasion does Cox think that the word "eternal" or "everlasting" would be appropriate to convey the meanings of the phrases in question. In particular, aeonial fire, aeonial destruction, and aeonial punishment are *age-long* consequences of living orientated away from God that are "proper to and distinctive of [the age]" (130), but there is no reason to consider them *ever*lasting. Indeed, they apply to gehenna, which Cox sees as part of Hades and thus an intermediate condition. The salting with fire in gehenna (Mark 9:42–50) is "a purifying and vivifying correction" (135).[16]

This extension of time far into the past and the future was a recovery of Origenist theology, but it also resonated very well with the vast

---

16. In a kind of Protestant one-upmanship move, he accused the traditional view of hell, so beloved by Evangelicals, to be a hangover from Catholicism, rather than a biblical doctrine. His critics repaid the favor by suggesting that it was Cox, with his quasi-purgatorial view, who was borrowing from Catholicism.

extensions of geological time that scientists were proposing, and with the ideas of evolution that were fast becoming popular in Cox's day—ideas to which Cox happily subscribed.

God is unchangeable—his saving purposes, his calling, and his election will not be revoked. With regard to that election, Cox is clear that election is for the sake of others: "when He elects and establishes a church, it is for the spiritual benefit of the whole world" (159). The saving work of Christ will eventually extend beyond the church to the whole world, "even the inanimate creation" (160).

God's punishments in Scripture are "corrective and even redemptive; . . . [they are] not simply penal and retributive, but corrective and remedial" (162–63).

> But will the unchangeable God change his attitude towards sinful men, when, despite his discipline, they have gone down into the pit? Can He? If we have once seen what his purpose is in chastening and punishing them for their sins, must not that be his eternal, his unalterable purpose? What right have we to assume that pain and wrath, and judgment will have another function in the age to come, or in any age, than that which we know them to have in this age? (164–65).

With regard to the cross, Cox is typical of many nineteenth-century theologians in seeking an account that avoids penal substitution.[17] He sees the cross as the revelation of the loving and saving will of an eternally kenotic God. The Father sorrows over our sin and the harm it causes us. For this divine passion to become redemptive, it must be revealed:

> Till we know that God is sorry for us, we shall not be sorry for ourselves with that godly sorrow that worketh life. . . . Hence, once in the ages, in the person of Jesus Christ, God became man to show His sympathy with men, His kinship with them, His care for them. To prove that He is verily afflicted in our afflictions, and that He is able to redeem us out of them all. . . . In short, the historical Cross of Christ is simply a disclosure within the bounds of time and space of the eternal passion of the unchangeable God: it is simply, the supreme manifestation of that

---

17. In fact, the notion of the cross as a revelation of divine self-giving love that we are to imitate as we take up our crosses can already be found in the writings of Hans Denck in the sixteenth century. This was part of Denck's concern that Reformed theology of the cross and justification can lead to antinomianism. George MacDonald's thought is also close to Denck in this regard.

> redeeming Love which always suffers in our sufferings, and is
> forever at work for our salvation from them. (168–69)

Cox finally moves on to sketch out the biblical hope of a glorious future for all humanity. This is simply a discussion of standard universalist texts (e.g., Gen 12:3; Ps 77:17; Isa 45:22–23 in Phil 2:6–11; John 1:29; 12:32; Acts 3:21; Rom 11; 1 Cor 15:24–28; 2 Cor 5:19; Eph 1:10; Col 1:20; 1 Tim 4:10). For instance, in 1 Timothy 2:1, 3, and 6, he writes:

> But if He is to be ultimately the Saviour of *all* men, as it is very
> certain that a countless multitude of men are not saved in this
> age, they must of necessity be excluded from that presence
> and glory of the Lord in the age to come which the righteous
> will enjoy, must be exposed to a far more severe and searching
> discipline than any they have known here. . . . God therefore,
> while the Saviour of all men, is specially the Saviour of them that
> believe, since these are saved in the present age, will pass into
> the blessedness of a perfecting discipline in the age to come, and
> may even be employed in errands of mercy to the spirits who
> are still in the bonds of their iniquity. Meanwhile the purpose of
> God stands sure. It is His will, His good pleasure, that all men
> should be saved by being led, through whatever correction and
> training may be necessary for that end . . . which truth will be
> testified to them in its appropriate seasons, and by appropriate
> methods, in the ages to come . . . so appropriately and so forcibly
> testified that at last they will no longer be able to withstand it.
> (188–89)

Our ultimate future is beyond our comprehension at this stage in our story, but Cox argues in the final chapter that what is clear is that:

1. There are degrees of bliss, or reward, in paradise, and degrees of punishment in gehenna.

2. In the spiritual world, the reward of the righteous is at once retributive and perfecting, and the punishment of the unrighteous at once retributive and remedial.

3. In the age or ages to come, there will be accorded a new and deeper revelation of the grace of God in Christ Jesus, a new and more penetrating proclamation of the gospel.

The God affirmed and proclaimed by Samuel Cox is one who is the Savior of all people.

Cox and Jukes, while both ministers, were pastor-scholars, men who sought to better exegete the teachings of Scripture with the tools of the academy. The final universalist we shall consider in this book was no academic, and contrasts those two men in numerous interesting ways. However, like them, she too was a preacher and an author, and while lacking their sophistication, she was considerably better known among Evangelicals than either of them—we speak of Hannah Whitall Smith.

HANNAH WHITALL SMITH (1832–1911) AND *THE UNSELFISHNESS OF GOD*

Hannah Whitall was not British at all, but had her biggest impact in the UK, which she made her home later in her life. Hannah was born in Philadelphia into a prominent Quaker family. Her childhood was, by her account, a very happy one. Indeed, she believes that she learned more about God from the love of her parents then from any formal teaching. In her spiritual autobiography, *The Unselfishness of God*, she divides her life into five stages. First comes her Quaker childhood, with all its focus on the "inward voice" of the Spirit in the heart of the individual. It was only much later in life that she began to fully appreciate the value of her Quaker heritage.

The second phase was what she referred to as her "awakening," a dark period from the age of sixteen to twenty-six (1848–58). This was what we may call a crisis of faith. Hannah always longed for God to speak to her through one of the prophetic Quaker preachers, but it never happened. She also found a great pressure to have a certain kind of emotional response to religious matters, yet found herself incapable of doing so, and the constant Quaker call to introspection only made her feel the inadequacy of her lack of experience—she could not affect the necessary inward change.[18] Hannah longed to know God, but seemed unable and

---

18. She later came to see a religion that was focused on having the right emotions as a tyrannous kind of faith that generates a self-focus and despair. Instead of focusing

eventually, with much agonizing and despair, became a religious skeptic around the age of twenty-three or twenty-four. If there was a God, she reasoned, he would not be as absent as he clearly was.

In 1851, aged nineteen, Hannah married Robert Pearsall Smith, another Quaker, and together they moved to Germantown, Pennsylvania. Her marriage managed to distract her somewhat from her religious inner torments. As we have seen, this town was a center of universalism in the eighteenth century, but Hannah gives no indication that this had any influence on her at the time or even that she was aware of it.

In 1858, Hannah entered the third phase of her spiritual life. She became acquainted with some Evangelical Christians and, after some wrestling, found a deep conviction that God was real, some months after which she had an Evangelical conversion experience. This transformed her. She fell in love with God, read the Bible avidly, and could not stop telling people about what God had done for her. Her religious enthusiasm alienated her somewhat from some of the elders among the Quakers, and Hannah and Robert became involved with the Plymouth Brethren, who had a presence in Philadelphia. Over a period of years, the Brethren had significant influence upon their lives.

In 1864 the couple moved to Millville, New Jersey, where Robert managed Hannah's father's glass factories. The fifth epoch of her spiritual life took place here. (We shall deal with the fourth phase in a moment.) It was her discovery in 1865 of how to live a Christian life of victory over sin. Here it was Methodist revivalists whose teaching made a big impact. She was struggling with her inability to live a life of victory over sin, and found the council of some Christians—that we cannot fully defeat sin in our lives—unpersuasive. But the Wesleyan doctrine of holiness seemed to offer hope. She became convinced that one could trust Christ for one's sanctification just as much for one's justification. Victory over sin comes not through trying harder, but through trusting Christ. This was the key to the higher life. It also proved to be the message that made Hannah internationally famous, as we shall see.

Some years after worshipping with the Brethren, Hannah had a second "conversion"—to universalism, a trust in the "unselfishness of God." She describes this as the fourth phase in her spiritual life, though as we shall see, it occurred chronologically later than her so-called fifth phase. It is here that our focus shall linger.

---

on God, the focus was on your own feelings about God.

During her years among the Brethren she had found herself increasingly disturbed by their Calvinist teaching on election. Try as she might to believe it, she found it revolting. "I felt that if this doctrine were true, I should be woefully disappointed in the God whom I had, with so much rapture, discovered" (196). She began to find her own salvation a burden, knowing that so many others who were in exactly the same undeserving condition as she was prior to her salvation would be damned forever simply because God had chosen not to rescue them.

To relieve the pressure on her faith created by the combination of Calvinism with everlasting hell, she resorted to annihilationism, but here she found herself convinced that God would have failed if his only solution to the problems of creation was to give up and destroy his creatures. This put her in a quandary:

> I felt hopeless of reconciling the love and justice of the Creator with the fate of His creatures, and I knew not which way to turn. ... I began to feel that the salvation in which I had been rejoicing was, after all, a very limited and a very selfish salvation, and as such, unworthy of the Creator who has declared so emphatically that His "tender mercies are over *all* His works." And above all unworthy of the Lord Jesus Christ, who came into the world for the sole and single purpose of saving the world. (198, 200)

Could Jesus' saving death prove so ineffective and fall so far short of putting the world right?

Everything changed for her in early 1873.[19] She writes, "one day a revelation came to me that vindicated Him, and that settled the whole question forever" (200). Perhaps there is some slight retrospective modification of the impact of the experience in this comment. From Hannah's letters, we see that the revelation was a transformative "intuition," just as

19. Hannah does not provide the date of her conversion to universal restoration in her autobiography. Readers can only infer that the revelation took place prior to her speaking at camp meetings in 1873 and the publication of *The Christian's Secret of a Happy Life* (1875) and some years after joining the Brethren around 1858. The incident took place in Philadelphia so it is plausible that it occurred while they were living nearby (i.e., before 1864 or after a move back in 1869). However, from her personal correspondence in 1873 she says that the revelation described in the autobiography occurred "at the beginning of the year" (letter to Anna Shipley, August 6, 1873). The earliest evidence we have of the theological shift is a letter from Hannah to her husband Robert dated April 3, 1873. My thanks to the Quaker historian Carole Spencer for uncovering the correspondence and sending me copies of the letters.

described in the autobiography.[20] However, the question may not have been *completely* settled as quickly as she suggests above. In letters to her husband Robert (who was away in England, convalescing on his doctor's advice), she seems to have acquired an immediate and clear inclination toward universal restitution, but was not fully committed to that stance. She wrote: "To me it looks like a very wide salvation at the least, if not universal" (April 3, 1873). She was also very quickly aware of the work of Andrew Jukes. She is eager to speak with him and asks Robert if he would be willing to make contact on her behalf (April 3). By June 4, she writes of her theological musings, "And oh, how all this does make me long to believe in Jukes' doctrine of the final restitution. I have got his book over here, & am going to read it, & thee need not be the least surprised if I am convinced." By June 6, she seems more confident in her theol-logic and appeals again to Robert to communicate with Mr. Jukes in a private letter about her ideas to see what he says. By July 17, she writes, "Jukes' book delights me. It is wonderful the [biblical] texts he brings forward. Do talk to him about it, & see if he wont convince thee. It would be too bad for us to differ on this subject, when we generally agree so entirely on all religious and doctrinal points." By August 6, she writes to Anna Shipley that "I am reading Jukes' 'Restitution of all things,' and am being convinced by it just as fast as possible." But, she continues, "I hardly needed the book though. The intuition came to me in the beginning of the year"—and she recounts her revelation.

To understand that transformative day, we need to wind the clock back a little further. After attending a revivalist meeting in which the congregants were asked to share in Christ's sufferings for the sake of others, she began to pray for this blessing. The answer to her prayer was not what she had been expecting. Instead, she had a revelation, not of Christ's sufferings, but of *humanity's* sufferings, the consequence of sin, and of Christ's sorrow for suffering humanity. She perceived Christ's anguish at our fate, but also his joy at being able to sacrifice himself to save us from it. She saw that both God's love and his justice motivated him to rescue his broken creatures. She grasped that "since God had permitted sin to enter into the world, it must necessarily be that He would be compelled, in common fairness, to provide a remedy that would be equal to the disease" (202–3). In a real sense, she writes, we are victims of the sin at work in the world. Hannah thought also of the love of mothers with diseased

---

20. Letter to Anna Shipley, her closet friend, dated August 6, 1873.

children, who would be willing to lay down their own lives for them if it would alleviate their afflictions. Could God do less? she reasoned.

All of this was incredibly vivid to her: "I *saw* it. It was a revelation of the *real* nature of things" (203). And how much more clearly, she understood, must God see reality in this way? "And I began to understand how it was that the least He could do would be to embrace with untold gladness anything that would help to deliver the beings He had created from such awful misery" (203).

This experience lasted for some protracted period, and it was crushing. She saw the story of human misery in every person's face, so she took to veiling herself in public to spare herself seeing people. However, on one occasion in a tram car in Philadelphia, she was compelled to look at two men and was overwhelmed with anguish and a deeper revelation of the misery caused by sin. She upbraided God—"Oh, God, how canst Thou bear it? Thou mightest have prevented it, but didst not. . . . I do not see how Thou *canst* go on living and ensure it" (204). Suddenly God seemed to answer her in an inward voice, saying "in tones of infinite love and tenderness,"

> "He shall see the travail of His soul and be satisfied" [Isa 53:11]. "Satisfied!" I cried in my heart, "Christ is to be satisfied! He will be able to look at the world's misery, and then at the travail through which He has passed because of it, and will be satisfied with the result! If I were Christ, nothing could satisfy me but that every human being should in the end be saved, and therefore I am sure that nothing less will satisfy Him." And with this a veil seemed to have been withdrawn from before the plans of the universe, and I saw that it was true, as the Bible says, that "as in Adam all die even so in Christ should all be made alive" [1 Cor 15:22]. As was the first, even so was the second. The "all" in one case could not in fairness mean less than the "all" in the other. I saw therefore that the remedy must necessarily be equal to the disease, the salvation must be as universal as the fall. (204–5)

This revelation was accompanied by a deep inner conviction as to its truth—"And from that moment I have never had one questioning thought as to the final destiny of the human race. . . . The how and the when I could not see; the one essential fact was all I needed—somewhere and somehow God was going to make everything right for all the creatures He had created. My heart was at rest about it forever" (205). Andrew Jukes's book served to consolidate and reinforce this conviction, resonating deeply with it, but the conviction itself was grounded in her spiritual experience, not his book.

She rushed to search the Scriptures and was amazed to find it illuminated in a new way, as her eyes were opened to perceive what had previously been hidden—the final restitution of all things. "I turned greedily from page to page of my Bible, fairly laughing aloud for joy at the blaze of light that illuminated it all. It became a new book" (206–7). This too reinforced her new conviction.

She continued to build up more arguments from the Bible and Christian theology to support this conclusion, including arguments for interpreting God's defeat of his enemies and his fiery wrath as part of the means of salvation, but the basic core conviction came in a moment of "insight" in Philadelphia. When she tried to encapsulate the insight in a single phrase it was this: "the unselfishness of God." She finally saw that God's love did not fall short of her ideal of love, as she had previously feared it did, but far exceeded it. "I found out that He was far more than loving;—He was love, love embodied and ingrained. I saw that He was, as it were, made out of love, so that in the very nature of things He could not do anything contrary to love. Not that He would not do it, but actually could not, because love was the very essence of His being" (211). This insight completely revitalized and reshaped Hannah's spiritual life.

Hannah's experience of motherhood was important in her theological reflections. "My feelings as a mother, which had heretofore seemed to war with what I believed of God, now came into perfect harmony" (213). Her tender feelings toward her children shaped the way she thought of the bliss of heaven and of the love of God: "I think this feeling has taught me more of what God's feelings are towards His children than anything else in the universe. . . . In fact most of my ideas of the love and goodness of God have come from my own experience as a mother." (213). She conceives of a mother's love as a reflection of God's love, for humans are divine images. God's love, therefore, cannot be inferior to a mother's own love for her children—for the latter is only a pale reflection of the former—it must infinitely exceed it. This divine love she calls "the mother-heart of God" (215).

Hannah quickly announced her views on Restitution and was met with great disapproval from the Plymouth Brethren, resulting in "what might be called persecution" (220). This did not put her off, as she saw herself as the enlightened one in the midst of those in darkness. "And on this ground I have always rather enjoyed being considered a heretic, and have never wanted to be endorsed by anyone" (220).

She did not shove her new views down people's throats, but if doors opened and opportunities arose, she took them. And she would not accept any speaking engagements unless those requesting her knew what her "heretical" views were. On one occasion, she was asked to speak in Brighton, England, on condition that she did not mention her views on Restitution while in Britain. She wrote back, refusing the condition, saying, "I compromise for nobody" (224). The committee immediately dropped the requirement and invited her anyway.

During their time in New Jersey, William E. Boardman (1810–86), an influential American holiness teacher and healer, became impressed by Robert and Hannah and persuaded them to come to England with him and speak on "the Higher Life." This they did in 1873–74, and an important door was opened up for them in England and Europe as a result.

Before Hannah could hold the "Higher Life" meetings in London, she met with some influential Evangelical women. Their task was to decide whether to endorse her. As a funeral went past the group, she expressed how she was not sad, but happy, for she trusts in the love of God for everybody. That was a risky thing to say in such a context, but she immediately won the respect and affection of the very wealthy Lady Mount Temple, who promptly invited Hannah to some meetings at Broadlands, her house in Hampshire. This was the start of a series of important conferences at Broadlands, which proved critical for Hannah's work in England and elsewhere. Indeed, her "heretical" views proved not to be an obstacle at all to her influential ministry in England.

The Broadlands conferences hosted by Lord and Lady Mount Temple were an important tributary feeding into the Keswick conventions, Evangelical holiness convocations that continue annually to this day in the UK. Their focus was the "Higher Life"—holiness, moral transformation, and entire surrender to God. What is interesting is that those initial conferences gathered an eclectic group of delegates with a range of theological views, often with a mystical bent, and included several prominent universalists. Not only was Hannah there as a key speaker, but so were George MacDonald and Andrew Jukes, Hannah's universalist guide. In addition, Julia Wedgewood and Emelia Russell Gurney, both strong devotees of Thomas Erskine's theology, were present, as was John Brash who, along with George MacDonald and the Mount Temples, was much-influenced by F. D. Maurice. The thought of all these thinkers fed into the brew that became Keswick's spirituality. And so it was that universalists played an important (though often unrealized) role in the launching of a significant British Evangelical movement with a strong conservative flavor. Perhaps there is some irony there.

Hannah's ministry in England was a major success in 1873–74 and again, after a brief return to America, in 1875. She and Robert addressed literally thousands of Christian ministers at key events in Brighton, Oxford, London, Manchester, Leicester, and Dublin. Hannah's Bible readings at these conventions made a major impression. Her influence through preaching and publishing reached very many thousands of Christians.

Then a scandal in which Robert was suspected of committing adultery broke, from which his ministry never fully recovered. Hannah's ministry, however, continued to flourish. Her book *The Christian's Secret of a Happy Life* (1875), a book on "the joy of obedience," became quite possibly *the* most influential text in the holiness movement (and foundational for the Keswick doctrine of sanctification), and remains read to this day.[21] She was often asked to speak on Christian spirituality and holiness and also became involved with proto-feminist campaigns through the Women's Christian Temperance Union, which she helped to found in 1874. Her teaching on holiness to the WCTU gave her direct input to around sixty thousand Christian women. The family moved permanently to England in 1888.[22]

In 1903, Hannah published her autobiography, *The Unselfishness of God and How I Discovered It*. The title itself puts Hannah's universalism front-and-center, and one of the major sections of the biography is devoted to her conversion to the larger hope. Indeed, she says, "If I were called upon to state in one sentence the sum and

21. Though she wrote it only reluctantly, in response to her husband's persistent requests.

22. In 1894, one of her daughters, Alys Pearsall Smith, married the mathematician and philosopher Bertrand Russell. Their marriage began to come apart in 1901, when Russell decided that he no longer loved Alys and embarked on a lifestyle of numerous affairs. Russell and Alys were finally divorced in 1921. Russell never hid his strong dislike for Hannah.

substance of my religious experience, it is this sentence [i.e., the unselfishness of God]" (ch. 1). However, subsequent editions removed the offending three chapters for fear that they were too controversial. In this way, while Hannah's teaching on the higher life continued to influence the Christian public, that public was protected from her dangerous eschatological hope.

Hannah takes her place as one of several influential female believers in the larger hope, alongside the likes of Ann Conway (1631–79), Jane Lead (1624–1704), Johanna Eleonora Petersen (1644–1724), Judith Sargent Murray (1751–1820), and Josephine Butler (1828–1906), not to mention the many society-shaping women in the Universalist denomination in America.[23] In a patriarchal world in which a woman's place was very clearly demarcated and prescribed, these women were exceptional and ground breaking, finding a certain level of acceptance in their unusual vocations, just as their early-church and medieval precursors, such as Macrina the Younger (324–379) and Julian of Norwich (1342–1416), had before them. And Hannah has no qualms about bringing her insights as a woman, as a mother, to the task of theological reflection, offering an insight that the male-dominated theology of the church has often been blind to.

Hannah is not the most significant theologian with universalist instincts, but she represents the irrepressible vitality of that instinct, how even when it is deliberately locked away deep underground in a theological prison, kept out of sight and mind, it refuses to stay locked up and keeps on breaking out. It is an irrepressible "heresy." Why this should be so will depend on the analyst. For some its constant reappearing reflects the ever-rebellious sinful desires of humans, who seem constitutionally incapable of submitting to divine revelation. For others, it is that universal salvation is an idea implicit in the biblical gospel itself, an idea that the core doctrines of Christian theology reach out toward in hope. As such, as long as the gospel is proclaimed in the church, there will be those who find themselves swept along by its wave in the direction of a larger hope.

23. See http://uuhhs.org/womens-history/notable-women-biographies/.

Conclusion

LOOKING BACK ACROSS THE period from the Reformation to the end of the nineteenth century, we can see that right from the start a tiny spring of universalist thinking began to bubble up among some of the grass roots. The spring became a small-but-steady stream of hopeful Christians that continued to flow across the centuries. Its journey was one of twists and turns, and its fortune was afflicted by droughts and floods; sometimes it became a mere trickle, sometimes it even seemed to disappear out of sight in one place only to reappear somewhere else, and at one point it included a fairly sizable denomination. The stream took on different appearances in different contexts, under different conditions, but on it flowed.[1]

GENEALOGIES OF HOPE

Throughout this tour, I have aimed to clarify the connections that the various individuals we have considered had with each other, whether directly or indirectly. This enables us to trace some lines of influence, genealogies if you will. We can also observe some "intermarriages" of different universalist families as some individuals combine aspects of more than one family line.

One line of influence that reaches back beyond our period is the Origenian tradition itself, which experienced something of a revival in certain quarters in the seventeenth century. Among the Cambridge Platonists, who esteemed Origen, some were drawn to his theology of

1. Perhaps, however, we should exercise some caution in speaking of this as the story of a *single* stream. It may possibly be better to consider it as several different streams—flowing in the same vicinity and containing similar elements in the water—that combine and divide in complex ways.

apokatastasis. This never caught on in Protestantism as a whole, but once the ideas were put forth again, they began to have a shaping effect. We have seen how even those who may not have read Origen for themselves could have been influenced by those ideas. This was illustrated through Jane Lead, who, while she never once mentions Origen, actually has multiple points of convergence with his theology and with his exegesis of certain texts. Origen was not the *major* influence on many of the eighteenth- and nineteenth-century believers in the larger hope that we have considered; nevertheless, a lot of them were aware of him and had read parts of his work, so his theology did continue to exert some direct influence. His presence did increase in the twentieth century, especially among some Orthodox and Catholic theologians, as the result of a major restoration of Origen's reputation among patristics scholars, stripping away centuries of suspicion and fear. In our day, Origen is at last being reclaimed as a saintly and important theologian for the church. But that story belongs to another book.

It can sometimes be hard to know whether similarities between the patristic doctrine of *apokatastasis* and later universalisms are a case of "descent" or of "convergent evolution." After all, once one has started to pursue that kind of theology, certain similarities with *apokatastasis* are inevitable. So a good dose of caution is required. Nevertheless, certain notions—such as the idea common to most versions of eighteenth-century universalism that the final restoration, in which God is "all in all," would occur *after* the end of all ages, including the age to come—resonate so strongly with patristic theology, and are not in any sense demanded by universal salvation *per se* that an Origenian influence, either direct or indirect, seems possible.

Another notable influence for many universalists in the period covered is Jakob Böhme, the Lutheran mystic. Of course, some disliked Böhme (e.g., Relly, Murray, and Chauncy), and others were appreciative but very cautious (e.g., Peter Sterry), while many were enamored (especially Jane Lead, the various Pietist groups, and William Law) or at least selectively appreciative (Thomas Erskine, George MacDonald, Andrew Jukes). Why the recurring interest in Böhme? In many ways, it is not surprising. He was esteemed by the Philadelphians in Britain and Germany before they embraced universalism. Consequently, they did not simply spread the message of universal salvation, but also a Christianity with varying degrees of a Böhmist tinge. Similarly, William Law's influence on certain later universalists mediated some of that tinge to those outside the direct line of descent from Radical Pietists (Erskine, MacDonald, Jukes). Böhme was not the source of their belief in universal salvation, but he did flavor some important strands of their theology and spirituality to varying degrees. (See the appendix for a response to what I consider a recent over-estimation of Böhme's role.)

Other genealogical lines are straightforward. For instance, we have seen the direct link between Jane Lead's mystical theology and the conversion of the Petersens to the cause of final restitution. We saw, too, that they took their modified version of Lead's theology far and wide, influencing many Radical Pietists. Large numbers of those Pietists, in turn, migrated from Europe to the United States and preached their brands of Christianity there, in word and in print. Through their witness, some American colonists, such as Elhanan Winchester, became subscribers to and disseminators of the "everlasting gospel." Winchester in particular had a relatively sizable impact in America and Britain, stamping a certain shape on the developing universalisms in both countries.

James Relly represents a very different family tree. His was an idiosyncratic Calvinistic universalism, though rather different from and unrelated to that of Peter Sterry and Jeremiah White in the seventeenth century. Relly's theology was passed along, largely uncontaminated, by his disciple John Murray. And it was Murray who is credited with leading the first formal universalist church in America. Yet despite his tireless effort and a major input into the early Universalist denomination, he had little long-term impact when it came to the theology of the movement. The Pietist strand was always dominant.

Other lines of influence were somewhat messier. We have seen how, in nineteenth-century Britain, certain individuals were exploring a wider hope, and many of them knew each other well, or were at least acquainted with each other or with each other's work. But it is somewhat harder to get a clear sense of the nature of the influence in these matters. Thomas Erskine was acknowledged by F. D. Maurice to be a major inspiration, and Edward Plumptre, F. W. Farrar, and George MacDonald (among others) became aware of Erskine and his work, holding him in high esteem. And F. D. Maurice himself was clearly a big influence on Farrar, Plumptre, and MacDonald. All of those characters in turn were read and respected by Andrew Jukes, Samuel Cox, and Thomas Allin. What complicates matters is that all of these men were reading multiple authors on these issues, including patristic sources. So while there were clear and acknowledged influences in the directions indicated, the overall importance of each of the diverse influences in the final landscape of the audiences' own theologies is less clear. We simply do not know enough about the journeys of these people toward a wider hope and, consequently, we do not know whether they were *already* musing about such matters—perhaps even having their thoughts more or less in place—before coming across the work of others or whether that work was a trigger. George MacDonald, about whom we know more in this matter, was clearly moving in hopeful directions from his youth, long before he found likeminded theologians to engage. In his case, it seems that the work of Maurice and Erskine served to reinforce and clarify his *existing* theological dispositions. It would certainly not be correct to describe him as one in the Maurice family tree. All this said, it remains the case that those who were exploring these radical notions were guiding and inspiring each other in those explorations.

THE PERENNIAL "HERESY"

One striking aspect that stands out from our explorations in this volume is the way in which universalism seems to be spontaneously rediscovered over and over again. Of course, as just indicated, there are universalist genealogies, and it is not hard to find people who were converted to universalism directly through the preaching or the writing of another. Think, for instance, of the key role of Paul Siegvolk's book in Elhanan Winchester's conversion, or of James Relly's writing and preaching in John Murray's. Nevertheless, it is fascinating how many people seem to move into a belief in universal salvation seemingly without the influence of other Christians encouraging them to. One thinks, for instance, of Hans Denck (if he was a universalist), Gerrard Winstanley, Jeremiah White, Jane Lead, George de Benneville, George Stonehouse, James Relly, Charles Chauncy, Caleb Rich, Friedrich Schleiermacher, Johann Christoph Blumhardt, Thomas Erskine, George MacDonald, Andrew Jukes, and Hannah Whitall Smith. I am not suggesting that their diverse journeys into a belief in the final redemption of all were not influenced, indeed deeply influenced, by other Christians or by inherited Christian theological ideas. Of course they were—every one of them. My point, rather, is that each of these characters found their own way toward belief in universal salvation without the direct influence of other *universalists*. Their journeys were indeed pushed in such radical directions by other people and existing ideas, but those influential people and ideas were not themselves universalist. Rather, it was our lone travelers who took the baton and then ran with it into new and unanticipated territory. Subsequently, as we saw with Hannah Whitall Smith, the theology of other universalists can serve to refine and confirm that initial "insight," but the insight itself was not taught them by another.

What is fascinating is that this deviancy, running off course with the baton, keeps on happening. Perhaps we might even dare to speak of universal salvation as *the perennial "heresy,"* echoing the way that some have spoken of Platonism as the perennial philosophy. (Of course, I use the term "heresy" with my tongue in my cheek, for I do not believe that universalism is a formal heresy; rather, it occupies a space between heresy and dogma.) It is a theological idea that refuses to go away and keeps on raising its ugly/beautiful (delete as appropriate) head over and over again, throughout the centuries. One may wonder why this is so. It is almost as if the baton itself had some "pull" of its own, drawing runners off the prescribed course. Might it be that the chief impulses behind the deviancy, in its many Christian versions, are integrally related to deep Christian convictions—about God's love and goodness and justice, about the dignity of humans in God's image, about the victory of Christ over sin and death, and so on. It seems to be those very convictions that raise doubts about hell as eternal torment and push in the direction of a larger hope. In other words, perhaps the seeds of this hope lie in the gospel itself. If that is the case, then as long as Christians continue to believe in such things, there will remain an inherent temptation to follow them toward conclusions that push beyond the mainstream tradition, off the prescribed course, in the pursuit of a wider hope.

ROUTES INTO UNIVERSALISM

A third concluding observation that arises from these stories concerns the diversity of the journeys that different people took on their way into embracing universal restoration. We observe in all those journeys a complex and varied relationship between Scripture, tradition, reason, and experience. And while for certain individuals one or two elements in that quadrilateral may loom large, all four will be playing some role because they all interconnect and mutually inform one another. Consider, for instance, George de Benneville. Clearly his religious experiences were the primary explosive motivation in his conversion to universalism, but they are experiences that are clearly informed and shaped by Scripture and traditional Christian theological categories. They did not occur *ex nihilo*. And those experiences in turn shaped the way in which de Benneville subsequently interpreted Scripture and traditional Christian theology.

We could picture the relationship as in the diagram below. A little explanation is in order. I do not think that "reason" should be thought of as a separate element in the quadrilateral so much as the way in which the other elements are reflected upon and related to each other. So in the diagram below, think of reason as a part of what makes up the arrows. Thus, when one reads a philosopher or a theologian making out arguments for or against hell, he or she is using reason, but is reasoning *about* the teaching of Scripture, of tradition, and about our human experiences. Reason does not have its own content.

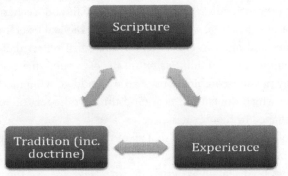

Of course, it is also true that the other three components cannot really be conceived adequately apart from each other. Scripture itself arose within the tradition of the community of Israel and of the church. Its component parts were written and edited by people shaped by that tradition, and those texts in turn reflected and preserved that tradition. Furthermore, the community itself selected—or, perhaps better, discerned under the guidance of God's Spirit—the books that were to be acknowledged as inspired Scripture. Without the community and its traditions, there would not *be* a canon of Scripture. The tradition then preserved the text and honored it as inspired and authoritative and passed on patterns for its use and interpretation. Scripture arose *from* and exists *within* the community, *for* the community. But the tradition, when it has been true to itself, has never considered itself somehow *above* the Bible. Rather, it has seen itself as accountable to biblical teaching and always under the divine authority mediated by scriptural teaching. So renewal movements

usually take the form of calling the church back to being true to its inspired text.

This interpenetration is also true of experience, which cannot be
sealed off from Scripture and tradition. The Bible itself reflects the experiences of the community and individuals within it as they journey
with God. It also shows the role that experience can play in theological
reflection. Consider, for instance, the way that Job's experience runs on
a collision course with the neat prepackaged theology of his comforters.
And the book vindicates Job for taking his experience seriously. Similarly,
previously revealed texts can shape the contours of profound charismatic
encounters with God. The book of Revelation illustrates this: its visions,
which we have good reason to believe were actual visionary experiences
rather than simple literary constructions, are overflowing with allusions
to earlier prophetic texts, such as those of Isaiah and Zechariah. John,
the author of Revelation, was deeply shaped by biblical texts from earlier
generations, and his own encounters in the Spirit reflect that input. In
these visions we see tradition, Scripture, and experience merged in one of
their many possible combinations. And it should go without saying that
the way in which the faithful hear God through the text of Scripture is
strongly shaped by their experience.

All of this is simply to say that all of these factors will play a part in
the story of an individual's conversion to belief in universal salvation, that
they cannot be disentangled in a tidy way. Nevertheless, the dominant
trigger-element will vary from one person to another.

The role of experiences

Everyday experiences can play a role in a Christian's reflections on hell
and salvation. Think, for instance, of experiences of the horrors of suffering, of love for those one believes will be damned, of the kindness
of unbelievers, of human empathy. This kind of experience-influenced
thinking was a recurring motif among all those we have considered who
began as Calvinists and found themselves struggling and repelled by the
vision of a God who chooses to torment unbelievers in hell forever when
he could just as easily have chosen to love and deliver them. Everything in
their human experience of love rebelled against that theology. Or, somewhat differently, think of George de Benneville's experience of meeting
pious Muslims and the way in which it made him realize the shallowness

of his own faith. Consider too Hannah Whitall Smith's experience as a mother with her children and how that shaped the way she came to think about God.

In addition to these mundane experiences, there are the more extraordinary spiritual experiences that play a role in some universalist conversions. The best known are the shewings of Julian of Norwich (see chapter 10 of the first volume of this series), but we have also seen the transformative role of the purported revelations given Jane Lead through her visions of divine Sophia, the impact of Johanna Petersen's dream about the end-time conversion of the Jews, the life-changing revelation of divine love in George de Benneville's Evangelical conversion experience and his subsequent near-death visionary journeys to heaven and hell, and Caleb Rich's angelic visitor, who proclaimed "the everlasting gospel" of the salvation of all Adam's descendants in Christ. Hannah Whitall Smith's revelation on the tram in Philadelphia that Jesus would see the travail of his soul and be satisfied was a moment of deep clarity for her on the issue, one from which she never looked back. Furthermore, sometimes earlier religious experiences can be seen in a new, universal perspective, after starting down *apokatastasis* road. Here one might ponder Elhanan Winchester as he looked back on his Evangelical conversion experience and saw universalist impulses in it that he felt he had wrongly suppressed in order to conform to his Calvinist context.

These experiences, both mundane and more exceptional, play differing roles in the journey of an individual toward embracing ultimate restoration. Some, like de Benneville's conversion experience or Jane Lead's visions, lead *directly* to an embracing of universalism. This tends to be the case with the more unusual religious experiences. They carry a sense of conviction and revelation with them that more mundane experiences do not. Other experiences prompt further reflection on Scripture and doctrine, which in its turn leads to universalism. One can track Elhanan Winchester's slow journey over at least two years in which various encounters and events played the role of provoking further reflection. A person's experience can also reinforce their existing universalist belief, as, for instance, de Benneville's near-death visions of heaven and hell did both for him and for those who heard them or read them.

Religious experience was much more prominent in seventeenth and eighteenth-century universalism than in the nineteenth century. The Universalist denomination, as it embraced the Enlightenment valuation of the centrality of a certain mode of rationality, actively distanced itself from the emotional excesses of revivalism, which they felt could bring the cause into disrepute. Similar suspicion of dreams, visions, and revivalist "emotionalism" can also be found in eighteenth-century universalists like Charles Chauncy and John Murray. In a similar way, some of the hopeful universalists in the nineteenth-century mainstream denominations were concerned with respectability and were not given to visionary religion. But for the most part, it would seem to be true that many universalists were open to the charismatic dimensions of Christian experience, and allowed them a place in the life of faith.

The role of Scripture

For some converts, intense study of the Bible was *the* key factor that led to their change in perspective. They may not have even been looking into the issue, but the issue came looking for them. Charles Chauncy claims that it was in his work on 1 Corinthians 15 that he became persuaded of universal salvation. And as he carefully explored the rest of the Bible, he found this unexpected view reinforced. George Stonehouse too appears to have come to the view from Bible study. Others may have been prompted by hearing the arguments or experiences of others to look again at the Bible. Johann Petersen, on reading of Jane Lead's visions, went to the Bible and found himself both persuaded of its central message, but also needing to offer some corrections to aspects of Lead's theology. This illustrates the way in which the Bible was seen to be an authority to which experiences were accountable and by which they could be assessed. Elhanan Winchester's conversion involved a range of factors, but the decisive key was his own diligent searching of Scripture and testing out of the various views against it. It was *this* that, in the end, was the main factor in persuading him to be an unwavering universalist. But the situation could run the other way: one's reading of the Bible could be opened up in fresh ways in the light of experience. That was Hannah Whitall Smith's story after her revelation on the tram—she went back to the Bible and suddenly found the wider hope all over the place. It felt like her eyes had been blind to it, but now she could see. Whenever it comes into the frame, Scripture traditionally played a fundamental role that *every* Christian universalist had to take seriously.

Tradition

In some ways, given the dominance of eternal conscious torment in the tradition, it would seem that a certain sitting loose to tradition would be a requirement for exploring the possibility of universal salvation. There is some truth in this suspicion. The Reformation, with its *sola Scriptura* and its rejection of certain traditions in the church, created the potential space within Protestant communities for imagining non-traditional possibilities regarding hell. One can see that many of the Protestant universalists were overt in dismissing traditional views in the name of fidelity to what they saw as the true teaching of the Bible. Many gloried in their rejection of tradition, finding great pleasure in mocking it, and boasting of their elevation of the Bible in opposition to tradition. Of course, it is also true that there was a certain amount of self-deception here because these believers were simultaneously profoundly indebted to the very tradition they thought they were rejecting in their theology. It shaped their faith at deeper levels than they realized. They *thought* they were Bible-only believers, but there is no such thing.

The place of tradition in our tale, however, is more complex. For some, it was the recovery of a sidelined part of the tradition, the teaching of Origen and his theological heirs, that opened the door to hope. This was the case with George Rust and some others influenced by the Cambridge Platonists. And we have witnessed in our tale the recovery of some Origenist interpretations of certain biblical texts and the role that these readings played in the rise of universalism in this period. Even those who may not have read Origen's work seem to have become at least indirectly influenced by its recovery. We suggested that this was the case with Jane Lead, and it was likely the case with numerous others. It is certainly not hard to find lots of parallels with Origenian theology in the writings of many of those discussed in this book. I avoided pointing them out *en route* simply to minimize tedium.

The importance of tradition was even more in focus for those nineteenth-century Anglicans who refused to shut out the possibility of the redemption of all, people such as Frederick W. Farrar, Edward Plumptre, and Thomas Allin. As good Anglicans, holding a deep respect for the catholic tradition, they invested considerable effort in demonstrating the presence of universalism in mainstream church history. Allin in particular argued in great detail that *apokatastasis* was far more widespread among the church fathers than is usually imagined. The recovery of the larger hope in the early church is a major factor behind the revival of hopeful universalism among some Orthodox and Catholics in the twentieth century and beyond—the likes of Sergius Bulgakov or Hans Urs von Balthasar. For them, unlike some of the characters in this book, tradition was perhaps the key provocation toward openness to universal salvation.

For Allin, the situation was starker still. He felt that eternal hell, although having been embraced by large parts of the church, was actually *incompatible* with the central creedal core of the tradition, generating impossible conflicts *within* Christian theology. In his mind, universal salvation was necessary precisely in order to preserve the core elements of the tradition, protecting them against the erosion caused by hell. Everlasting hell was the cuckoo in the nest of orthodoxy, an alien intruder threatening the tradition.

It was definitely the case that reflection on certain traditional doctrines and their implications played a large role in the rise of universalism and in many of the journeys we have followed. For some, this may have involved a more parochial doctrine, such as the critical role that the penal substitution theory, important in the classical Reformed tradition, played in driving James Relly into a kind of Calvinist universalism, or the way that reflection on the Reformed doctrines of predestination and election took Schleiermacher in creative new directions. Evangelical tradition also factored in the way that those like Elhanan Winchester played off Calvinism and Arminianism against each other—he argued that each theological tradition had its undesirable implications (Calvinism creates problems for God's love, while Arminianism creates problems for God's sovereignty and victory). Universalism affirmed the best insights, while rejecting the problematic aspects, of both traditions: the perfect *via media*.

For many, the traditional catholic Christian teachings about divine love, creation, fall, the work of Christ in his incarnation, death, and resurrection, God's final defeat of evil, and so on, played a critical role in their move to universalism. The perceived difficulty created for such catholic theology by attempting to assimilate the doctrine of eternal hell into it played some role for most of those whose stories we have considered.

So we end this volume hopefully with a better understanding of the diversity of the phenomenon of Christian universalism, of its roots, motivators, and theological shapes, and of its strengths and weaknesses.[2]

2. I have not tried to assess many of the strengths or weaknesses, but hopefully readers will now have enough data to make their own such assessments intelligently.

The twentieth and twenty-first centuries saw some further significant changes in both the theological contours and fortunes of the hope for the salvation of all. Reformed theologians continued to make a contribution, but their impact was considerably bigger, especially after Karl Barth, who—whether or not one considers him to believe in universal salvation—made a game-changing move in his doctrine of election, the ripple-effects of which have not faded with time.[3] Alongside that change some notable Catholic and Orthodox theologians, including a couple of popes, affirmed versions of hopeful universalism. This significant change was shaped by a major twentieth-century rehabilitation of Origen among patristics scholars.[4] As his brand was detoxified, his theology became more influential within churches holding a high view of tradition. Unrelated to all that, there was also a flowering of debate among philosophical theologians that marked several new directions in the development of the doctrine.[5] That philosophical discussion overflowed somewhat into the more popular streams of Christian thought, mingling with other changing cultural influences, such that the twenty-first century has begun to witness a growing openness to universal salvation even in constituencies considered among its greatest opponents—the Evangelicals.[6] The story of belief in universal salvation becomes especially interesting and complicated with the arrival of the internet and social media, enabling rapid global dissemination, cross-fertilization of ideas, and the connection of like-minded Christians. At the end of the nineteenth century, belief in

3. Some of the universalist Reformed thinkers influenced by Barth in this regard are Jacques Ellul, Jürgen Moltmann, and Jan Bonda. Barth was also influential on the Catholic Hans Urs von Balthasar's hopeful universalism. Balthasar, in turn, has exerted huge influence on many sections of post-Vatican II Catholicism. There is arguably also a Barthian influence in the universalism of J. A. T. Robinson, and certainly in what we might refer to as the "hopeful universalism" of T. F. Torrance (though he himself would strongly have objected to that language).

4. One of the most significant pioneers of this recovery is Catholic patristic scholar Ilaria Ramelli, herself a convinced universalist.

5. Directions exemplified, for instance, in the work of John Hick, Marilyn Adams, Thomas Talbott, Eric Reitan, and David Bentley Hart, with other notable Christian philosophers like Alvin Plantinga declaring as hopeful universalists.

6. At which point I ought to footnote my own book: MacDonald, *Evangelical Universalist*. But my turn-of-the-millennium Evangelical universalism had twentieth-century precursors in the likes of the British Pentecostal minister A. E. Saxby (see his *God in Creation, Redemption, Judgment, and Consummation*), Saddhu Sundar Singh, various little-known British Brethren universalists, and my own immediate inspiration, philosopher Thomas Talbott.

"the larger hope" was a little stream, but if one was to track it through the twentieth and twenty-first centuries, one would see it become a small (but growing) river. That is a story that needs telling.[7]

7. McClymond, *Devil's Redemption*, vol. 2 provides considerable detail on important parts of it, albeit with a view to offering a strong theological critique.

Appendix

Is Jakob Böhme the Father
of Modern Universalism?

A Response to the McClymond Model

I. INTRODUCTION

MICHAEL MCCLYMOND'S MASSIVE TWO-VOLUME work *The Devil's Redemption: A New History and Interpretation of Christian Universalism* is one of the most significant analyses and critiques of Christian universalism ever published.[1] It is very impressive in both the breadth and depth of its scholarship, and usually fair-minded in its attempt to understand carefully the ideas it criticizes. As such, no academic attempt to engage universal salvation in a Christian context can afford to ignore it. While I find the theological critique inadequate to the task of undermining Christian universalism *per se* (both because I reject its core thesis and because I think the specific theological accusations against universal salvation do not stand up), there is a lot in McClymond's book, including his critiques of various specific universalist theologies, with which I concur.[2]

Despite the length and detail of the book, the central thesis at its heart is very simple: universalism does not arise from biblical or Christian theological instincts, but is an alien import that first emerged and

1. I would like to express my thanks to Professor Michael McClymond and Revd. Dr. Alan Gregory for very helpful feedback on a first draft of this appendix.

2. For my critique of McClymond's theological case against universal restoration, see Parry, "A Response to Michael McClymond's Theological Critique of Universalism."

flourished in heretical gnostic sects and was subsequently planted into Christianity by Origen. (McClymond argues that Origen's theology of *apokatastasis* was considered very controversial from the first, was never more than a minority report, and was subsequently condemned by the church.) The modern revival of universalism from the late seventeenth century onwards similarly drank deeply from the wells of esotericism, especially from the poisoned well of Jakob Böhme, whose heterodox theology lies somewhere behind many, perhaps most, modern versions of universalism. "Böhme *laid the foundation* for much of modern universalism" (*DR*, 22, italics mine), and his teaching "contained the seeds of later universalist thinking" (*DR*, 200). "With only slight exaggeration, one could say that Christian universalism during the eighteenth and nineteenth centuries was a series of footnotes to Böhme" (*DR*, 445, cf. 7). Indeed, the twentieth-century Russians who were sympathetic to universalism were also deeply indebted to Böhme (*DR*, 685–747), so "one might speak of a Böhmist era in Christian universalism, roughly from 1700 to 1950" (*DR*, 445). Thus, despite the Christian language with which universal salvation dresses itself in an attempt to appear at home in the church, its origins and underlying theological structure are, according to McClymond, antithetical to orthodox Christianity. He hopes that once we see the dubious origins of the universalist idea, in both its ancient and modern versions, we will be enabled to see why it is so problematic. In this debate, argues McClymond, universalism is a Trojan horse—*everything* is at stake (*DR*, xxiv).[3]

In this appendix I have no intention of attempting an analysis of McClymond's book as a whole—that would be a massive undertaking! I will say nothing about his thesis that patristic universalism came from ancient Gnosticism, a thesis that Ilaria L. E. Ramelli has strongly criticized in the first volume of this series (and in more detail in various academic studies). Nor will I offer a response to his analysis of twentieth- and twenty-first-century universalist texts, including my own.[4] And I will not offer a critique of his theological case against universal salvation,

3. The doctrines he thinks are threatened by universalism include not just eschatology, but also the doctrines of God, creation, Christology, sin, atonement, and the like. I think he is mistaken on all these counts, even if one can find examples of particular universalists—some included in this volume—who went skiing off-piste on these various doctrines.

4. Though it will surprise no one to learn that I think his arguments against my own book are unpersuasive.

though I think that this is the area where his book is most vulnerable.[5] Rather, my focus here is on a matter directly relating to this volume of *A Larger Hope?* Namely, his core claim about the pivotal originating role of Jacob Böhme in the rise of modern universalism. I shall suggest that, while Böhme does have a part in this story, it is not that of foundation-layer or seed-planter.

II. JAKOB BÖHME AND THE MCCLYMOND THESIS

Jakob Böhme (1575–1624) was not the kind of man anyone would expect to exert much of an influence of the world of his day—he was not of noble birth, nor university-trained, nor ordained into the Lutheran church in which he was raised.[6] Rather, Böhme worked as a cobbler in a village in Upper Lusatia (in what is now Poland). A mystical experience in 1600, which lasted only a matter of minutes, was the transform-ing event that he felt gave him insight into the inner meanings of the cosmos.

However, it was not until 1612 that he began to write his first book, *Aurora*, and between 1619 and his death in 1624 he published numerous other works that blended theological, esoteric, mystical, alchemical, and biblical themes. Böhme's publications put him in conflict with the local Lutheran clergy of his day. However, those publications went on to exert a very widespread and long-lasting influence.[7] He is probably one of the most influential thinkers you've never heard of.

5. For such a response, see Parry, "A Response to Michael McClymond's Theological Critique of Universalism."

6. For those interested in the details and the context, the most helpful historical analyses of Böhme and his reception I have read are Weeks, *Boehme* and the essays in Hessayon and Apetrei (eds.), *An Introduction to Jacob Boehme*. All Böhme's works and a wealth of material about them can be accessed at Jacob Boehme Online (jacobboehmeonline.com).

7. His ideas gained devotees across Germany, France, England, Russia, and America. This was not merely among religious groups, but also in intellectual circles. Modern continental philosophy, for instance, owes him a considerable debt, not least through his influence on the likes of Hegel, Schelling, and Schopenhauer. So too, arguably, does

Böhme's writings are notoriously ambiguous and difficult to interpret, and various divergent interpretations of them have arisen.[8] Some interpreted him as an orthodox Lutheran, and many sought to present a way of reading him that was compatible with Christian orthodoxy. (William Law was one such reader.) Others more interpreted him as a gnostic-like cosmic dualist, who saw good and evil as eternal cosmic principles, both rooted in God's eternal being—a notion hard to reconcile with orthodoxy![9] I have no dog in this fight, but for the sake of argument I shall assume a worst-case scenario—that Böhme was indeed heterodox. There are certainly many *prima facie* problematic aspects in his thought for orthodox Christians, even if there is also much that they might find helpful.

McClymond's thesis is simply that modern universalism was (to a very considerable extent) forged in the fires of Böhme's esoteric theology, without which it would not have arisen, and it was passed on among those who continued to revere Böhme's writings, indicating how closely connected it is with his heterodox thought. McClymond shows how many, perhaps most, of the key universalists from the late seventeenth century through to the early twentieth century (and even later) have some connection, in one way or another, with Böhme's writings.[10] He writes that "Böhmist universalism (ca. 1700–ca. 1950) centered on a dialectic of *a divine self-differentiation and divine self-reconciliation*" (*DR*, 1008). And "it should not be surprising that the shift towards a conflictual or Böhmist conception of God should also involve a shift in the direction of universal salvation" (*DR*, 1022). There is, he alleges, a direct link between the eternal dualism within God that we find in Böhme and belief in universal salvation. I shall argue that the evidence indicates the exact opposite.

the psychoanalysis of Freud and Jung, on which see McGrath, "Böhme's Theology of Evil and Its Relevance for Psychoanalysis."

8. McClymond is very helpful in summarizing the diverse reception (*DR*, 451–59). See also the essays in Hessayon and Apetrei, *Introduction to Jacob Boehme*.

9. He has been compared to the ancient Manichaeans, with their eternal cosmic dualism between good and evil. The core difference is that Böhme saw the eternal principles that give rise to good and evil as united *within God*.

10. I need to make clear that McClymond's Böhme thesis is only one component in a much larger thesis in which esoteric mysticism is the inspiration behind Christian universalism.

III. RESPONSE

McClymond has done a service to scholarship to bring out the subtle influence of Böhme's writings on many seventeenth- to twentieth-century universalists. It is of interest and worthy of note. However, it is my contention that he has misunderstood and overplayed the nature of that influence.

1. Böhme was not a universalist

The first issue that needs to be grasped is that Böhme himself was *not a universalist*. McClymond writes that "[p]erhaps surprisingly, Böhme did not believe that hell would ever end" (*DR*, 477). However, it is not so surprising. His belief in eternal hell was arguably no mere accident but an integral aspect of his system of thought.[11] How so?

For Böhme, reality at its most fundamental level—in the one God—is a *duality*, a *conflict*. In God, the origin of all reality, we find the conflicting principles eternal *mercy* and eternal *wrath* held in a perfect and unified balance.[12] These eternal binaries are interpenetrating but distinct principles in God, yet they have a single root, which Böhme called the *Ungrund* (a German word meaning "groundless").

The *Ungrund* is the mysterious, ineffable, Absolute, which is undifferentiated, pure potential. The *Ungrund* "desires" to manifest itself and to know itself, but it can only do this if there is another to whom it can reveal itself. Thus, to know itself it must first negate itself in order to open up the space for an other to whom it can self-manifest. Thus, the *Ungrund*'s originating "will" to self-assertion generates a duality within God whereby God can know Godself and thereby become personal.

The *Ungrund* is not *aware* of anything—it does not *think* anything; it does not *know* anything. It moves unconsciously, stirring itself with a libidinous desire to relate to itself and thus know itself, driving towards self-differentiation and thereby self-knowledge. In the *Ungrund* there is

---

11. Now I have no intention of outlining much of Böhme's thinking, but McClymond's summary is helpful in its concision and clarity (*DR*, 459–79). The summary that follows here draws on McClymond and on McGrath, "Böhme's Theology of Evil."

12. This idea was also found in the mysticism of Jewish kabbalah, which was very influential in seventeenth-century Europe. How much Böhme was influenced by Jewish mysticism is disputed.

no conflict, but as it self-differentiates in order to know itself it bifurcates into a dark principle (wrath) and a light principle (mercy).

The dark principle tends inwards towards narcissistic, self-centered contraction; the light principle tends outwards in altruistic, self-giving expansion. The conflict between the two gives rise to a third principle of balance as the two rival principles are held in perfect tension. The first principle is prior: it is the self-assertion, the self-love that is the origin of the divine personality; the second principle is what holds it in check. Love requires both principles: without the dark principle of narcissism there is *no self* to give to others; without the light principle of self-giving altruism, narcissism becomes evil.

For Böhme, the narcissistic dark principle (wrath) is God the Father from whom the light principle (mercy), God the Son, is generated as its necessary opposite. The Spirit is the principle of balance that hold the two together as perfect love. This is a highly unusual spin on Augustinian trinitarian theology![13]

As creation originates in God, so the light and dark in God necessarily permeate everything in creation. Evil in creation arises from the sad reality that these principles are not held in balance as they are in God. God himself has no evil in him because his darkness is balanced by his light in a perfection of goodness. Lucifer, however, in his freedom, embraced narcissism without altruism, self-assertion without self-giving, and thereby became corrupted, evil. Evil is, in effect, a dis-order, a loss of balance—the first principle (wrath/self-love) overwhelming the second (mercy/other-love). It is a form of psychosis and necessarily degrades our personhood.

13. Böhme further spells out the three principles into seven forms of eternal nature (the seven spirits of God), as follows:

Father (dark principle/God's wrath)	Spirit (mediates)	Son (light principle/God's mercy)
Harshness		Light
Bitterness	Fire (unites the conflicting principles of God)	Sound
Angst		Figure

According to McGrath, "Böhme thus fuses the triadic structure of Christianity with the dark-light dualism typical of Gnosticism" ("Böhme's Theology of Evil," 10 in the online version). These seven forms of the eternal nature need one another to exist, but all arise from the *Ungrund*.

Eternal heaven and hell reflect the eternal light and darkness, mercy and wrath within God. Those like Lucifer who embrace the darkness without the light can only exist in hell, facing the wrath of God. To eradicate hell would risk messing up the balance at the heart of Böhme's theology.

Now McClymond is well aware that Böhme did not believe in universal salvation and, being a good scholar, is very open about this fact (e.g., *DR*, 7), but I shall argue that he has not fully appreciated its significance for his thesis.

McClymond helpfully discusses numerous problematic aspects of Böhme's thought, from the perspective of Christian orthodoxy (*DR*, 459–79). But what we need to be very clear about is that *universalism was not one of them*. More than that, universalism is *neither a deduction nor an induction from his ideas*.

One searches McClymond's analysis of Böhme in vain for a convincing exposition of how Böhme's teachings led to a belief in universal salvation. Section 5.4 is intended to perform this task, so it is worth paying it closer attention. What it shows is that the rejection by Böhme's admirers (e.g., Hans Martensen, William Law) of his metaphysical grounding of evil in God and his everlasting dualism of wrath and mercy led to a view of God as pure light. And *this* theology pointed to universalism. Sure, but this is *not a theology derived from Böhme*. It is an orthodox *fix* to such a theology. So if anything, this argument points in the exact *opposite* direction from McClymond's thesis.

McClymond seeks to strengthen his case by arguing that, in his late work *Mysterium Magnum*, Böhme's theology softened and opened up to a kind of salvific inclusivism, taking in those heathen, Jews, and Muslims who "remain within the light principle" (*DR*, 481). But inclusivism addresses the question of *how* one is saved, not *how many* are saved. Inclusivists can be universalists, but there is no reason why they must. Similarly, universalists can be inclusivists, but they do not have to be. Böhme's late inclusivism is neither universalism nor in itself a step closer to it.

McClymond further points out that some passages in Böhme's late text *The Election of Grace* indicate that he later started to see God as pure love and as containing no darkness. Now, if Böhme did change his mind and end up moving away from his earlier claims about eternal light and dark in God, then fair enough. But the extent to which he did so is the extent to which his theology took a step in a less problematic direction.

And if the answer to the question of how Böhme was the ancestor of universalism is "Because he eventually rejected his earlier views and came to teach that 'God is light and in him there is no darkness at all' (1 John 1:5)" then this is either uninteresting or harmless, because in effect all it is saying is that he inspired universalism by abandoning his earlier gnostic-like ideas and ended up promoting an ancient and orthodox Christian teaching.

Finally, McClymond points to a passage from *The Signature of Things*, chapter 16, in which Böhme argues that what is good or evil is relative to the subject. Thus, hell is evil for angels and good for demons; heaven is good for angels and evil for demons. McClymond argues that this subjectivization of good and evil leads to a view that heaven and hell are simply subjective perceptions and then it becomes hard to maintain a "no exit" view of hell because all that one needs to do to move from hell to heaven is to change one's mind. His claim is not that Böhme went in this direction—he did not—but that the potential was there in his thought for others to exploit. The first problem here is that the followers of Böhme that embraced universalism did not do so for this reason. The second problem is that Böhme seems to be speaking about good and evil being relative to *created natures*: "Hell is Evil to angels, *for they were not created thereunto*" (italics mine), and it is good for demons because they were created for that environment. Think about the way that living underwater is good for a fish and bad for a cat. That does not mean that cats simply need to change their mind about how they experience water to be able to take the plunge. So, this is seemingly part of Böhme's eternal cosmic dualism. It does not obviously convert into universalism in the way that McClymond suggests without some significant tinkering elsewhere in Böhme's system.[14]

In sum, I repeat, one searches McClymond's analysis in vain for a convincing exposition of how Böhme's teachings led to a belief in

---

14. McClymond argues that, although Böhme was not a universalist, his theology "could easily be marshalled to support the idea of a temporary hell" (*DR*, 490). His evidence for this claim is the Böhmist Johann Georg Gichtel. Gichtel argued that his dead friend did not have to remain in hell on the grounds that Böhme had rejected predestinarianism, and thus nobody was predestined to hell. However, anti-predestinarianism is a very dubious basis for arguing against the idea that our fates are sealed at death—just ask an Arminian. If this was Gichtel's argument, then it tells us more about his desire to have hope for his friend than it does about how easily Böhme's ideas engender belief in a temporary hell. Gichtel, like Böhme, believed in eternal hell, and he came to oppose the universalism of Jane Lead and the Petersens.

universal salvation. If there is a pathway, McClymond has failed to illuminate it.

Now universalists certainly drew *other* ideas from him—for instance, William Law's use of Böhme to develop an anti-deistic account of how Christ transforms us from within[15]—but, to repeat, they did not get universal reconciliation from him, either directly or indirectly. Universalism is to all appearances *incompatible* with Böhme's own system of thought *as he himself presented it*. To incorporate it properly, one needs to modify some important aspects of his theology. This too McClymond acknowledges: "Böhme identifies good and evil as 'one thing' . . . Yet later reception of Böhme's thought indicate that this idea did not play well. . . . It was too radical a notion for many of those who appreciated other aspects of Böhme's thought" (*DR*, 479). Instead, many admirers of Böhme swapped out this troubling idea for one in which God is unqualified love, light, and goodness. In so doing, they rejected Böhme's important idea of an eternal dualism of light and dark (*DR*, 479–80). This major move was necessary for the coherent affirmation of non-eternal hell and universal salvation.

William Law exemplifies the widespread shift very clearly with his strong declarations of God's goodness and love and his fervent denial of wrath in God (*DR*, 480).[16] Understood against the background of Böhme's duality of wrath and mercy in God one could plausibly see Law's declarations as a distancing of himself—whether intentional or not—from this important aspect of Böhme's teaching. Alternatively, he may simply be interpreting Böhme through a theological grid that filtered out ideas of duality and latched on to Böhme's declarations about God's goodness, mercy, and love.[17] Alan Gregory observes that "without referring to it in any way, Law abandons all the most obviously heterodox elements in Boehme's theology."[18] And we should note that it was Law's version

15. Gregory, "No New Truths of Religion." This essay is a helpful guide to Law's careful appropriation and transformation of Böhme's theology.

16. Law reads and seeks to present Böhme as an orthodox Christian. Irrespective of the merits of his interpretation as an accurate representation of Böhme, his own Böhmist Christian faith, while not without its problems, was arguably orthodox. For a helpful sympathetic explanation of Law's later Böhmist works, and for a rebuttal of John Wesley's critique of Law, see Gregory, *Quenching Hell*.

17 My thanks to Alan Gregory for this alternative suggestion. Email 8 Nov 2018.

18. Gregory, "No New Truths in Religion," 147. He continues, addressing one of McClymond's key concerns with Böhme: "Consequently, the most striking thing about Law's Behemism is the absence of almost everything that the Romantics and

of Böhmism that was such an inspiration for many of the nineteenth-century universalists like George MacDonald and Andrew Jukes.

It is perhaps ironic that the move to embrace universal salvation among some of Böhme's admirers and to reject Böhme's teaching on eternal hell and evil's origin in God's dark principle was precisely the move that brought sections of "Böhmism" closer to Christian orthodoxy.

2. Jane Lead and the shift to universalism

So what happened? McClymond is correct in arguing that the shift to universalism took place principally in and through the English Böhmist Jane Lead (1624–1704), "whose most important departure from the teaching of Jakob Böhme, by her own admission, was her affirmation of universal salvation" (DR, 503). It was she who had a life-changing vision that led her to embrace "the everlasting gospel." It was her influence that set off a chain reaction that eventually worked its way through the international networks of Böhme's admirers so that the Böhmian "tradition," such as it was, shifted in significant part in universalist directions.

What is somewhat obscured in McClymond's account is just how major this shift was—at least once it had reconfigured Böhme's thought around itself. To start with, Lead incorporated the idea within an insufficiently modified version of Böhmism, one that still sought the principles of light and dark in God, yielding a system that was now inconsistent. However, its full integration required a *fundamental* alteration to Böhme's doctrine of God. This was made explicit in Francis Lee (DR, 505), Lead's follower, who was clear that a dualism of darkness and light in God is incompatible with the temporal hell taught by Jane Lead. Universalism works best with a non-dual vision of the Deity (DR, 505). And such is what we find in the universalisms that trace their original spark back to Jane Lead.

We also need to observe that Jane Lead was very well aware that, with universal salvation, she was introducing an unexpected new idea to Böhme's readers. Their natural response would be this: If Böhme was inspired by God, why had God not made this truth clear to him? Indeed, why did he teach eternal hell? Thus, she felt the need to offer an apologetic for the move. "I must own that *Jacob Behmen* did open a deep

---

German Idealists were to admire in Boehme, most specifically his exposition of the 'living God' in developmental, narrative terms."

Foundation of the Eternal Principles, and was a worthy Instrument in his Day. But it [i.e., the revelation of universal restoration] was not given to him, neither was it Time for the unsealing of this Deep."[19] This, she claimed, was a *new* insight into the meaning of Scripture, given for the church of the last days.

In sum, universalism did not arise naturally as an entailment of Böhme's thought—indeed, it is hard to imagine it doing so. Rather, it was introduced into the communities of his admirers as a new idea from outside that purportedly came via a divine revelation. And its introduction led fairly rapidly to a shift in the doctrine of God away from that taught by Böhme to a theology in which God is pure light and love in God's essence. So it seems odd to describe Böhme as one who laid the foundation for modern universalism.

3. How Böhmist are McClymond's Böhmist universalists?

McClymond's thesis is that Böhme is the hidden inspiration behind vast swathes of Christian universalists since the seventeenth century. He lists twenty-five people in his Appendix G, and explores them and others in various degrees of depth in the main text. The implication is that the inspiration behind their universalism was his mystical theology. There are several things to say here.

First, McClymond is absolutely right to highlight that Böhme was read by many people, universalists and others, and was influential in some intellectual and religious circles. But of course, there is no neat link between Böhme and universalism. For starters, as McClymond himself shows, one could arrive at universalism without any Böhmist influence. James Relly (1722–78) and John Murray (1741–1816) strongly disliked Böhme, as did Charles Chauncy (1705–87) (*DR*, 564). Not all universalists got to their views through religious groups with Böhmist influences. As such, universalist ideas cannot be considered to sink or swim with Böhme's mysticism, but must be considered on their own theological merits and demerits.

Second, it is worth noting that not all on the list of "Böhmist universalists" are obviously influenced by Böhme at all. Take Gerald Winstanley. We have no direct evidence that he read Böhme or was influenced by his ideas, for he never refers to, quotes from, or alludes to the Teutonic

19. Lead, *Revelation*, 25.

mystic. However, McClymond speculates that he was influenced (*DR*, 494). We know that one of his associates in the Diggers, William Everard, knew John Poradge, the English Böhmist. So there is a potential indirect connection. And Winstanley's publications certainly have an esoteric flavor, like Böhme's. However, McClymond's suggestion is weakly founded. Winstanley's universalist book was published in 1648, while Böhme's works were only published in English in London from 1645 to 1662. So Winstanley would have had to have been at the very cutting-edge of positive reception of Böhme. Add to this the fact that, during the time of his writing, he had little financial means, so likely had few books. Ariel Hessayon, in a study of the dissemination and reception of Böhme's work in England during the seventeenth century, argues that "it seems certain that Winstanley did not consult any of Boehme's works while writing his own. It also seems very probable that he never read Boehme. The disparities between them [in content, vocabulary, and style] are far too great."[20] More to the point, even if there was some influence, Winstanley's universalist book was published almost fifty years before any Böhmists had moved to embrace universal salvation, so Winstanley's universalism was his own, not Böhme-inspired.

Third, we need to be attentive to the very different degrees to which Böhme's thought influenced those whom McClymond classifies as Böhmist universalists. Some were paid-up, card-carrying admirers and followers. Here one thinks of Anne Conway, Jane Lead, William Law, and Richard Roach, among others. (Though, to repeat, even in most of these cases, some of the more problematic aspects of the mystic's thought were toned down or eradicated or construed in more orthodox-friendly directions.) Others that McClymond considers to be Böhmist universalists were arguably only very marginally influenced by his ideas. All of them were people who had likely read something by Böhme (or by later Böhmists) and indeed had appreciated aspects of what they read, but to classify them as Böhmists would be misleading. In the whirling atmosphere of seventeenth-century Protestant thought, drawing some influences, direct and indirect, from esotericism (e.g., alchemy, Kabbalah, Böhme) was not at all unusual. But there is a big difference between suggesting some influence—perhaps a few ideas or some terminology—and seeing such sources as providing important or even structural elements.[21] As

20. Hessayon, "Jacob Boehme's Writings," 86.

21. An example from McClymond: Jewish kabbalah had the notion of a cycle of world ages lasting fifty thousand years, a number derived from the biblical idea of

an example, take Puritan universalist Peter Sterry. Sterry found profit in reading Böhme, encountering "rich Depths, Sweet Heights" in his texts. However, he also warns, "1. The Lord have him [Böhme] his Spirit by measure leaving much Darkness mingled with his light. 2. They yt reade him, had neede come to him well instructed in ye Mystery of Christ. . . . Others will bee perverted by him."[22] This ought to serve as a warning against the simplistic and hasty move of classifying anyone who drew inspiration from Böhme as a "Böhmist."

Consider Jeremiah White, another Puritan universalist. McClymond places him in the "Böhmist universalist" category (*DR*, 81, 1131) yet it is interesting that he does so without reference to anything in White's book save a posthumous introduction written by (we think) Richard Roach, a follower of Jane Lead (*DR*, 508). This may well suggest some links between White and people in Böhmist networks. But McClymond makes no mention of the *content* of the White's book and its arguments. Yet if one reads the book, one finds oneself in a very different world from that of Jakob Böhme. White's text owes far more to Puritanism, Reformed theology, and Scripture than it does to visions and esotericism. McClymond's readers would remain oblivious of this fact and would come away thinking of White in the same camp as Lead.

Another example: Elhanan Winchester. McClymond describes him as "the most wide-ranging and successful evangelist in early American and British universalism" (*DR*, 592). It is fascinating that, out of Winchester's massive publishing output, only the content of a single sermon is mentioned by McClymond—"The Seed of the Woman Bruising the Serpent's Head" (1781). This is the very first universalist publication from Winchester, and it does indeed contain some Böhmist themes (e.g., an androgynous Adam, heavenly Sophia, the principles of fire, water, and nature).[23] What is striking, however, is that if one was to read the rest of

the Year of Jubilee (Lev 25) multiplied by 1,000—7 x 7,000 years + 1,000 years for the climactic Jubilee itself (*DR*, 174–75). We find this fifty-thousand-year period in both Johann Petersen and (as tentative speculation) in Elhanan Winchester (*DR*, 5–6) when pondering the duration of hell. It is certainly possible that their speculations derive ultimately from a Jewish esoteric source. However, even if they did, (a) it is peripheral to their universalism and (b) it is a harmless speculation as far as questions of orthodoxy go.

22. Letter to Morgan Llwyd in Wrexham. National Library of Wales, MS 11438 D, letter 68. Quoted in Hessayon, "Jacob Boehme's Writings," 84.

23. McClymond also mentions as evidence of Winchester's Böhmism a disapproving comment from John Murray that Winchester "is full of Mr [William] Law" (*DR*,

Winchester's considerable and important output of universalist books, one is immediately struck by how anomalous this first sermon is. I have not found Böhmist themes in any of his other works. He seemed to briefly toy with them before losing interest. Instead, what one finds is a passion with mainstream evangelical theological themes of his day and with the interpretation of the Bible (understandable given that Winchester's shaping background was the Evangelical Revival, as a Baptist preacher). But readers of McClymond's book would have no idea at all of the way that Winchester sought to carefully build his case for universal salvation from Scripture, interpreted more or less in the plain sense. Instead, Winchester too would be seen as another example of an off-the-peg esoteric universalist.

Furthermore, even some of those closer to the Böhmist flame draw little on such mystical speculations *in their universalist theologizing*. Take Paul Siegvolck's influential book, *The Everlasting Gospel* (German, 1700; English, 1753). It was written, as McClymond notes, by a German Radical Pietist who inhabited circles in which Böhme's writings were much admired. But if one reads the book itself—and again McClymond says almost nothing about its actual content—it reads as a book primarily concerned with fairly mainstream issues in the Christian theology of its day and the interpretation of biblical texts and themes. To describe it as a "Böhmist tract" (*DR*, 486, 564) is as endarkening as it is enlightening.[24]

594n69). This comment, however, relates to no more than Winchester's belief that people could go to a temporary hell—something Murray vehemently rejected. It is not a complaint that Winchester is unduly influenced by Böhme's theology. After all, Böhme believed in an eternal hell.

24. It is important to note that McClymond's case for his Böhme's thesis is not restricted to the English-speaking world, which I have largely focused on above, but takes in France (536–58), Germany (509–16, 609–84), and Russia (558–63, 685–747) too. A brief word about that is needed. The general arguments I make in the main text above apply in these cases too. *France*: Böhme's thought influenced Louis-Claude de Saint-Martin (1743–1803), who inherited an esoteric-inspired (but non-Böhmist) version of universalism from Martines de Pasqually (1727?–74), which he then modified under the influence of Swedenborg and Böhme. It was Böhme's work that inspired him to move away from outward rituals to inner reality. McClymond's account is fascinating, and I have no disputes with it. But what it does not show is that Böhme's ideas contributed in any direct way to Saint-Martin's *universalism*. They served more to nuance and refine the wider framework and spirituality within which his existing esoteric universalism was understood. *Germany*: McClymond's impressive chapter surveys Kant, Julius Möller, Schleiermacher, Hegel, Schelling, and Paul Tillich. However, Kant and Hegel never addressed the issue of universal salvation (though Hegel was influenced by Böhme); Möller was definitely not a universalist; and Schleiermacher

The danger with McClymond's thesis is that he approaches each universalist looking for any and every connection he can make between them and Böhme. He draws attention to their awareness of Böhme's work and any possible Böhmian ideas and terminology in their work. This is interesting and worthwhile. The problem, however, is that on various occasions certain important question are not asked: *What role* do these ideas from Böhme play in the overall thought of this universalist? Are they central, peripheral, or something in between? Are they related to the notion of universal salvation in this thinker? If so, how? Instead, once a link with Böhme is found, the universalist is classified as a Böhmist and the implication drawn is that their universalism is built upon heterodox mystical speculations. But a careful study of their works indicates that the foundations of their universalist idea are not constructed in this way, so the theory can sometimes lead to searching for confirmatory evidence and ignoring the bread and butter of the books mentioned.[25]

At times, I wondered whether the Böhmist metanarrative was made to appear more powerful than it is by passing over significant universalist publications that do not fit the model. For instance, Charles Chauncy's *The Mystery Hid from Ages and Generations* (1784) received some passing mentions, but no discussion. Chauncy, who could not tolerate Böhme, became a universalist through his studies of the Bible, and his book was an unusually scholarly attempt to defend that thesis from Scripture. As such, it arguably warrants attention for being somewhat different from many others, as most universalist writers of the period were not academically

was a universalist, but *not under Böhme's influence*. Thus, only Schelling and Tillich fall into the category of universalists with Böhmist influences, and in both cases the caveats in the main text apply. *Russia*: Along with German idealism, Böhme and other strands of esotericism and occultism exerted a considerable influence among Russian churchmen and intellectuals. The first thing to say is that most of them did not thereby become universalists, and given the widespread influence of Böhme, that in itself is suggestive. The thinkers McClymond singles out for close attention are Vladimir Solovyov, Nikolai Berdyaev, and Sergius Bulgakov. The first two were clearly indebted to Böhme, and their writings certainly contained strong universalist impulses (though some ambiguity remains in both of them)—the latter is clear about his universalism, but is much less indebted to Böhme. Bulgakov's universalism is explored through patristic sources, so it seems better to look there for its foundation, even if esotericism played a role (perhaps indirectly, via Solovyov?) in shaping his controversial Sophiology.

25. I should add that, when McClymond picks out universalist books for special concentration, he does pay careful attention to their content. So the criticism in the main text needs to be tempered by that important qualification.

trained. The same could be said about George Stonehouse's three publications (1761, 1768, 1773), which only receive a single footnote reference in McClymond.[26] Yet Stonehouse was a serious biblical scholar and arguably deserved some attention for his attempt to demonstrate the scriptural nature of universalism. Of course, McClymond could not possibly explore every person who published on universalism, and he rightly makes no attempt to do so, but that he did not discuss the merits of the two most academically rigorous eighteenth-century attempts to demonstrate the biblical nature of the idea is a little surprising.[27]

I have no intention of denying that Böhme's ideas exercised some influence on many universalists in the late seventeenth to early twentieth century, for it is clear that they did. In some cases, it was a strong influence; in others, a minor one. But in no cases did *the universalist idea itself* emerge from Böhme's thinking. Rather, Böhmist ideas were accommodated around a universalism that had other roots. And in most cases, the justifications offered for universalism were drawn from the Bible and Christian theology.

Perhaps you think I protest too much. After all, surely the recurring presence of Böhme, whether as a major or minor influence, must be more than a coincidence. Of course it is. After the universalist shift that came with Jane Lead, many of those who admired Böhme become universalists, so it is no surprise that the streams that flowed on from them were streams that carried versions of universalism influenced by varying degrees of (modified) Böhmism. One would expect to find many universalists also sympathetic to Böhme. His recurring presence does not mean that "in modern Christian universalism, almost all roads lead back to Böhme" (*DR*, 563), or that he "laid the foundation" for the various buildings of modern universalism. I think he is more like the person who provided some builders with important elements like a wall, doors, windows, and a chimney, others with wallpaper and carpet, still others with a few decorations, while some builders kicked him out on his backside.

26. *DR*, 593n64.

27. Speaking for myself, I think that while both studies have many merits and are worthy of attention, they are also riddled with problems, both exegetical and theological.

Bibliography

Allen, Ethan. *Reason: The Only Oracle of Man: A Compendious System of Natural Religion*. Bennington, VT: Haswell & Russell, 1784.

Allin, Thomas. *The Augustinian Revolution in Theology: Illustrated by a Comparison with the Teaching of the Antiochene Divines of the Fourth and Fifth Centuries*. London: James Clark, 1911.

———. *Christ Triumphant: Universalism Asserted as the Hope of the Gospel on the Authority of Reason, the Fathers, and Holy Scripture*. Edited and with an introductory essay and notes by Robin A. Parry. Eugene, OR: Wipf & Stock, 2015.

———. *Race and Religion: Hellenistic Theology: Its Place in Christian Thought*. London: James Clark, 1899.

Almond, Philip C. *Heaven and Hell in Enlightenment England*. Cambridge: Cambridge University Press, 1994.

Bailey, Philip James. *Festus: A Poem*. 9th ed. London: Longmans, Green & Co., 1875.

Ballou, Hosea. *An Examination of the Doctrine of Future Retribution, on the Principles of Morals, Analogy and the Scriptures*. Boston: Trumpet Office, 1834.

———. *A Treatise on Atonement: In Which the Finite Nature of Sin Is Argued, Its Cause and Consequence as Such; The Necessity and Nature of Atonement; and Its Glorious Consequences, in the Final Reconciliation of All Men to Holiness and Happiness*. 2nd ed. Portsmouth, NH: Oracle, 1812.

Ballou, Maturin Murray. *Biography of Rev. Hosea Ballou*. Boston: Abel Tompkins, 1852.

Beecher, Edward. *History of Opinions on the Scriptural Doctrine of Retribution*. New York: Appleton, 1878.

Bell, Albert D. *The Life and Times of Dr. George de Benneville (1703–1793)*. Boston: Universalist Church of America, 1953.

De Benneville, George. *A True and Most Remarkable Account of Some Passages in the Life of Mr. George De Benneville*. Translated by Elhanan Winchester. London: 1791.

Blanchard, Laurence M. *Will All Be Saved? An Assessment of Universalism in Western Theology*. Paternoster Theological Monographs. Milton Keynes, UK: Paternoster, 2015.

Blumhardt, Johann Christoph. *Blatter Aus Bad Boll, Vol. 4*. Blumhardt, Gesammelte Werke Reihe II: Verkundigung. Göttingen: Vandenhoeck & Ruphrect, 1993.

———. *Evangelien-predigten auf alle Sonn und Feiertage des Kirchenjahres*. Blumhardt-Zündelsches Handbuch zum Neuen Testament. Reprint, Reichl: Otto Der Leuchter, 2010.

————. *Gospel Sermons: On Faith, the Holy Spirit, and the Coming Kingdom.* Translated by Jörg and Renata Barth. Edited by Christian T. Collins Winn and Charles E. Moore. Eugene, OR: Cascade, 2017.

————. *Täglich Brod aus Bad Boll, Vol. 2.* Bad Boll: 1879.

————. *Die Verkündigung II–IV. Blätter aus Bad Boll.* Vandenhoeck & Ruprecht, 1969, 1993, 1994.

Boulton, David. *Gerrard Winstanley and the Republic of Heaven.* Dent, UK: Dales Historical Monographs, 1999.

Bouwsma, William J. *The Career and Thought of Guillaume Postell (1510–1581).* Cambridge: Harvard University Press, 1957.

Bradstock, Andrew. *Religious Radicalism in Cromwell's England: A Concise History from the English Civil War to the End of the Commonwealth.* London: Taurus, 2011.

————, ed. *Winstanley and the Diggers, 1649–1999.* London: Cass, 2000.

Bressler, Ann Lee. *The Universalist Movement in America, 1770–1880.* New York: Oxford University Press, 2001.

Brown, Raymond. *The English Baptists of the Eighteenth Century.* London: Baptist Historical Society, 1986.

Brumbaugh, Martin Grove. *A History of the German Baptist Brethren in Europe and America.* Mount Morris, IL: Brethren, 1899.

Burns, William E. "London's Barber-Elijah: Thomas Moor and Universal Salvation in the 1690s." *Harvard Theological Review* 95.3 (2002) 277–90.

Calamy, Edmund. *The Nonconformist's Memorial: Being an Account of the Lives, Sufferings, and Printed Works of the Two Thousand Ministers Ejected from the Church of England, Chiefly by the Act of Uniformity, August 24, 1666: Vol. I.* London: Harris, 1775.

Calvin, John. *De aeterna Dei praedestinatione.* Geneva: Jean Crespin, 1551.

Campbell, John McLeod. *The Nature of the Atonement and Its Relation to Remission of Sins and Eternal Life.* Cambridge: Macmillan, 1856.

Cassara, Ernest. *Hosea Ballou: The Challenge to Orthodoxy.* Washington, DC: University Press of America, 1982.

————, ed. *Universalism in America: A Documentary History.* Boston: Beacon, 1971.

Chauncy, Charles. *The Mystery Hid from Ages and Generations, Made Manifest in the Gospel-Revelation: Or, The Salvation of All Men. The Grand Thing Aimed at in the Scheme of God, as Opened in the New Testament Writings, and Entrusted with Jesus Christ to Bring into Effect.* London: Dilly, 1784.

Cole, Alfred S., and Clarence R. Skinner. *Hell's Ramparts Fell: The Life of John Murray.* Boston: Universalist, 1941.

Conway, Ann. *Principia philosophiae antiquissimae et recentissimae de Deo, Christo et Creatura id est de materia et spiritu in genere.* Amsterdam: 1690.

————. *The Principles of the Most Ancient and Modern Philosophy.* Edited by Peter Lopston. The Hague: Nijhoff, 1982.

————. *The Principles of the Most Ancient and Modern Philosophy.* Translated by Jonathan Bennett, 2017. https://www.earlymoderntexts.com/assets/pdfs/conway1692_1.pdf.

Cox, Samuel. *The Larger Hope: A Sequel to Salvator Mundi.* London: Paul, Trench & Co., 1883.

————. *The Resurrection: Twelve Expository Essays on the Fifteenth Chapter of St. Paul's First Epistle to the Corinthians.* London: Strahan & Co., 1869.

————. *Salvator Mundi: Or, Is Christ the Saviour of All Men?* 4th ed. New York: Dutton, 1878.

Cragg, Gerald R., ed. *The Cambridge Platonists.* New York: Oxford University Press, 1968.

Crouzel, Henri. *Une controverse sur Origène à la Renaissance: Jean Pic de La Mirandole et Pierre Garcia.* Paris: Vrin, 1977.

Darby, John Nelson. "Examination of the Book Entitled 'The Restitution of All Things.'" http://www.stempublishing.com/authors/darby/DOCTRINE/31002E.html.

Denck, Hans. *Hans Denck Schriften.* Edited by Georg Baring and Walter Fellman. 2 vols. Gütersloh: Bertelsmann, 1956–56.

————. "Divine Order." In *Selected Writings of Hans Denck,* translated by Walter Fellmann, edited by Edward Furcha, 73–98. Pittsburgh: Pickwick, 1976.

————. "Whether God Is the Cause of Evil." In *The Spiritual Legacy of Hans Denck: Interpretation and Translation of Key Texts,* edited by Clarence Bauman, 76–117. Studies in Medieval and Reformation Thought 47. Leiden: Brill, 1991.

Durnbaugh, Donald F. "Communication Networks as One Aspect of Piestist Definition: The Example of Radical Pietist Connection between Colonial North America and Europe." In *Pietism in Germany and North America, 1680–1820,* edited by Jonathan Strom et al., 33–50. Farnham, UK: Ashgate, 2009.

————. *European Origins of the Brethren.* Elgin, IL: Brethren, 1958.

Eddy, Richard. *Universalism in America: A History. Vol. 1, 1636–1800.* Boston: Universalist, 1884.

————. *Universalism in America: A History. Vol. 2, 1801–1886.* Boston: Universalist, 1886.

Edwards (the Younger), Jonathan. *The Salvation of All Men Strictly Examined; and the Endless Punishment of Those Who Die Impenitent, Argued and Defended against the Objections and Reasoning of the Late Rev. Doctor Chauncy of Boston, in His Book Entitled "The Salvation of All Men," &c.* Reprint, Boston: Ewer & Bedlington, 1824.

Erskine, Thomas. "The Bible in Relation to Faith." In *The Spiritual Order and Other Papers,* 76–99. Edinburgh: Edmonston & Douglas, 1871.

————. "The Divine Son." In *The Spiritual Order and Other Papers,* 28–46. Edinburgh: Edmonston & Douglas, 1871.

————. *The Doctrine of Election and Its Connection with the General Tenor of Christianity.* London: Duncan, 1837.

————. *An Essay on Faith.* 5th ed. Edinburgh: Waugh & Innes, 1829.

————. "The Father Revealed in the Son." In *The Spiritual Order and Other Papers,* 243–45. Edinburgh: Edmonston & Douglas, 1871.

————. *Letters of Thomas Erskine of Linlathen: Vol. 1, from 1800 til 1840.* Edited by William Hanna. Edinburgh: Douglas, 1877.

————. *Letters of Thomas Erskine of Linlathen: Vol. 2, from 1840 til 1870.* Edited by William Hanna. Edinburgh: Douglas, 1877.

————. "The Purpose of God." In *The Spiritual Order and Other Papers,* 47–75. Edinburgh: Edmonston & Douglas, 1871.

————. *The Unconditional Freeness of the Gospel in Three Essays.* Edinburgh: Waugh & Innes, 1828.

Farrar, Frederic W. *Eternal Hope: Five Sermons Preached in Westminster Abbey, November and December, 1877.* New York: Dutton, 1878.

————. *Mercy and Judgment: A Few Last Words on Christian Eschatology with Reference to Dr. Pusey's "What Is of Faith?"* London: Macmillan, 1881.

Finch, Anne. *The Principles of the Most Ancient and Modern Philosophy concerning God, Christ, and the Creatures, viz. of Spirit and Matter in General, Whereby May Be Resolved All Those Problems Or Difficulties, Which Neither by the School Nor Common Modern Philosophy, Nor by the Cartesian, Hobbesian, or Spinosian, Could Be Discussed.* London: 1692.

Finn, Nathan A. "The Making of a Baptist Universalist: The Curious Case of Elhanan Winchester." *Baptist History and Heritage* 47.3 (2012) 6–18.

Foster, John. *A Letter of the Celebrated John Foster to a Young Minister, on the Duration of Future Punishment [1841]: With an Introduction and Notes, Consisting Chiefly of Extracts From Orthodox Writers, and an Earnest Appeal to The American Tract Society in Regard to the Character of Its Publications.* Boston: Phillips, Sampson & Co., 1849.

Foster, Marian. "Representation and Substitution in Thomas Erskine of Linlathen." PhD thesis, King's College, London, 1992.

Fuller, Andrew. "Letters to Mr Vidler on the Doctrine of Universal Salvation." In *The Complete Works of Andrew Fuller, Vol. 2: Controversial Publications*, edited by Joseph Belcher, 292–327. Harrisonburg, VA: Sprinkle, 1988.

Gladstone, William E. *Studies Subsidiary to the Works of Bishop Butler.* Oxford: Clarendon, 1896.

Gregory, Alan. "'No New Truths of Religion': William Law's Appropriation of Jacob Boehme." In *An Introduction to Jacob Boehme: Four Centuries of Thought and Reception*, edited by Ariel Hessayon and Sarah Apetrei, 142–61. London: Routledge, 2014.

————. *Quenching Hell: The Mystical Theology of William Law.* New York: Seabury, 2008.

Gregory of Nyssa. *Gregorii Nysseni Opera.* Edited by Werner Jaeger et al. 10 vols. Leiden: Brill, 1960–90.

Groth, Friedhelm. "Die Apokatastasis panton, das Ziel der Werke Gottes. Bemerkungen zum eschatologischen Heilsuniversalismus bei Friedrich Christoph Oetinger." In *Wahrnehmungen: Theologische Perspektiven und Zusammenhänge*, edited by Werner Brändle, 79–95. Studien für Eckhard Lessing zum 50 Geburtstag. Münster: Eigendruck, 1985.

————. *Die Apokatastasis panton im württembergischen Pietismus: Theologiegeschichtliche Studien zum eschatologischen Heilsuniversalismus württembergischer Pietisten des 18 Jahrhunderts.* Münster: Vandenhoeck & Ruprecht, 1981.

————. "Chiliasmus und Apokatastasishoffnung in der Reich-Gottes-Verkündigung der beiden Blumhardts." *Pietismus und Neuzeit* 9 (1983) 56–116.

————. *Die Wiederbringung aller Dinge im Württembergischen Pietismus. Theologiegeschichtliche Studien zum eschatologischen Heilsuniversalismus württembergischer Pietisten des 18 Jahrhunderts.* Göttingen: Vandenhoeck & Ruprecht, 1984.

Gurney. John. *Brave Community: The Digger Movement in the English Revolution.* Manchester: Manchester University Press, 2007.

Guyon, Jeanne de la Mothe. *Jeanne Guyon's Apocalyptic Universe: Her Biblical Commentary on Revelation with Reflections on the Interior Life.* Translated by Nancy Carol James. Eugene, OR: Pickwick, 2019.

Hagan, Anette I. *Eternal Blessedness for All? A Historical-Systematic Examination of Schleiermacher's Understanding of Predestination.* Princeton Theological Monographs 195. Eugene, OR: Pickwick, 2013.

Heap, Jason. "Baptists and the Afterlife." MPhil thesis, University of Oxford, 2006.

Hein, Rolland. *George MacDonald: Victorian Mythmaker.* Nashville: Star Song, 1993.

Hessayon, Ariel. "Jacob Boehme's Writings during the English Revolution and Afterwards: Their Publication, Dissemination, and Influence." In *An Introduction to Jacob Boehme: Four Centuries of Thought and Reception,* edited by Ariel Hessayon and Sarah Apetrei, 57–76. London: Routledge, 2014.

———, ed. *Jane Lead and Her Transnational Legacy.* Christianities in the Trans-Atlantic World, 1500–1800. London: Palgrave Macmillan, 2016.

Hessayon, Ariel, and Sarah Apetrei, eds. *An Introduction to Jacob Boehme: Four Centuries of Thought and Reception.* London: Routledge, 2014.

Hill, Andrew. "The Obscure Mosaic of British Universalism: An Outline and Bibliographical Guide." *Transactions of the Unitarian Historical Society* 23.1 (2003) 421–44.

Hirst, Julie. *Jane Leade: Biography of a Seventeenth-Century Mystic.* Aldershot: Ashgate, 2005.

———. "Mysticism, Millenarianism, and the Visions of Sophia in the Works of Jane Lead (1624–1704)." PhD thesis, University of York, 2002.

Holyoake, Austin. *Heaven and Hell: Where Situated? A Search after the Objects of Man's Fervent Hope & Abiding Terror.* Pamphlet. 1873.

Horrocks, Don. *Laws of the Spiritual Order: Innovation and Reconstruction in the Soteriology of Thomas Erskine of Linlathen.* Studies in Evangelical History and Thought. Milton Keynes, UK: Paternoster, 2004.

———. "Postmortem Education: Universal Salvation in Thomas Erskine (1788–1870)." In *"All Shall Be Well": Explorations in Universal Salvation and Christian Theology, from Origen to Moltmann,* edited by Gregory MacDonald, 198–218. Eugene, OR: Cascade, 2011.

Hughes, Peter. "Elhanan Winchester." http://uudb.org/articles/elhananwinchester.html.

Huntingdon, William. *Advocates for Devils Refuted, and Their Hope of the Damned Demolished; or, An Everlasting Task for Winchester and All His Confederates.* London: 1794.

Huntington, Joseph. *Calvinism Improved; or The Gospel Illustrated as a System of Real Grace, Issuing in the Salvation of All Men.* New London, CT: Green, 1796.

Hurd Smith, Bonnie. *"Mingling Souls on Paper": An Eighteenth-Century Love Story.* Salem, MA: Judith Sargent Murray Society, 2007.

Hutton, Sarah. *Anne Conway: A Woman Philosopher.* Cambridge: Cambridge University Press, 2004.

———. "Lady Anne Conway." https://plato.stanford.edu/entries/conway/.

Irwin, Charlotte. "Pietist Origins of American Universalism." MA thesis, Tufts University, 1966.

Isaac, Daniel. *The Doctrine of Universal Restoration, Examined and Refuted; and the Objections to That of Endless Punishment Considered and Answered: Being a Reply to the Most Important Particulars Contained in the Writings of Winchester, Vidler, Wright, and Weaver.* London: 1808.

Ising, Dieter. *Johann Christoph Blumhardt, Life and Work: A New Biography.* Translated by Monty Ledford. Eugene, OR: Cascade, 2009.

Jackson, Thomas. *The Life of Charles Wesley, Vol. 2*. London: Wesleyan Conference Office, 1841.

Jeaffreson, Herbert H. *Letters of Andrew Jukes, Edited; with a Short Biography*. London: Longmans, Green & Co., 1903.

Jones, Thomas. *Funeral Sermon Sacred to the Memory of the Reverend Elhanan Winchester: Preached in the Universal Church, on Sunday, May 7th, 1797*. Philadelphia: Folwell, 1797.

Jones, Todd E. *The Cambridge Platonists: A Brief Introduction, with Eight Letters of Dr. Anthony Tuckney and Dr. Benjamin Whichcote*. Lanham, MD: University Press of America, 2004.

Jukes, Andrew John. *The Second Death and the Restitution of All Things, with Some Preliminary Remarks on the Nature and Inspiration of Holy Scripture: A Letter to a Friend*. Reprint, San Bernadino, CA: Ulan, 2012.

Kimel, Aidan. "The Salvation of Lilith." *Eclectic Orthodoxy* (blog), January 23, 2017. https://afkimel.wordpress.com/2017/01/23/fire-increate-and-the-salvation-of-lilith/.

Klassen, William. "Was Hans Denck a Universalist?" *Mennonite Quarterly Review* 39 (1965) 152–54.

Krulak, Todd. "Defining Competition in Neoplatonism." In *Religious Competition in the Greco-Roman World*, edited by Nathaniel P. DesRosiers and Lily C. Vuong, 79–84. Writings from the Greco-Roman World Supplement Series 10. Atlanta: SBL, 2016.

Kuntz, M. L. *Guillaume Postel: Prophet of the Restitution of All Things—His Life and Thought*. New York: Springer, 1981.

Laufer, Catherine Elle. *Hell's Destruction: An Exploration of Christ's Descent to the Dead*. London: Routledge, 2013.

Law, William. "An Appeal to All That Doubt or Disbelieve the Truths of the Gospel: Whether They Be Deists, Arians, Socinians, or Nominal Christians." In *The Works of William Law*, 6:57–155. Reprint, Eugene, OR: Wipf & Stock, 2001.

———. *An Humble, Earnest, and Affectionate Address to the Clergy*. London: Richardson, 1761.

———. *A Serious Call to a Devout and Holy Life; The Spirit of Love*. Edited by Paul Stanwood. New York: Paulist, 1978.

———. "The Spirit of Prayer, Parts I and II." In *The Works of William Law*, 7:3–48 and 49–143. Reprint, Eugene, OR: Wipf & Stock, 2001.

———. *The Way to Divine Knowledge: Being Several Dialogues between Humanus, Academicus, Rusticus, and Theophilus*. London: Innys & Richardson, 1752.

Lead, Jane. *The Enochian Walks with God: Found Out by a Spiritual Traveller, Whose Face towards Mount-Sion Was Set; with an Experimental Account of What Was Known, Seen and Met Withal There*. London: Edwards, 1694.

———. *The Laws of Paradise, Given Forth by Wisdom to a Translated Spirit*. London: Sowle, 1695.

———. "Lebenslauff der Autorin" [Life of the Author]. In *Sechs Unschätzbare Durch Göttliche Offenbarung und Befehl ans Liecht gebrachte Mystische Tractätlein*. Amsterdam: 1696.

———. *A Revelation of the Everlasting Gospel Message: Which Shall Never Cease to be Preach'd Till the Hour of Christ's Eternal Judgment Shall Come; Whereby Will Be Proclaim'd the Last-Love Jubilee, in Order to the Restitution of the Whole Lapsed*

Creation, Whether Human or Angelical. When by the Blood of the Everlasting Covenant, All Prisoners Shall Be Set Free. London: 1697.

———. *The Wonders of God's Creation: Manifest in the Variety of Eight Worlds*. London: 1695.

Locke, John. *Essay Concerning Human Understanding: Book 2*. London: 1690.

Ludlow, Morwenna. "Why Was Hans Denck Thought to be a Universalist?" *Journal of Ecclesiastical History* 2 (2004) 275–74.

Lum, Kathryn Gin. *Damned Nation: Hell in America from the Revolution to Reconstruction*. New York: Oxford University Press, 2014.

Luther, Martin. "Letter to Hans von Rechenberg." In *Luther's Works: Vol. 43, Devotional Writings 2*, edited by Helmut T. Lehmann and Gustav K. Wiencke, 51–55. Philadelphia: Fortress, 1968.

Macchia, Frank D. *Spirituality and Social Liberation: The Message of the Blumhardt's in the Light of Wuerttemberg*. Metuchen, NJ: Scarecrow, 1993.

MacDonald, George. *Alec Forbes of Howglen*. 3 vols. London: Hurst & Blackett, 1865.

———. "The Child in the Midst." In *Unspoken Sermons, First Series*. London: Strahan, 1867.

———. "The Consuming Fire." In *Unspoken Sermons, First Series*. London: Strahan, 1867.

———. "The Creation in Christ." In *Unspoken Sermons, Third Series*. London: Strahan, 1889.

———. *England's Antiphon*. London: MacMillan, 1868.

———. "Justice." In *Unspoken Sermons, Third Series*. London: Strahan, 1889.

———. "The Last Farthing." *Unspoken Sermons, Second Series*. London: Strahan, 1885.

———. "Light." In *Unspoken Sermons, Third Series*. London: Strahan, 1889.

———. *Lilith: A Romance*. 2nd ed. London: Chatto & Windus, 1896.

———. *Miracles of Our Lord*. New ed. London: Longmans, Green & Co., 1896.

———. "Righteousness." In *Unspoken Sermons, Third Series*. London: Strahan, 1889.

———. *Robert Falconer*. 3 vols. London: Hurst & Blackett, 1868.

———. *Robert Falconer*. Translated by David Jack. North Charleston, SC: CreateSpace, 2016.

———. "Salvation from Sin." In *The Hope of the Gospel*. London: Ward, Lock & Bowden, 1892.

———. "The Truth in Jesus." In *Unspoken Sermons, Second Series*. London: Strahan, 1885.

———. *Unspoken Sermons*. In Three Series. London: Strahan, 1867, 1885, 1889.

———. "The Voice of Job." In *Unspoken Sermons, Second Series*. London: Strahan, 1885.

———. *Weighed and Wanting, Vol. 1*. London: Routledge, 1882.

MacDonald, Gregory. *The Evangelical Universalist*. Eugene, OR: Cascade, 2006.

———, ed. *"All Shall Be Well": Explorations in Universal Salvation and Christian Theology, from Origen to Moltmann*. Eugene, OR: Cascade, 2011.

MacDonald, Grenville. *George MacDonald and His Wife*. London: Allen & Unwin, 1924.

Mack, Alexander. "Brief and Simple Exposition of the Outward But Yet Sacred Rights and Ordinances of the House of God." In *History of the Tunkers and the Brethren Church*, translated by H. R. Holsinger, 45–117. Oakland, CA: Pacific, 1901.

Marini, Stephen A. *Radical Sects of Revolutionary New England.* Cambridge: Harvard University Press, 1982.

Martin, Lucinda. "'God's Strange Providence': Jane Lead in the Correspondence of Johann Georg Gichtel." In *Jane Lead and Her Translational Legacy*, edited by Ariel Hessayon, 187–212. Christianities in the Trans-Atlantic World, 1500–1800. London: Palgrave-Macmillan, 2016.

Marx-Wolf, Heidi. *Spiritual Taxonomies and Ritual Authority: Platonists, Priests, and Gnostics in the Third Century, C.E.* Philadelphia: University of Pennsylvania, 2016.

Mason, William. *Antinomian Heresy Exploded in an Appeal to the Christian World; against the Unscriptural Doctrines, and Licentious Tenets of Mr. James Relly: Advanced in His Treatise of Union, &c.* London: Lewis, 1760.

Maurice, Frederick Denison. *Theological Essays.* 2nd ed. London: Macmillan, 1853.

McClymond, Michael J. *The Devil's Redemption: A New History and Interpretation of Christian Universalism.* 2 vols. Grand Rapids: Baker Academic, 2018.

McDowell, Paula. *The Women of Grub Street: Press, Politics, and Gender in the London Literary Marketplace 1678–1730.* Oxford: Oxford University Press, 1998.

McGrath, Sean J. "Böhme's Theology of Evil and Its Relevance for Psychoanalysis." In *The Psychoanalysis of Evil*, edited by Ronald C. Naso and Jon Mills, 49–68. London: Routledge, 2016. https://www.academia.edu/35709146/B%C3%B6hmes_Theology_of_Evil_and_its_Relevance_for_Psychoanalysis._1

Miller, Russell E. *The Larger Hope: The First Century of the Universalist Church in America, 1770–1870.* 2 vols. Boston: Unitarian Universalist Association, 1979.

Moltmann, Jürgen. "The Hope for the Kingdom of God and Signs of Hope in the World: The Relevance of Blumhardt's Theology Today." *Pneuma* 26.1 (2004) 4–16.

———. "The Logic of Hell." In *God Will Be All in All: The Eschatology of Jürgen Moltmann*, edited by Richard Bauckham, 42–47. Edinburgh: T. & T. Clark, 1999.

Moor, Thomas. *A Second Addition to the Clavis Aurea: Wherein the Mysteries of the Scriptures are Clearly Broken Open in this Present Year 1697, according to Dr. Beverley's Calculation in his Scriptural Line of Time.* London: 1697.

More, Henry. *Divine Dialogues Containing Sundry Disquisitions & Instructions Concerning the Attributes and Providence of God: The Three First Dialogues Treating of the Attributes of God and His Providence at Large.* London: Flesher, 1668.

Müller, Gotthold. "Die Idee einer Apokatastasis ton panton in der europäischen Theologie von Schleiermacher bis Barth." *Zeitschrift für Religion und Geistesgeschichte* 16.1 (1964) 1–22.

Murray, John. *Letters and Sketches of Sermons, in Three Volumes.* Boston: Belcher, 1812.

———. *Records of the Life of the Rev. John Murray: Late Minister of the Reconciliation and Senior Pastor of the Universalists, Congregated in Boston. Written by Himself.* Boston: Munroe & Francis, 1816.

Murray, Judith. *Universalist Catechism.* Portsmouth, NH: privately published, 1782.

Needham, Nicholas R. *Thomas Erskine of Linlathen: His Life and Theology, 1788–1837.* Rutherford Studies in Historical Theology. Reprint, Lewiston, NY: Mellen, 1992.

Nicolson, Marjorie Hope, and Sarah Hutton. *The Conway Letters: The Correspondence of Anne, Viscountess Conway, Henry More, and Their Friends, 1642–1684.* Rev. ed. Oxford: Clarendon, 1992.

Nightingale, Florence. "A 'Note' of Interrogation." *Fraser's Magazine* 7.41 (May 1873) 567–77.

Parry, Robin A. "Between Calvinism and Arminianism: The Evangelical Universalism of Elhanan Winchester (1751–1778)." In *"All Shall Be Well": Explorations in Universal Salvation and Christian Theology, from Origen to Moltmann*, edited by Gregory MacDonald, 141–70. Eugene, OR: Cascade, 2011.

———. "A Response to Michael McClymond's Theological Critique of Universalism." On Academia.edu. https://www.academia.edu/37667049/A_Response_to_ Michael_McClymonds_Theological_Critique_of_Universalism.

Patrologia Graeca. Edited by J. P. Migne. 161 vols. Paris: Migne, 1857–66.

Petersen, Johann. *Das Leben Jo: Wilhelmi Petersen*. Halle: Renger, 1717.

———. *Mysterion Apokatastaseos Panton: Das ist, Das Geheimniß Der Wiederbringung aller Dinge, Darinnen in einer Unterredung zwischen Philaletham und Agathophilum gelehret wird, Wie das Böse und die Sünde, Die keine Ewige Wurtzel hat, sondern in der Zeit geuhrständet ist, wiederum gäntzlich solle auffgehoben, und vernichtet; Hergegen die Creaturen Gottes, Die nach seinem Willen das Wesen haben, doch eine jegliche in ihrer Ordnung, von der Sünde, und Strasse der Sünden, nach Verfliessung derer in der Göttlichen Oeconomie darzu bestimmten Perioden, und nach Außübung der Gerechtigkeit, krafft des ewigen Rath-Schlusses Gottes, durch Jesum Chrisum, Den Wiederbringer aller Dinge, Zum Lobe und Preiß seines herrlichen Namens, sollen befreyet und errette werden, auff daß da bleibe Das Gute, und Gott sey Alles in Allen, Offenbahret durch Einen Zeugen Gottes und seiner Warheit*. 3 vols. Offenbach: Brede, 1700, 1703, 1710.

Petersen, Johanna. *The Life of Lady Johanna Eleonora Petersen, Written by Herself*. Edited and translated by Barbara Becker-Cantarino. Chicago: University of Chicago Press, 2005.

Petry, Yvonne. *Gender, Kabbalah, and the Reformation: The Mystical Theology of Guillaume Postel*. Studies in Medieval and Reformation Traditions. Leiden: Brill, 2004.

Pfleiderer, Otto. *The Development of Theology in Germany since Kant, and Its Progress in Great Britain since 1825*. Translated by J. Frederick Smith. London: Sonnenschein, 1890.

Phillips, Michael. *Hope beyond Hell: A Novel*. Lowerstoft, UK: Sunrise, 2013.

Pinto, Vivian de Sola. *Peter Sterry: Platonist and Puritan, 1613–1672*. Cambridge: Cambridge University Press, 1934.

Plumptre, Edward H. *The Spirits in Prison and Other Studies on the Life After Death*. Rev. ed. New York: Thomas Whittaker, 1894.

Porter, Bertha. "White, Jeremiah (1629–1707)." In *Dictionary of National Biography, Vol. 61*. London: Smith, Elder & Co., 1900. https://en.wikisource.org/wiki/ White,_Jeremiah_(DNB00).

Postel, Guillaume. *De orbis terrae concordia libri quatuor, multiiuga eruditione ac pietate referti, quibus nihil hoc tam perturbato rerum statu uel utilius, uel accommodatius potuisse in publicum edi, quiuis aequus lector iudicabit. Adiectae sunt quoq[ue] annotationes in margine a pio atque erudito quodam viro*. Basel: Oporinus, 1544.

Pusey, E. B. *What Is of Faith as to Everlasting Punishment? In Reply to Dr. Farrar's Challenge in His 'Eternal Hope,' 1879*. 3rd ed. London: Rivingtons, 1880.

Rae, Murray. "Salvation-in-Community: The Tentative Universalism of Friedrich Schleiermacher." In *"All Shall Be Well": Explorations in Universal Salvation and Christian Theology, from Origen to Moltmann*, edited by Gregory MacDonald, 171–97. Eugene, OR: Cascade, 2011.

Raeper, William. *George MacDonald*. Oxford: Lion, 1987.

Ramelli, Ilaria L. E. *The Christian Doctrine of Apokatastasis*. Supplements to Vigiliae Christianae 120. Leiden: Brill, 2013.

———. "Good/Beauty." In *The Brill Dictionary of Gregory of Nyssa*, edited by Lucas Francisco Mateo-Seco and Giulio Maspero, 356–63. Leiden: Brill, 2010.

———. *Gregorio di Nissa sull'anima e la resurrezione*. Milan: Bompiani-Catolic University, 2007.

———. *The Larger Hope? Universal Salvation from Christian Beginnings to Julian of Norwich*. Eugene, OR: Cascade, 2019.

———. "Origen's Exegesis of Jeremiah: Resurrection Announced through the Bible and Its Twofold Conception." *Augustinianum* 48 (2008) 59–78.

———. *Preexistence of Souls? The ἀρχή and τέλος of Rational Creatures in Origen and Some Origenians*. Studia Patristica 56, vol. 4. Leuven: Peeters, 2013.

Ramsey, The Chevalier. *The Philosophical Principles of Natural and Revealed Religion, Unfolded in a Geometrical Order*. 2 vols. Glasgow: Foulis, 1748.

Randall, Ian. "'I Felt Bound to Receive All True Christians as Brethren': The Expansive Ecclesiology of Andrew Jukes (1815–1901)." Paper presented at the Brethren Archivists and Historians Network (BAHN) in Maynooth, Ireland, 3–5 July 2017.

Renkewwitz, Heinz. *Hochmann von Hochenau (1670–1721): Quellenstudien zur Geschichte des Pietismus*. Bresslau: Maruschke & Brendt, 1935.

Relly, James. *Antichrist Resisted in a Reply to a Pamphlet, Wrote by W. Mason, Entitled Antinomian Heresy Exploded: in an Appeal to the Christian World; against the Unscriptural Doctrines, and Licentious Tenet of Mr. James Relly, Advanced in His Treatise of Union*. London: 1761.

———. *Christian Liberty; or The Liberty wherewith Christ Hath Made Us Free*. London: 1775.

———. *Epistles: or The Great Salvation Contemplated; in a Series of Letters to a Christian Society*. London: Lewis, 1776.

———. "Eunuch for the Kingdom of Heaven's Sake." In *Remarks on the Works of Richard Coppin*. London: 1764.

———. *The Life of Christ; The Perseverance of the Christian*. London: 1762.

———. "The Sadducee Detected and Refuted." In *Remarks on the Works of Richard Coppin*. London: 1764.

———. *Salt of the Sacrifice; Or, the True Christian Baptism Delineated According to Reason and Spirit: As Gathered from Sundry Discourses on that Subject*. London: 1776.

———. *Salvation Compleated: and Secured in Christ, as the Covenant of the People. Considered in a Discourse on that Subject*. London: Witts, 1760.

———. *Thoughts on the Cherubimical Mystery; or an Attempt to Prove That the Cherubims Were the Emblems of Salvation by the Blood of Jesus*. London: 1780.

———. *Union; or, a Treatise of the Consanguinity and Affinity between Christ and His Church*. London: 1759.

———. *Written on Hearing of the Much-Lamented Death of the Rev. Mr. George Whitefield*. London: 1770.

Renkewwitz, Heinz. *Hochmann von Hochenau (1670–1721)*. Bresslau: Maruschke & Brendt, 1935.

Rich, Caleb. "A Narrative of Elder Caleb Rich." *Candid Examiner* 2 (April 30–June 18, 1827).

Rioli, Giorgio. *Epistla alli cittadini della riva Trento*. Bologna: 1550.

[Roach, Richard(?)]. "Preface." In *The Restoration of All Things, or a Vindication of the Goodness and Grace of God, to be Manifest at Last, in the Recovery of His Whole Creation Out of Their Fall*, Jeremiah White, i–xxx. 3rd ed. London: Denis, 1779. (The preface was anonymous.)

Robinson, James. *Divine Healing: The Formative Years: 1830–1890. Theological Roots in the Transatlantic World*. Eugene, OR: Pickwick, 2011.

Rowell, Geoffrey. *Hell and the Victorians: A Study of Nineteenth-Century Theological Controversies Concerning Eternal Punishment and the Future Life*. Oxford: Clarendon, 1974.

Rush, Benjamin. *Essays, Literary, Moral, and Philosophical*. 2nd ed. Philadelphia: Bradford, 1806.

[Rust, George]. *Letter of Resolution Concerning Origen and the Chief of His Opinions*. London: Esquire, 1661. (Published anonymously.)

Safford, Oscar F. *Hosea Ballou: A Marvellous Life Story*. 4th ed. Boston: Universalist, 1890.

Saxby, A. E. *God in Creation, Redemption, Judgment, and Consummation*. http://www.theheraldofgodsgrace.org/Saxby/GodInCreationRedemptionJudgment AndConsummation.htm.

Schär, Max. *Das Nachleben des Origenes im Zeitalter des Humanismus*. Basel: Helbing & Lichtenhahn, 1979.

Schleiermacher, Friedrich. *The Christian Faith*. Translated by H. R. MacIntosh and J. S. Stewart. Reprint, Edinburgh: T. & T. Clark, 1999.

————. *The Life of Schleiermacher, as Unfolded in His Autobiography and Letters*. Translated by Frederica Rowan. 2 vols. London: Smith. Elder & Co., 1860.

————. *On the Doctrine of Election: With Special Reference to the Aphorisms of Dr. Bretschneider*. Translated with an introduction and notes by Iain G. Nicol and Allen G. Jorgenson. Columbia Series in Reformed Theology. Louisville: Westminster John Knox, 2012.

Shantz, Douglas H. *An Introduction to German Pietism*. Baltimore: John Hopkins University Press, 2013.

Siegvolck, Paul. *The Everlasting Gospel, Commanded to be Preached by Jesus Christ, Judge of the Living and the Dead, unto All Creatures, Mark xvi.15. Concerning the Eternal Redemption Found Out by Him, whereby Devil, Sin, Hell, and Death, Shall at Last be Abolished, and the Whole Creation Restored to Its Primal Purity; Being a Testimony against the Present Anti-Christian World*. London: Gillet, 1792.

Sinclair, A. G. *A Letter to Elhanan Winchester, in which His Theological Tenets and Opinions Are Fairly and Candidly Examined and Confuted, as Inconclusive and Sophistical*. London: 1790.

Skemp, Sheila L. *Judith Sargent Murray: A Brief Biography with Documents*. The Bedford Series in History and Culture. Boston: Bedford, 1998.

Smith, C. F. "A Note on Jane Lead with Selections from Her Writings." *Studia Mystica* 3.4 (1980) 79–82.

Smith, Hannah Whitall. *The Christian's Secret of a Happy Life*. Chicago: Christian Witness, 1875.

————. *The Unselfishness of God and How I Discovered It: A Spiritual Autobiography*. 1st ed. London: Revell, 1903.

Spalding, Josiah. *Universalism Confounds and Destroys Itself, or Letters to a Friend in Four Parts*. Northampton, MA: 1805.

Steenbuch, Johannes. "Reconciling Conflicting Convictions on the Sovereignty of God and the Freedom of Human Beings: Three Centuries (16th-18th) of Baptist Universalism." http://www.mercyuponall.org/2018/06/07/reconciling-conflicting-convictions-on-the-sovereignty-of-god-and-the-freedom-of-human-beings-three-centuries-16th-18th-of-baptist-universalism/.

Sterry, Peter. *The Appearance of God to Man in the Gospel and the Gospel Change* London: 1710.

———. *A Discourse on the Freedom of the Will*. London: Starkey, 1675.

———. *The Rise, Race, and Royalty of the Kingdom of God in the Soul of Man*. Edited and with an introduction by Jeremiah White. London: Cockerill, 1683.

———. "That the State of Wicked Men After This Life Is Mixt of Evill, and Good Things." Unpublished manuscript. Cambridge, Emmanuel College Library MS 294, Fol. 84.

Stone, Martin. *Biography of Rev. Elhanan Winchester*. Boston: Brewster, 1836.

Stonehouse, George. *Universal Restitution, A Scripture Doctrine: This Prov'd in Several Letters Written on the Nature and Extent of Christ's Kingdom; Wherein the Scripture Passages, Falsely Alleged in Proof of the Eternity of Hell's Torments, Are Truly Translated and Explained*. London: 1761.

———. *Universal Restitution Farther Defended: Being a Supplement to the Book Intitled Universal Restitution, A Scripture Doctrine*. Bristol: Pine, 1768.

———. *Universal Restitution Vindicated Against the Calvinists in Five Dialogues*. Bristol: Farley, 1773.

Stoudt, John Joseph. *Jacob Boehme: His Life and Thought*. Reprint, Eugene, OR: Wipf & Stock, 2004.

Talbott, Thomas. "The Just Mercy of God: Universal Salvation in George MacDonald (1824–1905)." In *"All Shall Be Well": Explorations in Universal Salvation and Christian Theology, from Origen to Moltmann*, edited by Gregory MacDonald, 219–48. Eugene, OR: Cascade, 2011.

Taylor, Dan. *The Eternity of Future Punishment Asserted and Improved: A Discourse on Matt xxv.46*. London: Cicero, 1789.

Tennent, Gilbert. *Some Account of the Principles of the Moravians*. London: Mason, 1743.

Tennyson, Alfred Lord. *In Memoriam*. Edited, with notes, by William J. Rolfe. Boston: Houghton Mifflin, 1895.

Thompson, R. *The Eternity of Hell Torments Vindicated, from Scripture and Reason: wherein Mr Winchester's Errors in Defence of Universal Restoration Are Refuted*. London: 1788.

Tyson, John, and Boyd Schlenther. *In the Midst of Early Methodism: Lady Huntingdon and Her Correspondence*. Plymouth, UK: Scarecrow, 2006.

Urbano, Arthur. "Difficulties in Writing the Life of Origen." *Oxford Handbook of Origen*, edited by Ronald E. Heine and Karen Jo Torjesen. Oxford: Oxford University Press, forthcoming.

[Van Helmont, F. M.]. *Two Hundred Queries Moderately Propounded concerning the Doctrine of the Revolution of Human Souls and Its Conformity with the Truth of the Christian Religion*. London: 1684. (Published anonymously.)

Vidler, William. *A Sketch of the Life of Elhanan Winchester, Preacher of the Universal Restoration, with a Review of His Writings*. London: Gillet, 1797.

Walker, D. P. *The Decline of Hell: Seventeenth-Century Discussions on Eternal Torment.* Chicago: University of Chicago Press, 1964.

Walton, Christopher. *Notes and Materials for an Adequate Biography of the Celebrated and Divine Theosopher William Law.* London: 1854.

Wedgewood, Julia. *Nineteenth-Century Teachers and Other Essays.* London: Hodder & Stoughton, 1909.

Weeks, Andrew. *Boehme: An Intellectual Biography of the Seventeenth-Century Philosopher and Mystic.* Albany, NY: State University of New York, 1991.

Wesley, John. *The Works of the Rev. John Wesley, Vol. II.* London: Jones, 1809.

Wheeler, Michael. *Heaven, Hell and the Victorians.* Cambridge: Cambridge University Press, 1994.

White, Jeremiah. *The Restoration of All Things, or a Vindication of the Goodness and Grace of God, to be Manifest at Last, in the Recovery of His Whole Creation Out of Their Fall.* 3rd ed. London: printed by John Denis, 1779.

Whitefield, George. *George Whitefield's Journals.* Edinburgh: Banner of Truth, 1986.

Whittemore, Thomas. *Life of Rev. Hosea Ballou: With Accounts of His Writings, and Biographical Sketches of His Seniors and Contemporaries in the Universalist Ministry.* 4 vols. Boston: Usher, 1854–55.

———. *The Modern History of Universalism from the Era of the Reformation to the Present Time.* Boston: Whittemore, 1830.

Williams, George Huntson. *American Universalism: A Bicentennial Historical Essay.* 4th ed. Boston: Skinner, 2002.

———. *The Radical Reformation.* 3rd ed. Kirksville, MO: Sixteenth Century Journal, 1992.

Wilson, Henry Bristow. "Séances Historiques de Genève: The National Church." In *Essays and Reviews*, edited by John William Parker, 145–206. London: Parker & Sons, 1860.

Wilson, Walter. *History and Antiquities of Dissenting Churches and Meeting Houses in London, Westminster, and Southwark; Including the Lives of Their Ministers, from the Rise of Nonconformity to the Present Time, Vol. 1.* London: printed for the author, 1808.

Winchester, Elhanan. *An Address to the Youth of Both Sexes in Philadelphia.* Philadelphia: Towne, 1785.

———. *An Attempt to Collect the Scripture Passages in Favour of the Universal Restoration: As Connected with the Doctrine of Rewards and Punishments: All Tending to Prove the Universal Empire of Christ, the Total Destruction of Evil, and the Final Reestablishment of Lapsed Intelligences.* Providence: 1786.

———. *God the Glorious, Holy, Wonder-Working God. A Century Sermon on the Glorious Revolution; Preached in London on November 16th, 1788 . . . and the Blessings of Civil and Religious Liberty Considered.* London: Johnson, 1788.

———. *A Course of Lectures on the Prophecies That Remain to be Fulfilled.* 4 vols. London: Hawes & Garner, 1789.

———. *A Defence of Revelation in Ten Letters to Thomas Paine; Being an Answer to His First Part of The Age of Reason.* London: Gillet, 1796.

———. *A Funeral Sermon for the Reverend Mr John Wesley, Who Departed This Life March 2, 1791, in the Eighty-eighth Year of His Age. Delivered March 10th, the Day after His Interment.* London: Gillet, 1791.

———. *Letter to the Rev. C. E. De Coetlogon, A. M. Editor of President Edwards's Lately Revised Sermon on the Eternity of Hell-torments.* London: Scollick, 1789.

————. *An Oration on the Discovery of America. Delivered in London, October the 12th, 1792.* London: Keeble & Acutts, 1792.

————. *A Plain Political Catechism. Intended for the Use of Schools in the United States of America.* Greenfield, MA: Dickman, 1796.

————. *Ten Sermons on Various Subjects. By the Late Elhanan Winchester, Preacher of the Universal Restoration.* London: Burton, 1799.

————. *The Divinity of Christ. Proved from the Scriptures of the Old and New Testament, in Several Letters to a Friend.* Philadelphia: Towne, 1784.

————. *The Holy Conversation, and High Expectation, of True Christians. A Discourse Delivered in London, April 29, 1789. To Which Are Added a Few Remarks on the Rev. Mr. Dan Taylor's Discourse, Entitled, "The Eternity of Future Punishment Asserted and Improved." In a Letter to a Friend.* London: Hawes, 1789.

————. *The Outcasts Comforted. A Sermon Delivered at the University of Philadelphia, January 4, 1782.* Philadelphia: Towne, 1782.

————. *The Process and Empire of Christ, From His Birth to the End of the Mediatorial Kingdom: A Poem, in Twelve Books.* London: Gillet, 1793.

————. *The Reigning Abominations, Especially the Slave Trade, Considered as Causes of Lamentations; Being the Substance of a Discourse Delivered in Fairfax County, Virginia, December 30, 1774.* London: Trapp, 1788.

————. *The Restitution of all Things (which God Hath Spoken by the Mouth of All His Holy Prophets since the World Began) Defended: Being an Attempt to Answer the Reverend Dan Taylor's Assertions and Re-assertions in Favour of Endless Misery, in Five Letters to Himself.* London: Parsons, 1790.

————. *The Seed of the Woman Bruising the Serpent's Head. Delivered at the Baptist Meeting House in Philadelphia, Sunday April 22, 1781.* Philadelphia: Towne, 1781.

————. *The Universal Restoration: Exhibited in a Series of Dialogues between a Minister and His Friend: Comprehending the Substance of Several Conversations that the Author Hath Had with Various Persons, both in America and Europe, on that Interesting Subject, Wherein the Most Formidable Objections are Stated and Fully Answered.* London: Gillet, 1788.

————. *Thirteen Hymns, Suited to the Present Times: The Past, Present, and Future State of America, with Advice to Soldiers and Christians: Dedicated to the Inhabitants of the United Colonies.* Baltimore: n.p., 1776.

————. *The Universalist's Hymnbook.* London: Gillet, 1794.

Winn, Christian T. Collins. "'Before Bloch there was Blumhardt': A Thesis on the Origins of the Theology of Hope." *Scottish Journal of Theology* 62.1 (2009) 26–39.

————. *Jesus Is Victor: The Significance of the Blumhardt's for the Theology of Karl Barth.* Princeton Theological Monographs. Eugene, OR: Pickwick, 2009.

Winstanley, Gerrard. *The Law of Freedom in a Platform.* London: 1652.

————. *The Mysterie of God, Concerning the Whole Creation, Mankinde: To Be Made Known to Every Man and Woman, after Seaven Dispensations and Seasons of Time are Passed Over, according to the Councell of God, Revealed to His Servants.* London: Calvert, 1648.

Zahl, Simeon. *Pneumatology and Theology of the Cross in the Preaching of Christoph Friedrich Blumhardt: The Holy Spirit between Wittenberg and Azusa Street.* London: T. & T. Clark, 2012.

Zinzendorf, Nicolaus. *Sixteen Discourses on the Redemption of Man by the Death of Christ.* London: James Hutton, 1740.

Index of Names